Pau

RAISING KANE
and other Essays

**Introduction by
Philip French**

**Marion Boyars
London • New York**

Published in Great Britain
in 1996 by Marion Boyars Publishers Ltd
24 Lacy Road, London SW15 1NL

Distributed in Australia and New Zealand by
Peribo Pty Ltd, 58 Beaumont Road, Mount Kuring-gai, NSW

'Fantasies of the Art-House Audience' and *'Hud*, Deep in the Divided Heart of
Hollywood' were originally published in *I Lost It At The Movies* (1965);
'Movie Brutalists', 'The Making of *The Group*', 'Movies on Television' and
'Bonnie and Clyde' in *Kiss Kiss Bang Bang* (1968). 'Trash, Art and the
Movies' was first published in *Going Steady* (1970), 'Raising Kane' in *The
Citizen Kane Book* (1971) and 'On the Future of Movies' in *Reeling* (1976).
'The Man from Dream City: Cary Grant' first appeared in *When the Lights
Go Down* (1980) and 'Why Are Movies So Bad? or, The Numbers' in
Taking It All In (1984).

British Library Cataloguing in Publication Data

Kael, Pauline
  Raising Kane and other essays
  1. Film criticism 2. Motion pictures—Evaluation
  I. Title
  791.4'375

    ISBN 0–7145–3014–X Original paperback

Typeset by Ann Buchan Typesetters, Shepperton, Middx.
Printed by The Lavenham Press Ltd, Suffolk

Contents

Author's Note

From time to time observations that didn't fit into my regular movie views started piling up in my head and I found myself writing a longer piece. This book is a selection of these pieces. William Shawn, the editor of *The New Yorker*, said they should be allowed to grow to their 'natural' length, and the reader can see that they took varied forms.

'Raising Kane' was intended to be a brief introduction to the first publication of the script of *Citizen Kane* and it grew into what was published in *The New Yorker* as a two-parter. It's a narrative union (I hope) of history and aesthetics. The Cary Grant profile grew out of my dissatisfaction with the usual press coverage of movie stars that told everything but what I wanted to know: what made them so effective in some roles, so ludicrous in others. I wanted to get at some of the personality elements that go into screen acting. 'Trash, Art and the Movies' came out of my feeling that reviews had become preposterously high-minded; I felt that they were falsifying what we hoped for when we went to the movies. This was a subject I'd got into when I wrote about *Hud*. Now I went into it from some other angles. We ought, I thought, to be able to enjoy trash without having to pretend that it's art. To take it further, trashiness is often what we respond to most in movies.

This is a speculative book. I say a lot of chancey things and I say them in a slang voice that is sometimes deliberately provocative — because who can say with any sureness how to talk about the movies we love the most? Movies can be so blissfully entertaining — movies such as Sturges' *The Lady Eve* or *Unfaithfully Yours* or Lubitsch's *Trouble in Paradise* — that we know they're not just trash. And movies can be so rightly sensual — Bertolucci's *The Conformist* or Coppola's *Godfather II* or Altman's *McCabe & Mrs Miller* — that they overwhelm our niggling anxieties about how they rank compared to great works in the other arts.

Even when I wrestled with questions about the movie industry, I felt the freedom that we felt as school children when we fled to the movies — an escape from uninvolvement into intensity and pleasure, into an expanded world. When movies are good, they can make you feel more alive, and writing about them can have the same effect.

Pauline Kael

Introduction by Philip French

Pauline Kael emerged from the San Francisco Bay area onto the international scene — the élite scene of small-circulation, high-brow film magazines — in 1954 with a characteristically combative article called 'Morality Plays Right and Left' in the British Film Institute's quarterly *Sight and Sound*. It was a devastating attack on two American movies, Nunnally Johnson's *Night People*, a Hollywood anti-Communist thriller set in a divided Berlin, and Herbert J. Biberman's *Salt of the Earth*, an independent production about a strike at a New Mexico copper mine, financed by a left-wing union and made by blacklisted artists. Coming at the height of the McCarthy Era when victims of the House Un-American Activities Committee were regarded in leftist circles as saintly heroes, the assault on *Salt of the Earth* as old-fashioned Communist propaganda attracted the largest, most hostile postbag in *Sight and Sound*'s history. In the first issue of 1955, the editor (noting that 'these protests are not entirely unexpected') published three pages of letters from, among others, the Ealing Studio editor and producer Sidney Cole (a Party member and union activist), the film-makers Ralph Bond and Christopher Brunel, the cinematographer Walter Lassally, and the formidable George Hoellering, director of the classic Hungarian documentary *Hortobagy* and manager of Britain's most prestigious art-house, the Academy, Oxford Street.

Kael had drawn blood and she evidently liked the taste: over the next forty years she went for the jugular. But her British critics had no idea of her background and they would have found it difficult to understand the political context from which she emerged. 'A bookish girl from a bookish family' is the way she described herself to Studs Terkel in *Hard Times* (1971), his oral history of the Depression. But in the same book we see her in a more complex light. The daughter of Jewish immigrant stock, she was raised on a northern Californian farm, and at the age of 16 began a four-year course in philosophy on a modest scholarship at the University of California's Berkeley campus in 1936. There she experienced at first-hand the in-fighting between Stalinists and Trotskyites, campaigned for a minimum 40 cents-an-hour wage for student employees (of which she was one), and often went hungry.

A further ten years passed before Kael's reputation extended beyond the coterie world of film magazines and beyond San Francisco, where she managed an art-house cinema (for which she wrote the programme notes), consorted with the local avant-garde (it included some notable film-makers and was to play host to the Beat Generation) and broadcast, at length and unpaid, on the public-service radio station run by the Pacifica Foundation and supported by public subscriptions. By the mid-1960s, largely due to the energizing force of European cinema (this was the heyday of Bergman, Fellini, Antonioni, the re-discovered Buñuel and the French New Wave), cinema became the fashionable interest of the educated middle-classes and the young. University film studies were expanding; the press and glossy magazines were taking cinema seriously; the media were bestowing on movie directors an attention hitherto reserved for their stars. The movies were becoming, as we would now say, the new rock'n'roll, except that at that very moment rock music — through the Beatles, the Rolling Stones, Bob Dylan and various West Coast groups — was embarking on its political, counter-cultural phase as the Vietnam War began to escalate.

It was in this heady, highly charged atmosphere that Kael's first book, *I Lost It At The Movies*, appeared in the early summer of 1965. Containing over a decade of reviews and essays, it brought her polemical style to the general public and Kael herself to New York to be lionized and fought over by the arts editors of nationally circulated magazines. She proposed the title somewhat facetiously, and her publishers responded with enthusiasm. Was it her heart or her virginity that she had lost? Having been pushed on stage clutching it like a vaudeville stripper's fan, Kael was to choose titles of a similarly playful *double-entendre* over the next thirty years. Along with the vociferous attacks on the New York critical establishment and the iconoclasm, these titles contributed to an air of sensationalism. We should remember, however, that by this time Kael was in her mid-forties.

I recall attending a landmark occasion, a Sunday night forum on film criticism held in October 1965 at the YMHA on Manhattan's Upper East Side, an important venue for poetry readings and intellectual symposia as, I imagine, the Manhattan YMCA is not. The speakers were Dwight Macdonald, John Simon, Andrew Sarris and, the new gun in town, Pauline Kael. The bearded, bear-like Macdonald, who had helped Kael secure the grant that enabled her to compile *I Lost It At The Movies*, was the very embodiment of the pre-war left-wing, Trotskyist, anti-Communist intellectual; he'd been writing about movies since the 1920s and was now, in the margins of a busy life, contributing a film column to *Esquire*. Macdonald saw little difference between Soviet conformity and the Hollywood production line, and he was a vociferous enemy of the American bourgeois values he dubbed Mid-Cult. Simon, a fair-haired, neatly-dressed European emigré polymath with a Harvard PhD, was writing waspishly everywhere on everything, and had just published a collection of essays with an introduction by Macdonald. He championed the cinema as art, had no truck with popular culture, and saw himself as a member of a praetorian élite, engaged in a rear-guard action against the Philistines. Sarris, dark-haired with a sallow complexion, was film critic of *The Village Voice*, the man who had introduced the French *nouvelle vague* critics' *politique des auteurs* to America as 'the auteur theory'. Shortly thereafter he was to become a Professor of Film at New York University, editor of the briefly successful English language version of *Cahiers du Cinéma*, and author of the seminal *The American Cinema: Directors and Directions 1929–1968*, an expanded version of his reappraisal of American cinema in the Spring 1963 number of the experimental movie quarterly *Film Culture*. And sitting with them was Kael, small, bird-like, with the deceptive fragility of a steel leaf.

Macdonald and Sarris had been the target of numerous barbs in *I Lost It At The Movies*; both were to write harshly of her, Macdonald in a deeply divided critique of that first book (while nevertheless declaring it the best collection of movie criticism since the posthumous selection of reviews by his closest friend, James Agee), Sarris much later. Simon, who admired her sharp intelligence (in much the same terms as Macdonald), would also lay into her a number of times in the 1970s. (Over the years Macdonald turns up in several novels, most memorably in Saul Bellow's *Humboldt's Gift*. Simon and Kael became the butt of private jokes in public places. Director Melvin Frank mocked Simon in a joke about the venomous critic 'John Schuster' (a play on the publishing house of Simon and Schuster) in the 1979 comedy *Lost and Found*; George Lucas and Ron Howard named the villain of the 1988 sword-and-sorcery movie *Willow*, General Kael.

The usual questions were asked that evening about the function of criticism and the responsibility of the reviewer, though it was probably the last time that anyone in New York would ask if film criticism could be as serious an activity as reviewing the other arts. Especially memorable was the civilized, ameliorative tone: this aggressive, combative panel had assembled to establish the crucial cultural significance of the movies and, without stating it, they had for a brief, historical moment, buried their considerable differences. Macdonald died in 1982 at the age of 76, his last published piece an essay on Buster Keaton. Simon and Sarris still write regular columns and teach at universities, and each has written several books on the cinema. But of that 1965 YMHA quartet it is Pauline Kael who has emerged triumphant, despite or because of the fact that what we would now call her 'agenda' was less clearly defined.

She prevailed against the odds. Kael got in ahead of most others with her book (Macdonald's collected film criticism didn't appear until 1970). But her views proved too tough for the East Coast publications that courted her. She began writing for *McCalls*, the family journal that in the 1950s proclaimed itself 'The Magazine of Togetherness', but didn't survive her hostile notice of *The Sound of Music*. The rejection by the liberal weekly, *New Republic*, of her 1967 analysis of *Bonnie and Clyde*, for its unseemly enthusiasm, was a blessing in disguise. She passed it to William Shawn, editor of *The New Yorker*, where a few months earlier she had made her debut with the article 'Movies on Television' (subsequently given the OUP imprimatur through inclusion in John Gross's 1991 *Oxford Book of Essays*.) As a result she became a *New Yorker* film critic. For a decade she and Penelope Gilliatt (who had been signed up the previous year) shared the job at 20 West 43rd St, doing six-monthly stints. This neat arrangement came to a messy end in the late 70s. Gilliatt suffered a mental breakdown and *The New Yorker* decided it would only publish her fiction. (She died in 1993 at the age of 60.) A little earlier, feeling that she was getting stale, Kael had been lured to Hollywood to work as a producer for Warren Beatty's company, but she decided against the arrangement and worked instead for Paramount as an executive consultant for five months; she missed writing, and returned to *The New Yorker*, appearing usually every other week. The simple announcement of her retirement, in a March 1991 issue of *The New Yorker*, produced a wave of sadness through the magazine's readership and became a national news story.

Until Gilliatt and Kael joined *The New Yorker*, the paper had usually taken a flip, dismissive approach to the cinema in its critical columns. The prevailing attitude was especially contemptuous of American films, though over the years — starting with its drama critic, Herman Mankiewicz, in 1927 — a stream of *New Yorker* writers decamped for Hollywood, most of them never to return. Kael and Gilliatt were a double-act, once compared by a British observer to Stanley Kowalski and Blanche Dubois in Tennessee Williams' *A Streetcar Named Desire* — a tough, demotic, commonsensical Kael wading into the movies with a barroom aggressiveness; the delicate, whimsical, ladylike Gilliatt fluttering around her subjects with quivering antennae. Gilliatt was not, I think, a great critic; her best writing is to be found in her short stories. Kael, however, helped change the nature and status of film criticism in the English-speaking world. She transformed it into an exciting, vital, essential activity, an argument with our times and our culture. More than any other writer of the past thirty years (probably since Salinger, whose last story appeared the same year as *I Lost It At The Movies*), she brought younger readers to *The New Yorker*. I became aware of this in 1972 when, as a visiting professor at the University of Texas, I discovered that she was the only critic all my students read, and for a number of them she was the only critic of any sort they could name. Willy-nilly her columns became essential texts for the classes I taught. When she became cognisant of her transcontinental influence on undergraduate critics, she took to holding back peculiarly hostile reviews of current films so that students would have to form their own opinions before reading her in *The New Yorker*.

Week after week she brought the whole of her heart, mind and experience to bear on what she saw. And given her extraordinary memory (she apparently doesn't take notes and rarely sees a film twice), her reviews seem like instant replays in which she argues, meditates, analyzes, enthuses and agonizes over what she has seen. The space *The New Yorker* gave her for a quarter of a century was an essential part of this activity — like the members of Peckinpah's *Wild Bunch*, she could play her rope out to the end. (Length was never connected to remuneration — Shawn agreed from the start to let Kael go to her limit, while paying her a basic fee. It was said that it was the same sum as her tight-lipped colleague, Penelope Gilliatt.) She writes with passion, sometimes angrily, but also joyfully, and from the perspective of a proud, provincial American. Realistic as to national faults, Kael properly resents those who unjustly disparage the national inheritance.

She reminds me of another American critic of her generation I greatly admire, Robert Warshow (the only other film critic represented in Gross's 1991 *Oxford Book of Essays*), who died in 1955 at the age of 37, leaving a handful of articles on film and popular culture that were posthumously collected in 1962 as *The Immediate Experience*. In the application for a Guggenheim Fellowship to write the book he was never even to embark on (it is used as the Author's Preface to *The Immediate Experience*), Warshow wrote

> The movies — and the American movies in particular — stand at the centre of that unresolved problem of 'popular culture' which has come to be a kind of nagging embarrassment to criticism, intruding itself into all our efforts to understand the special qualities of our culture and to define our own relations to it.

Kael, who got a grant from the Guggenheim Foundation to put together her first book, has, I think, pursued the project that Warshow intended to embark upon. He also said that the sociological aesthetic approaches to cinema

> in their separate ways, have tended to slight the fundamental *fact* of the movies, a fact at once aesthetic and sociological but also something more. This is the actual, immediate experience of seeing and responding to the movies as most of us see them and respond to them. A critic may extend his frame of reference as far as it will bear extension, but it seems to me almost self-evident that he should start with the simple acknowledgement of his own relation to the object he criticizes; at the centre of all truly successful criticism there is always a man reading a book, a man looking at a picture, a man watching a movie. Critics of the films, caught in the conflict between 'high culture' and 'popular culture,' have too often sought to evade this confrontation.

This again is something of which Kael has been consistently aware.

In 1968, Kael abandoned her assaults on fellow critics. 'She appears to consider them, almost without exception, as either rivals, or butts, or usually, both', Dwight Macdonald wrote in 1965, 'as if her security depended upon eliminating all rivals to the throne'. Once she was installed at *The New Yorker*, it soon became apparent that there were no longer any serious professional rivals. The subsequent battles were closer to home, indeed internecine.

Publicly, fellow *New Yorker* writers took pot-shots at her. Brendan

Gill in his unauthorised 50th Anniversary history of the journal, *Here At The New Yorker* (1975), starts off by celebrating 'the two brilliant women, Pauline Kael and Penelope Gilliatt, who, seven or eight years ago, took my place reviewing movies for the magazine'. He describes Kael as 'always witty and sometimes a holy terror; among other things, she has the distinction of being the only person I know who has made her fellow-reviewer John Simon blanch with terror. . .' Her 'only fault as a writer', Gill goes on, 'is an occasional garrulousness' which he blames on 'the fact that in youth she used to give talks about movies over the radio; the ear forgives much more than the eye and welcomes repetition as a necessary *aide-mémoire*; on the page it implies that the reader cannot follow a straightforward line of reasoning'. In 1979 her *New Yorker* colleague Renata Adler (who had spent a year in the 1960s as film critic of *The New York Times*) made an unpleasant attack on her style and public persona in *The New York Review of Books*. None of this affected Kael. By this time, her constituency extended far beyond Manhattan's West 43rd Street. But during her early years at *The New Yorker* (as she relates in the introduction to her anthology *For Keeps*, 1994) 'the editors tried to turn me into just what I'd been struggling not to be: a genteel, fuddy-duddy stylist'. As a result she 'spent more time and effort restoring what I'd written than writing it'. But as we know, she won the battle. Fortunately, and for our mutual good.

Everything she has written for *The New Yorker* has been collected and (in Britain, though not in the States) virtually all of it — some eleven volumes — remains in print. This new collection is of her longer, more general essays, which grew fewer when she gave up writing for film magazines, and it includes her nearest thing to a book — *Raising Kane*, the lengthy essay she wrote in 1971 to accompany the screenplay of *Citizen Kane*. This article was written at a time when screenwriters were not getting their due (they still aren't) and when directors were being elevated to something approaching sainthood in books with titles like *The Film Director As Super Star* and *The Directors' Event*. In putting the case for Herman Mankiewicz as co-author of *Kane*, Kael was saluting a neglected artist, whom she found congenial and even heroic. Orson Welles wrote an angry thousand-word letter to the London *Times* when part of the essay was serialized there in 1971, but no one reading the piece objectively could think its aim was to diminish the film's star and director. *Raising Kane* shows Kael to be a gifted historian and reporter, as well as a critic. And what comes through in this collection is her knowledge and feeling for the American experience in this century, whether she is taking a retrospective look, as in the *Bonnie and Clyde* and *Kane* essays, or catching it on the wing in the two despairing essays, *On the Future of Movies* and *Why Are Movies So Bad?* If I have a criticism of Kael (and I have a few, because arguing with her is part of the fun and stimulation we get from reading her) it is that where some critics mistake a couple of minor swallows for a glorious summer, she can be persuaded by a few moulting swallows to predict an indefinite future of silent springs.

All these essays are personal in different ways, but the most overtly autobiographical is the piece on *Hud*, which in a most moving fashion tells us about where Kael comes from and the rural West of the interwar years that shaped her worldview. As she remarks in *Movies On Television* 'everyone's 'golden age of the movies' is the period of his first movie-going'. Re-reading that essay after three decades, I noticed for the first time the relaxed, confident use of 'his'.

There is in *Projections 5* (Faber & Faber, 1996), the annual anthology of reflections by film-makers on their craft, the transcript of a conversation between Brian De Palma and Quentin Tarantino that includes a revealing exchange on what Kael meant to serious American cinéastes.

> De Palma: It's an unfortunate thing for your generation of film-makers, but we had Pauline Kael and whatever you say about her, whether you liked her opinions or not, she wrote with such passion and such excitement about movies. And for the life of me, I cannot find a writer today who I can read with as much interest and excitement.
>
> Tarantino: In some ways Kael was as influential on me as any film-maker. She helped me at a young age to develop my aesthetic, which doesn't mean I didn't disagree with her, but that she was like a teacher to me.
>
> De Palma: Exactly.
>
> Tarantino: She quit the business when I was in pre-production on *Reservoir Dogs*, and I feel weird about it. Maybe because she was so important to me, I don't want to know what she thought of it! But when I was younger, I always used to fantasize about her picking my movie to review, because she didn't review everything, and that Pauline Kael would refer to me by my last name — 'When Tarantino does da, da, da, da' — and how cool that would be!

Fantasies of the Art-House Audience

For several decades now educated people have been condescending toward the children, the shopgirls, all those with 'humdrum' or 'impoverished' lives — the mass audience — who turned to movies for 'ready-made' dreams. The educated might admit that they sometimes went to the movies designed for the infantile mass audience — the number of famous people who relax with detective fiction makes this admission easy — but presumably they were not 'taken in'; they went to get away from the tensions of their complex lives and work. But of course when they really want to enjoy movies as an art, they go to foreign films, or 'adult' or unusual or experimental American films.

I would like to suggest that the educated audience often uses 'art' films in much the same self-indulgent way as the mass audience uses the Hollywood 'product,' finding wish fulfillment in the form of cheap and easy congratulation on their sensitivities and their liberalism. (Obviously any of my generalizations are subject to numerous exceptions and infinite qualifications; let's assume that I know this, and that I use large generalizations in order to be suggestive rather than definitive.)

By the time Alain Resnais's *Hiroshima Mon Amour* reached American art houses, expectations were extraordinarily high. Dwight Macdonald in *Esquire* had said: 'It is the most original, moving, exciting and important movie I've seen in years, somehow managing to combine a love story with propaganda against war and the atomic bomb without either losing its full force.' The rest of the press seemed to concur. The *Saturday Review* considered it 'a masterpiece.' The New York *Herald Tribune* decided that 'it establishes beyond any man's cavilling the potentialities of the film as an art' — something one might have thought already established. *Time* decided that the theme was that 'Hiroshima, like God, is love. It is the Calvary of the atomic age. It died for man's sins . . . .' I met a couple who had seen the film five nights in a row; a University of California professor informed me that if I didn't like *this* one, he would never speak to me again. Dwight Macdonald wrote more and went further:

> It is as stylized as *Potemkin* or *Ten Days that Shook the World*, as pure and powerful as cinema . . . It is also a novelistic exploration of memory, a *recherche du temps perdu* comparable to Proust . . . For the first time since Eisenstein — we have a cinematic intelligence so quick, so subtle, so original, so at once passionate and sophisticated that it can be compared with Joyce, with Picasso, with Berg and Bartok and Stravinsky. The audience was extraordinarily quiet — no coughing, whispering, rustling of paper; a hypnotic trance . . . It was oddly like a religious service, and if someone had made a wisecrack, it would have seemed not an irritation but a blasphemy.

Surely movies — even the greatest movies — are rarely received in such an atmosphere of incense burning. *Breathless* and *L'Aventura* were to be either admired or disliked or ignored, but *Hiroshima Mon Amour* was described in hushed tones; it was some sort of ineffable deep experience. Why?

The picture opened with those intertwined nude bodies — this could be symbolic of a true intermingling, but it irresistibly set off some lewd speculations about just *what* was going on. And what was that stuff they were covered with? Beach sand? Gold dust? Ashes? Finally, I accepted it as symbolic bomb ash, but I wasn't happy with it. (Later I discovered that it was supposed to be 'sweat, ashes and dew.') Then the French girl said she had seen everything in Hiroshima, and the Japanese man told her she had seen nothing in Hiroshima. Then they said the same things over again, and again, and perhaps again. And I lost patience. I have never understood why writers assume that repetition creates a lyric mood or underlines meaning with profundity. My reaction is simply, 'OK, I got it the first time, let's get on with it.' Now, this is obviously not how we are supposed to react to Marguerite Duras' dialogue, which is clearly intended to be musical and contrapuntal, and I was going to try to get in the right, passive, receptive mood for a ritual experience, when some outright fraud made me sit up and pay attention. The action — or inaction — in bed was intercut with what purported to be documentary shots of the effect of the bomb on Hiroshima. Only I had seen some of the footage before in a Japanese atrocity movie that was about as documentary as *Peyton Place*. This clumsily staged imposture made me suspect that the Japanese man didn't know Hiroshima either, and I began to look askance at the truth he was supposed to represent. Where did he get this metaphysical identity with Hiroshima? As the film went on, and the heroine recounted her first love for a German soldier, how he had been killed on the last day of fighting, how she had been dragged away and her head shaved, how she had gone mad and been hidden away in the cellar by her shamed parents, I began to think less and less of the movie and more about why so many people were bowled over by it.

Was it possibly an elaborate, masochistic fantasy for intellectuals? Surely both sexes could identify with the girl's sexual desperation, her sensitivity and confusion — and had anyone dreamed up worse punishments for sexuality? Only a few years ago it had looked as if James Dean in *East of Eden* and *Rebel Without a Cause* had gone just about as far as anybody could in being misunderstood. But this heroine not only had her head shaved by people who didn't understand her love and need of the German, but she went *crazy* and was locked in a cellar. You can't go much further in being misunderstood. And, at the risk of giving offense, is this not what sends so many people to analysts — the fear that they'll go crazy if they don't get love?

The Japanese, it may be noted, is rather dull and uninteresting: he says no more than an analyst might; he is simply a sounding board. And if, being Japanese, he is supposed to represent the world's conscience, he brings an unsuitably bland, professionally sympathetic and upper-class manner to the function. But everybody who has suffered sexual deprivation — and who hasn't? — can identify with her and perhaps fantasize brutal parents and cellars. Even her insantiy can be equated with those rough nights when a love affair fell apart or that nervous exhaustion at the end of the academic year that sends so many to the hospital or the psychiatric clinic.

It seemed to be a woman's picture — in the most derogatory sense of the term. And still she went on talking: her feelings, her doubts, her memories, kept pouring out. It began to seem like True Confession at the higher levels of spiritual and sexual communion; and I decided the great lesson for us all was to shut up. This woman (beautifully as Emmanuelle Riva interpreted her) was exposing one of the worst faults of intelligent modern women: she was talking all her emotions out — as if bed were the place to demonstrate sensibility. It's unfortunate that what people believe to be the most important things about themselves, their innermost truths and secrets — the real you or me — that we dish up when somebody looks sympathetic, is very likely to be the driveling nonsense that we generally have enough brains to forget about. The real you or me that we conceal because we think people won't accept it is slop — and why *should* anybody want it?

But here was the audience soaking it up — audiences of social workers, scientists, doctors, architects, professors — living and loving and suffering just like the stenographer watching Susan Hayward. Are the experiences involved really so different? Few of us have seen our lovers killed by partisan bullets, but something kills love anyway — something always does — and it's probably highly gratifying for many people to identify with a heroine who isn't responsible: it is the insane world that has punished her for her sexual expression. Emmanuelle Riva's sexual expression is far more forthright than a Hollywood heroine's, which makes it more appealing to an educated audience, and, of course, her character and her manner of indicating her emotional problems have a higher 'tone.' (It may be relevant to note that the educated audience, which generally ignores Miss Hayward, did turn out for *I Want to Live*, in which the character of Barbara Graham was turned into a sort of modern Tess of the d'Urbervilles — not only innocent of crime but horribly sinned against and *nobler* than anybody else.)

But what does her sad story have to do with Hiroshima and the bomb? Would not some other psychosexual story of deprivation (say, *Camille* or *Stella Dallas*) be just as relevant to the horrors of war if it were set in Hiroshima? It would seem so. However, the setting itself explains another aspect of the film's strong appeal, particularly to liberal intellectuals. There is a crucial bit of dialogue: 'They make movies to sell soap, why not a movie to sell peace?' I don't know how many movies you have gone to lately that were made to sell soap, but American movies *are* like advertisements, and we can certainly assume that indirectly they sell a way of life that includes soap as well as an infinity of other products. But what makes the dialogue crucial is that the audience for *Hiroshima Mon Amour* feels virtuous because they want to buy peace. And the question I want to ask is: who's selling it?

Recently, at a cocktail party of artists and professors, I noticed displayed on a table right next to the pickled Jerusalem artichokes, two French publications — Lo Duca's new volume on *Eroticism in the Cinema* and Kenneth Anger's *Hollywood Babylon*. Both books are like more elegantly laid-out issues of *Confidential* and all those semi-nameless magazines which feature hideously outsized mammary glands, only these books are supposed to be chic — the latest intellectual camp. The Lo Duca book features stills from a Kenneth Anger movie in which nude ladies are wrapped in chains. Anger, you may recall, made his reputation with a film called *Fireworks*, in which a roman candle explodes inside a sailor's fly. His own book has a dust jacket photograph of Jayne Mansfield — an aerial view down her dress that makes her breasts look like long strips of cooked tripe. The book itself is a recounting of the legends (that is to say the dirty stories, scandals, and gossip) that Anger heard while growing up in southern California.

What struck me about these books, which function as entertainment to what might be called highbrows, was that their chic seemed to consist largely in a degradation of the female image. The stars and starlets are displayed at their most grotesque, just as they are in the cheapest American publications (in fact the photos are probably derived from those sources). This female image is a parody of woman — lascivious face, wet open mouth, gigantic drooping breasts. She has no character, no individuality: she's blonde or brunette or red-head, as one might consume a martini, an old-fashioned, or a gin and tonic.

Now I am told that even the junior-high-school boys of America use photographs like these as pinups, and that this is their idea of the desirable female. I don't believe it. I would guess that they pretend to this ideal because they're afraid they won't be considered manly and sexy if they admit they find this image disgusting. I don't believe that these photographs are erotic in any ordinary sense. I think that the grotesqueness of this female image is what people enjoy. Here are some possible reasons. First, these spongy, subhuman sex images reduce women to the lowest animal level. And in the modern world, where women are competent, independent, and free and equal, the men have a solid, competitive hostility — they want to see women degraded even lower than they were in the Victorian era. Here is woman reduced to nothing but a blob that will gratify any male impulse. And, of course, a woman who has no interest in life but love presents no challenge to the male ego. Second, there's the old split between sacred and profane love — and many men feel that the more degraded the female, the more potent they would become. Third, there's the vast homosexual audience which enjoys derision of the female. I would guess, and here's a big generalization, that more homosexuals than heterosexuals love to chortle over the nude photos of Anita Ekberg. She's so preposterous — a living satire of the female. It's my guess that the audience for nudie-cutie magazines uses them in much the same way the wealthy and educated use expensive French publications on the same theme: They want to laugh at the subjects and/or feel superior to them.

When the parodied female becomes known, becomes a 'personality,' derision gives way to admiration and sympathy and 'understanding.' In publications like the British *Sunday Times* you will find discussions with passages like 'Marilyn Monroe grew up without affection and at times she was near suicide. When she talks about herself the awareness of her bitter past is never quite absent.' *Time* and *Life* present her psychoanalytical comments on herself. And Dwight Macdonald in *Esquire* explains that 'the expensive difficulties she makes for her employers are not so much prima donna assertiveness as symptoms of resentment and boredom.' Sociologists read Zolotow's book on her character changes, and Cecil Beaton rhapsodizes that 'she was born the postwar day we had need of her. Certainly she has no knowledge of the past. Like Giraudoux's Ondine, she is only fifteen years old; and she will never die.' He's right, at least, about her not having knowledge of the past: she seems to have swallowed all the psychoanalytical clichés about maltreated children, and when she talks about her past she simply spews them up. And the educated public loves these burbling bits of Freudian 'insight' when they come out of the mouths of 'babes.' In *The Misfits*, our heroine, with the sure instincts of the faithful dog, and the uncorrupted clarity of the good clean peasant, looks at each character in the film and knows him for what he is. The innocent eye can see the inner man — she's the female of the species of the strong, silent hero, but she's also the traditional whore with the heart of gold. Her performance in *The Misfits* appears uncontrollably nervous, but it's almost as if her confused state were the final proof of her sincerity. The public loves her the more because life seems too much for her.

La Vérité is a tired and trite and mechanical piece of slick moviemaking. Conceptually, it's rather like *Of Human Bondage* —

seen from Mildred's point of view. Although the title and the film's structure suggest that we are going to see the relativity of truth, the movie seems designed to show us the truth about Brigitte Bardot, just as *The Misfits* was written around Monroe. (These ladies are then congratulated for their histrionic achievements in playing themselves; certainly they are perfect in the roles — no one else could play them so well — but then, could they play anyone else?) This confusion of art and life which takes the form of sensationalism is becoming very popular in this Freudianized period. (Clouzot coyly plays with this confusion by having Bardot, the subject of a book by Simone de Beauvoir, accused in the courtroom of *La Vérité* of having read a book by de Beauvoir.)

It is supposed to be daring and modern to make these messed-up accounts of messed-up lives — though they may seem very much like the old Sunday supplements with their daring exposés. In this new form, however, the appeal is not only to the mass audience but also to the more literate, who are led to believe that they are getting some inside psychological dope.

Apparently these screen incarnations of male fantasies, Monroe (once a calendar girl come to comic strip life, an implausible but delicious affront to respectability) and Bardot (the distillation of all those irresponsible, petulant teen-agers who may never know that human experience has depth and expressiveness and potentialities beyond their immediate range of impulses) are objects of enthusiasm not so much for their (former or present) polymorphous-perverse physical charms and their (former or present) comedy talents, as for their messy, confused public-private lives — the nervous break-downs, miscarriages, overweight problems, husband troubles, and all those mental and physical ills which now comprise the image of a great star. The new heroine of our films is becoming the wretched star herself. In the pre-Freudian age, the exploitation of personal ailments in films like *The Misfits* and *La Vérité* would have been regarded as disgusting. It *is* disgusting, and the condescending type of sympathetic 'understanding' which is now widely purveyed is an insult to Freud and man. In the frivolous, absurd old days, stars were photographed in their bubble baths: now they bathe in tears of self-pity — while intellectual critics tap their understanding typewriters.

The 'mass' audience looks up at the 'stars'; the educated audience looks down sympathetically, as if reading a case history. They all stew in their own narcissism. The mass audience is beginning to catch up.

On a recent television program Ed Sullivan clucked sympathetically at Brigitte Bardot and told her how much he sympathized with the hard life of glamour girls like her and Monroe and Taylor, and, final irony, told her how much he admired the way she had 'handled herself.'

The educated American is a social worker at heart: he feels especially sympathetic toward these slovenly ladies because their slovenliness marks them as misfits who couldn't function in his orderly world. The same man who is enchanted with Monroe in the seduction scene of *Some Like It Hot* — crawling all over Tony Curtis while hanging out of her dress both fore and aft — expects his girl friends or wife to be trim, slender and well-groomed. The decor in the homes and offices of the American professional classes is clean and functional — Scandinavian with a guilty dash of Japanese (as reparation for the bomb, we sit close to the earth). Upon occasion, the American will desert the art house for an American picture, particularly if it is advertised with the intellectually fashionable decor. For this decor is an article of faith: it is progressive and important; it calls businessmen and artists to conferences at Aspen, where it is linked with discussions of such topics as 'Man the Problem Solver.' And so American movies now often come, packaged as it were, with several minutes of ingenious, abstract, eye-catching titles. This send-off — the graphics look provided by Saul Bass and other designers — has virtually nothing to do with the style or mood of the picture, but it makes the movie look more *modern*. (How can the picture be dismissed as trash when it looks like your own expensive living room?) This type of design, using basic colors and almost no soft lines, was, of course, devised so that advertising would be clear and effective with a minimum of cost. In movies, a photographic medium, complexity and variety and shadings of beauty are no more expensive than simplification. But modern graphic design, which has built an aesthetic on advertising economics, has triumphed: new big productions (like *The Misfits*) open with such a proud array of flashy designs that the movie itself comes on rather apologetically.

The advertising campaign for new films often uses a motif that appears again at the opening of the film: presumably, if the ad was good enough to get you there, you'll appreciate having it amplified. Perhaps the next Hollywood 'genius' will be the man who can design the whole movie to look like a high-powered ad. At present, the movie that begins when the packaging is out of the way is in a different, and older, style of advertising art. This style was summed up by a member of the audience a few weeks ago when I was looking at a frightfully expensive, elaborately staged movie. The beautiful heroine, in pale blue, was descending an elegant beige staircase, when a voice from the dark piped up — 'Modess, because . . . .' When the beautiful heroine in pale blue finally got into her creamy white lace and the properly nondenominational clergyman intoned, 'Wilt thou, Robert, take this woman . . . ,' another voice in the theater groaned, 'I wilt.'

The social worker-at-heart finds true reassurance when the modern-designed movie also has modern design built into the theme: a movie like *Twelve Angry Men*. Ask an educated American what he thought of *Twelve Angry Men* and more likely than not he will reply, 'That movie made some good points' or 'It got some important ideas across.' His assumption is that it carried these ideas, which also happen to be his ideas, to the masses. Actually, it didn't: this tense, ingenious juryroom melodrama was a flop with the mass audience, a success only at revivals in art houses.

The social psychology of *Twelve Angry Men* is perfectly attuned to the educated audience. The hero, Henry Fonda — the one against the eleven — is lean, intelligent, gentle but strong; this liberal, fair-minded architect is *their* hero. And the boy on trial is their dream of a victim: he is of some unspecified minority, he is a slum product who never had a chance, and, to clinch the case, his father didn't love him. It isn't often that professional people can see themselves on the screen as the hero — in this case the Lincolnesque architect of the future — and how they love it! They are so delighted to see a movie that demonstrates a proposition they have already accepted that they cite *Twelve Angry Men* and *The Defiant Ones* as evidence that American movies are really growing up.

It is a depressing fact that Americans tend to confuse morality and art (to the detriment of both), and that, among the educated, morality tends to mean social consciousness. Not implicit social awareness (Antonioni isn't 'saying anything,' they complain of *L'Aventura*) but explicit, machine-tooled, commercialized social consciousness. 'The old payola won't work any more,' announces the hero of *The Apartment*, and even people who should know better are happy to receive the message. How reassuring *The Apartment* is, with its cute, soft-hearted Jewish doctor and his cute, soft-hearted, fat, mama-comic Jewish wife — so unworldly and lovable that they take the poor frustrated sap for a satyr (almost as deadly in its 'humor' as Rock

Hudson being mistaken for a homosexual in *Pillow Talk*). In *The Apartment*, the little people are little dolls; the guys at the top are vicious and corrupt and unfaithful to their wives as well. The moral is, stick at the bottom and you don't have to do the dirty. This is the pre-bomb universe; and its concept of the 'dirty' is so old-fashioned and irrelevant, its notions of virtue and of vice so smugly limited, that it's positively cozy to see people for whom deciding to quit a plushy job is a big moral decision. The 'social consciousness' of the educated is so unwieldy, so overstuffed, that the mass audience may well catch up before the intellectuals have found any grounds to move on to — though surely many should be happy to vacate the premises of Freud and Marx.

The art-house audience is at its dreamiest for Russian films like *Ballad of a Soldier* and *The Cranes Are Flying*. How eager they are to believe the best about the Soviet Union, to believe that love is back, propaganda is out, and it's all right to like Russian movies because the Russians are really nice people, very much like us, only better. These sentiments have been encouraged by the theaters and by the cultural exchange agreement, and at showings of *The Cranes Are Flying* there was a queasy little prefatory note: 'At the same time you are watching this Soviet film, Soviet audiences are watching an American motion picture.' I was happy for the voice in the theater which piped up, 'But it's six a.m. in the Soviet Union.'

The Cranes Are Flying and *Ballad of a Soldier* are both good examples of nineteenth-century patriotism and nineteenth-century family values; neither seems to belong to the Communist period at all — they're reminiscent of American war epics of the silent era. And sophisticated Americans love the simple, dutiful characters that they would laugh at in American movies. It's a long time since audiences at art houses accepted the poor, ravished unhappy heroine who has to marry the cad who rapes her. They go even farther toward primitivism at *Ballad of a Soldier*: they love the 'touching' and 'charming' hero and heroine who express such priggish repugnance at a soldier's unfaithful wife (how would these two react if they caught the wife sleeping with a German, like the heroine of *Hiroshima Mon Amour*?). *Ballad of a Soldier* takes us back to the days when love was sweet and innocent, authority was good, only people without principles thought about sex, and it was the highest honor to fight and die for your country. These homely values, set in handsome, well-photographed landscapes, apparently are novel and refreshing — perhaps they're even exotic — to art-house audiences. It's a world that never was, but hopeful people would love to associate it with life in the Soviet Union.

Are these recruiting posters so morally superior to American lingerie ads like *Butterfield 8*? Are they as effective in the U.S.S.R. as in the outside world? We can see the results of *Butterfield 8*: half the junior-high-school girls in America are made up to look like Elizabeth Taylor, and at the Academy Award Show it was hard to tell the stars apart — there were so many little tin Lizzies. It's more difficult to gauge the effects of Russia's antique middle-class morality. Perhaps educated Americans love the Russians more than the Russians do. All over America people are suddenly studying Russian; and they sometimes give the impression that the first word they want to learn is 'Welcome.'

A congressional subcommittee headed by Kathryn Granahan, a Democrat from Pennsylvania who is known as America's leading lady smut-hunter, is exploring the possibility that the influx of foreign films, most especially the French film *Les Liaisons Dangereuses*, may be a Communist plot to undermine American moral structure — that is to say that Americans are being offered a preoccupation with sex so that they will become degenerate, corrupt, too weak to combat the Communist threat. Mrs Granahan has stated that the social, cultural and moral standards of France are among the greatest impediments to a strong NATO stand against international Communism.

In other words, she takes the position that a strong state, a state capable of defending itself, must be a Puritan state, and that individual freedom and the loosening of sexual standards threaten the state. This is, of course, the present Communist position: even American jazz is regarded as a threat. Nothing could be *cleaner* — in nineteenth-century terms — than Russian movies. Observers at the Moscow Film Festival reported that the Russians were quite upset after the showing of *The Trials of Oscar Wilde*: they had been under the impression that Wilde was imprisoned for his revolutionary politics — for socialism, not for sodomy. Russians have been protected from just such information, discussion and art as Mrs Granahan would protect us from. Apart from what appears to be a wholly unfounded notion that the Russians are trying to poison us via French sexual standards, there is an interesting issue here. For absurd as the Granahan position seems to be, I have heard a variant of it from many people who would scoff at the way she puts it.

Everywhere in the United States enthusiasts for *La Dolce Vita* explain that it's a great lesson to us — that Rome fell because of sexual promiscuity and high living, and we will too — that the Communists are going to win because of our moral laxity, our decay. It's as if poor Gibbon had labored in vain, and the churches' attitudes have triumphed. Even those who no longer believe in God seem to accept the idea that European and American habits and values are loose and sinful and will bring destruction down upon us.

May I suggest that this is just as nonsensical as the Granahan line? If all Europeans and all Americans suddenly became heterosexual and monogamous — if everyone took the pledge and there were no more drinking, if all nightclubs were closed, and if the rich turned their wealth over to the poor — I cannot see that our *power* position in this nuclear age would in any way be affected. And it's astonishing that sensible people can get so sentimental about Russian movies with their Puritan standards, the bourgeois morality that developed out of the rising salaried classes and the Stalinist drive to stamp out individual freedom. Queen Victoria squats on the Kremlin; and Americans who fought to rid themselves of all that repressive Victorianism now beat their breasts and cry, look how *good* they are, look how *terrible* we are — why, we don't *deserve* to win. Has Puritanism so infected our thinking that we believe a nuclear war would be won by the pure in heart?

Sight and Sound, 1962

Hud
Deep in the Divided Heart of Hollywood

As a schoolgirl, my suspiciousness about those who attack American 'materialism' was first aroused by the refugees from Hitler who so often contrasted their 'culture' with our 'vulgar materialism' when I discovered that their 'culture' consisted of their having had servants in Europe, and a swooning acquaintance with the poems of Rilke, the novels of Stefan Zweig and Lion Feuchtwanger, the music of Mahler and Bruckner. And as the cultural treasures they brought over with them were likely to be Meissen porcelain, Biedermeier furniture, oriental carpets, wax fruit, and bookcases with glass doors, it wasn't too difficult to reconstruct their 'culture' and discover that it was a stuffier, more middle-class materialism and sentimentality than they could afford in the new world.

These suspicions were intensified by later experience: the most grasping Europeans were, almost inevitably, the ones who leveled the charge of American materialism. Just recently, at a film festival, a behind-the-iron-curtain movie director, who interrupted my interview with him to fawn over every Hollywood dignitary (or supposed dignitary) who came in sight, concluded the interview with, 'You Americans won't understand this, but I don't make movies just for money.'

Americans are so vulnerable, so confused and defensive about prosperity — and nowhere more so than in Hollywood, where they seem to feel they can cleanse it, justify their right to it, by gilding it with 'culture,' as if to say, see, we're not materialistic, we appreciate the finer things. ('The hunting scene on the wall of the cabana isn't wallpaper: it's handpainted.') Those who live by making movies showing a luxurious way of life worry over the American 'image' abroad. But, the economics of moviemaking being what they are, usually all the producers do about it is worry — which is probably just as well because films made out of social conscience have generally given an even more distorted view of America than those made out of business sense, and are much less amusing.

The most conspicuous recent exception is *Hud* — one of the few entertaining American movies released in 1963 and just possibly the most completely schizoid movie produced anywhere anytime. *Hud* is a commercial Hollywood movie that is ostensibly an indictment of materialism, and it has been accepted as that by most of the critics. But those who made it protected their material interest in the film so well that they turned it into the opposite: a celebration and glorification of materialism — of the man who looks out for himself — which probably appeals to movie audiences just because it confirms their own feelings. This response to *Hud* may be the only time the general audience has understood film makers better than they understood themselves. Audiences ignored the cant of the makers' liberal, serious intentions, and enjoyed the film for its vital element: the nihilistic 'heel' who wants the good things of life and doesn't give a damn for the general welfare. The writers' and director's 'anti-materialism' turns out to be a lot like the refugees' anti-materialism: they had their Stefan Zweig side — young, tender Lon (Brandon de Wilde) and Melvyn Douglas's Homer, a representative of the 'good' as prating and tedious as Polonius; and they had their protection, their solid salable property of Meissen and Biedermeier, in Paul Newman.

Somehow it all reminds one of the old apocryphal story conference — 'It's a modern western, see, with this hell-raising, pleasure-loving man who doesn't respect any of the virtues, and, at the end, we'll fool them, he doesn't get the girl and he doesn't change!'

'But who'll want to see *that* ?'

'Oh, that's all fixed — we've got Paul Newman for the part.'

They could cast him as a mean man and know that the audience would never believe in his meanness. For there are certain actors who have such extraordinary audience rapport that the audience does not believe in their villainy except to relish it, as with Brando; and there are others, like Newman, who in addition to this rapport, project such a traditional heroic frankness and sweetness that the audience dotes on them, seeks to protect them from harm or pain. Casting Newman as a mean materialist is like writing a manifesto against the banking system while juggling your investments so you can break the bank. *Hud*'s shouted last remark, his poor credo, 'The world's so full of crap a man's going to get into it sooner or later, whether he's careful or not,' has, at least, the ring of *his* truth. The generalized pious principles of the good old codger belong to nobody.

The day *Hud* opened in San Francisco the theatre was packed with an audience that laughed and reacted with pleasure to the verve and speed and economy, and (although I can't be sure of this) enjoyed the surprise of the slightly perverse ending as much as I did. It was like the split movies of the war years — with those cynical heel-heroes whom we liked because they expressed contempt for the sanctimonious goody guys and overstuffed family values, and whom we still liked (because they were played by actors who *seemed* contemptuous) even when they reformed.

It's not likely that those earlier commercial writers and directors were self-deceived about what they were doing: they were trying to put something over, and knew they could only go so far. They made the hero a 'heel' so that we would identify with his rejection of official values, and then slyly squared everything by having him turn into a conventional hero. And it seems to me that we (my college friends) and perhaps the audience at large didn't take all this very seriously, that we enjoyed it for its obvious hokum and glamour and excitement and romance, and for the wisecracking American idiom, and the tempo and rhythm of slick style. We enjoyed the *pretense* that the world was like this — fast and funny; this pretense which was necessary for its enjoyment separated the good American commercial movie — the good 'hack' job like *Casablanca* or *To Have and Have Not* — from film art and other art. This was the best kind of Hollywood *product*: the result of the teamwork of talented, highly paid professional hacks who were making a living; and we enjoyed it as a product, and assumed that those involved in it enjoyed the money they made.

What gave the Hollywood movie its vitality and its distinctive flavor was that despite the melodramatic situations, the absurd triumphs of virtue and the inordinate punishments for trivial vice — perhaps even because of the stale conventions and the necessity to infuse some life that would make the picture seem new within them — the 'feel' of the time and place (Hollywood, whatever the locale of the story) came through, and often the attitudes, the problems, the tensions. Sometimes more of American life came through in routine thrillers and prison-break films and even in the yachting-set comedies than in important, 'serious' films like *The Best Years of Our Lives* or *A Place in the Sun*, paralyzed, self-conscious imitations of European art, or films like *Gentleman's Agreement*, with the indigenous paralysis of the Hollywood 'problem' picture, which is morally solved in advance. And when the commercial film makers had some freedom and leeway, as well as talent, an extraordinary amount came through — the rhythm of American life that give films like *She Done Him Wrong, I'm No Angel*, the Rogers-Astaire musicals, *Bringing Up Baby, The Thin Man, The Lady Eve, Double Indemnity, Strangers on a Train, Pat and Mike, The Crimson Pirate, Singin' in the Rain, The Big Sleep*, or the more recent *The Manchurian Candidate* and *Charade* a freshness and spirit that makes them unlike the films of any other country. Our movies are the best proof that Americans are liveliest and freest when we don't take ourselves too seriously.

Taking *Hud* as a commercial movie, I was interested to see that the audience reacted to Hud as a Stanley Kowalski on the range, laughing with his coarseness and sexual assertiveness, and sharing his contempt for social values. Years before, when I saw the movie version of *A Streetcar Named Desire*, I was shocked and outraged at those in the audience who expressed their delight when Brando as Stanley jeered at Blanche. At the time, I didn't understand it when they laughed their agreement as Stanley exploded in rage and smashed things. It was only later, away from the spell of Vivien Leigh's performance, that I could reflect that Stanley was clinging to his brute's bit of truth, his sense that her gentility and coquetry were intolerably fake. And it seemed to me that this was one of the reasons why *Streetcar* was a great play — that Blanche and Stanley upset us, and complicated our responses. This was no Lillian Hellman melodrama with good and evil clay pigeons. The conflict was genuine and dramatic. But Hud didn't have a dramatic adversary; his adversaries *were* out of Lillian Hellmanland.

The setting, however, wasn't melodramatic, it was comic — not the legendary west of myth-making movies like the sluggish *Shane* but the modern West I grew up in, the ludicrous real West. The comedy was in the realism: the incongruities of Cadillacs and cattle, crickets and transistor radios, juke-boxes, Dr Pepper signs, paperback books — all emphasizing the standardization of culture in the loneliness of vast spaces. My West wasn't Texas; it was northern California, but our Sonoma County ranch was very much like this one — with the frame house, and 'the couple's' cabin like the housekeeper's cabin, and the hired hands' bunkhouse, and my father and older brothers charging over dirt roads, not in Cadillacs but in Studebakers, and the Saturday nights in the dead little town with its movie house and ice cream parlor. This was the small-town West I and so many of my friends came out of — escaping from the swaggering small-town hotshots like Hud. But I didn't remember any boys like Brandon de Wilde's Lon: he wasn't born in the West or in anybody's imagination; that seventeen-year-old blank sheet of paper has been handed down from generations of lazy hack writers. His only 'reality' is from de Wilde's having played the part before: from *Shane* to *Hud*, he has been our observer, our boy in the West, testing heroes. But in *Hud*, he can't fill even this cardboard role of representing the spectator because Newman's Hud has himself come to represent the audience. And I didn't remember any clean old man like Melvyn Douglas's Homer: his principles and rectitude weren't created either, they were handed down from the authors' mouthpieces of the socially conscious plays and movies of the thirties and forties. Occupied towns in the war movies frequently spawned these righteous, prophetic elder citizens.

Somewhere in the back of my mind, Hud began to stand for the people who would vote for Goldwater, while Homer was clearly an upstanding Stevensonian. And it seemed rather typical of the weakness of the whole message picture idea that the good liberals who made the film made their own spokesman a fuddy-duddy, worse, made him inhuman — except for the brief sequences when he isn't a spokesman for anything, when he follows the bouncing ball and sings 'Clementine' at the movies. Hud, the 'villain' of the piece, is less phony than Homer.

In the next few days I recommended *Hud* to friends (and now 'friends' no longer means college students but academic and professional people) and was bewildered when they came back indignant that I'd wasted their time. I was even more bewildered when the reviews started coming out; what were the critics talking about? Unlike the laughing audience, they were taking *Hud* at serious message value as a work of integrity, and, even in some cases, as a tragedy. In the New York *Herald Tribune*, Judith Crist found that 'Both the portraits and the people are completely without compromise — and therein is not only the foundation but also the rare achievement of this film.' In the *Saturday Review*, Arthur Knight said that 'it is the kind of creative collaboration too long absent from our screen . . . by the end of the film, there can be no two thoughts about Hud: he's purely and simply a bastard. And by the end of the film, for all his charm, he has succeeded in alienating everyone, including the audience.' According to Bosley Crowther in the *New York Times*:

> Hud is a rancher who is fully and foully diseased with all the germs of materialism that are infecting and sickening modern man. . . . And the place where he lives is not just Texas. It is the whole country today. It is the soil in which grows a gimcrack culture that nurtures indulgence and greed. Here is the essence of this picture. While it looks like a modern Western, and is an outdoor drama, indeed, *Hud* is as wide and profound a contemplation of the human condition as one of the New England plays of Eugene O'Neill. . . . The striking, important thing about it is the clarity with which it unreels. The sureness and integrity of it are as crystal-clear as the plot is spare . . . the great key scene of the film, a scene in which [the] entire herd of cattle is deliberately and dutifully destroyed . . . helps fill the screen with an emotion that I've seldom felt from any film. It brings the theme of infection and destruction into focus with dazzling clarity.

As usual, with that reverse acumen that makes him invaluable, Crowther has put his finger on a sore spot. The director carefully builds up the emotion that Crowther and probably audiences in general feel when the cattle, confused and trying to escape, are forced into the mass grave that has been dug by a bulldozer, and are there systematically shot down, covered with lime, and buried. This is the movie's big scene, and it can be no accident that the scene derives some of its emotional power from the Nazis' final solution of the Jewish problem; it's inconceivable that these overtones would not have occurred to the group — predominantly Jewish — who made the film. Within the terms of the story, this emotion that is worked up is wrong, because it is not Hud the bad man who wants to destroy the herd; it is Homer the good man who accedes to what is necessary to stop the spread of infection. And is all this emotion appropriate to the slaughter of animals who were, after all, raised to be slaughtered and would, in the normal course of events, be even more *brutally* slaughtered in a few weeks? What's involved is simply the difference in money between what the government pays for the killing of the animals and their market value. It would not have been difficult for the writers and director to arrange the action so that the audience would feel quick relief at the destruction of the herd. But I would guess that they couldn't resist the opportunity for a big emotional scene, a scene with *impact*, even though the emotions don't support the meaning of the story. They got their big scene: it didn't matter what it meant.

So it's pretty hard to figure out the critical congratulations for clarity and integrity, or such statements as Penelope Gilliatt's in the *Observer*, 'Hud is the most sober and powerful film from America for a long time. The line of it is very skillfully controlled: the scene when Melvyn Douglas's diseased cattle have to be shot arrives like the descent of a Greek plague.' Whose error are the gods punishing? Was Homer, in buying Mexican cattle, merely taking a risk, or committing hubris? One of the things you learn on a ranch, or any other place, is that nobody is responsible for natural catastrophes; one of the things you learn in movies and other dramatic forms is the symbolic use of catastrophe. The locusts descended on Paul Muni in *The Good Earth* because he had gotten rich and *bad*: a farmer in the movies who neglects his humble wife and goes in for high living is sure to lose his crops. *Hud* plays it both ways: the texture of the film is wisecracking naturalism, but when a powerful sequence is needed to jack up the action values, a disaster is used for all the symbolic overtones that can be hit — and without any significant story meaning. I don't think the line of *Hud* is so much 'controlled' as adjusted, set by conflicting aims at seriousness and success.

It hardly seems possible but perhaps Crowther thought the *cattle* were symbolically 'fully and foully diseased with all the germs of materialism that are infecting and sickening modern man.' Those sick cattle must have *something* to do with the language he uses in describing the film. 'It is a drama of moral corruption — of the debilitating disease of avaricious self-seeking — that is creeping across the land and infecting the minds of young people in this complex, materialistic age. It is forged in the smoldering confrontation of an aging cattleman and his corrupted son.' Scriptwriters have only to toss in a few bitter asides about our expense-account civilization and strew a few platitudes like, 'Little by little the country changes because of the men people admire,' and the movie becomes 'a drama or moral corruption.'

The English critics got even more out of it: Derek Prouse experienced a 'catharsis' in *The Sunday Times*, as did Peter John Dyer in

Sight and Sound. Dyer seems to react to cues from his experience at *other* movies; his review, suggesting as it does a super-fan's identification with the film makers' highest aspirations, is worth a little examination. 'From the ominous discovery of the first dead heifer, to the massacre of the diseased herd, to Homer's own end and Hud's empty inheritance of a land he passively stood by and watched die, the story methodically unwinds like a python lying sated in the sun.' People will be going to *Hud*, as Charles Addams was reported to have gone to *Cleopatra*, 'to seek the snake.' Dyer squeezes out more meaning and lots more symbolism than the film makers could squeeze in. (A) Homer just suddenly up and died, of a broken heart, one supposes. It wasn't prepared for, it was merely convenient. (B) Hud's inheritance isn't empty: he has a large ranch, and the land has oil. Dyer projects the notion of Hud's emptiness as a human being onto his inheritance. (C) Hud didn't passively stand by and watch the land die. The *land* hasn't changed. Nor was Hud passive: he worked the ranch, and he certainly couldn't be held responsible for the cattle becoming infected — unless Dyer wants to go so far as to view that infection as a symbol of or a punishment for Hud's sickness. Even Homer, who had blamed Hud for just about everything else, didn't accuse him of infecting the cattle. Dyer would perhaps go that far, because somehow 'the aridity of the cattle-less landscape mirrors his own barren future.' Why couldn't it equally mirror Homer's barren past? In this scheme of symbolic interpretation, if there was a dog on the ranch, and it had worms, Hud the worm would be the reason. Writing of the 'terse and elemental polarity of the film,' Dyer says, 'The earth is livelihood, freedom and death to Homer; an impacably hostile prison to Hud' — though it would be just as easy, and perhaps more true to the audience's experience of the film, to interpret Hud's opportunism as love of life and Homer's righteousness as rigid and life-destroying — and *unfair*. The scriptwriters give Homer principles (which are hardly likely to move the audience); but they're careful to show that Hud is misunderstood and rejected when he makes affectionate overtures to his father.

Dyer loads meaning onto Hud's actions and behavior: for example, 'Instead of bronco-busting he goes in for a (doubtless) metaphorical bout of pig-wrestling.' Why 'instead of' — as if there were bronco-busting to do and he dodged it — when there is nothing of the kind in the film? And what would the pig-wrestling be a metaphor for? Does Dyer takes pigs to represent women, or does he mean that the pig-wrestling shows Hud's swinishness? Having watched my older brothers trying to catch greased pigs in this traditional western small-town sport, I took the sequence as an indication of how boring and empty small-town life is, and how coarse the games in which the boys work off a little steam. I had seen the same boys who wrestled greased pigs and who had fairly crude ideas of sex and sport enter a blazing building to save the lives of panic-stricken horses, and emerge charred but at peace with the world and themselves.

Are the reviewers trying to justify having enjoyed the movie, or just looking for an angle, when they interpret the illustrative details *morally* ? Any number of them got their tip on Hud's character by his taking advantage of a husband's absence to go to bed with the wife. But he couldn't very well make love to her when her husband was home — although that would be par for the course of 'art' movies these days. The summer nights are very long on a western ranch. As a child, I could stretch out on a hammock on the porch and read an Oz book from cover to cover while my grandparents and uncles and aunts and parents didn't stir from their card game. The young men get tired of playing cards. They either think about sex or try to do something about it. There isn't much else to do — the life doesn't exactly stimulate the imagination, though it does stimulate the senses. Dyer takes as proof of Hud's bad character that 'his appetites are reserved for married women.' What alternatives are there for a young man in a small town? Would it be proof of a *good* character to seduce young girls and wreck their reputations? There are always a few widows, of course, and, sometimes, a divorcee like Alma, the housekeeper. (Perhaps the first female equivalent of the 'white Negro' in our films: Patricia Neal plays Alma as the original author Larry McMurtry described the Negro housekeeper, the 'chuckling' Halmea with 'her rich teasing laugh.') But they can hardly supply the demand from the married men, who are in a better position to give them favors, jobs, presents, houses, and even farms. I remember my father taking me along when he visited our local widow: I played in the new barn which was being constructed by workmen who seemed to take their orders from my father. At six or seven, I was very proud of my father for being the protector of widows.

I assumed the audience enjoyed and responded to Hud's chasing women because this represented a break with western movie conventions and myths, and as the film was flouting these conventions and teasing the audience to enjoy the change, it didn't occur to me that in *this* movie his activity would be construed as 'bad.' But Crowther finds that the way Hud 'indulges himself with his neighbor's wife' is 'one of the sure, unmistakable tokens of a dangerous social predator.' Is this knowledge derived from the film (where I didn't discover it) or from Crowther's knowledge of life? If the latter, I can only supply evidence against him from my own life. My father who was adulterous, and a Republican who, like Hud, was opposed to any government interference, was in no sense and in no one's eyes a social predator. He was generous and kind, and democratic in the western way that Easterners still don't understand: it was not out of guilty condescension that mealtimes were communal affairs with the Mexican and Indian ranchhands joining the family, it was the way Westerners lived.

If Homer, like my father, had frequented married women or widows, would Dyer interpret that as a symbol of Homer's evil? Or, as Homer voiced sentiments dear to the scriptwriters and critics, would his 'transgressions' be interpreted as a touching indication of human frailty? What Dyer and others took for symbols were the clichés of melodrama — where character traits are sorted out and separated, one set of attitudes and behavior for the good characters, another for the bad characters. In melodrama, human desires and drives make a person weak or corrupt: the heroic must be the unblemished good like Homer, whose goodness is not tainted with understanding. Reading the cues this way, these critics missed what audiences were reacting to, just as Richard Whitehall in *Films and Filming* describes Newman's Hud as 'the-hair-on-the-chest-male' — although the most exposed movie chest since Valentino's is just as hairless.

I suppose we're all supposed to react on cue to movie rape (or as is usually the case, attempted rape); rape, like a cattle massacre, is a box-office value. No doubt in *Hud* we're really supposed to believe that Alma is, as Stanley Kauffmann says, 'driven off by his [Hud's] vicious physical assault.' But in terms of the modernity of the settings and the characters, as well as the age of the protagonists (they're at least in their middle thirties), it was more probable that Alma left the ranch because a frustrated rape is just too sordid and embarrassing for all concerned — for the drunken Hud who forced himself upon her, for her for defending herself so titanically, for young Lon the innocent who 'saved' her. Alma obviously wants to go to bed with Hud, but she has been rejecting his propositions because she doesn't want to be just another casual dame to him; she wants to be treated differently from the others. If Lon hadn't rushed to protect his idealized view of her, chances are that the next morning Hud would have felt guilty and repentant, and Alma would have been grateful to him for having used the violence necessary to break down her resistance, thus proving that she *was* different. They might have been celebrating ritual rapes annually on their anniversaries.

Rape is a strong word when a man knows that a woman wants him but won't accept him unless he commits himself emotionally. Alma's mixture of provocative camaraderie plus reservations invites 'rape.' (Just as, in a different way, Blanche DuBois did — though Williams erred in having her go mad: it was enough, it was really *more*, that she was broken, finished.) The scriptwriters for *Hud*, who, I daresay, are as familiar as critics with theories of melodrama, know that heroes and villains both want the same things and that it is their way of trying to get them that separates one from the other. They impart this knowledge to Alma, who tells Hud that she wanted him and he could have had her if he'd gone about it differently. But this kind of knowingness, employed to make the script more clever, more frank, more modern, puts a strain on the credibility of the melodramatic actions it explicates — and embellishes. Similarly, the writers invite a laugh by having Alma, seeing the nudes Lon has on his wall, say, 'I'm a girl, they don't do a thing for me.' Before the Kinsey report on women, a woman might say, 'They don't do a thing for me,' but she wouldn't have prefaced it with 'I'm a girl' because she wouldn't have known that erotic reactions to pictures are not characteristic of women.

The Ravetches have been highly praised for the screenplay: Penelope Gilliatt considers it 'American writing at its abrasive best'; Brendan Gill says it is 'honestly written'; *Time* calls it 'a no-compromise script.' Dyer expresses a fairly general view when he says it's 'on a level of sophistication totally unexpected from their scripts for two of Ritt's least successful, Faulkner-inspired films.' This has some special irony because not only is their technique in *Hud* a continuation of the episodic method they used in combining disparate Faulkner stories into *The Long Hot Summer*, but the dialogue quoted most appreciatively by the reviewers to illustrate their new skill (Alma's rebuff of Hud, 'No thanks, I've had one cold-hearted bastard in my life, I don't want another') is lifted almost verbatim from that earlier script (when it was Joanne Woodward telling off Paul Newman).

They didn't get acclaim for their integrity and honesty that time because, although the movie was entertaining and a box-office hit, the material was resolved as a jolly comedy, the actors and actresses were paired off, and Newman as Ben Quick the barn burner turned out not really to be a barn burner after all. They hadn't yet found the 'courage' that keeps Hud what *Time* called him, 'an unregenerate heel' and 'a cad to the end.' It may have taken them several years to learn that with enough close-ups of his blue, blue eyes and his hurt, sensitive mouth, Newman's Ben Quick could have burned barns all right, and audiences would have loved him more for it.

In neither film do the episodes and characters hold together, but Ritt, in the interim having made Hemingway's *Adventures of a Young Man* and failed to find a style appropriate to it, has now, with the aid of James Wong Howe's black and white cinematography, found something like a reasonably clean visual equivalent for Hemingway's prose. Visually *Hud* is so apparently simple and precise and unadorned, so skeletonic, that we may admire the bones without being quite sure of the name of the beast. This Westerner is part gangster, part *Champion*, part rebel-without-a-cause, part the traditional cynic-hero who pretends not to care because he cares so much. (And it is also part *Edge of the City*, at least the part about Hud's having accidentally killed his brother and Homer's blaming him for it. Ritt has plagiarized his first film in true hack style: the episode was integral in *Edge of the City* and the friendship of Cassavetes and Poitier — probably the most beautiful scenes Ritt has directed — drew meaning from it; in *Hud* it's a fancy 'traumatic' substitute for explaining why Hud and Homer don't get along.)

When *Time* says *Hud* is 'the most brazenly honest picture to be made in the U.S. this season' the key word is brazenly. The film brazens it out. In *The New Yorker* Brendan Gill writes, 'It's an attractive irony of the situation that, despite the integrity of its makers, *Hud* is bound to prove a box-office smash. I find this coincidence gratifying. Virtue is said to be its own reward, but money is nice, too, and I'm always pleased to see it flowing toward people who have had other things on their minds.' Believing in this coincidence is like believing in Santa Claus. Gill's last sentence lacks another final 'too.' In Hollywood, a 'picture with integrity' is a moneymaking message picture. And that's what Crowther means when he says, '*Hud* is a film that does its makers, the medium and Hollywood proud.' He means something similar when he calls his own praise of the film a 'daring endorsement' — as if it placed him in some kind of jeopardy to be so forthright.

If most of the critics who acclaimed the film appeared as innocent as Lon and as moralistic as Homer, Dwight Macdonald, who perceived that 'it is poor Hud who is forced by the script to openly practice the actual as against the mythical American Way of Life' regarded this perception as proof of the stupidity of the film.

But the movie wouldn't necessarily be a good movie if its moral message was dramatically sustained in the story and action, and perhaps it isn't necessarily a bad movie if its moral message is not sustained in the story and action. By all formal theories, a work that is split cannot be a work of art, but leaving the validity of these principles aside, do they hold for lesser works — not works of art but works of commerce and craftsmanship, sometimes fused by artistry? Is a commercial piece of entertainment (which may or may not aspire to be, or pretend to be, a work of art) necessarily a poor one if its material is confused or duplicit, or reveals elements at variance with its stated theme, or shows the divided intentions of the craftsmen who made it? My answer is no, that in some films the more ambivalence that comes through, the more the film may mean to us or the more fun it may be. The process by which an idea for a movie is turned into the product that reaches us is so involved, and so many compromises, cuts, and changes may have taken place, so much hope and disgust and spoilage and waste may be embodied in it or mummified in it, that the tension in the product, or some sense of urgency still left in it, may be our only contact with the life in which the product was processed. Commercial products in which we do not sense or experience divided hopes and aims and ideas may be the dullest — ones in which everything alive was processed out, or perhaps ones that were never alive even at the beginning. *Hud* is so astutely made and yet such a mess that it tells us much more than its message. It is redeemed by its fundamental dishonesty. It is perhaps an archetypal Hollywood movie: split in so many revealing ways that, like *On the Waterfront* or *From Here to Eternity*, it is the movie of its year (even though it's shallow and not nearly so good a film as either of them).

My friends were angry that I'd sent them to *Hud* because, like Macdonald, they 'saw through it,' they saw that Hud was not the villain, and they knew that though he expressed vulgar notions that offended *them*, these notions might not be unpopular. The film itself flirts with this realization: when Homer is berating Hud, Lon asks, 'Why pick on Hud, Grandpa? Nearly everybody around town is like him.'

My friends, more or less socialist, detest a crude Hud who doesn't believe in government interference because they believe in more, and more drastic, government action to integrate the schools and end discrimination in housing and employment. However, they are so anti-CIA that at Thanksgiving dinner a respected professor could drunkenly insist that he had positive proof that the CIA had engineered the murder of Kennedy with no voice but mine raised in doubt. They want centralized power when it works for their civil-libertarian aims, but they dread and fear its international policies. They hate cops but call them at the first hint of a prowler: they are split, and it shows in a million ways. I imagine they're very like the people who made *Hud*, and like them they do rather well for themselves. They're so careful to play the game at their jobs that if they hadn't told you that they're *really* screwing the system, you'd never guess it.

Film Quarterly, 1964

Movie Brutalists

The basic ideas among young American film-makers are simple: the big movies we grew up on are corrupt, obsolete or dead, or are beyond our reach (we can't get a chance to make Hollywood films) — so we'll make films of our own, cheap films that we can make in our own way. For some this is an attempt to break into the 'industry'; for others it is a different approach to movies, a view of movies not as a popular art or a mass medium but as an art form to be explored.

Much of the movie style of young American film-makers may be explained as a reaction against the banality and luxuriant wastefulness which are so often called the superior 'craftsmanship' of Hollywood. In reaction, the young become movie brutalists.

They, and many in their audiences, may prefer the rough messiness — the uneven lighting, awkward editing, flat camera work, the undramatic succession of scenes, unexplained actions, and confusion about what, if anything, is going on — because it makes their movies seem so different from Hollywood movies. This inexpensive, inexperienced, untrained look serves as a kind of testimonial to sincerity, poverty, even purity of intentions. It is like the sackcloth of true believers which they wear in moral revulsion against the rich in their fancy garments. The look of poverty is not necessarily a necessity. I once had the experience, as chairman of the jury at an experimental film festival, of getting on the stage, in the black silk dress I had carefully mended and ironed for the occasion, to present the check to the prizewinner, who came forward in patched, faded dungarees. He got an ovation, of course. I had seen him the night before in a good dark suit, but now he had dressed for his role (deserving artist) as I had dressed for mine (distinguished critic).

Although many of the American experimentalists have developed extraordinary kinds of technique, it is no accident that the virtuoso technicians who can apparently do almost anything with drawing board or camera are not taken up as the heroes of youth in the way that brutalists are. Little is heard about Bruce Baillie or Carroll Ballard whose camera skills expose how inept, inefficient, and unimaginative much of Hollywood's self-praised work is, or about the elegance and grandeur of Jordan Belson's short abstract films, like *Allures*, that demonstrate that one man working in a basement can make Hollywood's vaunted special effects departments look archaic. Craftsmanship and skill don't, in themselves, have much appeal to youth. Rough work looks rebellious and sometimes it is: there's anger and frustration and passion, too, in those scratches and stains and multiple superimpositions that make our eyes swim. The movie brutalists, it's all too apparent, are hurting our eyes to save our souls.

They are basically right, of course, in what they're *against*. Aesthetically and morally, disgust with Hollywood's fabled craftsmanship is long overdue. I say fabled because the 'craft' claims of Hollywood, and the notion that the expensiveness of studio-produced movies is necessary for some sort of technical perfection or 'finish,' are just hucksterism. The reverse is closer to the truth: it's becoming almost impossible to produce a decent-looking movie in a Hollywood studio. In addition to the touched-up corpses of old dramatic ideas, big movies carry the dead weight of immobile cameras, all-purpose light, whorehouse décor. The production values are often ludicrously inappropriate to the subject matter, but studio executives, who charge off roughly 30 percent of a film's budget to studio overhead, are very keen on these production values which they frequently remind us are the hallmark of American movies.

In many foreign countries it is this very luxuriousness that is most envied and admired in American movies: the big cars, the fancy food, the opulent bachelor lairs, the gadget-packed family homes, even the loaded freeways and the noisy big cities. What is not so generally understood is the studio executives' implicit assumption that this is also what American audiences like. The story may not involve more than a few spies and counterspies, but the wide screen will be filled. The set decorator will pack the sides of the image with fruit and flowers and furniture.

When Hollywood cameramen and editors want to show their expertise, they imitate the effects of Japanese or European craftsmen, and then the result is pointed to with cries of 'See, we can do anything in Hollywood.' The principal demonstration of art and ingenuity among these 'craftsmen' is likely to be in getting their sons and nephews into the unions and in resisting any attempt to make Hollywood movie-making flexible enough for artists to work there. If there are no cinematographers in modern Hollywood who can be discussed in the same terms as Henri Decaë or Raoul Coutard or the late Gianni di Venanzo, it's because the studio methods and the union restrictions and regulations don't make it possible for talent to function. The talent is strangled in the business bureaucracy, and the best of our cinematographers perform safe, sane academic exercises. If the most that a gifted colorist like Lucien Ballard can hope for is to beautify a John Michael Hayes screenplay — giving an old tart a fresh complexion — why not scratch up the image?

The younger generation doesn't seem much interested in the obstacles to art in Hollywood, however. They don't much care about why the older directors do what they do or whether some of the most talented young directors in Hollywood, like Sam Peckinpah (*Ride the High Country, Major Dundee*) or Irvin Kershner (*The Hoodlum Priest, The Luck of Ginger Coffey, A Fine Madness*), will break through and do the work they should be doing. There is little interest in the work of gifted, intelligent men outside the industry, like James Blue (*The Olive Trees of Justice*) or John Korty (*The Crazy Quilt*), who are attempting to make inexpensive feature films as honestly and independently as they can. These men (and their films) are not flamboyant; they don't issue manifestos, and they don't catch the imagination of youth. Probably, like the students in film courses who often do fresh and lively work, they're not surprising enough, not different enough. The new film enthusiasts are, when it comes down to it, not any more interested in simple, small, inexpensive pictures than Hollywood is. The workmen's clothes and crude movie techniques may cry out, 'We're poor and honest. They're rich and rotten.' But, of course, you can be poor and not so very honest and, although it's harder to believe, you can even be rich and not so very rotten. What the young seem to be interested in is brutalism. In certain groups, automatic writing with a camera has come to be considered the most creative kind of film-making.

Their hero, Jean-Luc Godard — one of the most original talents ever to work in film and one of the most uneven — is not a brutalist at so simple a level, yet he comprises the attitudes of a new generation. Godard is what is meant by a 'film-maker.' The concept of a 'film-maker' — as distinguished from a director (or even writer-directors like Bergman or Fellini) — is a response and reaction to traditional methods of financing as well as shooting, and to traditional concepts of what a movie is. Godard works with a small crew and shifts ideas and attitudes from movie to movie and even within movies. While Hollywood producers straddle huge fences trying to figure out where the action is supposed to be — and never find out — Godard in himself is where the action is.

There is a disturbing quality in Godard's work that perhaps helps to explain why the young are drawn to his films and identify with them, and why so many older people call him a 'coterie' artist and don't think his films are important. *His characters don't seem to have any future.* They are most alive (and most appealing) just because they don't conceive of the day after tomorrow; they have no careers, no plans, only fantasies of roles they could play — of careers, thefts, romance, politics, adventure, pleasure, a life like in the movies. Even his world of the future, *Alphaville*, is, photographically, a documentary of Paris in the present. (All of his films are in that sense documentaries — as were also, and also by necessity, the grade B American gangster films that influenced him.) And even before *Alphaville*, the people in *A Married Woman* were already science fiction — so blank and affectless no mad scientist was required to destroy their souls.

His characters are young, unrelated to families and background. Whether deliberately or unconsciously, he makes his characters orphans who, like the students in the theatres, feel only attachments to friends, to lovers — attachments that will end with a chance word or the close of the semester. They're orphans, by extension, in a larger sense, too, unconnected with the world, feeling out of relationship to it. They're a generation of familiar strangers.

An elderly gentleman recently wrote me, 'Oh, they're such a bore, bore, bore, modern youth! All attitudes and nothing behind the attitudes. When I was in my twenties, I didn't just loaf around, being a rebel, I went places and did things. The reason they all hate the squares is because the squares remind them of the one thing they are trying to forget: there *is* a Future and you must build for it.'

He's wrong, I think. The young are not 'trying to forget': they just don't think in those terms. Godard's power — and possibly his limitation — as an artist is that he so intensely expresses how they do feel and think. His characters don't plan or worry about careers or responsibilities; they just live. Youth makes them natural aristocrats in their indifference to sustenance, security, hard work; and prosperity has turned a whole generation — or at least the middle-class part of it — into aristocrats. And it's astonishing how many places they do go to and how many things they can do. The difference is in how easily they do it all. Even their notion of creativity — as what comes naturally — is surprisingly similar to the aristocratic artist's conde-scension toward those middle-class plodders who have to labor for a living, for an education, for 'culture.'

Here, too, Godard is the symbol, exemplar, and proof. He makes it all seem so effortless, so personal — just one movie after another. Because he is so skillful and so incredibly disciplined that he can make his pictures for under a hundred thousand dollars, and because there is enough of a youthful audience in France to support these pictures, he can do almost anything he wants within those budgetary limits. In this achievement of independence, he is almost alone among movie direc-tors: it is a truly heroic achievement. For a younger generation he is the proof that it is possible to make and go on making films your own way. And yet they don't seem aware of how rare he is or how hard it is to get in that position. Even if colleges and foundations make it easier than it has ever been, they will need not only talent but toughness to be independent.

As Godard has been able to solve the problems of economic freedom, his work now poses the problems of artistic freedom — problems that few artists in the history of movies have been fortunate enough to face. The history of great film directors is a history of economic and political obstacles — of compromises, defeats, despair, even disgrace. Griffith, Eisenstein, von Stroheim, von Sternberg, Cocteau, Renoir, Max Ophuls, Orson Welles — they were defeated because they weren't in a position to do what they wanted to do. If Godard fails, it will be because what he wants to do — which is what he *does* — isn't good enough.

Maybe he is attempting to escape from freedom when he makes a beautiful work and then, to all appearances, just throws it away. There is a self-destructive urgency in his treatment of themes, a drive toward a quick finish. Even if it's suicidal for the hero or the work, Godard is impatient for the ending: the mood of his films is that there's no way for things to work out anyway, something must be done even if it's disastrous, no action is intolerable.

It seems likely that many of the young who don't wait for others to call them artists, but simply announce that they are, don't have the patience to make art. A student's idea of a film-maker isn't someone who has to sit home and study and think and work — as in most of the arts — but someone who goes out with friends and shoots — a social activity. It is an extroverted and egotistic image of the genius-creator. It is the Fellini-Guido figure of *8½*, the movie director as star. Few seem to have noticed that by the time of *Juliet of the Spirits* he had turned into a professional party-giver. Film-making, carried out the way a lot of kids do it, is like having a party. And their movie 'ideas' are frequently no more than staging and shooting a wild, weird party.

'Creativity' is a quick route to power and celebrity. The pop singer or composer, the mod designer, says of his work, 'It's a creative way to make a living' — meaning it didn't take a dull lot of study and planning, that he was able to use his own inventiveness or ingenuity or talent to get to the top without much sweat. I heard a young film-maker put it this way to a teen-age art student: 'What do you go to life class for? Either you can draw or you can't. What you should do is have a show. It's important to get exposure.' One can imagine their faces if they had to listen to those teachers who used to tell us that you had to be able to do things the traditional ways before you earned the right to break loose and do things *your* way. They simply take shortcuts into other art forms or into pop arts where they can 'express themselves' now. Like cool Peter Pans, they just take off and fly.

Godard's conception of technique can be taken as a highly intellec-tualized rationale for these attitudes. 'The ideal for me,' he says, 'is to obtain right away what will work — and without retakes. If they are necessary, it falls short of the mark. The immediate is chance. At the same time it is definitive. What I want is the definitive by chance.' Sometimes, almost magically, he seems to get it — as in many scenes of *Breathless* and *Band of Outsiders* — but often, as in *A Married Woman*, he seems to settle for arbitrary effects.

A caricature of this way of talking is common among young American film-makers. Some of them believe that everything they catch on film is definitive, so they do not edit at all. As proof that they do not mar their instinct with pedantry or judgment, they may retain the blank leader to the roll of film. As proof of their creative sincerity they may leave in the blurred shots.

Preposterous as much of this seems, it is theoretically not so far from Godard's way of working. Although his technical control is

superb, so complete that one cannot tell improvisation from planning, the ideas and bits of business are often so arbitrary that they
appear to be (and probably are) just things that he chanced to think
of that day, or that he came across in a book he happened to be
reading. At times there is a disarming, an almost ecstatic innocence
about the way he uses quotes as if he had just heard of these beautiful
ideas and wanted to share his enthusiasm with the world. After
smiling with pleasure as we do when a child's discovery of the
beauty of a leaf or a poem enables us to re-experience the wonder of
responsiveness, we may sink in spirit right down to incredulity. For
this is the rapture with 'thoughts' of those whose minds aren't much
sullied by thought. These are 'thoughts' without thought: they don't
come out of a line of thought or a process of thinking, they don't
arise from the situation. They're 'inspirations' — bright illumina-
tions from nowhere — and this is what kids who think of themselves
as poetic or artistic or creative think ideas are: noble sentiments.
They decorate a movie and it is easy for viewers to feel that they give
it depth, that if followed, these clues lead to understanding of the
work. But if those who follow the clues come out with odd and
disjunctive interpretations, this is because the 'clues' are *not* integral
to the movie but are clues to what else the artist was involved in
while he was making the movie.

Putting into the work whatever just occurred to the artist is its own
rationale and needs no justification for young Americans encouraged
from childhood to express themselves creatively and to say whatever
came into their heads. Good liberal parents didn't want to push their
kids in academic subjects but oohed and aahed with false delight when
their children presented them with a baked ashtray or a woven doily.
Did anyone guess or foresee what narcissistic confidence this generation would develop in its banal 'creativity'? Now we're surrounded,
inundated by artists. And a staggering number of them wish to be or
already call themselves 'film-makers.'

A few years ago a young man informed me that he was going to
'give up' poetry and avant-garde film (which couldn't have been
much of a sacrifice as he hadn't done anything more than talk about
them) and devote himself to writing 'art songs.' I remember asking,
'Do you read music?' and not being especially surprised to hear that
he didn't. I knew from other young men that the term 'art' used as an
adjective meant that they were bypassing even the most rudimentary
knowledge in the field. Those who said they were going to make art

movies not only didn't consider it worth their while to go to see ordinary commercial movies, but usually didn't even know anything much about avant-garde film. I did not pursue the subject of 'art songs' with this young man because it was perfectly clear that he wasn't going to do anything. But some of the young who say they're going to make 'art movies' are actually beginning to make movies. Kids who can't write, who have never developed any competence in photography, who have never acted in nor directed a play, see no deterrent to making movies. And although most of the results are bad beyond our wildest fears, as if to destroy all our powers of prediction a few, even of the most ignorant, pretentious young men and women, are doing some interesting things.

Yet why are the Hollywood movies, even the worst overstuffed ones, often easier to sit through than the short experimental ones? Because they have actors and a story. Through what is almost a technological fluke, 16 mm movie cameras give the experimental film-maker greater flexibility than the 'professional' 35 mm camera user, but he cannot get adequate synchronous sound. And so the experimentalists, as if to convert this liability into an advantage, have asserted that their partial use of the capabilities of the medium is the true art of the cinema, which is said to be purely visual. But their visual explorations of their states of consciousness (with the usual implicit social protest) get boring, the mind begins to wander, and though this lapse in attention can be explained to us as a new kind of experience, as even the purpose of cinema, our desire to see a movie hasn't been satisfied. (There are, of course, some young film-makers who are not interested in movies as we ordinarily think of them, but in film as an art medium like painting or music, and this kind of work must be looked at a different way — without the expectation of story content or meaning.) They probably won't be able to make satisfying *movies* until the problems of sound are solved not only technically but in terms of drama, structure, meaning, relevance.

It is not an answer to toss on a spoofing semi-synchronous sound track as a number of young film-makers do. It can be funny in a cheap sort of way — as in Robert Downey's *Chafed Elbows* where the images and sound are, at least, in the same style; but this isn't fundamentally different from the way George Axelrod works in *Lord Love a Duck* or Blake Edwards in *What Did You Do in the War, Daddy?*, and there's no special reason to congratulate people for doing underground what is driving us down there. Total satire is opportunistic and easy; what's difficult is to make a movie in which something is taken seriously without making a fool of yourself.

Is Hollywood interested in the young movement? If it attracts customers, Hollywood will eat it up, the way *The Wild Angels* has already fed upon *Scorpio Rising*. At a party combining the commercial and noncommercial worlds of film, a Hollywood screen writer watched as an underground film-maker and his wife entered. The wife was wearing one of those classic film-makers' wives' outfits: a simple sack of burlap in natural brown, with scarecrow sleeves. The screen writer greeted her enthusiastically, 'I really dig your dress, honey,' he said, 'I used to have a dress like that once.'

The New Republic, 1966

The Making of *The Group*

Those who get disgusted with American movies may often be heard asking why America isn't producing great film directors — as if we had a shortage of *talent*, as if artists were yet to be attracted to the medium. The more relevant question might be: does the American film industry foster mediocrity and make it almost impossible for artists to work?

What kind of people get to make movies, and what gives a movie its particular shape? I hoped to find some possible answers by observing how Mary McCarthy's novel *The Group* became the movie *The Group*.

The Package

By August 28, 1963, when the novel was published, every major American motion picture studio had considered it and turned it down. Charles K. Feldman, an agent turned independent packager of movie properties — a function sometimes described as 'executive producer' — bought it for $162,500 (partly in deferred payments) plus 10 percent of the distributor's gross after the break-even point, and proceeded to try to convince the companies that had already rejected the book to finance the production. *The Group* had just reached the bookstores: Feldman hired publicity men to promote it. In addition to the publishers' advertising expenditures, he says he put $50,000 into advertising in the United States, $12,000 in England, and sizable amounts into other countries where the novel was coming out in translation. He claims that it was his money that made the book a bestseller. Several reasonably disinterested publishers I have talked with say that *The Group* would have made it without Feldman's money (though it may have helped in keeping the book so high on the lists for so long). Feldman's principal aim was to increase the value of his property so that he could make an advantageous deal with one of the studios. They would need convincing, of course, that the book which they had not thought would make a movie *could* be made into a movie. On the Riviera, he arranged with Sidney Buchman, a veteran Hollywood writer, to adapt the book and serve as producer. Long ago when Buchman had been head of production at Columbia, Feldman had been his agent. Now, Feldman hired Buchman for $185,000, plus a percentage.

Buchman is almost a one-man history of Hollywood. His first screenplay was for Cecil B. De Mille's *The Sign of the Cross* in 1932; his credits as writer or co-writer include such diverse films as *If I Had a Million, Theodora Goes Wild, Mr Smith Goes to Washington, Holiday, Here Comes Mr Jordan, Talk of the Town, Jolson Sings Again* and *A Song to Remember*. Buchman's career fell apart during the House Un-American Activities Committee hearings. He went abroad, made his home at Cannes, and except for the 1961 English film, *The Mark*, which he produced and co-authored, and perhaps a little bootleg job here or there, he was out of work (in a gentlemanly, comfortable way) for fifteen years. He was sixty-three when he took on the labor of *The Group* — a very tired and cynical sixty-three, and yet, curiously enough, determined to turn this new movie into some kind of progressive statement.

It might be asked at this point: why didn't Mary McCarthy adapt her own material for the screen? On the first page of her first book she had used an analogy with movies to describe her writing process, and her fiction — which is reportorial and semi-autobiographical — is peculiarly cinematic. She records characters and relationships from the outside and she details the costumes, furnishings, and locations that give the actions specific meanings. Is there a more completely worked-out scenario in modern fiction than 'The Man in the Brooks Brothers Shirt'? It's already a movie. However, there is no indication that she was asked to work on *The Group*. She told Feldman that she didn't think the novel could work as a movie without a lot of invention. But Buchman stayed very close to the book, hardly even inventing any dialogue, although transposing characters' thoughts into speech. She had not asked to see the screenplay. Buchman sent her a copy, anyway. She did not comment on it. Perhaps his fidelity to her material did not please her any more than infidelity might have; she is, notoriously, a writer given to seeing the faults in *any* course of action. And in this case it was obvious that neither inventiveness nor fidelity could be completely satisfactory. There were huge structural gaps in the book that in dramatic terms (and in terms of fiction also) cried out for invention; yet Buchman must have known that he could not invent in her style. He played it safe, preferring narrative holes to inadequate invention.

This was not exactly pleasing to Feldman, who admits publicly that he has no interest in Mary McCarthy's stature as a writer. Feldman's enthusiasm for the project had little to do with the literary qualities or dramatic potential of Miss McCarthy's work, but on the gorgeous possibility of getting options on a group of inexpensive, luscious young nobodies, building them up into stars, and then having them available for his own films and for handsome loan-out deals. He had had a similar intention when he bought *What's New, Pussycat?* — which he had also intended to cast with unknowns and little-knowns. But somehow things got out of hand, in the way movie financing-casting (a peculiarly linked process) often does, and he had wound up with Peter O'Toole, Peter Sellers, Capucine, Ursula Andress, Romy Schneider, and Paula Prentiss. This time, with a property featuring eight young girls, surely he would get his own young Capucines and Andresses; and with a stable of young beauties under option, a modern movie packager-producer could be richer than the greatest whoremasters of history. (There are even directors in Hollywood who make more money from the pieces they own of the stars they gave their first break to than from directing.) Feldman's ideas of casting are rather basic: 'You can always teach them to act.' He was so confident that this time he would get cheap stars out of the deal that when Buchman had completed a draft of the screenplay, and United Artists became interested, he stipulated as part of the package deal that UA should spend at least $100,000 to exploit the new talent (which he assumed would be *his* new talent).

There was another special interest that Feldman had in the book: a chance to exploit a lesbian theme. He assumed that the screenplay would center on Lakey's affairs — which would, of course, have to be invented for her. Instead, Buchman held so close to the text that waiting for Lakey to reappear in the movie is about like waiting for Godot. And the whole lesbian theme was handled with such discretion that when the movie was finished the United Artists publicity men threw out the campaign they had prepared to exploit it and prepared a new campaign featuring a true-confessions approach to each of the girls.

At the point when the deal was made, Charles K. Feldman became The Man in the background, and Sidney Buchman, more or less in charge of the production, began looking for a director. Most of the men interviewed were television directors who had never made a movie. This partly explains why recent movies are so bad: there is almost no way for young movie directors to get experience or make a reputation except on television (which is very different from movie-making, although movie-making is now becoming like television) or the theatre (which is even more different). But the older movie directors are dying off or are priced out of the market (they work on huge, slow super-epics). So for a production like this, TV and stage directors are considered and may get their first movie experience. Negotiations and discussions were going on with these men when Sidney Lumet, who has the same agent as Buchman, saw the script and leaped at the job. Lumet had not read the novel; it's doubtful if he'd ever read any Mary McCarthy. What he leaped at, evidently, was Sidney Buchman's screenplay, a job that would pay him $125,000, and a movie with a longer shooting schedule and a larger budget than he had ever had.

Why were they about to start on the cumbersome, tedious process of making a movie out of this novel? Why were they going to all the trouble of construction and reproduction to tell a story that had already been told in a simple, efficient, inexpensive way? Sometimes there are people who really want to bring their vision of a particular novel to life. But the filming of *The Group* was strictly a business proposition. Yet it presented aesthetic problems. In theory, there is little that a novel can do that a movie can't but, practically, American audiences won't sit for the length and detail and complexity of a novel. Almost all the details in this novel — the fads and fashions and chitchat — could be dramatically rendered, but how would the movie re-create the political climate, the sexual morality, the décor of the thirties — the so recent past — for the 'large' movie audience? Much distortion and simplification was inevitable; perhaps even more was accidental.

Sidney Lumet had been getting work directing movies for several years because he was cheap, fast, and reliable; but when he was signed for *The Group* he had still never had a box-office hit. And the people who put movie packages together are more concerned with box-office results than with the quality of the films. Lumet was known to critics and perhaps to the art-house audience for his first movie, the one-set, low-budget *Twelve Angry Men*, which, despite critical enthusiasm, hadn't shown a profit; the literate, uneven *Stage Struck*; the spectacular artistic and commercial disaster, the Brando-Magnani *The Fugitive Kind*; the ambitious and financially unsuccessful *A View from the Bridge*; and the superb transcription of O'Neill's *Long Day's Journey into Night*, which had cost less than a half million and still lost money. He had been making some of the most interesting movies coming out of the United States, but without at least one winner he had no standing in the world of big movies, big profits.

He was part of that earlier television-into-movies new generation of directors, but two other members of that generation, John Frankenheimer and Martin Ritt, had already made it into the big time with *hits*, and he was still in the young-promising category, i.e. hustling, taking the quick jobs (like *Fail-Safe*) that bigger directors didn't want. He could get these jobs because of his reputation for staying within budget and maybe even finishing *ahead* of schedule. Lumet wanted to work and he *liked* to work fast. He would not try to reshape the scenario or risk holding up production to do something unscheduled; he wouldn't plead for a few extra days to get something right.

If a director in another country has succeeded financially with an unusual project or approach, he is acclaimed as an artist and the big American companies are anxious to get him, but if a young American director shows any traces of really caring about what he does or how he does it — any signs of artistry — they become uneasy and clamp down on him. Art means risks; to businessmen, taking risks is unprofessional behavior. But by the time a man has made a TV reputation, he knows the score and there's very little he has left of his own to express. He has become a mechanic, and he'll approach making a movie as a job promotion, a step up from television. Businessmen want directors they can trust on the basis of past performance (and this, ironically, may be one of the reasons so many small pictures lose money). Lumet was television-trained; that meant he would do things the obvious ways that producers don't worry about. Or, if he did give them something to worry about, at least it would be something they could understand. And even without any hits on his record, Lumet was trustworthy because, for example, he never considered it a deterrent factor that when he read the novel he hated it. He was no dangerous artist; he was out to do a job.

Sidney Lumet's background was about as far from Mary McCarthy's Vassar as you can get. The son of an actor from Poland who appeared in the Yiddish theatre in New York (the elder Lumet appears as Mr Schneider in *The Group*), he had himself been an infant actor — indeed the infant Jesus in Max Reinhardt's New York production of *The Eternal Road*. He was Christ again, as a boy, in Maxwell Anderson's *Journey to Jerusalem*, with Arlene Francis as Mary. He was understudy to one of the Dead End Kids on Broadway, and it is not perhaps stretching the point to suggest that both of these roles are still visible in his behavior. He's messianic and driven, but like an understudy to a Dead End Kid, he's in a hurry to get there. Lumet, in the conventional sense, is probably not very well educated. But, in a way, untutored high intelligence may make a person seem even more 'creative,' as if it came out of nowhere, was 'genius.' And in show business people love the idea of 'genius': it's so much easier to throw the term about than to try to explain why certain people manage to get somewhere. Lumet, despite his almost ostentatious show-business streetboy's manner, is very well self-educated in terms of what he may be able to use. He reads for a purpose. A standard complaint of his earlier producers is: 'Sidney doesn't listen.' But he hears what he wants to, not what they want him to. In conversation, he doesn't respond to what doesn't immediately relate to his own interests, so the subject soon changes, or he simply changes it — as he is likely to be the dominating force anyway. He seems to have almost no intellectual curiosity of a more generalized or objective nature.

Working on *The Group*, Lumet was not scholarly — to put it mildly — about Mary McCarthy or about Vassar, but as a life-long actor and an experienced TV and movie director, he showed a professional respect for acting and his job. He and Buchman did the casting together, and, with the exception of Candice Bergen, a beauty glorious and young enough to gladden Feldman's and anyone else's heart, they selected for talent. Candy Bergen was hardly a poor struggling unknown who could be signed up for peanuts and promises and tied up for years of servitude. And the two Sidneys moved so fast in casting and getting underway that by the time Feldman's minions, uncertain and apprehensive about whether Feldman would want the other girls — actresses! — and *which* of them, got around to framing agreements, the girls were already in the picture and didn't need to sign away their futures in order to get this chance.

The Casting

The casting of movies is in some ways more important than the casting of plays: in the theatre a competent actor can make many roles his own, but in movies what an actor knows and can do is often less important than what he simply physically *is* — the way he looks, how he photographs, what he inadvertently projects. On stage he may be able to become a whole gallery of characters; but the camera exposes the actor as a man of a certain age, with definite physical assets and liabilities. There he is in close-up, huge on the screen, and if he's trying to play something that is physically different from what he is, he looks like a fool, and only if he is a good and subtle actor can he play something that is psychologically very different from how he is. When a movie is derived from a popular novel, the casting is even more complex: the roles have not been written with certain actors in mind; rather, the actors must somehow fit into the novelist's conception, or at least into a conception the public will accept as a reasonable facsimile. At best, in popular, commercial movies they should be like illustrations to the text — whose cover they will probably adorn in the paperback edition that is timed to the release of the film; or so popular in themselves that they will be stronger than the images in the text. All that was obvious from the outside — I knew it as a critic; these were simply the facts of the situation. But sitting in a little office with the producer and director as they interviewed actors and then discussed them, there were factors I had never really considered as a critic.

Everybody knows and talks about the state of the theatre; we all know there are few jobs, except in TV, which is now almost all in

California, but here was the living evidence — actors trying to get a job. Budgeted at $2,600,000, *The Group* was the most expensive movie yet made in New York; there were a lot of parts in it, and perhaps half the out-of-work actors in New York at one time or another must have had hopes. As each actor or actress came in for the prearranged interview, the air in the little room was heavy with strain and embarrassment. Many of them had worked with Lumet in his early days in the theatre or in radio, or had been directed by him in early live TV, so there were the tentative reminders of past association — uneasy good wishes to be conveyed to his father, an uncertainty about how far to press old intimacies with their former associate, now in a job-giving capacity. Powerlessness made them uncertain of how to deal with power; desperation made them transparent. The women in turbans or big, tricky hats all seemed to apologize for their hair; one after another explained how their agents had just notified them of the interview. Asked their height, most of the men gave the all-purpose five-eleven — wanting to be considered neither too short nor too tall for whatever the role might be. In fear of being considered wrong, and not knowing what they were being considered for, they tried to pass themselves off as Everyman. They had been preceded, of course, by photographs — large, glossy, glamorous photographs sent in by agents, and as Lumet said, 'What's heartbreaking is the pictures versus the people.' We saw them as they *had* looked or *could* look or had been *doctored* to look, and then we *saw* them. It was like people on TV commercials versus people in subways.

And I was horrified because they were people I knew: I had seen them in my childhood in the theatre in San Francisco, I had seen them touring with Katharine Cornell or acting in New York 'hits,' I had seen them long ago in the movies as juvenile leads, or in character roles — almost all of them were familiar names in the theatre, people I thought of as established, secure, honored. And here they were trying to get bit parts, eager for a few days' work, for a two-line role, and not knowing whether to conceal their desperation or whether to expose it. You could see them trying to calculate how much 'front' they should put on, or whether a naked appeal would be preferable. And they spoke in voices I knew so well, the voices that seemed to belong to their past more than to their present. Some of those familiar faces were aged, others just burnt-out. I think the worst thing to watch — because it was the most human, really — was when they tried uncertainly to play it both ways: to conceal what shape they were in and yet somehow to appeal. In succession, each applicant threw illumination on the others. It became like some terrible TV show in which the great, the famous, the celebrated expose their wrecked careers, their shameful poverty, their knowledge that they're drifting, waiting for a break, and maybe this show is it. It's as if they'd never had the breaks, never been famous, because now they scarcely expect to be remembered. Too many people have obviously forgotten them; they know how little it means in terms of getting jobs that they were once stars or almost-stars, that they're 'well known.'

Why do producers and directors begin to play God? Because they do play God.

I had only a couple of weeks of observing the casting in May: it had been going on since late February. (They had looked at over two hundred 'promising' young actresses for the eight leads; I didn't even want to think about what their pitches must have been like, how eager they must have been for a chance to make their names, change their fortunes. How cool they must have tried to appear, perhaps almost as cool as those who got the roles and then tried to appear indifferent to them. If one believed what they told the papers, several of the girls in the picture really didn't know why they bothered doing it at all.) I found two weeks of it hard to take — like living in a butcher shop with human meat. I had heard plenty of descriptions from actor friends, but I had never seen it from the other side. The casting director had selected the candidates for the meager little roles being cast: mothers or fathers of the girls of *The Group*, a butler, friends — roles that were later cut or reduced to a glimpse, anyway. And so sometimes it went to the actor who had exposed his need more, and then I couldn't help thinking, 'Suppose that other one who came on so prosperous and pleasant was really even more desperate and too proud to show it.' Most of the middle-aged performers were being considered for the parent roles, and unfortunately those who did not get the parts could not know — and probably they wouldn't have *believed* even if they were told — that they weren't picked because they didn't match up right with their 'daughters.' After a lifetime in the 'theatre' they were being picked not for what they could play, but for their physical types and for chance resemblances. And those who did get these small parts were of course really too good for the roles, which required almost no acting, and whenever they had a line they gave it so much full-throated voice and elegant gesture and presence that the lines generally had to be cut, because all that acting was florid and stagey and ridiculous. They were trying to turn movie bits into rich roles, and the results were generally disastrous: nonprofessionals type-cast might have done as well, or better. But then nonprofessionals probably wouldn't have needed the work so much.

What sustained these people in the most delusionary of all careers — 'acting'? There is a great deal written about the rich fantasy life and role playing in the childhood of actors, but actors may have nothing else to sustain them later on, either. Why do they stick with it? Many don't, of course, and I was to meet them shortly. They were the 'crew': from the director on down, they were almost all actors who had given up.

The Actresses

In the novel the girls are all satellites of Lakey, the rich aesthete who turns out to be that familiar skeleton in the closet of 'sophisticated' fiction, the International Lesbian. Several of the actresses were vaguely and some actively unhappy about not getting the Lakey role. They were even more unhappy when the studio publicity agents turned them into satellites of Candy Bergen, who is cast as Lakey.

Candice Bergen, the celebrated 19-year-old model and daughter of Edgar Bergen and ex-model Frances Westerman Bergen, is like some mythological creature. She's so inordinately beautiful that at first one is awe-struck just looking at this golden lioness of a girl. And she's perfectly pleasant to talk to, a nice big girl. But it's somewhat disconcerting — perhaps because you expect something extraordinary, expect that her conversation will be commensurate with her beauty. You want Candy to speak the lines of a *Deirdre of the Sorrows*, or of some heroine in history.

After a while I found her the least interesting to watch during rehearsals and shooting because she doesn't have the concentration or the self-awareness of a trained actress. Nothing happens when she 'acts' (yet her beauty on screen is quite enough). Something does happen to the other girls when they do a scene, and it is exciting to watch them focus into their roles. But Candy just walks through doing, as best she can, what she is told to do. The blandness of this attitude, the lack of interest in what is being done, makes her seem dull. Here she is, an intelligent young girl, beginning — despite her disclaimers — a career in the movies, and she doesn't appear interested enough even to stay awake and observe. It is as if she hasn't yet discovered what acting is all about, not even enough to pay attention to the other girls when they are doing it. And they are *good*, most of these girls; they are something to watch. They know how to control their bodies, how to make their moves mean something. They haven't got where they are by chance.

Here is the odd thing about movies. These seven are all lovely girls, used to playing the beautiful young ingenue, used to being the center of attention. I think that several, with any kind of luck, are destined for stardom and great fame. But Bergen is a natural goddess. And the movies, like religious myths, dote on goddesses. This is in the nature of the movies: the camera feasts on natural beauty. It seems unfair of course, but there it is — nature is unfair.

These girls are often brilliant on the screen but when Candy Bergen is on with them it is hard to take your eyes off her. She doesn't know how to move, she cannot say her lines so that one sounds different from the one before. As an actress, her only flair is in her nostrils. And she just naturally upstages the others. There she is, like a living act of God.

She wants these actresses, who have every reason to resent her for being a gorgeous amateur, to fuss over her when she squeezes out a few tears for a scene. (As one crew member said to me, 'What did she want? We followed her around, and said, "You were great, Candy, you were great." ') It's the start of a major movie-goddess career, to be both contemptuous of it all and to expect praise for the slightest effort.

She has described the director as a 'marmoset' and 'a rather loud captain who didn't want his rank forgotten.' Damn right he didn't: he'd worked too hard to get it. Everything has come easy to her. As Cocteau said, 'The privileges of beauty are enormous.'

Sidney Lumet will swallow his anger and go off to England to direct Candy Bergen again in a John Le Carré spy story; he'll cozen her and flatter her and try to keep her awake on the set so that she can move in front of the cameras now and then. And she will probably be just as impersonally, ostentatiouslly bored as she had been on *The Group* — that boredom which is a sign of privilege and which is an insult to every kid in the world who would give half her soul for the chance she has, that boredom of the gods which is so appropriate to movie queens.

Despite the publicity accorded Candy Bergen, Jessica Walter and Shirley Knight, the favorite of the crew is undoubtedly Kathleen Widdoes. She has the beautiful little Buddha face of a young Merle Oberon. In profile she is delicately implacable — a priestess of some nameless foreign country. Despite the sensitive, reserved performance she gives as Helena, her charm is that she is an unusually unself-conscious girl. Smiling and relaxed, she seems to be that rare creature, the intelligent extrovert. To make her movie debut as the sexless Helena cannot please her much, but she doesn't make a big thing about it. The camera crew loves her so much they often run a few extra feet after she's finished a scene, just for the pleasure of capturing her ravishing smiles. (Director Sidney Lumet kept saying, 'She's such a good actress!' When the movie was over, Sidney Buchman, the writer-producer, said, 'That girl could have played any one of the parts.')

Joan Hackett is perhaps the strangest of the girls. During the first weeks she looked so frightened and dedicated she seemed more like a nun than an acress. She never just asked a question; she moved up to Lumet and murmured something to him: it was inaudible but she seemed so serious and worried I always thought she was telling him she was ill. Lumet was remarkably patient; he adapted to her intensely shy manner, talking to her very quietly.

Some of this anxiety of hers was apparently centered on the decision to use color, because she seemed to be afraid that she was allergic to color makeup. (Her anxiety was allayed by ordering some special makeup flown in from France, which she never used.) She seemed totally unworldly, all huddled up in clothes and terrors. She had been a very successful model and I had seen her do brilliant work on TV, and so I couldn't imagine what she was carrying on about. She seemed almost passionate in her withdrawn way. No smiles, no small amenities — as if she was too serious for any of that. Possibly it was some kind of reverse temperament, and perhaps she was so worried simply because her big scenes were among the first to be shot.

I never figured out if Joan Hackett's unworldliness was genuine fright or just a way of making herself seem different from the other girls. (As each was concerned to seem different, it had the reverse effect: it became just something they shared.) But after the first few weeks, a new and remarkably assured, casual, flippant and chic Joan Hackett emerged smiling. The same girl who had had the set practically shrouded when she did her seduction scene — though she was wearing a Merry Widow — now appeared for the rushes wearing pink bell-bottom slacks, and on the set modeled for *Harper's Bazaar* in one elegant gown after another, with the blank-faced imperial nothing look of an accomplished professional model.

She is simply great in rehearsals: I find myself smiling with pleasure, watching her and listening to her. Her humor is radiant, shy and schoolgirlish. There is only one trouble: she sets her own rhythm. The performance all seems to come out of her (without relationship to the other actors or the script) and, although she's marvelous, she takes forever. What is the camera going to do during the pauses in her sentences?

There wasn't enough for it to do, and it was hell in the editing room, trying to save her performance. She even took too long entering a room, and I never could tell if she was thinking it out during all those pauses or if she was trying to milk her scenes. I wondered at the time why Lumet didn't try to speed her up. Her readings got to be a joke among the crew. They would ask Maggie James (the script girl and a former chorine), 'What did that sentence clock in at?' Lumet may have been right to be cautious. I suspect he didn't know the answer either and wasn't going to risk having her fly apart or walk off or whatever. The results, though they scarcely even suggest some of her marvelous inventiveness, justify his letting her do it her way.

Mary-Robin Redd is much prettier than she looks as Pokey. She has a little Carole Lombard, Eve Arden, Mary Boland in her. About as non-method as you can be, she is a traditional kind of good-humored young comedienne, and she walks on sensational, traffic-stopping legs. Eyes follow those legs about the set.

Something went wrong at the start of the casting. Shirley Knight, as the best-known actress in the group and the recipient of two Academy Award nominations, was considered for the two biggest roles, Kay and Polly. Had she been selected for the central role of Kay, the picture might have had a center. Shirley Knight has the strength to play Kay. But she was cast as the sweeter character, dear little likeable Polly; and this decision, made right at the beginning and not necessarily a wrong one for *her* in terms of her career, was wrong for the story the picture is presumably telling.

Kay is not easy to like, and almost impossible to play; it needs a young Katharine Hepburn perhaps, someone who could be intensely wrong about just about everything. She is, I think, one of the author's bad dreams of herself, the epitome of all pushing women who are really unsure of themselves and who devote their energies to the careers of 'genius' husbands. A difficult role, it is nevertheless the key role, for Kay, with all her delusions and needs to be a leader, is the suffering center of the novel, the poor witch whose story is told from wedding to funeral.

As Kay, Joanna Pettet had a miserable experience in her first movie role. A perfect type for frivolous, lightheaded comedy roles — giddy, bouncy girls with naturally bee-stung lips and a twinkly smile like Stella Stevens, she became more and more frantic trying to carry out the director's instructions.

Lumet, so patient with most of the cast, grew tense and irritable with her, doing retake after retake. I thought his directions to her — which mainly just made her talk too fast and move too much, were not so very different from the TV concept of how you show a villainess — keep the actress smoking.

Shirley Knight, too strong for Polly's early scenes, played them coyly, but has fine moments later in the film. She has rather startling ways of showing her experience: she could complete a semi-nude love scene and then, as the director called 'cut,' turn her head, without taking a breath, and call out, 'Sidney, you're printing this take, aren't you?'

Elizabeth Hartman's beauty is not fully caught in the role of Priss. She stays in character. She has the kind of timid, dainty loveliness that almost suggests heroines of the silent movie period, and a red-haired glowing quality when she isn't timid that is like a blossoming. She has almost ideal attributes for a movie actress; she doesn't project too much, she concentrates on the role. And she's a good, subtle actress. Whether she can develop the toughness necessary for a real acting career is the only doubt one might feel for her future.

It wasn't necessary for the girls to be tough on *The Group* because the Sidneys — Lumet and Buchman — protected them. Buchman is a gentleman and, despite his newsboy's manner, Lumet is, too. The actresses were always treated as ladies — if they are ladies.

Jessica Walter has what Buchman calls 'a brute talent.' Everything she reacts to is in her face and big enough to reach over the rafters. It's a gift of a kind. As Libby she has the pure old M-G-M look — the restorative vitality of vulgarity. And she often has it on the set — talking to someone, she gives a professional reflex of a smile, turns into Ann-Margret or Miss Rheingold, says the silly things that starlets are always quoted as saying, like, 'If plays stop coming along, I'll just have to swallow my pride and make movies.' She has had five years as a heavy in daytime TV, and I've run into several members of a Jessica Walter cult, people who are absolutely fascinated by her bad, bad girls — the traditional primrose path to movie stardom.

But when Jessica Walter isn't 'on' with people, when she's just watching what's going on around her, her face is opaque and you can't tell what she's receiving. And sometimes when she is tired, without makeup and in repose, you can imagine her in Chekhov or in Greek tragedy; she is as darkly beautiful as a tragic muse. Perhaps Joan Crawford once was, too?

Watching these eight actresses become the visual embodiment of Mary McCarthy's girls, I began to see that there might be a difference between stage and screen that I hadn't considered before. It's simply that miscasting is not so obvious on screen as on stage. In a play, you can see an actress in a role and think of another actress who should have played it; in a movie, the physical qualities of the actress dominate the role; she is more vivid than any concept of the role and she becomes your idea of the character. In a sense, the screen actress *is* her role in a way the stage actress isn't. In a play you separate the two — particularly in a bad performance.

These actresses are now the Mary McCarthy girls, and will be seen in the mind's eye of those who now read the book.

The Planning

Under modern production conditions, the key figures in movie-making, who on this film were the producer-writer and the director, are businessmen who claim the prestige and the latitude of the genius-artist role. Buchman and Lumet were already negotiating for their next projects when this one actually got underway. The crucial work for them seemed to be finished before the shooting started: the 'deal' and the planning of the production (which, like running a war, involves an almost incredible amount of detail, ledgers full of plans and calculations, including everything from transporting and feeding the actresses to having thirties cars ready at a certain place at a certain date). Like other businessmen, they were already planning their winter line while turning out the summer product. Buchman said he could hardly wait for this to be over so he could 'get on to some real work.' Eager to get back into his old harness, he was working on a Howard Fast novel. Lumet, while hoping to line up something that 'really excited' him — the production of a John Hersey book — was planning his next job, a John Le Carré spy thriller. But, though priding themselves on being good businessmen — which in movie business is what is usually meant by 'profession-alism' — they did not necessarily recognize how completely they were businessmen, perhaps because they felt that they really be-lieved, if not in this project, at least in those future hoped-for Howard Fast and John Hersey projects.

For Lumet, planning includes the camera position for each shot, the lens to be used, and just about everything the technicians need to know. The camera will rarely move within a shot; 'movement' will be accomplished by the actors moving within the frame and by the rapid juxtaposition of shots. During the actual shooting, the director puts the actors through their paces, trying to get some sense of life — mainly by encouraging the actors to come on strong — into this mechanized plan. The director who has enough training and self-confidence to face an army of technicians and experiment or improvise is rare — and what company wants him if his methods lose time, which is money? Tough, bright men like Sidney Lumet can get their effects, not by what we used to think of as the movie director's art, but by 'turning on,' i.e., turning loose the actors, and by emphasizing certain powerful 'big' scenes — emphatic climaxes, shocks, excessive and thus surprising bits of action. Lumet is not so vulgar as most of the new television-trained movie directors who just keep the actors shouting in close-up. And unlike the pretentious ones among them, he knows that he is just shooting a script, that he is not discovering the possibilities in the material and shaping it. Neverthe-less, he enthusiastically invited me to observe how the crew would begin to 'intermesh' as the shooting went on, and talked often of 'the rhythm' that the footage would reveal when it was edited. After observing a few days of shooting, I knew that if the editing would reveal rhythm in the footage, it would be luck; and luck was only likely in bits of sequences, it couldn't be counted on for the total structure.

There *are* movie directors who try to plan out every detail in advance: Hitchcock, for example, conceives the movie visually from the beginning of the script preparation, designing the production like a complicated mousetrap, then building it. His script is a set of plans representing the completed film, including the editing, and if he doesn't need to depart from it, that is because he works for exactly calculated effects of suspense and perversity. He is an ingenious, masterly builder of mousetraps, and more often than not, the audience is caught tight; his techniques, however, probably have more to do with gamesmanship than with art, and they are almost the opposite of the working methods of most great directors for whom making the movie is itself a process of discovery.

That process of discovery is not part of studio movie-making; in Hollywood even Jean Renoir, whose greatest work has been free and improvisatory, was expected to stick to plan, and his American movies showed what happens to an artist in such conditions. If a director is forced to follow a plan, whether another's or even his own, when, at the time of shooting, he wants to do it some other way — to use an idea that occurs to him when he sees the actors together on the set or sees the possibility of using the landscape in a way he hadn't thought of before — the necessity to do it according to specifications is crippling. It means he can't use his wits, he can't be spontaneous or inventive, he can't think and feel as an artist. This is one of the business practices that makes hacks out of American directors. And if the director knows that his being in a position to make movies at all is dependent on sticking to plan, probably after a while he doesn't even think of how he might like to do it; he just does it. These are the men who, in Hollywood, are considered the true pros.

From what I observed, Lumet's planning is based on the hope that he'll come out of the shooting with something he can pull together in the editing room. The precision of his method is illusory: mechanically, the shots are neatly scheduled, but their precise effect in terms of the finished film is not calculated. When he can't match them up properly later, when 'the rhythm' isn't revealed, audiences may experience the confusion of not knowing how to react to the action. For example, passages of comedy in *The Group* were often so awkward when assembled that some audiences thought the humor was inadvertent.

That tight schedule looks very businesslike on paper; everything seems to be worked out. But when you watch the shooting, as later when you watch the rushes, and finally when you see the movie, you know he operates on a wing and a prayer — and not just in an emergency but every day. For sheer guts, Lumet is awe-inspiring.

The Novel

Lumet and Buchman had finished their thinking about *The Group*; their minds were already turning on the future. At one level, I was more interested in this film than they were: at the level of what it was all about — how they were interpreting the novel. Except for conversations in which I brought up this subject, I never heard it discussed during the production. Nor did anyone ever talk about Mary McCarthy. Several of the girls (and their stand-ins too) were reading *The Group* during their waiting time at rehearsals — I could not tell whether for the first time. I did not *ask* because, after some early conversations with Lumet, he requested that I not discuss the author or novel with the actresses, and I held to this religiously. This was astute of him: he sensed some danger in my questioning his interpretations not only with him but with them. The remarks that I had made which led to this restriction were during a discussion with him in which I had demurred from Buchman's view of Mary McCarthy and referred to her autobiographical *Memories of a Catholic Girlhood* — Lumet did not know the book.

Whenever the subject of the movie came up among the girls or among the crew it was usually referred to contemptuously as a soap opera — which I gradually came to understand meant not only that they didn't see more to the novel than soap opera but that that was how they referred to something when they felt superior to it, when they considered it commercial rather than artistic. Was it possible that no one around had any notion of Mary McCarthy's position in the literary world? She was not only a writer: she was a culture heroine, with pride in intelligence, and wit that cleaned away commonplaces. She was direct, a liberator who brought women's experiences out into the open. But her smartness carried a threat to conventionality, and she was often penalized for it. *Time* had expressed what so many felt, that Mary McCarthy is, 'quite possibly the cleverest woman America has ever produced.' This made her a favorite voodoo doll: anyone who wanted to prove his superiority jabbed at her, and indeed *Time* did it with the needle of 'cleverest' — which, though accurate, is also wounding. Clever so often means 'merely' clever, not profound or truly important, certainly not 'sincere.' In the twenty-odd years since the publication of 'The Man in the Brooks Brothers Shirt' she was frequently jabbed in the wrong places by the sort of people who say, 'So she got laid on a train, does she have to *tell* about it?' — as if she had violated the gentleman's code. (Those who don't believe in the single standard have no qualms about using it to reinforce their double standard.)

No one around the movie seemed to connect to *this* Mary McCarthy or to be aware of how the publication of *The Group* had altered her position, puzzling her long-time admirers and bringing her a different, a best-seller audience. In *The Group* she parodies the motives, the aspirations, the styles in ideas of a group of girls who graduated from Vassar in 1933 into the midst of the Depression and the New Deal. Her Vassar girls seemed to be the women as victims so dearly beloved of middle-class fiction. Aggressive, determined Kay ('Kay was a frightful dancer and always tried to lead') goes mad; good sweet Polly gets a dear understanding husband to depend on. It was like a Hollywood movie; the girl who wants 'too much' gets nothing, is destroyed; the girl waiting for the right man gets the Best of Everything. She wins an undogmatic psychiatrist — the same role so often filled in movies by a Forward-Looking Architect. This Prince Charming even sets up a test — that she wouldn't send her loony papa to an institution. It seemed as if *The Group* could almost have been written by a female equivalent of 'The Man in the Brooks Brothers Shirt.' Mary McCarthy's attitude to her characters had become embarrassingly like his — from his disapproval of the heroine's suitcase with a missing handle to his final plea: 'Forget all this red nonsense and remember that you're just your father's little girl at heart.' Her earlier trouble-maker-heroine had split into impossible Kay and ludicrous Libby, and 'father's little girl at heart' — Polly — had now become the heroine.

Although pieces of the novel had appeared in print almost a decade before book publication, the direction it took was a surprise, and many of her former admirers thought the girls of *The Group* as cold and calculating, and as irrational and defenseless and inept, as if conceived by an anti-feminist male writer. It was depressing to find the book praised by those who thought it showed what happened to girls who 'insist on meeting life free from parental protection or guidance' — as if a Victorian training in domestic skills might have equipped them better than their Vassar education and kept them home and out of trouble. This way of reading the book — though naïve — was common, and it was the usual best-seller/Hollywood view of women. And this view, mixed with the idea that it was also a sensational book — 'dirty' in places — seemed to be prevalent around the studio.

The Producer-Writer

As a screenwriter, Sidney Buchman is known as a good man at 'construction' — i.e., clearing through the underbrush of a novel to locate or design a simplified, neat screenplay. This was hardly possible with *The Group*; still, he reduced it without undue vulgarization. But what he had thought or hoped to do was something very different — and rather bewildering.

On our first meeting, Sidney Buchman, courtly and urbane, told me that after his third reading of the novel and after discussion with Granville Hicks, he and Hicks agreed that the theme of *The Group* was: 'Higher education does not fit women for life.' Not being used to the role of an observer (I never did get used to it), I shot back, 'What does? Does higher education fit *men* for life?' He didn't reply and was taken up with another matter: accepting congratulations from someone who had just recently seen *The Mark* in revival and told him how great it was, that there was 'not a false note in it.' When Buchman had finished shaking hands on this, he turned back to me with a rather belligerent stance and asked, 'Just what did you have against *The Mark*?' (He had apparently heard that I had written a less than favorable review but he had not read it). Before I could reply, he went on, 'All I was trying to do was get people to feel compassion for the mentally ill.'

I said, 'But what sort of compassion is necessary when they know that the man is innocent of any wrongdoing?'

'Well,' he said, 'in the actual case it was based on, the man *did* rape a child, but if I told the truth, I wouldn't have any movie, I couldn't get people to feel compassion for him.'

I didn't want to tell him that that was almost a definition of the artist's task, so I just let it drop. But it occurred to me that this preposterous mixture of wanting to do good and yet evading the real problems — not even telling the simple truth if it might prejudice your case — was the basic cheat of Hollywood message movies.

Asked why he's got involved in this particular project, Buchman said, 'I have been interested in the education of the young for many years.' And he *had* been: he'd been on the board of Sarah Lawrence when his daughter was there. But I'd have been more reassured if he said he'd been interested in Mary McCarthy's writing for many years; or just said it was a job. He talked a tremendous amount about the problem of contraception; he had somehow convinced himself that the movie would make some sort of contribution to progress and enlightenment. Listening to him, you'd think you were going to get a contraceptive and a birth control pamphlet with your movie ticket. A few days after my abrupt 'Does higher education fit *men* for life?', he came over to me and said he'd been giving it a great deal of thought (God knows *why*!) and that, no, it didn't. Still, he went on and on during the production about his favorite theme of education, and how the movie was 'about these foolish, shallow girls having their lives wasted.' So I put it to him again, a little differently: 'Would it have been different for men?' And a few days later, he said he'd thought it over, and 'Yes, it could be eight men. You know, Pauline, I don't know what the damn thing's about.'

I said that I didn't think Mary McCarthy could resist her impulse to ridicule, that she was driven by the same kind of wicked logic whether she was dealing with the anarchists and socialists of *The Oasis* or the professors of *The Groves of Academe* or the girls of *The Group*, and that I didn't think her concentration on women this time was intended as an attack on education for women — that she herself was a triumphant demonstration that women can and do think without parroting men. He dropped the education-for-women line when we were alone, but I still heard it brought out for public occasions. I would hear him talking about 'does not fit women properly' and I would think, is it education or contraception this time? He still wanted the movie to prove something. It wasn't enough for him just to tell a story. He felt guilty that he wasn't doing something *worthwhile*, like getting compassion for the innocent.

I first heard of his next solution to the problem of how he would give the movie 'depth' when Lumet announced it to the girls. The girls nodded gravely as he explained it, and indeed, it was one of those superficially plausible ideas that young kids *would* think was brilliant. The idea was that while the girls were going on about their affairs, there would be Depression details in the background — pickets, soup kitchens, apple sellers — *and the girls would never even notice them*. This is just the sort of easy irony that the theatre and movies are full of, those fancy little effects — the products of theatrical training — that are considered 'moving' or 'deep.' Surely anyone who thought about Mary McCarthy's Group would realize that social consciousness was just what Vassar had given them. The novel is not about a bunch of rich girls who don't even notice the Depression; it's about a group of girls who come out of college full of awareness and idealism (mixed with priggishness and pride), and the ways in which their weaknesses and entrapment in ordinary human problems destroy their plans. I said most of this to Buchman and I told him, too, that I was damned tired of movies that made the audience feel so much smarter than the characters. 'Gee, look, they didn't even *notice* that poor apple seller. If I'd been there, I would have.' After all, what *could* you do except buy an apple? The irony they planned would be particularly grotesque, since the novel had satirized the political activities of the girls, and although the script eliminated much of this, it retained the structure so that the ones who are outside or above it all, the ones who don't get into the political movements of their time come off best — Lakey, Dr Ridgeley, Polly. Lumet often stressed that Lakey and Polly were 'the only ones of the Group who completed themselves. The others are all wrecked by trying to be something else, something they're not.'

Later on, I was happy to observe that the 'ironic' use of the Depression details was minimized. But the author's curious ambivalence to her material was reflected in these confusions. Although Lumet was delighted with Polly and Lakey for just going on about their own affairs, I don't think he recognized that Mary McCarthy was satirizing the social consciousness of the other girls, not their lack of it. I rather doubt that the author herself intended to do that when she started the book. But in ten years it's all too easy to become an uninvolved, amused aesthete toward even one's own past.

Buchman had another big problem with the material — a central problem. I had been startled to discover on the first day that, according to the producer-writer, 'Mary McCarthy is poison . . . she's competitive.' With whom, I wondered? Not Buchman, surely. Although Lumet seemed to share in this view of the author and had frequently said to the press that he would not have done the picture if he'd read the book before seeing the script (which he may have believed, though I didn't), in his case it seemed to be not so much grounded in any specific knowledge as in a general feeling about the *kind* of woman she was. As I got to know him, I concluded that, for Lumet, a woman shouldn't have any problems a real man can't take care of. If she does, she's sick. (Kay wanted to be a director . . .) With Buchman, I felt, it was different. Mary McCarthy, the anti-Communist intellectual, seemed to be a threat he had to fight. He referred to 'her vicious attack on Simone de Beauvoir' as something 'he would never forgive,' as if it were going on right this minute. It was, somehow, as if she were the enemy.

Neither Buchman nor Lumet was comfortable on the subject of Kay, and not just because of the miscasting of a charming giddy blonde who was emotionally too light for the role. The publicity stories all said Lakey was the leader of the group, and even in group photos, the actress who plays Kay seemed to fade away. I think the role was miscast partly because of their discomfort. The discomfort probably went very deep and although they didn't consciously relate Kay to Mary McCarthy, they used the same terms about both. Buchman (who felt that Truffaut's films *Shoot the Piano Player* and *Jules and Jim* were both betrayals of the social point of view for which he had admired Truffaut's first feature, *The 400 Blows*) used exactly the same rancorous terms to describe Catherine of *Jules and Jim*. On this subject, this extraordinarily sophisticated man sounded like a cabdriver or shopgirl — denouncing the movie because he hated the heroine. The cast took the cue: Kay was referred to as 'messy and scatterbrained,' 'a disorderly, disorganized nothing.' And when I admired one of Kay's thirties suits, the actress stared in surprise and said, 'Of course, Kay was such a schlunk she didn't have any taste.' Buchman looked blank at my comment that perhaps Kay could use a little of the self-destructive force that Jeanne Moreau had brought to Catherine. 'They were both,' he said, 'just silly, self-deceived women.'

The first day of rehearsals the girls sat around a table — serious, quiet, attentive faces — as Lumet talked. He gave them a little orientation course, not about the screenplay or its point of view or how it was to be interpreted, but about the Depression and Roosevelt and the banks closing and all. He went into his own life during that period as if *The Group* were about The Group Theatre. Then he took up the characters of Gus LeRoy and Mr Schneider and the antagonism between the Stalinists and Trotskyites. He ended with a description of his only YCL meeting at the age of fourteen, where he asserted that 'Soviet artists were a privileged class so the Soviet Union wasn't a classless society' and 'I got thrown out.'

Buchman spoke up, 'You got thrown out? I wasn't. That was my tragedy.'

Then he turned and said just to me, qualifying it a bit, 'It's not true. I wasn't young enough to be in the YCL.'

For the girls, 1933 was obviously as strange as fifth century Rome: they hadn't been born yet.

Sidney Lumet, Director

Though Sidney Lumet was, at the beginning of *The Group* project, still known as the director producers settled for when they couldn't get the one they wanted — everybody's second choice, the driving little guy who talked himself into jobs and then finished them before the producers even got to know him — by the time *The Group* was finished everybody knew he was going to be a big director. Two pictures he had slammed through opened in New York while he was working on *The Group*: in late April, *The Pawnbroker*; in October, *The Hill*. *The Pawnbroker*, which ranked high on many best-of-the-year lists, was not only a controversial film (it secured a Production Code Seal only after a group of directors, led by Joseph L. Mankiewicz, put up a fight for it and is still causing embarrassment to the Catholics who proscribed it), it even made some money. *The Hill*, his brutal study of an English military prison camp, made abroad, created considerable excitement before it arrived when word got out that Rex Harrison, on the Cannes Film Festival jury, had wired the Queen about the danger of its getting the grand prize. Lumet was talked about in reviews, even in the not too enthusiastic ones, in a way he hadn't been before.

And yet he is still, in his methods of work, basically a TV director — and it is possible that in the next few years television will wreck movies, not, as was thought possible earlier, by taking the audience away, but by its simplified methods and by killing B movies, which were the training ground for directors, and then inflicting its TV-trained directors on movies. Now that television executives have realized that people prefer old movies to television shows and are going to produce movies for later use on television, this dominance of the TV director may actually convert movies into TV shows, rather than the hoped-for reverse. The difference between the two media is becoming a matter of budget, not technique. The television play type of movie just uses the camera as a recording device for staged action. The director follows a script like a general carrying out a plan who shoots hoping to hit something: he moves the people or the camera around to get some 'movement' and hammers some simple points home. And you are cued to react, you're kept so busy reacting you may not even notice that there's *nothing* on the screen for your eye to linger on, no distances, no action in the background, no sense of life or landscape mingling with the foreground action. It's all in the foreground, put there for you to grasp at once. It's all on the surface, it's jumping out of the frame at you. If they want you to notice something, the actor shouts or holds a double-take, and the music accents it further. You don't have to do a thing. You hardly need to look. And if you were deaf, they'd probably shovel it onto your lap.

Lumet, after nine movies — and he is one of the best and most flexible of the TV-trained movie directors — still directs one-dimensionally. He cannot use crowds or details to convey the illusion of life. His backgrounds are always just an empty space; he doesn't even know how to make the principals stand out of a crowd. If he moves the camera, it's just a form of conspicuous expenditure — to prove he can do it. He has only TV foreground action — without intrusions even, and, of course, although this looks fine when the movies later turn up on TV, it basically represents a loss of the whole illusionary delight of movies.

When *The Group* was finished, Lumet told me about some of his plans, and one in particular for a difficult, epic subject, and I said, 'But Sidney, you can't *do* that — you can hardly handle more than two people on camera. I saw what happened to the party scenes in *The Group* — they had to be cut down to nothing because nothing was going on in them.'

And Lumet, with that surprising boyish honesty which is one of his most engaging qualities, said sheepishly, 'I know, but I can learn. I just have to give it some time.'

But it's more than just a matter of taking a few weeks or a few months (which I'm convinced he won't do anyway); it's a matter of a different approach to how movies are made, learning to see and compose differently, opening up a movie — in a way that TV just doesn't open up. Lumet can admit this limitation of his technique because he does not recognize its seriousness. It's no accident that he works well with plays; they don't have the texture of novels — so difficult to create on the screen. It makes sense that he preferred the screenplay of *The Group* to the book. That saved him from worrying about problems he didn't want to concern himself with. He'll go on faking it, I think, using the abilities he has to cover up what he doesn't know; he'll go on using space as stage space hyped up with a few tricks, treating movies as just a bigger canvas than TV. For even his honesty about his limitations is probably the result of his not really thinking they are limitations.

The only movie director trained specifically in TV who has at times transcended this limitation has done it in a singular way. Frankenheimer (*The Manchurian Candidate, Seven Days in May*) has converted TV technique into a new look, a new kind of movie style. Lumet's course is a different one. By temperament, he likes the TV speed and the slapdash intensity. He has the temperament to make this system of production work successfully for him because it doesn't frustrate him — he doesn't really want to work any other way. Personally, he's charged. He will take the easiest way to get a powerful effect; in some conventional, terribly obvious way he will be 'daring.' Chances are, he'll get by with it: he's fearless and dogged, he has a phenomenal memory, and he has an instinct. Lumet surpasses most of the new TV-into-movie directors because he genuinely is not interested in making ordinary movies and because of his energy, his feeling, and principally, his excesses. What he thinks is emotion is excess. He goes a little farther

than others do. Because Lumet can believe in coarse effects, he
can bring them off. Sidney Lumet may be one of the next *big*
directors because of a basic emotional vulgarity in his work that
audiences may respond to. This is a very uncommon man with a
common touch. Lumet is a man with a bad ear for dialogue and no
eye. Genius? Yes, the genius necessary to convince people he's a
genius. Or, to put it more favorably, the determination to convince
whoever needs convincing that, whatever it is, he can do it. And
that *is* genius, of a kind. You don't get to do much in this world
without it. There are a great many sensitive, talented people around
who will never do anything but treasure the superiority they feel to
people like Lumet, who has pragmatic genius: he'll get it done. It
won't be exquisite, it won't be perfect, but it will reflect the
energetic, 'vulgar' confidence he put into it: it will have some
charge or energy which may in some crazy way be more important
than perfection anyway.

Lumet made his TV reputation in *live* TV. He's a live wire, he
works best under pressure; when it isn't there, he invents it for
himself, racing to be *ahead* of schedule. He is happy on the set
when everything is going fast, even though the speed may be
spurious because the work is slovenly. He isn't reflective, and he
doesn't have more to give it if he takes longer. On the contrary, that
just makes him impatient and irritable. When directing movies, he
re-creates the conditions of live TV — not going back. Other
directors plead for retakes; the producer has to force him. He
accepts the passable. The advantage is that he gets something live
into movies and enjoys what he's doing because of the excitement
of the high pressure, the sheer activity of it. Precision seems almost
irrelevant to his methods. It's the spirit — or some spirit — that
satisfies him, not the exact line of dialogue or careful emphasis on
the words. He lets the words fall where they may — which means
they must often be post-synchronized because they have been articulated so inaccurately. When you watch scenes being shot and
see and hear what's the matter with them, you realize how much
bad and negligent work that could be corrected is allowed to pass
because of the mystique of movies being the editor's art. There are
possibilities for long, fluid scenes in several places in *The Group*.
Instead, the scenes will be chopped up with reaction shots and
close-ups to conceal the static camera setups and the faults in
timing, in acting, in rhythm of performances. Fast editing *can* be

done for aesthetic purposes, but too much of it *is* done these days to cover up bad staging and shooting, and the effect is jerky and confusing. But, as it calls so much attention to itself, it is often taken to be brilliant technique. Explaining something he wants done, Lumet will say, 'It can be very exciting' — which means what will *work*, not what may relate to any larger conception but simply something that will be effective here and now, in itself. The emphasis on immediate results may explain the almost total absence of nuance, subtlety, and even rhythmic and structural development in his work.

Perhaps because of his live TV approach, his work looks or rather feels somehow *dated* — too derivative, too familiar, too easily accessible as *powerful*. This, in *The Group*, is a commercial advantage, because for a mass audience this material needs some warmth that is not present in the novel. And though the production — and some of the settings in particular — give several of the girls a surprisingly, vulgarly opulent background, this increases the commonplaceness. It is an expression of common fantasies about the rich. And Lumet, by having the girls behave like stenographers or middle-class girls from the Bronx in the midst of this wealth, probably reaches the large audience directly, even if this is not entirely conscious on his part. In watching Lumet work, I was torn between detesting his fundamental tastelessness and opportunism and recognizing the fact that at some level it all *works*. It obviously, too obviously, wants to be moving, but damn it, it is.

Perhaps Lumet does so well with O'Neill (the famous TV production of *The Iceman Cometh*, the movie version of *Long Day's Journey into Night*) because O'Neill's plays don't depend on precision either, but on cumulative emotional power. They're pedestrian, simple, basic, forceful — solid meat and potatoes so honestly served it's great. O'Neill's writing is tenacious, obsessed, determined to get *at* something, to move you. It doesn't depend on a good ear or eye, either. And, of course, Lumet is pedestrian too: what fools you is that he's a fast pedestrian.

During the last week of the shooting, he invited me to his home to see a 16 mm print of the TV *The Iceman Cometh*. The guests were very quiet, very attentive, but Lumet kept laughing. Where O'Neill used comedy to make us more aware of pain, Lumet laughed at the bad jokes. I heard someone near me whisper, 'He laughs at places where you have to be insensitive to laugh.' Yet he had *directed* it. Probably what we couldn't accept was the crudeness of his enjoyment — he enjoys playing practical jokes on the set, too — a crudeness which, I think, is integral to his strengths as well as his weaknesses as a director. A great many important people now, and throughout history, would probably, up close, seem very crude to the people who admire them from a distance.

The direction of *The Iceman Cometh* showed the same strengths and weaknesses that I had been seeing each day on the set of *The Group*. He hadn't learned, really; he'd just raced ahead. The groupings were stagey, the lines often misread or overemphasized, but there was an overall intensity. And he gave the actors their chance. This was one of the peculiarities of his approach that I had been discovering: he gave his principal thought to the actors during casting. he looked for trained people, and once he'd cast them he expected them to know their business. He directed the actors' readings and interpretations hardly at all. It's as if he couldn't take the time for that, as if it had very little to do with him, it's *their* job — although how they were supposed to learn to work together I couldn't discover nor, obviously, could they. The results are, at worst, amateur theatricals and garbled readings; at average, pressure and excitement; but, at best, an actor who understands his role and can act gets a chance to soar — like Robards in *The Iceman Cometh* and the great family quartet of *Long Day's Journey*. Viewing acting as the responsibility of the actors is an extraordinary attitude for a movie director but not so extraordinary if thought of in terms of live TV, where it's up to them: sink or swim. When they sink — when the lines begin to sound 'literary' — he just lets it go, blaming it on their lack of training. But in some cases in *The Group* it's not that simple: they're miscast or they don't understand the roles — which are not necessarily made more comprehensible by Lumet's singularly 'instinctive' style of interpretation during the rehearsal period.

Lumet's Rehearsal Period

Lumet is rather unusual among movie directors in insisting on a rehearsal period; it was two weeks on *The Group*. This rehearsal period does not serve the same function as rehearsals in the theatre. It is, rather, an attempt to compensate for modern out-of-sequence shooting methods, which are dictated by business considerations, not aesthetic ones. For example, during the actual shooting, sequences involving the same locations or sets will be shot the same day or within a few days, even though they may, as in the case of Kay's wedding and funeral, represent a seven-year interval and will appear at the beginning and end of the finished film. Thrift, Horatio. In movies made in New York, even tiny sets are struck immediately, because space is so precious: all the scenes to be shot in one room are photographed, while another set is constructed right next to it, and the next day that room is dismantled as action shifts to the corner of a restaurant, while workmen try as quietly as possible to construct a doctor's waiting room or a W.P.A. office that will come and go just as fast. In a theatre, the stage goes through the same cycle of transformations each performance of the play. The studio for *The Group* was never the same for two days; construction was always going on. Actors in the same movie may not even meet each other unless they happen to be in the same shot, because their time is scheduled with alarming dexterity, so that they need only be paid for two or three days' work. An actor whose scenes appear to be years apart in the movie may have performed his total duties in a day or two. The elaborate scheduling combines the elements of actors and sets and crew for maximum economy. There is none of that old Hollywood contract-player life of sitting around for weeks in order to pop in and out of a few scenes. Partly because of soaring union costs, it has all been computerized. None of the cast of *The Group* was on salary for the full production: one by one, each said his farewell.

Even the rehearsal period — an attempt to help the actors go through the entire story-action in sequence, so that they can work out the development of their roles — is subject to this calculation. Only the eight girls and a few of the key men were considered essential for the rehearsals. It is at these rehearsals that Lumet explains the movie, as each day it is acted out, and it's here that he is in his element — papa-father, indoctrinator, principal performer, circus ringmaster. Lumet explaining *The Group* to the eight girls who were to embody the roles provided the gloss Mary McCarthy's writing had never had: a thoroughly male, gutsy, folksy, Yiddish interpretation, like the sort of thing one sometimes overhears in buses or restaurants when people are talking about a movie and you think, where did they get that from?

'Dottie is a sweet girl who falls in love. She gets laid and goes home. Bed works for her — first crack out of the box. Dottie thinks Dick Brown did it, and because she thinks so, he becomes the love of her life. . . . Her lack of any self-estimation is so enormous, she thought he did it. Dottie is one of those girls who are so wowed by this orgasm that she doesn't know it would have happened with any man, that she could have done it herself. She doesn't know that she carried this seed of pleasure in her from the beginning.'

'Helena uses art for hiding rather than for self-revelation.' And then solemnly, as if with insight (indeed, second sight) about the girls way beyond the pages of the book: 'She'll drop the newsletter after Kay's death.'

'When Helena doesn't scratch Norine's eyes out, that's when she nails her coffin.' On this one, I wanted to protest, I wanted to interrupt, 'But, Sidney, she scratches Norine's eyes out in her own way, when Norine asks her not to repeat their conversation and she replies that of course she won't, "But *you* will." ' And I wanted to say that if her 'coffin' is 'nailed' it's when she lets her father talk her into going to Europe, and that really it's been nailed pretty much from the beginning. Instead I looked at Buchman, who was listening with an amazement akin to my own. Our eyes met: he shrugged.

'Let's talk about one of the winners, Lakey. I think she does marvellously. By the way, the Baroness is going to be beautiful.' As it turned out, he was not able to be so generous to Lakey: the beautiful Swedish actress selected to be her lover was out of town when, through a change in the shooting schedule, the Baroness was required.

'Lakey and Polly kid themselves less than the others. They're more true to their own nature. Polly lets herself be used — and as soon as she can use someone, by God, it's great. She takes care of people because she wants to be taken care of. . . Her strength comes from great sureness. She thinks it's weakness; she doesn't know it's strength . . . I'm thinking of having her play Gus LeRoy's leave-taking scene — the whole thing — with a terrible smile on her face.' I looked at the girls as he said this and they seemed to be deeply impressed, and I thought back to how impressed we were in high school when the drama coach used to come up with that 'terrible smile' routine. And, of course, Andrea Leeds had actually used it in *Stage Door*. Fortunately, Lumet is prodigal with bad ideas. He seemed to have forgotten all about this one when he shot the scene.

He gave the material his own homey sense of life: rehearsing the graduation sequence, he explained to the actresses that while Helena is giving the valedictory address they should 'tell her with their eyes that she's doing great' and some of them should 'start applauding when she says "all shades of opinion are entitled to a hearing." ' Somehow it seems more like a Bronx high school than Vassar.

He was, in other words, a Method director: he looked for the meaning and motivation of everything in himself and his own experience; he thought of the girls in terms of what *he* felt he knew about them. And because most of his experience was in show business, he drew not only upon his own experiences — mostly with show business people — but also upon his second-hand experience, which was, I think, more real to him that his first: all the shored-up memories of old plays, radio, television, old movies. His 'experience' was full of terrible smiles. And because his mind lived in all this treasure trove of trash — just as I suspect many Method actors draw upon 'theatre' more than they realize — he could use it as if it *were* life. It *is*, in a way, for him. In *The Pawnbroker* he had had Rod Steiger use a soundless scream, and it had *almost* worked — even for those of us with good memories who filled the silence by thinking 'Ah, yes, that must be the famous Berliner Ensemble scream. I've heard of it but I've never not heard it before.' Terrible smiles and soundless screams, what would show business do without them? Maybe it would do better. When they almost work, they're distracting bits of schtik; when they don't work at all, like Buchman's version of the terrible smile — the 'ironic' use of a choral group on the soundtrack to comment on the action (the idea was that the music accelerates to frenzy, getting gayer and gayer as each life goes to pieces) — the idea is totally separable from the result.

Sometimes Lumet's experience worked rather well with the girls: though it had almost no connection with Mary McCarthy's girls, it gave the actresses a sense of how to play, and it was often rather shrewd.

On Libby: 'Whatever becomes her bitchiness later on, I want to look for the legitimate reasons for it. I have a friend who everytime you go to a restaurant with her, she orders and then when you do, she feels she's made a mistake. She always feels she's missing some-thing.' He has another friend 'who can't resist a wisecrack.'

On Kay, when asked whether she falls or jumps to her death: 'We'll take her as a suicide . . . . I have known four suicides in my life and they all had one thing in common — an increasing isolation.'

The flaw in his method is that, as he doesn't look to the original material to try to understand anything but pulls it all out of his *own* background, when the characters are alien to him, when they require some thought or even a little research, he simply neglects them or uses facile explanations of their behavior that just confuse the actors. He never made much sense on the subject of Kay, and then he got more and more impatient with the actress for her inability to become something that was never clearly formulated. This failure caused another failure: because Kay never developed the necessary charac-ter, she didn't provide the provocation for her husband, Harald, to beat her up, and the actor kept trying out different readings without any visible clue from the director as to what was wanted. Harald in the movie is, inexplicably, a weakling and a monster. What was the problem of Kay as a character? Well, there are certain kinds of female pushers who arouse more horror than pity: women who push their children to fulfill their own ambitions (stage mothers are perhaps the most glaring example); and women who push their husbands, like those good sacrificial ladies who devote their youth to dull jobs so that their husbands can achieve professional training only to discover that the new M.D. or Ph.D. or LL.B. must abandon them for women to whom they don't feel so horribly indebted. Kay is of this breed, but, a social climber to the Group's standards which she cannot fill so must attempt to overfill — to be ahead of the others — she wants not a mere professional status for her husband but the genius-artist status. And that, given the period and the field — the Depression and the theatre — doesn't even allow for the compromises and shifts of interest which usually enable such ambitions to work themselves out in appropriate ways — like teaching drama in a college or working in radio or television. There's a real pressure for men like Harald — pushed and sacrificed to — to betray, to beat up, to desert the too-helpful little woman.

Questions that might have concerned another director — such as, What had brought these particular girls together and made them a group, or In what ways were Vassar girls different from other college girls and other girls of the period — didn't, I believe, ever exist for

Lumet. The answers to questions like these go into the texture of a
work, into the nuances, the details. If he'd thought about the milieu
and the tastes of these girls, would he have OK'd the set for Libby's
bedroom, which is Joan Crawford forties, or for Libby's living room,
which is like a Loew's State lounge? In many of the sets, the *art
moderne* décor of the thirties, which was such an important part of the
novel, had been carefully and often amusingly prepared, and he didn't
bother to *use* it. Nor did he observe that the dress designer's unobtrusive good taste was often spoiled by the girls' hair styles. I wondered
why Lumet didn't notice that Kay's coiffures in some of the scenes
were derived from *My Fair Lady*, and I couldn't imagine why he let
Shirley Knight as Polly wear her hair down loose like Alice in
Wonderland when she's dressing the corpse. When asked, he says
indifferently, 'I don't care about things like that' — as if it wouldn't
be manly, somehow, as if only nits and nit-pickers noticed things like
that.

Lumet carried the Method to extravagance. He found psychological reasons for everything in the script — patterns of behavior and
consistent motivation, and even elaborate Freudian relationships between the girls and their parents and each other. He was sometimes
remarkably ingenious, like those people who prove that Francis
Bacon or Walt Disney wrote Shakespeare's plays. Anything the girls
were to say in the movie — even if Buchman had taken it out of
someone else's thoughts in the novel — had its origins in their
childhood, their repressions, their envy. It was as if God had plotted
every detail by a master plan and we must see his mysterious work-
ings. Lumet gave a glorious performance, as Buchman sat staring in
wonder, sometimes looking terribly fatigued.

The comedy now became watching the young actresses trying to
find the motivation in the lines and roles. Actresses of an earlier
generation would have *provided* it, but these girls thought it must be
there to be found, and Lumet encouraged them in this delusion by
seeking and finding whatever he put there. They were as misguided in
their 'Method' as The Group had been with their thirties ideas — yet
what else could they do? They're children of their time, too.

Lumet's great performance as a boring papa full of blather that the
impressionable may take for knowledge of life was counterpointed by
an appalling performance when the lines were not his own. He cued
the girls by reading the roles of almost all the missing actors and
actresses; and he read the Mary McCarthy lines with such animal

spirits, mixed with ready-made inflections, one might have taken them for radio drama circa 1938. I had asked him during one of our first talks why he had given up acting and he had begun a long explanation about how acting was a faggot's career and how he knew that if he was ever going to give a woman a real human relationship, etc, and I had simply jotted down 'too short for acting career.' Now, I decided that maybe his style of acting had dated before he had got old enough to face the problem of his height.

Between his own big role and all these other roles, he was 'on' all the time. He was 'on' even in the coffee breaks, going over charts, designs, schedules. He was indefatigable. And he loved it all.

His approach to speech — so totally at odds with Mary McCarthy's dialogue — was to cause trouble throughout the production. The girls, and many of the young men, were, like him, indifferent and insensitive to the value of words, the shadings of language. They produced sounds — as American Indians seem to — without real articulation; they did not time their dialogue for comprehension. They gave it some kind of emotional birth, during which they were quite likely to use their own words, which contrasted feebly with the author's. They did not seem to hear the difference. During casting, Lumet had asked one Method actor, 'Does your experience with improvisation get in the way when you're working with a script?' The actor's answer — worthy of the Sphinx — was, 'Only when the writing is bad. When it's good, your instinct should work with the dialogue.'

Because of actors' instinct, much of the dialogue had to be post-synchronized. Several of the girls took so long gestating their lines before delivery that good moments had to be cut because it was too absurd to switch from the potential speaker to reaction shots of the listener, and deathly dull just waiting on the speaker's face. The talk had to become faster in the editing room and, as a result, the movie became choppy and frenetic.

By the second week of rehearsals, the girls were whizzing through the whole movie, with the seedy old ballroom that had been rented for rehearsals turned into a maze of markings and charts, and chairs and tables and old mattresses simulating graduation exercises, church, restaurant, hotel, etc. They would do a complete run-through, quick, from sequence to sequence, hopping from one 'set' to the next. And I was puzzled: as the action covered seven years, why compress it to something like the running time of the movie in rehearsal? Why not do it scene by scene in sequence but allow them to think about it in between? They were so worn down from chasing around the markings, they didn't have time to think. Their anxieties about making their right positions took precedence over what the rehearsals were *for*. The rehearsals might have suggested movie conditions better and been much simpler if the actresses could have just stayed in one area and *imagined* that it was now a restaurant or a hotel — which actually is much closer to how a movie is shot, because the same space becomes one thing or another. Less strain and tension about where they had to get to for the next scene and more concentration on how to read the lines would have served them better in the movie. But it was great training for live TV where the actors need to move around and get into different positions fast — if anybody was still doing live TV.

The Crew

A caricaturist, Mary McCarthy is funny at the expense of the girls: she records their pratfalls. But she does not even try to suggest what they may gain in humanity and experience, or what they may truly lose by defeat. The actresses of *The Group* are 'on their way up.' The crew, most of them failed actors, had had some pratfalls; they knew that they weren't going to do much, and certainly not what they'd hoped to do when they were younger. Only once did I hear one say he was considering going back to acting, and nobody believed him.

The crew were cool and ironic in their evaluation of the performers; they gave measured praise when it was due. The grips, carpenters, makeup men, disbursers, controllers, the little white-haired wardrobe mistress who had been in a sister-act in vaudeville were not the sort of people to be impressed by young actresses who might come on like starlets. Youth and beauty are not in short supply in the theatre, and many of the stand-ins and women who worked in one job or another on the sets — preparing Baked Alaska for the wedding breakfast or the hors d'oeuvres for Libby's party — were as beautiful, and often livelier and more interesting. When one of the flat-chested actresses exposed more of herself than was necessary for a scene, a member of the crew gave a W.C. Fields snarl: 'Two aspirin on an ironing board.'

There were so many short scenes that took so long to set up; if nothing really came off in the performance, there was a blank, dull feeling on the set. For, of course, it was all up to the performers, everything else was mechanized — and though there might be mechanical failures, there was no such thing as a mechanical success.

The person on the set who was talked about with unfailing respect was Boris Kaufman, the almost legendary Boris Kaufman, who was the cinematographer for *The Group*. In the early thirties, as the cameraman for Jean Vigo's *Zero for Conduct* and *L'Atalante*, Kaufman had brought new poetic lyricism to the screen. Many on the crew had had long experience with him; they were known as 'Kazan's crew' because they had first worked together with Kaufman on Elia Kazan's films (*On the Waterfront, Baby Doll, Splendor in the Grass*), and they had worked with him on most of Lumet's pictures. They worked quickly and respectfully. For the technicians and actors in the East, Boris Kaufman has been a godsend; he has been the cinematographer for *most* of the important pictures made in New York in the past decade. Without him, it is safe to say, New York would not have attracted even the few productions it had.

When Kaufman came into the rehearsal hall to announce the happy news that the budget had been increased to shoot in color, several of the girls reacted with disdain. Color, for them, was 'commercial.' They thought the picture would be more 'artistic' in black and white, but Joan Hackett said it should be in brown and white to suggest a faded old photograph album. Shirley Knight topped this by the lofty, definitive information that she had seen only one film that justified the use of color, *The Red Desert*. In that moment I hated those actresses for behaving just like The Group. And although I'm sure that Kaufman, a modest, sensitive, quietly efficient man, would be the first to admit that on this kind of production he is a craftsman, not an artist, I think I can guess a little of how he may have felt when even his craftsmanship was destroyed. The beautiful, modulated color he worked so hard to achieve was turned into even worse-than-standard American movie color in the prints that reached theatres, as simply and carelessly as turning the knob on color TV.

As the cinematographer is responsible for the lighting, he is in charge of most of the work that goes on on the set, which is preparation for the brief periods of shooting. While he works — and he is the hardest working person on the set — the director waits. I wondered why Lumet did not use this waiting time to work with the actors, but he seemed too impatient to get going, to get it shot. There were no rehearsals after that first two-week period (which meant that there were no rehearsals at all for most of the cast), only the run-throughs for the camera and lights before the take.

It would be difficult for people who have seen some of these pictures to believe that they were shot where they were — in spaces so small you can hardly move the camera. People think of movies being made in beautiful luxurious studios with the stars emerging from big dressing rooms. Even Hollywood studios don't look the way they do in movies about Hollywood; in New York, most of *The Group* was shot in the old Fox Movietone building on West 54th Street and Tenth Avenue, where 'the stars' ' dressing rooms were known as the cell-block, which is what they looked like. And when things got too crowded at Movietone, there'd be a few days' shooting in a building in the fur district where, if you didn't watch your step, you might stumble over Kay's coffin. Wherever the shooting was going on, at the St Regis or St Marks in the Bouwerie or Connecticut or Long Island, the technicians, the carpenters, the visitors, all froze during takes — as in *Marienbad*. And in those moments, and perhaps only in those moments, did there seem to be some magic in this movie-making.

For those who were interested in movie-making, this was just a job until they could get a chance at the real thing. The crew wanted to do a good job; they enjoyed the work and each other, but they were indifferent to the material they were working on. They didn't respect this way of working. But they were negative — like regular army men bitching about the army — with no real alternative in mind. The 'real thing' was a day dream — an idea of creative work somewhere, which, when it was expressed more definitely, usually turned out to be either 'something honest' — i.e., a documentary; or something 'experimental' — i.e., TV commercials and the Richard Lester kind of movie-making; or, something poetic, something strange. Yet if they wanted to try to do something of their own, there was equipment they could scrounge, there was no shortage of actors; why didn't they try something in 16 mm or in 35 mm instead of griping about the crap they were working on? Except for a very few — three or four, I think — who were writing or shooting on weekends, I don't think most of them had the drive. They wanted to get paid for work; and their idea of making movies was the same old megalomaniac-genius racket of power, fame, big profits, etc — only they wanted it to be 'creative' too.

Their contempt for what they were working on was intensified by the general knowledge that despite the superficially democratic spirit on the set — pet names and lots of kisses — they couldn't even make suggestions, which Lumet took as implied criticism. As Adlai Stevenson pointed out, 'Absolute powerlessness corrupts absolutely.' Probably not even the experienced and tactful assistant director Dan Eriksen felt that he could make any recommendations. Of course, there is nothing surprising in this. It is part of the paranoia of power that men at the top who have stolen from everyone and everywhere to get there can't accept anything that's freely offered.

Could the crew have helped? On specific matters, yes. There were very few of the errors or careless stupidities or miscalculations that had to be cut out, or that, remaining, mar the film, which were not remarked on and sometimes widely commented on by the people on the set. But I think it would be a mistake to think that the director cared that much. And there was the producer, Buchman, the only person with authority to challenge Lumet's judgment, sitting by, watching, and lifting his eyes to heaven. If he didn't care enough to prevent Kay's twirling around the walls of her hospital room like a trapped animal (another 'terrible smile' — and an effect which made the hospital room look large as a salon) or to raise hell about Kay's ludicrous purple sunset of a black eye, why should the actors or the crew members risk a put-down and disfavor by pointing it out except to each other?

How little the Sidneys cared about accuracy in terms of the meaning of the material may be indicated by citing a simple error which I naïvely and diligently tried to get corrected. In the scene between Helena and Norine, Helena is supposed to reply to Norine's charge that The Group were 'the aesthetes' as distinguished from 'the politicals' by saying, 'The whole group was for Roosevelt in the college poll — except Poke who forgot to vote.' But the actress said, 'The whole class was for Roosevelt. . .' I heard the error during the shooting, but mindful of my agreement with the director not to discuss the material with the girls, I didn't mention it to the actress — who, I am sure, would have consulted her script and discovered that she was making a mistake. Instead, I mentioned it as casually as possible to each of the Sidneys, and as the sound on this sequence was badly recorded and was obviously going to need looping (i.e., post-synchronization), I assumed the word would then be corrected. During the first screenings of the film — without the music and with some editing still to be done — I noted the error again, and this time pointed it out somewhat more forcefully to the Sidneys. Each assured me I must be hearing it wrong. Neither apparently took the trouble to check or listen, because when the film was screened for the press, there it was again. By then, Lumet was in London working on his next film, Buchman was back on the Riviera.

Thinking that *someone* might care about the blooper, I called around, and after three people involved in the production assured me that if the Sidneys had had Helena say 'class' that must have been what they wanted, I finally got hold of the editor Ralph Rosenblum, who realized at once that it was an error. But he had enough other problems to worry about: in the absence of the Sidneys, he was left to argue the cuts the National Catholic Office for Motion Pictures (a new euphemism for the Legion of Decency) wanted.

These negotiations are more ambivalent than is generally known. Because, of course, the distributing company may benefit from the publicity that accrues to a film if it is having Legion trouble. But at the same time, the company will certainly want the public to think that the 'dirty' parts haven't really been altered. Frequently scenes are put in a picture just for the purpose of mollifying the Legion by agreeing to remove them, and as a bargaining weapon to retain other crucial scenes. And ironically, the Legion sometimes passes over these deliberately flagrant scenes and insists on removing others essential to the material. On its side of the bargaining counter the Legion traditionally demands major, even thematic changes, and then settles for small excisions, usually of semi-nude scenes. The negotiations involve horse-trading, low cunning, and general hypocrisy. On *The Group* the National Catholic Office objected to 'eight or nine elements' and settled for two bits of flesh, and United Artists was able to defy 'anyone to discern any appreciable difference . . . even after three screenings. . .' — which nobody was likely to go to anyway.

The Results

Mary McCarthy has always satirized women. We all do, and men are happy to join us in it, and this is, I think, a terrible feminine weakness

— our coquettish way of ridiculing ourselves, hoping perhaps that we can thus be accepted as feminine, that we will not be lumped with those imaginary gorgons who are always held up as horrible examples of competitive, castrating women. We try to protect ourselves as women by betraying other women. And, of course, women who are good writers succeed in betrayal but fail to save themselves.

The most condescending, most sanctimonious, the phoniest dialogue in the movie (and it's right out of the book) is uttered by dear little Polly and is intended to show what a fine girl she is. She tells Gus LeRoy that she set out to be a doctor. And he says, 'Too late now?' and she says, 'Well, not if I had Libby's drive, I suppose — or Kay's.' Gus says, 'You think you haven't?' and she answers, 'Worse. In college, I never cared particularly for people with drive — or those most likely to succeed. The truth is, the only way I could like assured, aggressive girls was to feel sorry for them.' This dreadful nonsense — which would be called Uncle Tomism if uttered by a Negro — is very appealing to men and, of course, men like the Sidneys (rightly) include the author in the category she is condemning. I don't think there's any doubt that Polly is here speaking for the author because the structure of the book says the same thing: that the quiet girls who don't come on strong come off best as human beings. Although at the time she was writing *The Group*, she may have believed in this quietism and imagined that as the author of *Venice Observed* and *The Stones of Florence* she had become an elegant aesthete like Lakey, it is her inability to endow Polly and Lakey with the hideous believability of the others that gives the lie to the structure of the book. It is only when Polly is asking clear questions — like earlier Mary McCarthy heroines — that she has some stature as a character: Mary McCarthy can bring Polly to life when she's seeing through Dr Bijur but not when she's selling blood — or feeling 'sorry' for the other girls. That comes easier to Buchman and Lumet than to Mary McCarthy. If *The Group* had had a woman script-writer and director, it might have been much more satirical. But, ultimately, Buchman and Lumet have betrayed women in a more basic way: by treating the girls as poor, weak creatures, as insignificant 'little women.' For this, of course, is their way of being sympathetic, of making the movie more compassionate than the novel. (They don't feel the same condescending need to soften the men's roles, so these men seem like even worse bastards than the men in the novel, now that the women are so much more sympathetic.)

Mary McCarthy has said, 'What I really do is take real plums and put them in an imaginary cake.' In the movie, they have baked a different cake, using ready-mix, but the plums are still there — good juicy plums of real experience — recognizably real and familiar, so that we laugh with the pleasure of recognition. In a sense, the girls and crew in calling it a soap opera were more instinctively accurate than the Sidneys, with their meanings and interpretations. But, it isn't soap opera just because it deals with tangled lives and loves (almost all novels do — good as well as bad ones). The quality of observation, though at times at a soap-opera level, is generally much higher. Actually, the Sidneys' *ideas* are closer to soap opera than the material they're working with. When they 'think,' they dish out soap-opera interpretations, but what they worked with is interesting enough to make their interpretations seem silly and phony — which they are. Life — to the degree that Mary McCarthy catches it and they use her material — is not reducible to their ideas, which, oddly, they seem to feel are higher, more important than giving us something of the life of a period. They really are products of the thirties, using fashionable, liberal 'ideas' to explain and falsify what they're doing, which is what Mary McCarthy was exposing in the girls.

What gives the movie its vitality — and despite its carelessness and sloppy style, it is one of the few interesting American movies of recent years — is that the talented, fresh young performers are given some material to work with. There's solid observation in Mary McCarthy's writing, and the movie is a considerably more realistic and sophisticated account of modern male-female relationships and what goes wrong in them than we've had on the screen. It deals with the specific experiences of women in our time that Mary McCarthy has always specialized in: how a girl (Dottie) may want to lose her virginity but then feel unwanted and deserted when a casual affair doesn't turn into 'love'; how scared virgins may come on as the sexiest teasers (Libby); how a woman's life can be made a ridiculous martyrdom to theories of child care (Priss); how people now 'use' analysis in their relationships (Polly and Gus).

After his part of the editing was finished, a few days before he left for England, Sidney Lumet asked me to a ritual lunch — at the same restaurant where we had had our first. The United Artists executives had just seen the picture, and Sidney was chuckling in triumph. 'You know,' he said, 'at first they were afraid I couldn't do this picture, that I wasn't a woman's director.' In Hollywood that is generally a euphemism for a fussy, effeminate director. Although Lumet has given *The Group* something the usual woman's director wouldn't, I miss the clarity and detail a *good* woman's director might have given it. I have an awful feeling that in the movie when Libby protects her virginity by kneeing Nils in the groin, and Nils says, 'Did your lady teachers teach you that?' Sidney Lumet thinks they did. But if his sense of the material is a little primitive, some of its reality got to him, too. 'Funny thing' he said, 'you remember that day you mentioned the actor Harold that Mary McCarthy was married to, dying in a hotel fire. I didn't remember until later: I knew Harold Johnsrud. When I was a kid starring on Broadway in *My Heart's in the Highlands*, he had a small part in it.'

He asked if I had gotten what I wanted from following the course of the production and I didn't know what to answer because I had really got more than I wanted. When you see a movie, it has a certain inevitability; but when you see a movie being made, you see how it might be, how it could be, how it should be. The worst thing about movie-making is that it's like life: nobody can go back to correct the mistakes. I think now I know the answer to one question that always comes up when people discuss what has happened to novels when they become movies, and ask why did they leave out so and so? The obvious answers were: for length or unnecessary complication, because they couldn't include everything; for propriety, and to please church or pressure groups. To these I can add: because they didn't shoot it very well, and when the sets have been struck and the actors and technicians have gone on to other commitments, it's almost impossible to go back and redo it. They just hack it out. This problem of no return also explains why so many obviously bad things are in it. They were too integral to the story to be left out, so they just had to be used, no matter how bad. If an actor's reading is too awful, he may be dubbed. If performances are so disastrous that editing can't save them, the roles may be almost eliminated. They generally can't be totally eliminated because then sequences involving large numbers of people or sequences essential to the story line would have to be cut. When I asked what had happened to some particularly nice little scenes, Lumet tried out the gaudy explanation that he had learned not to be self-indulgent about retaining too many unusually good moments. But either he's too honest or my face gave me away because he began to laugh. When important material is cut — even crucial material — the justification is always that the movie is too long anyway. But when one persists and says why this rather than that, the plain truth generally comes out that because of negligence or some error in planning, the bit couldn't be properly made to fit. The editor takes the pieces for a jigsaw puzzle and, if they don't quite fit, forces them into place. We're supposed to ignore little holes as unimportant — as even more modern and jazzy. If a director is more concerned to get something on film than to get it right, the editing is going to be very tricky. The beginning of this movie is too fast and confusing for the simple reason that the big scenes of the graduation and Kay's announcement of her engagement to Harald were a shambles and were chopped to fragments. When asked how the audience would get its bearings, how they would be able to tell who the girls were and what was going on, Lumet said it didn't matter. The problem of the time transitions and how to link the episodes so that the audience might get some sense of the girls' lives didn't matter either. The material flying by so fast may even help Lumet's reputation as an 'artistic' director. This, more and more, is the way movies are going to be made, because it is more businesslike. Lumet has had the 'genius' to be a pioneer: he doesn't think 'the little things' matter.

Economy represents the decisive factor in the working arrangements, yet because of these working arrangements, there is one large area of waste. After watching a few weeks of shooting, I sat down with the script and calculated I could save close to a quarter of a million dollars in production costs just by cutting out, before it was shot, what I assumed would have to be cut out after it was shot. *The Group*, like most movies these days, began with a script for an unconscionably long movie — over three hours (many four-hour movies are shot). I gradually came to see that, given the working methods, they needed this extra footage because they were never sure of what would work out and what wouldn't. My calculations were posited on a coherent story line and the retention of the best material; the actual final cut removed much that I would have cut, but also a great deal I considered essential. And I realized that they had shot an over-three-hour script so that they could pull some kind of two-and-a-half-hour movie out of it. Economy, speed, nervousness, and desperation produce the final wasteful, semi-incoherent movies we see.

Carried much further, this pioneering could mean the death of what we now still know as the art of the film. The key word in that sentence is that little shrinking 'we.' Lumet has the right chemistry for the new kind of picture-making and the genius to know that for the really big audience, 'the little things' don't count. If vast audiences are indifferent to the absence of beauty on television, if they do not object to the loss of visual detail when they see old movies on television, if they do not object that the shape of the image destroys much of what remains of the compositions, if they do not object to the cuts which make the story line and characterization incoherent and to the interruptions for commercials which destroy the intensity, the suspense, the whole dramatic construction, then why not give them what, apparently, is all they really want: the immediacy of foreground action and as many climaxes as possible?

I would not have written this lengthy analysis if I did not feel that there are basic, crucially important reasons for not making movies in this way. I discovered that my subject was not so much what happens when a book becomes a movie but what happens when movies become television.

Life, 1966

Movies on Television

A few years ago, a jet on which I was returning to California after a trip to New York was instructed to delay landing for a half hour. The plane circled above the San Francisco area, and spread out under me were the farm where I was born, the little town where my grandparents were buried, the city where I had gone to school, the cemetery where my parents were, the homes of my brothers and sisters, Berkeley, where I had gone to college, and the house where at that moment, while I hovered high above, my little daughter and my dogs were awaiting my return. It was as though my whole life were suspended in time — as though no matter where you'd gone, what you'd done, the past were all still there, present, if you just got up high enough to attain the proper perspective.

Sometimes I get a comparable sensation when I turn from the news programs or the discussion shows on television to the old movies. So much of what formed our tastes and shaped our experiences, and so much of the garbage of our youth that we never thought we'd see again — preserved and exposed to eyes and minds that might well want not to believe that this was an important part of our past. Now these movies are there for new generations, to whom they cannot possibly have the same impact or meaning, because they are all jumbled together, out of historical sequence. Even what may deserve an honorable position in movie history is somehow dishonored by being so available, so meaninglessly present. Everything is in hopeless disorder, and that is the way new generations experience our movie past. In the other arts, something like natural selection takes place: only the best or the most significant or influential or successful works compete for our attention. Moreover, those from the past are likely to be touched up to accord with the taste of the present. In popular music, old tunes are newly orchestrated. A small repertory of plays is continually reinterpreted for contemporary meanings — the great ones for new relevance, the not so great rewritten, tackily 'brought up to date,' or deliberately treated as period pieces. By contrast, movies, through the accidents of commerce, are sold in blocks or packages to television, the worst with the mediocre and the best, the successes with the failures, the forgotten with the half forgotten, the ones so dreary you don't know whether you ever saw them or just others like them with some so famous you can't be sure whether you actually saw them or only imagined what they were like. A lot of this stuff never really made it with any audience; it played in small towns or it was used to soak up the time just the way TV in bars does.

There are so many things that we, having lived through them, or passed over them, never want to think about again. But in movies nothing is cleaned away, sorted out, purposefully discarded. (The destruction of negatives in studio fires or deliberately, to save space, was as indiscriminate as the preservation and resale.) There's a kind of hopelessness about it: what does not deserve to last lasts, and so it all begins to seem one big pile of junk, and some people say, 'Movies never really were any good — except maybe the Bogarts.' If the same thing had happened in literature or music or painting — if we were constantly surrounded by the piled-up inventory of the past — it's conceivable that modern man's notion of culture and civilization would be very different. Movies, most of them produced as fodder to satisfy the appetite for pleasure and relaxation, turned out to have magical properties — indeed, to *be* magical properties. This fodder can be fed to people over and over again. Yet, not altogether strangely, as the years wear on it doesn't please their palates, though many will go on swallowing it, just because nothing tastier is easily accessible. Watching old movies is like spending an evening with those people next door. They bore us, and we wouldn't go out of our way to see them; we drop in on them because they're so close. If it took some effort to see old movies, we might try to find out which were the good ones, and if people saw only the good ones maybe they would still respect old movies. As it is, people sit and watch movies that audiences walked out on thirty years ago. Like Lot's wife, we are tempted to take another look, attracted not by evil but by something that seems much more shameful — our own innocence. We don't try to reread the girls' and boys' 'series' books of our adolescence — the very look of them is dismaying. The textbooks we studied in grammar school are probably more 'dated' than the movies we saw then, but we never look

at the old schoolbooks, whereas we keep seeing on TV the movies that
represent the same stage in our lives and played much the same part in
them — as things we learned from and, in spite of, went beyond.

Not all old movies look bad now, of course; the good ones are
still good — surprisingly good, often, if you consider how much of
the detail is lost on television. Not only the size but the shape of the
image is changed, and, indeed, almost all the specifically visual
elements are so distorted as to be all but completely destroyed. On
television, a cattle drive or a cavalry charge or a chase — the
climax of so many a big movie — loses the dimensions of space and
distance that made it exciting, that sometimes made it great. And
since the structural elements — the rhythm, the buildup, the suspense — are also partly destroyed by deletions and commercial
breaks and the interruptions incidental to home viewing, it's amazing that the bare bones of performance, dialogue, story, good
directing, and (especially important for close-range viewing) good
editing can still make an old movie more entertaining than almost
anything new on television. (That's why old movies are taking over
television — or, more accurately, vice versa.) The verbal slapstick
of the newspaper-life comedies — *Blessed Event, Roxie Hart, His
Girl Friday* — may no longer be fresh (partly because it has been
so widely imitated), but it's still funny. Movies with good, fast,
energetic talk seem better than ever on television — still not great
but, on television, better than what *is* great. (And as we listen to the
tabloid journalists insulting the corrupt politicians, we respond
once again to the happy effrontery of that period when the targets of
popular satire were still small enough for us to laugh at without
choking.) The wit of dialogue comedies like Preston Sturges's
Unfaithfully Yours isn't much diminished, nor does a tight melodrama like *Double Indemnity* lose a great deal. Movies like Joseph
L. Mankiewicz's *A Letter to Three Wives* and *All About Eve* look
practically the same on television as in theatres, because they have
almost no visual dimensions to lose. In them the camera serves
primarily to show us the person who is going to speak the next
presumably bright line — a scheme that on television, as in theatres, is acceptable only when the line *is* bright. Horror and fantasy
films like Karl Freund's *The Mummy* or Robert Florey's *The Mur-
ders in the Rue Morgue* — even with the loss, through
miniaturization, of imaginative special effects — are surprisingly
effective, perhaps because they are so primitive in their appeal that

the qualities of the imagery matter less than the basic suggestions. Fear counts for more than finesse, and viewing horror films is far more frightening at home than in the shared comfort of an audience that breaks the tension with derision.

Other kinds of movies lose much of what made them worth looking at — the films of von Sternberg, for example, designed in light and shadow, or the subtleties of Max Ophuls, or the lyricism of Satyajit Ray. In the box the work of these men is not as lively or as satisfying as the plain good movies of lesser directors. Reduced to the dead grays of a cheap television print, Orson Welles's *The Magnificent Ambersons* — an uneven work that is nevertheless a triumphant conquest of the movie medium — is as lifelessly dull as a newspaper Wirephoto of a great painting. But when people say of a 'bit' movie like *High Noon* that it has dated or that it doesn't hold up, what they are really saying is that their judgment was faulty or has changed. They may have overresponded to its publicity and reputation or to its attempt to deal with a social problem or an idea, and may have ignored the banalities surrounding that attempt; now that the idea doesn't seem so daring, they notice the rest. Perhaps it was a traditional drama that was new to them and that they thought was new to the world; everyone's 'golden age of movies' is the period of his first moviegoing and just before — what he just missed or wasn't allowed to see. (The Bogart films came out just before today's college kids started going.)

Sometimes we suspect, and sometimes rightly, that our memory has improved a picture — that imaginatively we made it what we knew it could have been or should have been — and, fearing this, we may prefer memory to new contact. We'll remember it better if we don't see it again — we'll remember what it meant to us. The nostalgia we may have poured over a performer or over our recollections of a movie has a way of congealing when we try to renew the contact. But sometimes the experience of reseeing is wonderful — a confirmation of the general feeling that was all that remained with us from childhood. And we enjoy the fresh proof of the rightness of our responses that reseeing the film gives us. We re-experience what we once felt, and memories flood back. Then movies seem magical — all those *madeleines* waiting to be dipped in tea. What looks bad in old movies is the culture of which they were part and which they expressed — a tone of American life that we have forgotten. When we see First World War posters, we are far enough away from their patriotic primitivism to be amused at the emotions and sentiments to which they appealed. We can feel charmed but superior. It's not so easy to cut ourselves off from old movies and the old selves who responded to them, because they're not an isolated part of the past held up for derision and amusement and wonder. Although they belong to the same world as stories in *Liberty*, old radio shows, old phonograph records, an America still divided between hayseeds and city slickers, and although they may seem archaic, their pastness isn't so very past. It includes the last decade, last year, yesterday.

Though in advertising movies for TV the recentness is the lure, for many of us what constitutes the attraction is the datedness, and the earlier movies are more compelling than the ones of the fifties or the early sixties. Also, of course, the movies of the thirties and forties look better technically, because, ironically, the competition with television that made movies of the fifties and sixties enlarge their scope and their subject matter has resulted in their looking like a mess in the box — the sides of the image lopped off, the crowds and vistas a boring blur, the color altered, the epic themes incongruous and absurd on the little home screen. In a movie like *The Robe*, the large-scale production values that were depended on to attract TV viewers away from their sets become a negative factor. But even if the quality of the image were improved, these movies are too much like the ones we can see in theatres to be interesting at home. At home, we like to look at those stiff, carefully groomed actors of the thirties, with their clipped, Anglophile stage speech and their regular, clean-cut features — walking profiles, like the figures on Etruscan vases and almost as remote. And there is the faithless wife — how will she decide between her lover and her husband, when they seem as alike as two wax grooms on a wedding cake? For us, all three are doomed not by sin and disgrace but by history. Audiences of the period may have enjoyed these movies for their action, their story, their thrills, their wit, and all this high living. But through our window on the past we see the actors acting out other dramas as well. The Middle European immigrants had children who didn't speak the king's English and, after the Second World War, didn't even respect it so much. A flick of the dial and we are in the fifties amid the slouchers, with their thick lips, shapeless noses, and shaggy haircuts, waiting to say their lines until they think them out, then mumbling something that is barely speech. How long, O Warren Beatty, must we wait before we turn back to beautiful stick figures like Phillips Holmes?

We can take a shortcut through the hell of many lives, turning the dial from the social protest of the thirties to the films of the same writers and directors in the fifties — full of justifications for blabbing, which they shifted onto characters in oddly unrelated situations. We can see in the films of the forties the displaced artists of Europe — the anti-Nazi exiles like Conrad Veidt, the refugees like Peter Lorre, Fritz Kortner, and Alexander Granach. And what are they playing? Nazis, of course, because they have accents, and so for Americans — for the whole world — they become images of Nazi brutes. Or we can look at the patriotic sentiments of the Second World War years and those actresses, in their orgies of ersatz nobility, giving their lives — or, at the very least, their bodies — to save their country. It was sickening at the time; it's perversely amusing now — part of the spectacle of our common culture.

Probably in a few years some kid watching *The Sandpiper* on television will say what I recently heard a kid say about *Mrs Miniver*: 'And to think they really believed it in those days.' Of course, we didn't. Many of us went to see big-name pictures just as we went to *The Night of the Iguana*, without believing a minute of it. The James Bond pictures are not to be 'believed,' but they tell us a lot about the conventions that audiences now accept, just as the confessional films of the thirties dealing with sin and illegitimacy and motherhood tell us about the sickly-sentimental tone of American entertainment in the midst of the Depression. Movies indicate what the producers thought people would pay to see — which was not always the same as what they *would* pay to see. Even what they enjoyed seeing does not tell us directly what they believed but only indirectly hints at the tone and style of a culture. There is no reason to assume that people twenty or thirty years ago were stupider than we are now. (Consider how *we* may be judged by people twenty years from now looking at today's movies.) Though it may not seem obvious to us now, part of the original appeal of old movies — which we certainly understood and responded to as children — was that, despite their sentimental tone, they helped to form the liberalized modern consciousness. This trash — and most of it was, and is, trash —probably taught us more about the world, and even about values, than our 'education' did. Movies broke down barriers of all kinds, opened up the world, helped to make us aware. And they were almost always on the side of the mistreated, the socially despised. Almost all drama is. And, because movies were a mass medium, they had to be on the side of the poor.

Nor does it necessarily go without saying that the glimpses of something really good even in mediocre movies — the quickening of excitement at a great performance, the discovery of beauty in a gesture or a phrase or an image — made us understand the meaning of art as our teachers in appreciation courses never could. And — what is more difficult for those who are not movie lovers to grasp — even after this sense of the greater and the higher is developed, we still do not want to live only on the heights. We still want the pleasure of discovering things for ourselves; we need the sustenance of the ordinary, the commonplace, the almost-good as part of the anticipatory atmosphere. And though it all helps us to respond to the moments of greatness, it is not only for this that we want it. The educated person who became interested in cinema as an art form through Bergman or Fellini or Resnais is an alien to me (and my mind goes blank with hostility and indifference when he begins to talk). There isn't much for the art-cinema person on television; to look at a great movie, or even a poor movie carefully designed in terms of textures and contrasts, on television is, in general, maddening, because those movies lose too much. (Educational television, though, persists in this misguided effort to bring the television viewer movie classics.) There are few such movies anyway. But there are all the not-great movies, which we probably wouldn't bother going to see in museums or in theatre revivals — they're just not that important. Seeing them on television is a different kind of experience, with different values — partly because the movie past hasn't been filtered to conform to anyone's convenient favorite notions of film art. We made our own, admittedly small, discoveries or rediscoveries. There's Dan Dailey doing his advertising-wise number in *It's Always Fair Weather*, or Gene Kelly and Fred Astaire singing and dancing 'The Babbitt and the Bromide' in *Ziegfeld Follies*. And it's like putting on a record of Ray Charles singing 'Georgia on My Mind' or Frank Sinatra singing 'Bim Bam Baby' or Elisabeth Schwarzkopf singing operetta, and feeling again the elation we felt the first time. Why should we deny these pleasures because there are other, more complex kinds of pleasure possible? It's true that these pleasures don't deepen, and that they don't change *us*, but maybe that is part of what makes them seem our own — we realize that we have some emotions and responses that *don't* change as we get older.

People who see a movie for the first time on television don't remember it the same way that people do who saw it in a theatre. Even without the specific visual loss that results from the transfer to another medium, it's doubtful whether a movie could have as intense an impact as it had in its own time. Probably by definition, works that are not truly great cannot be as compelling out of their time. Sinclair Lewis's and Hemingway's novels were becoming archaic while their authors lived. Can *On the Waterfront* have the impact now that it had in 1954? Not quite. And revivals in movie theatres don't have the same kind of charge, either. There's something a little stale in the air, there's a different kind of audience. At a revival, we must allow for the period, or care because of the period. Television viewers seeing old movies for the first time can have very little sense of how and why new stars moved us when they appeared, of the excitement of new themes, of what these movies meant to us. They don't even know which were important in their time, which were 'hits.'

But they can discover *something* in old movies, and there are few discoveries to be made on dramatic shows produced for television. In comedies, the nervous tic of canned laughter neutralizes everything; the laughter is as false for the funny as for the unfunny and prevents us from responding to either. In general, performances in old movies don't suffer horribly on television except from cuts, and what kindles something like the early flash fire is the power of personality that comes through in those roles that made a star. Today's high school and college students seeing *East of Eden* and *Rebel Without a Cause* for the first time are almost as caught up in James Dean as the first generation of adolescent viewers was, experiencing that tender, romantic, marvelously masochistic identification with the boy who does everything wrong because he cares so much. And because Dean died young and hard, he is not just another actor who outlived his myth and became ordinary in stale roles — he is the symbol of misunderstood youth. He is inside the skin of moviegoing and television-watching youth — even educated youth — in a way that Keats and Shelley or John Cornford and Julian Bell are not. Youth can respond — though not so strongly — to many of our old heroes and heroines: to Gary Cooper, say, as the elegant, lean, amusingly silent romantic loner of his early Western and aviation films. (And they can more easily ignore the actor who sacrificed that character for blubbering righteous bathos.) Bogart found his myth late, and Dean fulfilled the romantic myth of self-destructiveness, so they look good on television. More often, television, by showing us actors before and after their key starring roles, is a myth-killer. But it keeps acting ability alive.

There is a kind of young television watcher seeing old movies for the first time who is surprisingly sensitive to their values and responds almost with the intensity of a moviegoer. But he's different from the moviegoer. For one thing, he's housebound, inactive, solitary. Unlike a moviegoer, he seems to have no need to discuss what he sees. The kind of television watcher I mean (and the ones I've met are all boys) seem to have extreme empathy with the material in the box (new TV shows as well as old movies, though rarely news), but he may not know how to enter into a conversation, or even how to come into a room or go out of it. He fell in love with his baby-sitter, so he remains a baby. He's unusually polite and intelligent, but in a mechanical way — just going through the motions, without interest. He gives the impression that he wants to withdraw from this human interference and get back to his real life — the box. He is like a prisoner who has everything he wants in prison and is content to stay there. Yet, oddly, he and his fellows seem to be tuned in to each other; just as it sometimes seems that even a teenager locked in a closet would pick up the new dance steps at the same moment as other teenagers, these television watchers react to the same things at the same time. If they can find more intensity in this box than in their own living, then this box can provide *constantly* what we got at the movies only a few times a week. Why should they move away from it, or talk, or go out of the house, when they will only experience that as a loss? Of course, we can see why they should, and their inability to make connections outside is frighteningly suggestive of ways in which we, too, are cut off. It's a matter of degree. If we stay up half the night to watch old movies and can't face the next day, it's partly, at least, because of the fascination of our own movie past; *they* live in a past they never had, like people who become obsessed by places they have only imaginative connections with — Brazil, Venezuela, Arabia Deserta. Either way, there is always something a little shameful about living in the past; we feel guilty, stupid — as if the pleasure we get needed some justification that we can't provide.

For some moviegoers, movies probably contribute to that self-defeating romanticizing of expectations which makes life a series of disappointments. They watch the same movies over and over on television, as if they were constantly returning to the scene of the crime — the life they were so busy dreaming about that they never lived it. They are paralyzed by longing, while those less romantic can leap the hurdle. I heard a story the other day about a man who ever since his school days had been worshipfully 'in love with' a famous movie star, talking about her, fantasizing about her, following her career, with its ups and downs and its stormy romances and marriages to producers and agents and wealthy sportsmen and rich businessmen. Though he became successful himself, it never occurred to him that he could enter her terrain — she was so glamorously above him. Last week, he got a letter from an old classmate, to whom, years before, he had confided his adoration of the star; the classmate — an unattractive guy who had never done anything with his life and had a crummy job in a crummy business — had just married her.

Movies are a combination of art and mass medium, but television is so single in its purpose — selling — that it operates without that painful, poignant mixture of aspiration and effort and compromise. We almost never think of calling a television show 'beautiful,' or even of complaining about the absence of beauty, because we take it for granted that television operates without beauty. When we see on television photographic records of the past, like the pictures of Scott's Antarctic expedition or those series on the First World War, they seem almost too strong for the box, too pure for it. The past has a terror and a fascination and a beauty beyond almost anything else. We are looking at the dead, and they move and grin and wave at us; it's an almost unbearable experience. When our wonder and our grief are interrupted or followed by a commercial, we want to destroy the ugly box. Old movies don't tear us apart like that. They do something else, which we can take more of and take more easily: they give us a sense of the passage of life. Here is Elizabeth Taylor as a plump matron and here, an hour later, as an exquisite child. That charmingly petulant little gigolo with the skinny face and the mustache that seems the most substantial part of him — can he have developed into the great Laurence Olivier? Here is Orson Welles as a young man, playing a handsome old man, and here is Orson Welles as he has really aged. Here are Bette Davis and Charles Boyer traversing the course of their lives from ingenue and juvenile, through major roles, into character parts — back and forth, endlessly, embodying the good and bad characters of many styles, many periods. We see the old character actors put out to pasture in television serials, playing gossipy neighbors or grumpy grandpas, and then we see them in their youth or middle age, in the roles that made them famous — and it's startling to find how good they were, how vital, after we've encountered them carica-turing themselves, feeding off their old roles. They have almost nothing left of that young actor we responded to — and still find ourselves responding to — except the distinctive voice and a few crotchets. There are those of us who, when we watch old movies, sit there murmuring the names as the actors appear (Florence Bates, Henry Daniell, Ernest Thesiger, Constance Collier, Edna May Oliver, Douglas Fowley), or we recognize them but can't remember their names, yet know how well we once knew them, experiencing the failure of memory as a loss of our own past until we can supply it (Maude Eburne or Porter Hall) — with great relief. After a few seconds, I can always remember them, though I cannot remember the names of my childhood companions or of the prizefighter I once dated, or even of the boy who took me to the senior prom. We are eager to hear again that line we know is coming. We hate to miss anything. Our memories are jarred by cuts. We want to see the movie to the end.

The graveyard of *Our Town* affords such a tiny perspective compared to this. Old movies on television are a gigantic, panoramic novel that we can tune in to and out of. People watch avidly for a few weeks or months or years and then give up; others tune in when they're away from home in lonely hotel rooms, or regularly, at home, a few nights a week or every night. The rest of the family may ignore the passing show, may often interrupt, because individual lines of dialogue or details of plot hardly seem to matter as they did originally. A movie on television is no longer just a drama in itself; it is part of a huge ongoing parade. To a new generation, what does it matter if a few gestures and a nuance are lost, when they know they can't watch the parade on all the channels at all hours anyway? It's like traffic on the street. The television generation knows there is no end; it all just goes on. When television watchers are surveyed and asked what kind of programming they want or how they feel television can be improved, some of them not only have no answers but can't understand the questions. What they get on their sets is television — that's it.

The New Yorker, 1967

Bonnie and Clyde

How do you make a good movie in this country without being jumped on? *Bonnie and Clyde* is the most excitingly American American movie since *The Manchurian Candidate*. The audience is alive to it. Our experience as we watch it has some connection with the way we reacted to movies in childhood: with how we came to love them and to feel they were ours — not an art that we learned over the years to appreciate but simply and immediately ours. When an American movie is contemporary in feeling, like this one, it makes a different kind of contact with an American audience from the kind that is made by European films, however contemporary. Yet any movie that is contemporary in feeling is likely to go further than other movies — go too far for some tastes — and *Bonnie and Clyde* divides audiences, as *The Manchurian Candidate* did, and it is being jumped on almost as hard. Though we may dismiss the attacks with 'What good movie doesn't give some offense?,' the fact that it is generally *only* good movies that provoke attacks by many people suggests that the innocuousness of most of our movies is accepted with such complacence that when an American movie reaches people, when it makes them react, some of them think there must be something the matter with it — perhaps a law should be passed against it. *Bonnie and Clyde* brings into the almost frighteningly public world of movies things that people have been feeling and saying and writing about. And once something is said or done on the screens of the world, once it has entered mass art, it can never again belong to a minority, never again be the private possession of an educated, or 'knowing,' group. But even for that group there is an excitement in hearing its own private thoughts expressed out loud and in seeing something of its own sensibility become part of our common culture.

Our best movies have always made entertainment out of the anti-heroism of American life; they bring to the surface what, in its newest forms and fashions, is always just below the surface. The romanticism in American movies lies in the cynical tough guy's independence; the sentimentality lies, traditionally, in the falsified finish when the anti-hero turns hero. In 1967, this kind of sentimentality wouldn't work with the audience, and *Bonnie and Clyde* substitutes sexual fulfillment for a change of heart. (This doesn't quite work, either; audiences sophisticated enough to enjoy a movie like this one are too sophisticated for the dramatic uplift of the triumph over impotence.)

Structurally, *Bonnie and Clyde* is a story of love on the run, like the old Clark Gable–Claudette Colbert *It Happened One Night* but turned inside out; the walls of Jericho are psychological this time, but they fall anyway. If the story of Bonnie Parker and Clyde Barrow seemed almost from the start, and even to them while they were living it, to be the material of legend, it's because robbers who are loyal to each other — like the James brothers — are a grade up from garden-variety robbers, and if they're male and female partners in crime and young and attractive they're a rare breed. The Barrow gang had both family loyalty and sex appeal working for their legend. David Newman and Robert Benton, who wrote the script for *Bonnie and Clyde*, were able to use the knowledge that, like many of our other famous outlaws and gangsters, the real Bonnie and Clyde seemed to others to be acting out forbidden roles and to relish their roles. In contrast with secret criminals — the furtive embezzlers and other crooks who lead seemingly honest lives — the known outlaws capture the public imagination, because they take chances, and because, often, they enjoy dramatizing their lives. They know that newspaper readers want all the details they can get about the criminals who do the terrible things they themselves don't dare to do, and also want the satisfaction of reading about the punishment after feasting on the crimes. Outlaws play to this public; they show off their big guns and fancy clothes and their defiance of the law. Bonnie and Clyde established the images for their own legend in the photographs they posed for: the gunman and the gun moll. The naïve, touching doggerel ballad that Bonnie Parker wrote and had published in newspapers is about the roles they play for other people contrasted with the coming end for them. It concludes:

> Someday they'll go down together;
> They'll bury them side by side;
> To few it'll be grief —

> To the law a relief —
> But it's death for Bonnie and Clyde

That they did capture the public imagination is evidenced by the many movies based on their lives. In the late forties, there were *They Live by Night*, with Farley Granger and Cathy O'Donnell, and *Gun Crazy*, with John Dall and Peggy Cummins. (Alfred Hitchcock, in the same period, cast these two Clyde Barrows, Dall and Granger, as Loeb and Leopold, in *Rope*.) And there was a cheap — in every sense — 1958 exploitation film, *The Bonnie Parker Story*, starring Dorothy Provine. But the most important earlier version was Fritz Lang's *You Only Live Once*, starring Sylvia Sidney as 'Joan' and Henry Fonda as 'Eddie,' which was made in 1937; this version, which was one of the best American films of the thirties, as *Bonnie and Clyde* is of the sixties, expressed certain feelings of its time, as this film expresses certain feelings of ours. (*They Live by Night*, produced by John Houseman under the aegis of Dore Schary, and directed by Nicholas Ray, was a very serious and socially significant tragic melodrama, but its attitudes were already dated thirties attitudes: the lovers were very young and pure and frightened and underprivileged; the hardened criminals were sordid; the settings were committedly grim. It made no impact on the postwar audience, though it was a great success in England, where our moldy socially significant movies could pass for courageous.)

Just how contemporary in feeling *Bonnie and Clyde* is may be indicated by contrasting it with *You Only Live Once*, which, though almost totally false to the historical facts, was *told* straight. It is a peculiarity of our times — perhaps it's one of the few specifically modern characteristics — that we don't take our stories straight any more. This isn't necessarily bad. *Bonnie and Clyde* is the first film demonstration that the put-on can be used for the purposes of art. *The Manchurian Candidate almost* succeeded in that, but what was implicitly wild and far-out in the material was nevertheless presented on screen as a straight thriller. *Bonnie and Clyde* keeps the audience in a kind of eager, nervous imbalance — holds our attention by throwing our disbelief back in our faces. To be put on is to be put on the spot, put on the stage, made the stooge in a comedy act. People in the audience at *Bonnie and Clyde* are laughing, demonstrating that they're not stooges — that they appreciate the joke — when they catch the first bullet right in the face. The movie keeps them off balance to the end.

During the first part of the picture, a woman in my row was gleefully assuring her companions, 'It's a comedy. It's a comedy.' After a while, she didn't say anything. Instead of the movie spoof, which tells the audience that it doesn't need to feel or care, that it's all just in fun, that 'we were only kidding,' *Bonnie and Clyde* disrupts us with 'And you thought we were only kidding.'

This is the way the story was told in 1937. Eddie (Clyde) is a three-time loser who wants to work for a living, but nobody will give him a chance. Once you get on the wrong side of the law, 'they' won't let you get back. Eddie knows it's hopeless — once a loser, always a loser. But his girl, Joan (Bonnie) — the only person who believes in him — thinks that an innocent man has nothing to fear. She marries him, and learns better. Arrested again and sentenced to death for a crime he didn't commit, Eddie asks her to smuggle a gun to him in prison, and she protests, 'If I get you a gun, you'll kill somebody.' He stares at her sullenly and asks, 'What do you think they're going to do to me?' He becomes a murderer while escaping from prison; 'society' has made him what it thought he was all along. *You Only Live Once* was an indictment of 'society,' of the forces of order that will not give Eddie the outcast a chance. 'We have a right to live,' Joan says as they set out across the country. During the time they are on the run, they become notorious outlaws; they are blamed for a series of crimes they didn't commit. (They do commit holdups, but only to get gas or groceries or medicine.) While the press pictures them as desperadoes robbing and killing and living high on the proceeds of crime, she is having a baby in a shack in a hobo jungle, and Eddie brings her a bouquet of wild flowers. Caught in a police trap, they die in each other's arms; they have been denied the right to live.

Because *You Only Live Once* was so well done, and because the audience in the thirties shared this view of the indifference and cruelty of 'society,' there were no protests against the sympathetic way the outlaws were pictured — and, indeed, there was no reason for any. In 1958, in *I Want to Live!* (a very popular, though not very good, movie), Barbara Graham, a drug-addict prostitute who had been executed for her share in the bludgeoning to death of an elderly woman, was presented as gallant, wronged, morally superior to everybody else in the movie, in order to strengthen the argument against capital punishment, and the director, Robert Wise, and his associates weren't accused of glorifying criminals, because the 'criminals,' as in *You Only Live Once*, weren't criminals but innocent victims. Why the protests, why are so many people upset (and not just the people who enjoy indignation), about *Bonnie and Clyde*, in which the criminals *are* criminals — Clyde an ignorant, sly near psychopath who thinks his crimes are accomplishments, and Bonnie a bored, restless waitress-slut who robs for excitement? And why so many accusations of historical inaccuracy, particularly against a work that is far more accurate historically than most and in which historical accuracy hardly matters anyway? There is always an issue of historical accuracy involved in any dramatic or literary work set in the past; indeed, it's fun to read about Richard III vs Shakespeare's Richard III. The issue is always with us, and will always be with us as long as artists find stimulus in historical figures and want to present their versions of them. But why didn't movie critics attack, for example, *A Man for All Seasons* — which involves material of much more historical importance — for being historically inaccurate? Why attack *Bonnie and Clyde* more than the other movies based on the same pair, or more than the movie treatments of Jesse James or Billy the Kid or Dillinger or Capone or any of our other fictionalized outlaws? I would suggest that when a movie so clearly conceived as a new version of a legend is attacked as historically inaccurate, it's because it shakes people a little. I know this is based on some pretty sneaky psychological suppositions, but I don't see how else to account for the use only against a *good* movie of arguments that could be used against almost all movies. When I asked a nineteen-year-old boy who was raging against the movie as 'a cliché-ridden fraud' if he got so worked up about other movies, he informed me that that was an argument *ad hominem*. And it is indeed. To ask why people react so angrily to the best movies and have so little negative reaction to poor ones is to imply that they are so unused to the experience of art in movies that they fight it.

Audiences at *Bonnie and Clyde* are not given a simple, secure basis for identification; they are made to feel but are not told *how* to feel. *Bonnie and Clyde* is not a serious melodrama involving us in the plight of the innocent but a movie that assumes — as William Wellman did in 1931 when he made *The Public Enemy*, with James Cagney as a smart, cocky, mean little crook — that we don't need to pretend we're interested only in the falsely accused, as if real criminals had no connection with us. There wouldn't be the popular excitement there is about outlaws if we didn't all suspect that — in some cases, at least — gangsters must take pleasure in the profits and glory of a life of crime. Outlaws wouldn't become legendary figures if we didn't suspect that there's more to crime than the social workers' case studies may show. And though what we've always been told will happen to them — that they'll come to a bad end — does seem to happen, some part of us wants to believe in the tiny possibility that they can get away with it. Is that really so terrible? Yet when it comes to movies people get nervous about acknowledging that there must be some fun in crime (though the gleam in Cagney's eye told its own story). *Bonnie and Clyde* shows the fun but uses it, too, making comedy out of the banality and conventionality of that fun. What looks ludicrous in this movie isn't *merely* ludicrous, and after we have laughed at ignorance and helplessness and emptiness and stupidity and idiotic devilry, the laughs keep sticking in our throats, because what's funny isn't only funny.

In 1937, the movie-makers knew that the audience wanted to believe in the innocence of Joan and Eddie, because these two were lovers, and innocent lovers hunted down like animals made a tragic love story. In 1967, the movie-makers know that the audience wants to believe — maybe even prefers to believe — that Bonnie and Clyde were guilty of crimes, all right, but that they were innocent in general; that is, naïve and ignorant *compared with us*. The distancing of the sixties version shows the gangsters in an already legendary period, and part of what makes a legend for Americans is viewing anything that happened in the past as much simpler than what we are involved in now. We tend to find the past funny and the recent past campy-funny. The getaway cars of the early thirties are made to seem hilarious. (Imagine anyone getting away from a bank holdup in a tin lizzie like that!) In *You Only Live Once*, the outlaws existed in the same present as the audience, and there was (and still is, I'm sure) nothing funny about them; in *Bonnie and Clyde* that audience is in the movie, transformed into the poor people, the Depression people, of legend — with faces and poses out of Dorothea Lange and Walker Evans and *Let Us Now Praise Famous Men*. In 1937, the audience felt sympathy for the fugitives because they weren't allowed to lead normal lives; in 1967, the 'normality' of the Barrow gang and their individual aspirations toward respectability are the craziest things about them — not just because they're killers but because thirties 'normality' is in itself funny to us. The writers and the director of *Bonnie and Clyde* play upon our attitudes toward the American past by making the hats and guns and holdups look as dated as two-reel comedy; emphasizing the absurdity with banjo music, they make the period seem even farther away than it is. The Depression reminiscences are not used for purposes of social consciousness; hard times are not the reason for the Barrows' crimes, just the excuse. 'We' didn't make Clyde a killer; the movie deliberately avoids easy sympathy by picking up Clyde when he is already a cheap crook. But Clyde is not the urban sharpster of *The Public Enemy*; he is the hick as bank robber — a countrified gangster, a hillbilly killer who doesn't mean any harm. People so simple that they are alienated from the results of their actions — like the primitives who don't connect babies with copulation — provide a kind of archetypal comedy for us. It may seem like a minor point that Bonnie and Clyde are presented as not mean and sadistic, as having killed only when cornered; but in terms of legend, and particularly movie legend, it's a major one. The 'classic' gangster films showed gang members betraying each other and viciously murdering the renegade who left to join another gang; the gang-leader hero no sooner got to the top than he was betrayed by someone he had trusted or someone he had double-crossed. In contrast, the Barrow gang represent family-style crime. And Newman and Benton have been acute in emphasizing this — not making them victims of society (they are never that, despite Penn's cloudy efforts along these lines) but making them absurdly 'just-folks' ordinary. When Bonnie tells Clyde to pull off the road — 'I want to talk to you' — they are in a getaway car, leaving the scene of a robbery, with the police right behind them, but they are absorbed in family bickering: the traditional all-American use of the family automobile. In a sense, it is the absence of sadism — it is the violence without sadism — that throws the audience off balance at *Bonnie and Clyde*. The brutality that comes out of this innocence is far more shocking than the calculated brutalities of mean killers.

Playfully posing with their guns, the real Bonnie and Clyde mocked the 'Bloody Barrows' of the Hearst press. One photograph shows slim, pretty Bonnie, smiling and impeccably dressed, pointing a huge gun at Clyde's chest as he, a dimpled dude with a cigar, smiles back. The famous picture of Bonnie in the same clothes but looking ugly squinting into the sun, with a foot on the car, a gun on her hip, and a cigar in her mouth, is obviously a joke — her caricature of herself as a gun moll. Probably, since they never meant to kill, they thought the 'Bloody Barrows' were a joke — a creation of the lying newspapers.

There's something new working for the Bonnie-and-Clyde legend now: our nostalgia for the thirties — the unpredictable, contrary affection of the prosperous for poverty, or at least for the artifacts, the tokens, of poverty, for Pop culture seen in the dreariest rural settings, where it truly seems to belong. Did people in the cities listen to the Eddie Cantor show? No doubt they did, but the sound of his voice, like the sound of Ed Sullivan now, evokes a primordial, pre-urban existence — the childhood of the race. Our comic-melancholic affection for thirties Pop has become sixties Pop, and those who made *Bonnie and Clyde* are smart enough to use it that way. Being knowing is not an artist's highest gift, but it can make a hell of a lot of difference in a movie. In the American experience, the miseries of the Depression are funny in the way that the Army is funny to draftees — a shared catastrophe, a leveling, forming part of our common background. Those too young to remember the Depression have heard about it from their parents. (When I was at college, we used to top each other's stories about how our families had survived: the father who had committed suicide so that their wives and children could live off the insurance; the mothers trying to make a game out of the meals of potatoes cooked on an open fire.) Though the American derision of the past has many offensive aspects, it has some good ones, too, because it's a way of making fun not only of our forebears but of ourselves and our pretensions. The toughness about what we've come out of and what we've been through — the honesty to see ourselves as the Yahoo children of yokels — is a good part of American popular art. There is a kind of American poetry in a stickup gang seen chasing across the bedraggled backdrop of the Depression (as true in its way as Nabokov's vision of Humbert Humbert and Lolita in the cross-country world of motels) — as if crime were the only activity in a country stupefied by poverty. But Arthur Penn doesn't quite have the toughness of mind to know it; it's not what he means by poetry. His squatters'-jungle scene is too 'eloquent,' like a poster making an appeal, and the Parker-family-reunion sequence is poetic in the gauzy mode. He makes the sequence a fancy lyric interlude, like a number in a musical (*Funny Face*, to be exact); it's too 'imaginative' — a literal dust bowl, as thoroughly becalmed as Sleeping Beauty's garden. The movie becomes dreamy-soft where it should be hard (and hard-edged).

If there is such a thing as an American tragedy, it must be funny. O'Neill undoubtedly felt this when he had James Tyrone get up to turn off the lights in *Long Day's Journey into Night*. We are bumpkins, haunted by the bottle of ketchup on the dining table at San Simeon. We garble our foreign words and phrases and hope that at least we've used them right. Our heroes pick up the wrong fork, and the basic figure of fun in the American theatre and American movies is the man who puts on airs. Children of peddlers and hod carriers don't feel at home in tragedy; we are used to failure. But, because of the quality of American life at the present time, perhaps there can be no real comedy — nothing more than stupidity and 'spoof' — without true horror in it. Bonnie and Clyde and their partners in crime are comically bad bank robbers, and the backdrop of poverty makes their holdups seem pathetically tacky, yet they rob banks and kill people; Clyde and his good-natured brother are so shallow they never think much about anything, yet they suffer and die.

If this way of holding more than one attitude toward life is already familiar to us — if we recognize the make-believe robbers whose toy guns produce real blood, and the Keystone Cops who shoot them dead, from Truffaut's *Shoot the Piano Player* and Godard's gangster pictures, *Breathless* and *Band of Outsiders* — it's because the young French directors discovered the poetry of crime in American life (from our movies) and showed the Americans how to put it on the screen in a new, 'existential' way. Melodramas and gangster movies and comedies were always more our speed than 'prestigious,' 'distinguished' pictures; the French directors who grew up on American pictures found poetry in our fast action, laconic speech, plain gestures. And because they understood that you don't express your love of life by denying the comedy or the horror of it, they brought out the poetry in our tawdry subjects. Now Arthur Penn, working with a script heavily influenced — one might almost say inspired — by Truffaut's *Shoot the Piano Player*, unfortunately imitates Truffaut's artistry instead of going back to its tough American sources. The French may tenderize their American material, but we shouldn't. That turns into another way of making 'prestigious,' 'distinguished' pictures.

Probably part of the discomfort that people feel about *Bonnie and Clyde* grows out of its compromises and its failures. I wish the script hadn't provided the upbeat of the hero's sexual success as a kind of sop to the audience. I think what makes us not believe in it is that it isn't consistent with the intelligence of the rest of the writing — that it isn't on the same level, because it's too manipulatively clever, too much of a gimmick. (The scene that shows the gnomish gang member called C.W. sleeping in the same room with Bonnie and Clyde suggests other possibilities, perhaps discarded, as does C.W.'s reference to Bonnie's liking his tattoo.) Compromises are not new to the Bonnie-and-Clyde story; *You Only Live Once* had a tacked-on coda featuring a Heavenly choir and William Gargan as a dead priest, patronizing Eddie even in the afterlife, welcoming him to Heaven with 'You're free, Eddie!' The kind of people who make a movie like *You Only Live Once* are not the kind who write endings like that, and, by the same sort of internal evidence, I'd guess that Newman and Benton, whose Bonnie seems to owe so much to Catherine in *Jules and Jim*, had more interesting ideas originally about Bonnie's and Clyde's (and maybe C.W.'s) sex lives.

But people also feel uncomfortable about the violence, and here I think they're wrong. That is to say, they *should* feel uncomfortable, but this isn't an argument *against* the movie. Only a few years ago, a good director would have suggested the violence obliquely, with reaction shots (like the famous one in *The Golden Coach*, when we see a whole bullfight reflected in Anna Magnani's face), and death might have been symbolized by a light going out, or stylized, with blood and wounds kept to a minimum. In many ways, this method is more effective; we feel the violence more because so much is left to our imaginations. But the whole point of *Bonnie and Clyde* is to rub our noses in it, to make us pay our dues for laughing. The dirty reality of death — not suggestions but blood and holes — is necessary. Though I generally respect a director's skill and intelligence in inverse ratio to the violence he shows on the screen, and though I questioned even the Annie Sullivan–Helen Keller fight scenes in Arthur Penn's *The Miracle Worker*, I think that this time Penn is right. (I think he was also right when he showed violence in his first film, *The Left Handed Gun*, in 1958.) Suddenly, in the last few years, our view of the world has gone beyond 'good taste.' Tasteful suggestions of violence would at this point be a more grotesque form of comedy than *Bonnie and Clyde* attempts. *Bonnie and Clyde* needs violence; violence is its meaning. When, during a comically botched-up getaway, a man is shot in the face, the image is obviously based on one of the most famous sequences in Eisenstein's *Potemkin*, and the startled face is used the same way it was in *Potemkin* — to convey in an instant how someone who just happens to be in the wrong place at the wrong time, the irrelevant 'innocent' bystander, can get it full in the face. And at that instant the meaning of Clyde

Barrow's character changes; he's still a clown, but *we've* become the butt of the joke.

It is a kind of violence that says something to us; it is something that movies must be free to use. And it is just because artists must be free to use violence — a legal right that is beginning to come under attack — that we must also defend the legal rights of those film-makers who use violence to sell tickets, for it is not the province of the law to decide that one man is an artist and another man a no-talent. The no-talent has as much right to produce works as the artist has, and not only because he has a surprising way of shifting from one category to the other but also because men have an inalienable right to be untalented, and the law should not discriminate against lousy 'artists.' I am not saying that the violence in *Bonnie and Clyde* is legally acceptable because the film is a work of art, but I think that the violence in *The Dirty Dozen*, which isn't a work of art, and whose violence offends me *personally*, should also be legally defensible, however morally questionable. Too many people — including some movie reviewers — want the law to take over the job of movie criticism; perhaps what they really want is for their own criticisms to have the force of law. Such people see *Bonnie and Clyde* as a danger to public morality; they think an audience goes to a play or a movie and takes the actions in it as examples for imitation. They look at the world and blame the movies. But if women who are angry with their husbands take it out on the kids, I don't think we can blame *Medea* for it; if, as has been said, we are a nation of mother-lovers, I don't think we can place the blame on *Oedipus Rex*. Part of the power of art lies in showing us what we are *not* capable of. We see that killers are not a different breed but are *us* without the insight or understanding or self-control that works of art strengthen. The tragedy of *Macbeth* is in the fall from nobility to horror; the comic tragedy of *Bonnie and Clyde* is that although you can't fall from the bottom you can reach the same horror. The movies may set styles in dress- or love-making, they may advertise cars or beverages, but art is not examples for imitation — that is not what a work of art does for us — though that is what guardians of morality *think* art is and what they want it to be and why they think a good movie is one that sets 'healthy,' 'cheerful' examples of behavior, like a giant all-purpose commercial for the American way of life. But people don't 'buy' what they see in a movie quite so simply; Louis B. Mayer did not turn us into a nation of Andy Hardys, and if, in a film, we see a frightened man wantonly take the life of another, it does not encourage us to do the same, any more than seeing an ivory hunter shoot an elephant makes us want to shoot one. It may, on the contrary, so sensitize us that we get a pang in the gut if we accidentally step on a moth.

Will we, as some people have suggested, be lured into imitating the violent crimes of Clyde and Bonnie because Warren Beatty and Faye Dunaway are 'glamorous'? Do they, as some people have charged, confer glamour on violence? It's difficult to see how, since the characters they play are horrified by it and ultimately destroyed by it. Nobody in the movie gets pleasure from violence. Is the charge based on the notion that simply by their presence in the movie Warren Beatty and Faye Dunaway make crime attractive? If movie stars can't play criminals without our all wanting to be criminals, then maybe the only safe roles for them to play are movie stars — which, in this assumption, everybody wants to be anyway. After all, if they played factory workers, the economy might be dislocated by everybody's trying to become a factory worker. (Would having criminals played by dwarfs or fatties discourage crime? It seems rather doubtful.) The accusation that the beauty of movie stars makes the anti-social acts of their characters dangerously attractive is the kind of contrived argument we get from people who are bothered by something and are clutching at straws. Actors and actresses are *usually* more beautiful than ordinary people. And why not? Garbo's beauty notwithstanding, her Anna Christie did not turn us into whores, her Mata Hari did not turn us into spies, her Anna Karenina did not make us suicides. We did not want her to be ordinary looking. Why should we be deprived of the pleasure of beauty? Garbo could be all women in love because, being more beautiful than life, she could more beautifully express emotions. It is a supreme asset for actors and actresses to be beautiful; it gives them greater range and greater possibilities for expressiveness. The handsomer they are, the more roles they can play; Olivier can be anything, but who would want to see Ralph Richardson, great as he is, play Antony? Actors and actresses who are beautiful start with an enormous advantage, because we love to look at them. The joke in the glamour charge is that Faye Dunaway has the magazine-illustration look of countless uninterestingly pretty girls, and Warren Beatty has the kind of high-school good looks that are generally lost fast. It's the roles that make *them* seem glamorous. Good roles do that for actors.

There is a story told against Beatty in a recent *Esquire* — how during the shooting of *Lilith* he 'delayed a scene for three days demanding the line "I've read *Crime and Punishment* and *The Brothers Karamazov*" be changed to "I've read *Crime and Punishment* and *half* of *The Brothers Karamazov*." ' Considerations of professional conduct aside, what is odd is why his adversaries waited three days to give in, because, of course, he was right. That's what the character he played *should* say; the other way, the line has no point at all. But this kind of intuition isn't enough to make an actor, and in a number of roles Beatty, probably because he doesn't have the technique to make the most of his lines in the least possible time, has depended too much on intuitive non-acting — holding the screen far too long as he acted out self-preoccupied characters in a lifelike, boringly self-conscious way. He has a gift for slyness, though, as he showed in *The Roman Spring of Mrs Stone*, and in most of his films he could hold the screen — maybe because there seemed to be something going on in his mind, some kind of calculation. There was something smart about him — something shrewdly private in those squeezed-up little non-actor's eyes — that didn't fit the clean-cut juvenile roles. Beatty was the producer of *Bonnie and Clyde*, responsible for keeping the company on schedule, and he has been quoted as saying, 'There's not a scene that we have done that we couldn't do better by taking another day.' This is the hell of the expensive way of making movies, but it probably helps to explain why Beatty is more intense than he has been before and why he has picked up his pace. His business sense may have improved his timing. The role of Clyde Barrow seems to have released something in him. As Clyde, Beatty is good with his eyes and mouth and his hat, but his body is still inexpressive; he doesn't have a trained actor's use of his body, and, watching him move, one is never for a minute convinced he's impotent. It is, however, a tribute to his performance that one singles this failure out. His slow timing works perfectly in the sequence in which he offers the dispossessed farmer his gun; there may not be another actor who would have dared to prolong the scene that way, and the prolongation until the final 'We rob banks' gives the sequence its comic force. I have suggested elsewhere that one of the reasons that rules are impossible in the arts is that in movies (and in the other arts, too) the new 'genius' — the genuine as well as the fraudulent or the dubious — is often the man who has enough audacity, or is simpleminded enough, to do what others had the good taste not to do. Actors before Brando did not mumble and scratch and show their sweat; dramatists before Tennessee Williams did not make explicit a particular substratum of American erotic fantasy; movie directors before Orson Welles did not dramatize the techniques of film-making; directors before Richard Lester did not lay out the whole movie as cleverly as the opening credits; actresses before Marilyn Monroe did not make an asset of their ineptitude by turning faltering misreadings into an appealing style. Each, in a large way, did something that people had always enjoyed and were often embarrassed or ashamed about enjoying. Their 'bad taste' shaped a new accepted taste. Beatty's non-actor's 'bad' timing may be this kind of 'genius'; we seem to be watching him *think out* his next move.

It's difficult to know how Bonnie should have been played, because the character isn't worked out. Here the script seems weak. She is made too warmly sympathetic — and sympathetic in a style that antedates the style of the movie. Being frustrated and moody, she's not funny enough — neither ordinary, which, in the circumstances, would be comic, nor perverse, which might be rather funny, too. Her attitude toward her mother is too loving. There could be something funny about her wanting to run home to her mama, but, as it has been done, her heading home, running off through the fields, is unconvincing — incompletely motivated. And because the element of the ridiculous that makes the others so individual has been left out of her character she doesn't seem to belong to the period as the others do. Faye Dunaway has a sixties look anyway — not just because her eyes are made up in a sixties way and her hair is wrong but because her personal style and her acting are sixties. (This may help to make her popular; she can seem prettier to those who don't recognize prettiness except in the latest styles.) Furthermore, in some difficult-to-define way, Faye Dunaway as Bonnie doesn't keep her distance — that is to say, an *actor's* distance — either from the role or from the audience. She doesn't hold a characterization; she's in and out of emotions all the time, and though she often hits effective ones, the emotions seem *hers*, not the character's. She has some talent, but she comes on too strong; she makes one conscious that she's a willing worker, but she doesn't seem to know what she's doing — rather like Bonnie in her attempts to overcome Clyde's sexual difficulties.

Although many daily movie reviewers judge a movie in isolation, as if the people who made it had no previous history, more serious critics now commonly attempt to judge a movie as an expressive vehicle of the director, and a working out of his personal themes. Auden has written, 'Our judgment of an established author is never simply an aesthetic judgment. In addition to any literary merit it may have, a new book by him has a historic interest for us as the act of a person in whom we have long been interested. He is not only a poet . . . he is also a character in our biography.' For a while, people went to the newest Bergman and the newest Fellini that way; these movies were greeted like the latest novels of a favorite author. But Arthur Penn is not a writer-director like Bergman or Fellini, both of whom began as writers, and who (even though Fellini employs several collaborators) compose their spiritual autobiographies step by step on film. Penn is far more dependent on the talents of others, and his primary material — what he starts with — does not come out of his own experience. If the popular audience is generally uninterested in the director (unless he is heavily publicized, like De Mille or Hitchcock), the audience that is interested in the art of movies has begun, with many of the critics, to think of movies as a directors' medium to the point where they tend to ignore the contribution of the writers — and the directors may be almost obscenely content to omit mention of the writers. The history of the movies is being rewritten to disregard facts in favor of celebrating the director as the sole 'creative' force. One can read Josef von Sternberg's autobiography and the text of the latest books on his movies without ever finding the name of Jules Furthman, the writer who worked on nine of his most famous movies (including *Morocco* and *Shanghai Express*). Yet the appearance of Furthman's name in the credits of such Howard Hawks films as *Only Angels Have Wings, To Have and Have Not, The Big Sleep*, and *Rio Bravo* suggests the reason for the similar qualities of good-bad-girl glamour in the roles played by Dietrich and Bacall and in other von Sternberg and Hawks hero-ines, and also in the Jean Harlow and Constance Bennett roles in the movies he wrote for *them*. Furthman, who has written about half of the most entertaining movies to come out of Hollywood (Ben Hecht wrote most of the other half), isn't even listed in new encyclopedias of the film. David Newman and Robert Benton may be good enough to join this category of unmentionable men who do what the directors are glorified for. The Hollywood writer is becoming a ghostwriter. The writers who succeed in the struggle to protect their identity and their material by becoming writer-directors or writer-producers soon be-come too rich and powerful to bother doing their own writing. And they rarely have the visual sense or the training to make good movie directors.

Anyone who goes to big American movies like *Grand Prix* and *The*

Sand Pebbles recognizes that movies with scripts like those don't have a chance to be anything more than exercises in technology, and that this is what is meant by the decadence of American movies. In the past, directors used to say that they were no better than their material. (Sometimes they said it when they weren't even up to their material.) A good director can attempt to camouflage poor writing with craftsmanship and style, but ultimately no amount of director's skill can conceal a writer's failure; a poor script, even well directed, results in a stupid movie — as, unfortunately, does a good script poorly directed. Despite the new notion that the direction is everything, Penn can't redeem bad material, nor, as one may surmise from his *Mickey One*, does he necessarily know when it's bad. It is not fair to judge Penn by a film like *The Chase*, because he evidently did not have artistic control over the production, but what happens when he does have control and is working with a poor, pretentious mess of a script is painfully apparent in *Mickey One* — an art film in the worst sense of that term. Though one cannot say of *Bonnie and Clyde* to what degree it shows the work of Newman and Benton and to what degree they merely enabled Penn to 'express himself,' there are ways of making guesses. As we hear the lines, we can detect the intentions even when the intentions are not quite carried out. Penn is a little clumsy and rather too fancy; he's too much interested in being cinematically creative and artistic to know when to trust the script. *Bonnie and Clyde* could be better if it were simpler. Nevertheless, Penn is a remarkable director when he has something to work with. His most interesting previous work was in his first film, *The Left Handed Gun* (and a few bits of *The Miracle Worker*, a good movie version of the William Gibson play, which he had also directed on the stage and on television). *The Left Handed Gun*, with Paul Newman as an ignorant Billy the Kid in the sex-starved, male-dominated Old West, has the same kind of violent, legendary, nostalgic material as *Bonnie and Clyde*; its script, a rather startling one, was adapted by Leslie Stevens from a Gore Vidal television play. In interviews, Penn makes high, dull sounds — more like a politician than a movie director. But he has a gift for violence, and, despite all the violence in movies, a gift for it is rare. Eisenstein had it, and Dovzhenko, and Buñuel, but not many others.) There are few memorable violent moments in American movies, but there is one in Penn's first film: Billy's shotgun blasts a man right out of one of his boots; the man falls in the street, but his boot remains upright; a little girl's giggle at the boot is interrupted by her mother's slapping her. The mother's slap — the seal of the awareness of horror — says that even children must learn that some things that look funny are not only funny. That slap, saying that only idiots would laugh at pain and death, that a child must develop sensibility, is the same slap that *Bonnie and Clyde* delivers to the woman saying 'It's a comedy.' In *The Left Handed Gun*, the slap is itself funny, and yet we suck in our breath; we do not dare to laugh.

Some of the best American movies show the seams of cuts and the confusions of compromises and still hold together, because there is enough energy and spirit to carry the audience over each of the weak episodes to the next good one. The solid intelligence of the writing and Penn's aura of sensitivity help *Bonnie and Clyde* triumph over many poorly directed scenes: Bonnie posing for the photograph with the Texas Ranger, or — the worst sequence — the Ranger getting information out of Blanche Barrow in the hospital. The attempt to make the Texas Ranger an old-time villain doesn't work. He's in the tradition of the mustachioed heavy who foreclosed mortgages and pursued heroines in turn-of-the-century plays, and this one-dimensional villainy belongs, glaringly, to spoof. In some cases, I think, the writing and the conception of the scenes are better (potentially, that is) than the way the scenes have been directed and acted. If Gene Hackman's Buck Barrow is a beautifully controlled performance, the best in the film, several of the other players — though they are very good — needed a tighter rein. They act too much. But it is in other ways that Penn's limitations show — in his excessive reliance on meaning-laden closeups, for one. And it's no wonder he wasn't able to bring out the character of Bonnie in scenes like the one showing her appreciation of the fingernails on the figurine, for in other scenes his own sense of beauty appears to be only a few rungs farther up that same cultural ladder.

The showpiece sequence, Bonnie's visit to her mother (which is a bit reminiscent of Humphrey Bogart's confrontation with his mother, Marjorie Main, in the movie version of *Dead End*), aims for an effect of alienation, but that effect is confused by all the other things attempted in the sequence: the poetic echoes of childhood (which also echo the child sliding down the hill in *Jules and Jim*) and a general attempt to create a frieze from our national past — a poetry of poverty. Penn isn't quite up to it, though he is at least good enough to communicate what he is trying to do, and it is an attempt that one can respect. In 1939, John Ford attempted a similar poetic evocation of the legendary American past in *Young Mr Lincoln*; this kind of evocation, by getting at how we *feel* about the past, moves us far more than attempts at historical re-creation. When Ford's Western evocations fail, they become languorous; when they succeed, they are the West of our dreams, and his Lincoln, the man so humane and so smart that he can outwit the unjust and save the innocent, is the Lincoln of our dreams, and the Depression of *Bonnie and Clyde* is the Depression of our dreams — the nation in a kind of trance, as in a dim memory. In this sense, the effect of blur is justified, is 'right.' Our memories *have* become hazy; this is what the Depression has faded into. But we are too conscious of the technical means used to achieve this blur, of the *attempt* at poetry. We are aware that the filtered effects already include our responses, and it's too easy; the lines are good enough so that the stylization wouldn't have been necessary if the scene had been played right. A simple frozen frame might have been more appropriate.

The editing of this movie is, however, the best editing in an American movie in a long time, and one may assume that Penn deserves credit for it along with the editor, Dede Allen. It's particularly inventive in the robberies and in the comedy sequence of Blanche running through the police barricades with her kitchen spatula in her hand. (There is, however, one bad bit of editing: the end of the hospital scene, when Blanche's voice makes an emotional shift without a corresponding change in her facial position.) The quick panic of Bonnie and Clyde looking at each other's face for the last time is a stunning example of the art of editing.

The end of the picture, the rag-doll dance of death as the gun blasts keep the bodies of Bonnie and Clyde in motion, is brilliant. It is a horror that seems to go on for eternity, and yet it doesn't last a second beyond what it should. The audience leaving the theatre is the quietest audience imaginable.

Still, that woman near me was saying 'It's a comedy' for a little too long, and although this could have been, and probably was, a demonstration of plain old-fashioned insensitivity, it suggests that those who have attuned themselves to the 'total' comedy of the last few years may not know when to stop laughing. Movie audiences have been getting a steady diet of 'black' comedy since 1964 and *Dr Strangelove, Or: How I Learned to Stop Worrying and Love the Bomb*. Spoof and satire have been entertaining audiences since the two-reelers; because it is so easy to do on film things that are difficult or impossible in nature, movies are ideally suited to exaggerations of heroic prowess and to the kind of lighthearted nonsense we used to get when even the newsreels couldn't resist the kidding finish of the speeded-up athletic competition or the diver flying up from the water. The targets have usually been social and political fads and abuses, together with the heroes and the clichés of the just preceding period of film-making. *Dr Strangelove* opened a new movie era. It ridiculed *everything* and *everybody* it showed, but concealed its own liberal pieties, thus protecting itself from ridicule. A professor who had told me that *The Manchurian Candidate* was 'irresponsible,' adding, 'I didn't like it — I can suspend disbelief only so far,' was overwhelmed by *Dr Strangelove*: 'I've never been so involved. I had to keep reminding myself it was only a movie.' *Dr Strangelove* was clearly intended as a cautionary movie; it meant to jolt us awake to the dangers of the bomb by showing us the insanity of the course we were pursuing. But artists' warnings about war and the dangers of total annihilation never tell us how we are supposed to regain control, and *Dr Strangelove*, chortling over madness, did not indicate any possibilities for sanity. It was experienced not as satire but as a confirmation of fears. Total laughter carried the day. A new generation enjoyed seeing the world as insane; they *literally* learned to stop worrying and love the bomb. Conceptually, we had already been living with the bomb; now the mass audience of the movies — which is the youth of America — grasped the idea that the threat of extinction can be used to devaluate everything, to turn it all into a joke. And the members of this audience do love the bomb; they love feeling that the worst has happened and the irrational are the sane, because there is the bomb as the proof that the rational are insane. They love the bomb because it intensifies their feelings of hopelessness and powerlessness and innocence. It's only three years since Lewis Mumford was widely acclaimed for saying about *Dr Strangelove* that 'unless the spectator was purged by laughter he would be paralyzed by the unendurable anxiety this policy, once it were honestly appraised, would produce.' Far from being purged, the spectators are paralyzed, but they're still laughing. And how odd it is now to read, '*Dr Strangelove* would be a silly, ineffective picture if its purpose were to ridicule the characters of our military and political leaders by showing them as clownish monsters — stupid, psychotic, obsessed.' From *Dr Strangelove* it's a quick leap to *MacBird* and to a belief in exactly what it was said we weren't meant to find in

Dr Strangelove. It is not war that has been laughed to scorn but the possibility of sane action.

Once something enters mass culture, it travels fast. In the spoofs of the last few years, everything is gross, ridiculous, insane; to make sense would be to risk being square. A brutal new melodrama is called *Point Blank* and it is. So are most of the new movies. This is the context in which *Bonnie and Clyde*, an entertaining movie that has some feeling in it, upsets people — people who didn't get upset even by *Mondo Cane*. Maybe it's because *Bonnie and Clyde*, by making us care about the robber lovers, has put the sting back into death.

The New Yorker, 1967

Trash, Art and the Movies

I

Like those cynical heroes who were idealists before they discovered that the world was more rotten than they had been led to expect, we're just about all of us displaced persons, 'a long way from home.' When we feel defeated, when we imagine we could now perhaps settle for home and what it represents, that home no longer exists. But there are movie houses. In whatever city we find ourselves we can duck into a theatre and see on the screen our familiars — our old 'ideals' aging as we are and no longer looking so ideal. Where could we better stoke the fires of our masochism than at rotten movies in gaudy seedy picture palaces in cities that run together, movies and anonymity a common denominator. Movies — a tawdry corrupt art for a tawdry corrupt world — fit the way we feel. The world doesn't work the way the schoolbooks said it did and we are different from what our parents and teachers expected us to be. Movies are our cheap and easy expression, the sullen art of displaced persons. Because we feel low we sink in the boredom, relax in the irresponsibility, and maybe grin for a minute when the gunman lines up three men and kills them with a single bullet, which is no more 'real' to us than the nursery-school story of the brave little tailor.

We don't have to be told those are photographs of actors impersonating characters. We know, and we often know much more about both the actors and the characters they're impersonating and about how and why the movie has been made than is consistent with theatrical illusion. Hitchcock teased us by killing off the one marquee-name star early in *Psycho*, a gambit which startled us not just because of the suddenness of the murder or how it was committed but because it broke a box-office convention and so it was a joke played on what audiences have learned to expect. He broke the rules of the movie game and our response demonstrated how aware we are of commercial considerations. When movies are bad (and in the bad parts of good movies) our awareness of the mechanics and our cynicism about the aims and values is peculiarly alienating. The audience talks right back to the phony 'outspoken' condescending *The Detective*; there are groans of dejection at *The Legend of Lylah Clare*, with, now and then, a desperate little titter. How well we all know that cheap depression that settles on us when our hopes and expectations are disappointed *again*. Alienation is the most common state of the knowledgeable movie audience, and though it has the peculiar rewards of low connoisseurship, a miser's delight in small favors, we long to be surprised out of it — not to suspension of disbelief nor to a Brechtian kind of alienation, but to pleasure, something a man can call good without self-disgust.

A good movie can take you out of your dull funk and the hopelessness that so often goes with slipping into a theatre; a good movie can make you feel alive again, in contact, not just lost in another city. Good movies make you care, make you believe in possibilities again. If somewhere in the Hollywood-entertainment world someone has managed to break through with something that speaks to you, then it isn't *all* corruption. The movie doesn't have to be great; it can be stupid and empty and you can still have the joy of a good performance, or the joy in just a good line. An actor's scowl, a small subversive gesture, a dirty remark that someone tosses off with a mock-innocent face, and the world makes a little bit of sense. Sitting there alone or painfully alone because those with you do not react as you do, you know there must be others perhaps in this very theatre or in this city, surely in other theatres in other cities, now, in the past or future, who react as you do. And because movies are the most total and encompassing art form we have, these reactions can seem the most personal and, maybe the most important, imaginable. The romance of movies is not just in those stories and those people on the screen but in the adolescent dream of meeting others who feel as you do about what you've seen. You do meet them, of course, and you know each other at once because you talk less about good movies than about what you love in bad movies.

II

There is so much talk now about the art of the film that we may be in danger of forgetting that most of the movies we enjoy are not works of art. *The Scalphunters*, for example, was one of the few entertaining

American movies this past year, but skillful though it was, one could hardly call it a work of art — if such terms are to have any useful meaning. Or, to take a really gross example, a movie that is as crudely made as *Wild in the Streets* — slammed together with spit and hysteria and opportunism — can nevertheless be enjoyable, though it is almost a classic example of an unartistic movie. What makes these movies — that are not works of art — enjoyable? *The Scalphunters* was more entertaining than most Westerns largely because Burt Lancaster and Ossie Davis were peculiarly funny together; part of the pleasure of the movie was trying to figure out what made them so funny. Burt Lancaster is an odd kind of comedian: what's distinctive about him is that his comedy seems to come out of his physicality. In serious roles an undistinguished and too obviously hard-working actor, he has an apparently effortless flair for comedy and nothing is more infectious than an actor who can relax in front of the camera as if he were having a good time. (George Segal sometimes seems to have this gift of a wonderful amiability, and Brigitte Bardot was radiant with it in *Viva Maria!*) Somehow the alchemy of personality in the pairing of Lancaster and Ossie Davis — another powerfully funny actor of tremendous physical presence — worked, and the director Sydney Pollack kept tight control so that it wasn't overdone.

And *Wild in the Streets*? It's a blatantly crummy-looking picture, but that somehow works for it instead of against it because it's smart in a lot of ways that better-made pictures aren't. It looks like other recent products from American International Pictures but it's as if one were reading a comic strip that looked just like the strip of the day before, and yet on this new one there are surprising expressions on the faces and some of the balloons are really witty. There's not a trace of sensitivity in the drawing or in the ideas, and there's something rather specially funny about wit without *any* grace at all; it can be enjoyed in a particularly crude way — as Pop wit. The basic idea is corny — *It Can't Happen Here* with the freaked-out young as a new breed of fascists — but it's treated in the paranoid style of editorials about youth (it even begins by blaming everything on the parents). And a cheap idea that is this current and widespread has an almost lunatic charm, a nightmare gaiety. There's a relish that people have for the idea of drug-taking kids as monsters threatening them — the daily papers merging into *Village of the Damned*. Tapping and exploiting this kind of hysteria for a satirical fantasy, the writer Robert Thom has used what is available and obvious but he's done it with just enough

mockery and style to make it funny. He throws in touches of characterization and occasional lines that are not there just to further the plot,
and these throwaways make odd connections so that the movie
becomes almost frolicsome in its paranoia (and in its delight in its own
cleverness).

If you went to *Wild in the Streets* expecting a good movie, you'd
probably be appalled because the directing is unskilled and the music
is banal and many of the ideas in the script are scarcely even carried
out, and almost every detail is messed up (the casting director has used
bit players and extras who are decades too old for their roles). It's a
paste-up job of cheap movie-making, but it has genuinely funny
performers who seize their opportunities and throw their good lines
like boomerangs — Diane Varsi (like an even more zonked-out
Geraldine Page) doing a perfectly quietly convincing freak-out as if it
were truly a put-on of the whole straight world; Hal Holbrook with his
inexpressive actorish face that is opaque and uninteresting in long
shot but in closeup reveals tiny little shifts of expression, slight
tightenings of the features that are like the movement of thought; and
Shelley Winters, of course, and Christopher Jones. It's not so terrible
— it may even be a relief — for a movie to be without the look of art;
there are much worse things aesthetically than the crude good-natured
crumminess, the undisguised reach for a fast buck, of movies without
art. From *I Was a Teen-Age Werewolf* through the beach parties to
Wild in the Streets and *The Savage Seven*, American International
Pictures has sold a cheap commodity, which in its lack of artistry and
in its blatant and sometimes funny way of delivering action serves to
remind us that one of the great appeals of movies is that we don't have
to take them too seriously.

Wild in the Streets is a fluke — a borderline, special case of a movie
that is entertaining because some talented people got a chance to do
something at American International that the more respectable companies were too nervous to try. But though I don't enjoy a movie so obvious
and badly done as the big American International hit, *The Wild Angels*,
it's easy to see why kids do and why many people in other countries do.
Their reasons are basically why we all started going to the movies. After
a time, we may want more, but audiences who have been forced to wade
through the thick middle-class padding of more expensively made
movies to get to the action enjoy the nose-thumbing at 'good taste' of
cheap movies that stick to the raw materials. At some basic level they
like the pictures to be cheaply done, they enjoy the crudeness; it's a

breather, a vacation from proper behavior and good taste and required responses. Patrons of burlesque applaud politely for the graceful erotic dancer but go wild for the lewd lummox who bangs her big hips around. That's what they go to burlesque for. Personally, I hope for a reasonable minimum of finesse, and movies like *Planet of the Apes* or *The Scalphunters* or *The Thomas Crown Affair* seem to me minimal entertainment for a relaxed evening's pleasure. These are, to use traditional common-sense language, 'good movies' or 'good bad movies' — slick, reasonably inventive, well-crafted. They are not art. But they are almost the maximum of what we're now getting from American movies, and not only these but much worse movies are talked about as 'art' — and are beginning to be taken seriously in our schools.

It's preposterously egocentric to call anything we enjoy art — as if we could not be entertained by it if it were not; it's just as preposterous to let prestigious, expensive advertising snow us into thinking we're getting art for our money when we haven't even had a good time. I did have a good time at *Wild in the Streets*, which is more than I can say for *Petulia* or *2001* or a lot of other highly praised pictures. *Wild in the Streets* is not a work of art, but then I don't think *Petulia* or *2001* is either, though *Petulia* has that kaleidoscopic hip look and *2001* that new-techniques look which combined with 'swinging' or 'serious' ideas often pass for motion picture art.

III

Let's clear away a few misconceptions. Movies make hash of the schoolmarm's approach of how well the artist fulfilled his intentions. Whatever the original intention of the writers and director, it is usually supplanted, as the production gets under way, by the intention to make money — and the industry judges the film by how well it fulfills that intention. But if you could see the 'artist's intentions' you'd probably wish you couldn't anyway. Nothing is so deathly to enjoyment as the relentless march of a movie to fulfill its obvious purpose. This is, indeed, almost a defining characteristic of the hack director, as distinguished from an artist.

The intention to make money is generally all too obvious. One of the excruciating comedies of our time is attending the new classes in cinema at the high schools where the students may quite shrewdly and accurately interpret the plot developments in a mediocre movie in terms of manipulation for a desired response while the teacher tries to explain everything in terms of the creative artist working out his theme — as if the conditions under which a movie is made and the market for which it is designed were irrelevant, as if the latest product from Warners or Universal should be analyzed like a lyric poem.

People who are just getting 'seriously interested' in film always ask a critic, 'Why don't you talk about technique and "the visuals" more?' The answer is that American movie technique is generally more like technology and it usually isn't very interesting. Hollywood movies often have the look of the studio that produced them — they have a studio style. Many current Warner films are noisy and have a bright look of cheerful ugliness, Universal films the cheap blur of money-saving processes, and so forth. Sometimes there is even a *spirit* that seems to belong to the studio. We can speak of the Paramount comedies of the thirties or the Twentieth-Century Fox family entertainment of the forties and CinemaScope comedies of the fifties or the old M-G-M gloss, pretty much as we speak of Chevvies or Studebakers. These movies look alike, they move the same way, they have just about the same engines because of the studio policies and the *kind* of material the studio heads bought, the ideas they imposed, the way they had the films written, directed, photographed, and the labs where the prints were processed, and, of course, because of the presence of the studio stable of stars for whom the material was often purchased and shaped and who dominated the output of the studio. In some cases, as at Paramount in the thirties, studio style was plain and rather tacky and the output — those comedies with Mary Boland and Mae West and Alison Skipworth and W.C. Fields — looks the better for it now. Those economical comedies weren't slowed down by a lot of fancy lighting or the adornments of 'production values.' Simply to be enjoyable, movies don't need a very high level of craftsmanship: wit, imagination, fresh subject matter, skillful performers, a good idea — either alone or in any combination — can more than compensate for lack of technical knowledge or a big budget.

The craftsmanship that Hollywood has always used as a selling point not only doesn't have much to do with art — the expressive use of techniques — it probably doesn't have very much to do with actual box-office appeal, either. A dull movie like Sidney Furie's *The Naked Runner* is technically competent. The appalling *Half a Sixpence* is technically astonishing. Though the large popular audience has generally been respectful of expenditure (so much so that a critic who wasn't impressed by the money and effort that went into a *Dr Zhivago* might be sharply reprimanded by readers), people who like *The*

President's Analyst or *The Producers* or *The Odd Couple* don't seem
to be bothered by their technical ineptitude and visual ugliness. And
on the other hand, the expensive slick techniques of ornately empty
movies like *A Dandy in Aspic* can actually work against one's enjoyment, because such extravagance and waste are morally ugly. If one
compares movies one likes to movies one doesn't like, craftsmanship
of the big-studio variety is hardly a decisive factor. And if one
compares a movie one likes by a competent director such as John
Sturges or Franklin Schaffner or John Frankenheimer to a movie one
doesn't much like by the same director, his technique is probably not
the decisive factor. After directing *The Manchurian Candidate*
Frankenheimer directed another political thriller, *Seven Days in May*,
which, considered just as a piece of direction, was considerably more
confident. While seeing it, one could take pleasure in Frankenheimer's
smooth showmanship. But the material (Rod Serling out of Fletcher
Knebel and Charles W. Bailey II) was like a straight (i.e., square)
version of *The Manchurian Candidate*. I have to chase around the
corridors of memory to summon up images from *Seven Days in May*;
despite the brilliant technique, all that is clear to mind is the touch-
ingly, desperately anxious face of Ava Gardner — how when she
smiled you couldn't be sure if you were seeing dimples or tics. But *The
Manchurian Candidate*, despite Frankenheimer's uneven, often barely
adequate, staging, is still vivid because of the script. It took off from
a political double entendre that everybody had been thinking of
('Why, if Joe McCarthy were working for the Communists, he couldn't
be doing them more good!') and carried it to startling absurdity, and
the extravagances and conceits and conversational non sequiturs (by
George Axelrod out of Richard Condon) were ambivalent and funny
in a way that was trashy yet liberating.

Technique is hardly worth talking about unless it's used for something worth doing: that's why most of the theorizing about the new art
of television commercials is such nonsense. The effects are impersonal — dexterous, sometimes clever, but empty of art. It's because of
their emptiness that commercials call so much attention to their
camera angles and quick cutting — which is why people get impressed by 'the art' of it. Movies are now often made in terms of what
television viewers have learned to settle for. Despite a great deal that
is spoken and written about young people responding visually, the
influence of TV is to make movies visually less imaginative and
complex. Television is a very noisy medium and viewers listen, while

getting used to a poor quality of visual reproduction, to the absence of visual detail, to visual obviousness and overemphasis on simple compositions, and to atrociously simplified and distorted color systems. The shifting camera styles, the movement, and the fast cutting of a film like *Finian's Rainbow* — one of the better big productions — are like the 'visuals' of TV commercials, a disguise for static material, expressive of nothing so much as the need to keep you from getting bored and leaving. Men are now beginning their careers as directors by working on commercials — which, if one cares to speculate on it, may be almost a one-sentence résumé of the future of American motion pictures.

I don't mean to suggest that there is not such a thing as movie technique or that craftsmanship doesn't contribute to the pleasures of movies, but simply that most audiences, if they enjoy the acting and the 'story' or the theme or the funny lines, don't notice or care about how well or how badly the movie is made, and because they don't care, a hit makes a director a 'genius' and everybody talks about his brilliant technique (i.e., the technique of grabbing an audience). In the brief history of movies there has probably never been so astonishingly gifted a large group of directors as the current Italians, and not just the famous ones or Pontecorvo (*The Battle of Algiers*) or Francesco Rosi (*The Moment of Truth*) or the young prodigies, Bertolucci and Bellocchio, but dozens of others, men like Elio Petri (*We Still Kill the Old Way*) and Carlo Lizzani (*The Violent Four*). *The Violent Four* is a gangster genre picture. And it may be a form of aestheticism — losing sight of what people go to movies for, and particularly what they go to foreign movies for — for a critic to say, 'His handling of crowds and street scenes is superb,' or, 'It has a great semi-documentary chase sequence.' It does, but the movie is basically derived from our old gangster movies, and beautifully made as it is, one would have a hard time convincing educated people to go see a movie that features a stunning performance by Gian Maria Volonte which is based on Paul Muni and James Cagney. Presumably they want something different from movies than a genre picture that offers images of modern urban decay and is smashingly directed. If a movie is interesting primarily in terms of technique then it isn't worth talking about except to students who can learn from seeing how a good director works. And to talk about a movie like *The Graduate* in terms of movie technique is really a bad joke. Technique at this level is not of any aesthetic importance; it's not the ability to achieve what you're after but the skill to find something acceptable. One must talk about a film like this in terms of what audiences enjoy it for or one is talking gibberish — and might as well be analyzing the 'art' of commercials. And for the greatest movie artists where there is a unity of technique and subject, one doesn't need to talk about technique much because it has been subsumed in the art. One doesn't want to talk about how Tolstoy got his effects but about the work itself. One doesn't want to talk about how Jean Renoir does it; one wants to talk about what he has done. One can try to separate it all out, of course, distinguish form and content for purposes of analysis. But that is a secondary, analytic function, a scholarly function, and hardly needs to be done explicitly in criticism. Taking it apart is far less important than trying to see it whole. The critic shouldn't need to tear a work apart to demonstrate that he knows how it was put together. The important thing is to convey what is new and beautiful in the work, not how it was made — which is more or less implicit.

Just as there are good actors — possibly potentially great actors — who have never become big stars because they've just never been lucky enough to get the roles they needed (Brian Keith is a striking example) there are good directors who never got the scripts and the casts that could make their reputations. The question people ask when they consider going to a movie is not 'How's it made?' but 'What's it about?' and that's a perfectly legitimate question. (The next question — sometimes the first — is generally, 'Who's in it?' and that's a good, honest question, too.) When you're at a movie, you don't have to believe in it to enjoy it but you do have to be interested. (Just as you have to be interested in the human material, too. Why should you go see *another* picture with James Stewart?) I don't want to see another samurai epic in exactly the same way I never want to read *Kristin Lavransdatter*. Though it's conceivable that a truly great movie director could make any subject interesting, there are few such artists working in movies and if they did work on unpromising subjects I'm not sure we'd really enjoy the results even if we did *admire* their artistry. (I recognize the greatness of se-quences in several films by Eisenstein but it's a rather cold admiration.) The many brilliant Italian directors who are working within a commercial framework on crime and action movies are obviously not going to be of any great interest unless we get a chance to work on a subject we care about. Ironically the Czech successes here (*The Shop on Main Street, Loves of a Blonde, Closely Watched*

Trains) are acclaimed for their techniques, which are fairly simple and rather limited, when it's obviously their human concern and the basic modesty and decency of their attitudes plus a little barnyard humor which audiences respond to. They may even respond partly because of the *simplicity* of the techniques.

IV

When we are children, though there are categories of films we don't like — documentaries generally (they're too much like education) and, of course, movies especially designed for children — by the time we can go on our own we have learned to avoid them. Children are often put down by adults when the children say they enjoyed a particular movie; adults who are short on empathy are quick to point out aspects of the plot or theme that the child didn't understand, and it's easy to humiliate a child in this way. But it is one of the glories of eclectic arts like opera and movies that they include so many possible kinds and combinations of pleasure. One may be enthralled by Leontyne Price in *La Forza del Destino* even if one hasn't boned up on the libretto, or entranced by *The Magic Flute* even if one has boned up on the libretto, and a movie may be enjoyed for many reasons that have little to do with the story or the subtleties (if any) of theme or character. Unlike 'pure' arts which are often defined in terms of what only they can do, movies are open and unlimited. Probably everything that can be done in movies can be done some other way, but — and this is what's so miraculous and so expedient about them — they can do almost anything any other art can do (alone or in combination) and they can take on some of the functions of exploration, of journalism, of anthropology, of almost any branch of knowledge as well. We go to the movies for the variety of what they can provide, and for their marvellous ability to give us easily and inexpensively (and usually painlessly) what we can get from other arts also. They are a wonderfully *convenient* art.

Movies are used by cultures where they are foreign films in a much more primitive way than in their own; they may be enjoyed as travelogues or as initiations into how others live or in ways we might not even guess. The sophisticated and knowledgeable moviegoer is likely to forget how new and how amazing the different worlds up there once seemed to him, and to forget how much a child reacts to, how many elements he is taking in, often for the first time. And even adults who have seen many movies may think a movie is 'great' if it introduces them to unfamiliar subject matter; thus many moviegoers react as naïvely as children to *Portrait of Jason* or *The Queen*. They think they're wonderful. The oldest plots and corniest comedy bits can be full of wonder for a child, just as the freeway traffic in a grade Z melodrama can be magical to a villager who has never seen a car. A child may enjoy even a movie like *Jules and Jim* for its sense of fun, without comprehending it as his parents do, just as we may enjoy an Italian movie as a sex comedy although in Italy it is considered social criticism or political satire. Jean-Luc Godard liked the movie of *Pal Joey*, and I suppose that a miserable American movie musical like *Pal Joey* might look good in France because I can't think of a single good dance number performed by French dancers in a French movie. The French enjoy what they're unable to do and we enjoy the French studies of the pangs of adolescent love that would be corny if made in Hollywood. A movie like *The Young Girls of Rochefort* demonstrates how even a gifted Frenchman who adores American musicals misunderstands their conventions. Yet it would be as stupid to say that the director Jacques Demy couldn't love American musicals because he doesn't understand their conventions as to tell a child he couldn't have liked *Planet of the Apes* because he didn't get the jokey references to the Scopes trial.

Every once in a while I see an anthropologist's report on how some preliterate tribe reacts to movies; they may, for example, be disturbed about where the actor has gone when he leaves the movie frame, or they may respond with enthusiasm to the noise and congestions of big-city life which in the film story are meant to show the depths of depersonalization to which we are sinking, but which they find funny or very jolly indeed. Different cultures have their own ways of enjoying movies. A few years ago the new 'tribalists' here responded to the gaudy fantasies of *Juliet of the Spirits* by using the movie to turn on. A few had already made a trip of *8½*, but *Juliet*, which was, conveniently and perhaps not entirely accidentally, in electric, psych-edelic color, caught on because of it. (The color was awful, like in bad M-G-M musicals — so one may wonder about the quality of the trips.)

The new tribalism in the age of the media is not necessarily the enemy of commercialism; it is a direct outgrowth of commercialism and its ally, perhaps even its instrument. If a movie has enough clout, reviewers and columnists who were bored are likely to give it another chance, until on the second or third viewing, they discover that it affects them 'viscerally' — and a big expensive movie is likely to do just that. *2001* is said to have caught on with youth (which can make it happen); and it's said that the movie will stone you — which is meant to be a recommendation. Despite a few dissident voices — I've heard it said, for example, that *2001* 'gives you a bad trip because the visuals don't go with the music' — the promotion has been remarkably effective with students. 'The tribes' tune in so fast that college students thousands of miles apart 'have heard' what a great trip *2001* is before it has even reached their city.

Using movies to go on a trip has about as much connection with the art of the film as using one of those Doris Day–Rock Hudson jobs for ideas on how to redecorate your home — an earlier way of stoning yourself. But it is relevant to an understanding of movies to try to separate out, for purposes of discussion at least, how we may personally *use* a film — to learn how to dress or how to speak more elegantly or how to make a grand entrance or even what kind of coffee maker we wish to purchase, or to take off from the movie into a romantic fantasy or a trip — from what makes it a good movie or a poor one, because, of course, we can *use* poor films as easily as good ones, perhaps *more* easily for such non-aesthetic purposes as shopping guides or aids to tripping.

V

We generally become interested in movies because we *enjoy* them and what we enjoy them for has little to do with what we think of as art. The movies we respond to, even in childhood, don't have the same values as the official culture supported at school and in the middle-class home. At the movies we get low life and high life, while David Susskind and the moralistic reviewers chastise us for not patronizing what they think we should, 'realistic' movies that would be good for us — like *A Raisin in the Sun*, where we could learn the lesson that a Negro family can be as dreary as a white family. Movie audiences will take a lot of garbage, but it's pretty hard to make us queue up for pedagogy. At the movies we want a different kind of truth, something that surprises us and registers with us as funny or accurate or maybe amazing, maybe even amazingly beautiful. We get little things even in mediocre and terrible movies — José Ferrer sipping his booze through a straw in *Enter Laughing*, Scott Wilson's hard scary all-American-boy-you-can't-reach face cutting through the pretensions of *In Cold Blood* with all its fancy bleak cinematography. We got, and still have embedded in memory, Tony Randall's surprising depth of feeling in *The Seven Faces of Dr Lao*, Keenan Wynn and Moyna MacGill in the lunch-counter sequence of *The Clock*, John W. Bubbles on the dance floor in *Cabin in the Sky*, the inflection Gene Kelly gave to the line, 'I'm a rising young man' in *DuBarry Was a Lady*, Tony Curtis saying 'avidly' in *Sweet Smell of Success*. Though the director may have been responsible for releasing it, it's the human material we react to most and remember longest. The art of the performers stays fresh for us, their beauty as beautiful as ever. There are so many kinds of things we get — the hangover sequence wittily designed for the CinemaScope screen in *The Tender Trap*, the atmosphere of the newspaper offices in *The Luck of Ginger Coffey*, the Automat gone mad in *Easy Living*. Do we need to lie and shift things to false terms — like those who have to say Sophia Loren is a great actress as if her *acting* had made her a star? Wouldn't we rather watch her than better actresses because she's so incredibly charming and because she's probably the greatest model the world has ever known? There are great moments — Angela Lansbury singing 'Little Yellow Bird' in *Dorian Gray*. (I don't think I've ever had a friend who didn't also treasure that girl and that song.) And there are absurdly right little moments — in *Saratoga Trunk* when Curt Bois says to Ingrid Bergman, 'You're very beautiful,' and she says, 'Yes, isn't it lucky?' And those things have closer relationships to art than what the schoolteachers told us was true and beautiful. Not that the works we studied in school weren't often great (as we discovered *later*) but that what the teachers told us to admire them for (and if current texts are any indication, are still telling students to admire them for) was generally so false and prettified and moralistic that what might have been moments of pleasure in them, and what might have been cleansing in them, and subversive, too, had been coated over.

Because of the photographic nature of the medium and the cheap admission prices, movies took their impetus not from the desiccated imitation European high culture, but from the peep show, the Wild West show, the music hall, the comic strip — from what was coarse and common. The early Chaplin two-reelers still look surprisingly lewd, with bathroom jokes and drunkenness and hatred of work and proprieties. And the Western shoot-'em-ups certainly weren't the schoolteachers' notions of art — which in my school days, ran more to didactic poetry and 'perfectly proportioned' statues and which over the years have progressed through nice stories to 'good taste' and 'excellence' — which may be more poisonous than homilies and dainty figurines because then you had a clearer idea of what you were up against and it was easier to fight. And this, of course, is what we were running away from when we went to the movies. All week we longed for Saturday afternoon and sanctuary — the anonymity and impersonality of sitting in a theatre, just enjoying ourselves, not having to be responsible, not having to be 'good.' Maybe you just want to look at people on the screen and know they're not looking back at you, that they're not going to turn on you and criticize you.

Perhaps the single most intense pleasure of moviegoing is this non-aesthetic one of escaping from the responsibilities of having the proper responses required of us in our official (school) culture. And yet this is probably the best and most common basis for developing an aesthetic sense because responsibility to pay attention and to appreciate is anti-art, it makes us too anxious for pleasure, too bored for response. Far from supervision and official culture, in the darkness at the movies where nothing is asked of us and we are left alone, the liberation from duty and constraint allows us to develop our own aesthetic responses. Unsupervised enjoyment is probably not the only kind there is but it may feel like the only kind. Irresponsibility is part of the pleasure of all art; it is the part the schools cannot recognize. I don't like to buy 'hard tickets' for a 'road show' movie because I hate treating a movie as an occasion. I don't want to be pinned down days in advance; I enjoy the casualness of moviegoing — of going in when I feel like it, when I'm in the mood for a movie. It's the feeling of freedom from respectability we have always enjoyed at the movies that is carried to an extreme by American International Pictures and the Clint Eastwood Italian Westerns; they are stripped of cultural values. We may want more from movies than this negative virtue but we know the feeling from childhood moviegoing when we loved the gamblers and pimps and the cons' suggestions of muttered obscenities as the guards walked by. The appeal of movies was in the details of crime and high living and wicked cities and in the language of toughs and urchins; it was in the dirty smile of the city girl who lured the hero away from Janet Gaynor. What draws us to movies in the first place, the opening into other, forbidden or surprising, kinds of experience, and the vitality and corruption and irreverence of that experience are so direct and immediate and have so little connection with what we have been taught is art that many people feel more secure, feel that their tastes are becoming more cultivated when they begin to *appreciate* foreign films. One foundation executive told me that he was quite upset that his teen-agers had chosen to go to *Bonnie and Clyde* rather than with him to *Closely Watched Trains*. He took it as a sign of lack of maturity. I think his kids made an honest choice, and not only because *Bonnie and Clyde* is a good movie, but because it is closer to us, it has some of the qualities of direct involvement that made us care about movies. But it's understandable that it's easier for us, as Americans, to see *art* in foreign films than in our own, because of how we, as Americans, think of art. Art is still what teachers and ladies and foundations believe in, it's civilized and refined, cultivated and serious, cultural, beautiful, European, Oriental: it's what America isn't, and it's especially what American movies are not. Still, if those kids had chosen *Wild in the Streets* over *Closely Watched Trains* I would think that was a sound and honest choice, too, even though *Wild in the Streets* is in most ways a terrible picture. It connects with their lives in an immediate even if a grossly frivolous way, and if we don't go to movies for excitement, if, even as children, we accept the cultural standards of refined adults, if we have so little drive that we accept 'good taste,' then we will probably never really begin to care about movies at all. We will become like those people who 'may go to American movies sometimes to relax' but when they want 'a little more' from a movie, are delighted by how colorful and artistic Franco Zeffirelli's *The Taming of the Shrew* is, just as a couple of decades ago they were impressed by *The Red Shoes*, made by Powell and Pressburger, the Zeffirellis of their day. Or, if they like the cozy feeling of uplift to be had from mildly whimsical movies about timid people, there's generally a *Hot Millions* or something musty and faintly boring from Eastern Europe — one of those movies set in World War II but so remote from our ways of thinking that it seems to be set in World War I. Afterward, the moviegoer can feel as decent and virtuous as if he's spent an evening visiting a deaf old friend of the family. It's a way of taking movies back into the approved culture of the schoolroom — into gentility — and the voices of schoolteachers and reviewers rise up to ask why America can't make such movies.

VI

Movie art is not the opposite of what we have always enjoyed in movies, it is not to be found in a return to that official high culture, it is what we have always found good in movies only more so. It's the subversive gesture carried further, the moments of excitement sustained longer and extended into new meanings. At best, the movie is totally informed by the kind of pleasure we have been taking from bits and pieces of movies. But we are so used to reaching out to the few good bits in a movie that we don't need formal perfection to be dazzled. There are so many arts and crafts that go into movies and there are so many things that can go wrong that they're not an art for purists. We want to experience that elation we feel when a movie (or even a performer in a movie) goes farther than we had expected and makes the leap successfully. Even a film like Godard's *Les Carabiniers*, hell to watch for the first hour, is exciting to think about after because its one good sequence, the long picture-postcard sequence near the end, is so incredible and so brilliantly prolonged. The picture has been crawling and stumbling along and then it climbs a high wire and walks it and keeps walking it until we're almost dizzy from admiration. The tightrope is rarely stretched so high in movies, but there must be a sense of tension somewhere in the movie, if only in a bit player's face, not just mechanical suspense, or the movie is just more hours down the drain. It's the rare movie we really *go* with, the movie that keeps us tense and attentive. We learn to dread Hollywood 'realism' and all that it implies. When, in the dark, we concentrate our attention, we are driven frantic by events on the level of ordinary life that pass at the rhythm of ordinary life. That's the self-conscious striving for integrity of humorless, untalented people. When we go to a play we expect a heightened, stylized language; the dull realism of the streets is unendurably boring, though we may escape from the play to the nearest bar to listen to the same language with relief. Better life than art imitating life.

If we go back and think over the movies we've enjoyed — even the ones we knew were terrible movies while we enjoyed them — what we enjoyed in them, the little part that was good, had, in some rudimentary way, some freshness, some hint of style, some trace of beauty, some audacity, some craziness. It's there in the interplay between Burt Lancaster and Ossie Davis, or, in *Wild in the Streets*, in Diane Varsi rattling her tambourine, in Hal Holbrook's faint twitch when he smells trouble, in a few of Robert Thom's lines; and they have some relation to art though they don't look like what we've been taught is 'quality.' They have the joy of playfulness. In a mediocre or rotten movie, the good things may give the impression that they come out of nowhere; the better the movie, the more they seem to belong to the world of the movie. Without this kind of playfulness and the pleasure we take from it, art isn't art at all, it's something punishing, as it so often is in school where even artists' little *jokes* become leaden from explanation.

Keeping in mind that simple, good distinction that all art is entertainment but not all entertainment is art, it might be a good idea to keep in mind also that if a movie is said to be a work of art and you don't enjoy it, the fault may be in you, but it's probably in the movie. Because of the money and advertising pressures involved, many reviewers discover a fresh masterpiece every week, and there's that cultural snobbery, that hunger for respectability that determines the selection of the even bigger annual masterpieces. In foreign movies what is most often mistaken for 'quality' is an imitation of earlier movie art or a derivation from respectable, approved work in the other arts — like the demented, suffering painter-hero of *Hour of the Wolf* smearing his lipstick in a facsimile of expressionist anguish. Kicked in the ribs, the press says 'art' when 'ouch' would be more appropriate. When a director is said to be an artist (generally on the basis of earlier work which the press failed to recognize) and especially when he picks artistic subjects like the pain of creation, there is a tendency to acclaim his new bad work. This way the press, in trying to make up for its past mistakes, manages to be wrong all the time. And so a revenge-of-a-sour-virgin movie like Truffaut's *The Bride Wore Black* is treated respectfully as if it somehow revealed an artist's sensibility in every frame. Reviewers who would laugh at Lana Turner going through her *femme fatale* act in another Ross Hunter movie swoon when Jeanne Moreau casts significant blank looks for Truffaut.

In American movies what is most often mistaken for artistic quality is box-office success, especially if it's combined with a genuflection to importance; then you have 'a movie the industry can be proud of' like *To Kill a Mockingbird* or such Academy Award winners as *West Side Story, My Fair Lady,* or *A Man for All Seasons*. Fred Zinnemann made a fine modern variant of a Western, *The Sundowners*, and hardly anybody saw it until it got on television; but *A Man for All Seasons* had the look of prestige and the press felt honored to praise it. I'm not sure most movie reviewers consider what they honestly enjoy as being central to criticism. Some at least appear to think that that would be relying too much on their own tastes, being too personal instead of being 'objective' — relying on the ready-made terms of cultural respectability and on consensus judgment (which, to a rather shocking degree, can be arranged by publicists creating a climate of importance around a movie). Just as movie directors, as they age, hunger for what was meant by respectability in their youth, and aspire to prestigious cultural properties, so, too, the movie press longs to be elevated in terms of the cultural values of their old high schools. And so they, along with the industry, applaud ghastly 'tour-de-force' performances, movies based on 'distinguished' stage successes or prize-winning novels, or movies that are 'worthwhile,' that make a 'contribution' — 'serious' messagy movies. This often involves praise of bad movies, of dull movies, or even the praise in good movies of what was worst in them.

This last mechanism can be seen in the honors bestowed on *In the Heat of the Night*. The best thing in the movie is that high comic moment when, Poitier says, 'I'm a police officer,' because it's a reversal of audience expectations and we laugh in delighted relief that the movie is not going to be another self-righteous, self-congratulatory exercise in the gloomy old Stanley Kramer tradition. At that point the audience sparks to life. The movie is fun largely because of the amusing central idea of a black Sherlock Holmes in a Tom and Jerry cartoon of reversals. Poitier's color is used for comedy instead of for that extra dimension of irony and pathos that made movies like *To Sir, with Love* unbearably sentimental. He doesn't really play the super sleuth very well: he's much too straight even when spouting the kind of higher scientific nonsense about right-handedness and left-handedness that would have kept Basil Rathbone in an ecstasy of clipped diction, blinking eyes and raised eyebrows. Like Bogart in *Beat the Devil* Poitier doesn't seem to be in on the joke. But Rod Steiger compensated with a comic performance that was even funnier for being so unexpected — not only from Steiger's career which had been going in other directions, but after the apparently serious opening of the film. The movie was, however, praised by the press as if it had been exactly the kind of picture that the audience was so relieved to discover it wasn't going to be (except in its routine melodramatic sequences full of fake courage and the climaxes such as Poitier slapping a rich white Southerner or being attacked by white thugs; except that is, in its worst parts). When I saw it, the audience, both black and white, enjoyed the joke of the fast-witted, hyper-educated black detective explaining matters to the backward, blundering Southern-chief-of-police slob. This racial joke is far more open and inoffensive than the usual 'irony' of Poitier being so good and so black. For once it's *funny* (instead of embarrassing) that he's so superior to everybody.

In the Heat of the Night isn't in itself a particularly important movie; amazingly alive photographically, it's an entertaining, somewhat messed-up comedy-thriller. The director Norman Jewison destroys the final joke when Steiger plays redcap to Poitier by infusing it with tender feeling, so it comes out sickly sweet, and it's too bad that a whodunit in which the whole point is the demonstration of the Negro detective's ability to unravel what the white man can't, is never clearly unraveled. Maybe it needed a negro super director. (The picture might have been more than just a lively whodunit if the detective had proceeded to solve the crime not by 'scientific' means but by an understanding of relationships in the South that the white chief of police didn't have.) What makes it interesting for my purposes here is that the audience enjoyed the movie for the vitality of its surprising playfulness, while the industry congratulated itself because the film was 'hard-hitting' — that is to say, it flirted with seriousness and spouted warm, worthwhile ideas.

Those who can accept *In the Heat of the Night* as the socially conscious movie that the industry pointed to with pride can probably also go along with the way the press attacked Jewison's subsequent film, *The Thomas Crown Affair*, as trash and a failure. One could even play the same game that was played on *In the Heat of the Night* and convert the *Crown* trifle into a subfascist exercise because, of course, Crown, the superman, who turns to crime out of boredom, is the crooked son of *The Fountainhead*, out of Raffles. But that's taking glossy summer-evening fantasies much too seriously; we haven't had a junior executive's fantasy-life movie for a long time and to attack this return to the worldly gentlemen-thieves genre of Ronald Colman and William Powell *politically* is to fail to have a sense of humor about the little romantic-adolescent fascist lurking in most of us. Part of the fun of movies is that they allow us to see how silly many of our fantasies are and how widely they're shared. A light romantic entertainment like *The Thomas Crown Affair*, trash undisguised, is the kind of chic crappy movie which (one would have thought) nobody could be fooled into thinking was art. Seeing it is like lying in the sun flicking through fashion magazines and, as we used to say, feeling rich and beautiful beyond your wildest dreams.

But it isn't easy to come to terms with what one enjoys in films, and if an older generation was persuaded to *dismiss* trash, now a younger generation, with the press and the schools in hot pursuit, has begun to talk about trash as if it were really very serious art. College newspapers and the new press all across the country are full of a hilarious new form of scholasticism, with students using their education to cook up impressive reasons for enjoying very simple, traditional dishes. Here is a communication from Cambridge to a Boston paper:

> To the Editor:
>   *The Thomas Crown Affair* is fundamentally a film about faith between people. In many ways, it reminds me of a kind of updated old fable, or tale, about an ultimate test of faith. It is a film about a love affair (note the title), with a subplot of a bank robbery, rather than the reverse. The subtlety of the film is in the way the external plot is used as a matrix to develop serious motifs, much in the same way that the *Heat of the Night* functioned.
>   Although Thomas Crown is an attractive and fascinating character, Vicki is the protagonist. Crown is consistent, predictable: he courts personal danger to feel superior to the system of which he is a part, and to make his otherwise overly comfortable life more interesting. Vicki is caught between two opposing elements within her, which, for convenience, I would call masculine and feminine. In spite of her glamour, at the outset she is basically masculine, in a man's type of job, ruthless, after prestige and wealth. But Crown looses the female in her. His test is a test of her femininity. The masculine responds to the challenge. Therein lies the pathos of her final revelation. Her egocentrism had not yielded to his.
>   In this psychic context, the possibility of establishing faith is explored. The movement of the film is towards Vicki's final enigma. Her ambivalence is commensurate with the increasing danger to Crown. The suspense lies in how she will respond to her dilemma, rather than whether Crown will escape.
>   I find *The Thomas Crown Affair* to be a unique and haunting film, superb in its visual and technical design, and fascinating for the allegorical problem of human faith.

The Thomas Crown Affair is pretty good trash, but we shouldn't convert what we enjoy it for into false terms derived from our study of the other arts. That's being false to what we enjoy. If it was priggish for an older generation of reviewers to be ashamed of what they enjoyed and to feel they had to be contemptuous of popular entertainment, it's even more priggish for a new movie generation to be so proud of what they enjoy that they use their education to try to place

trash within the acceptable academic tradition. What the Cambridge
boy is doing is a more devious form of that elevating and falsifying of
people who talk about Loren as a great actress instead of as a
gorgeous, funny woman. Trash doesn't belong to the academic tradition, and that's part of the *fun* of trash — that you know (or *should*
know) that you don't have to take it seriously, that it was never meant
to be any more than frivolous and trifling and entertaining.

It's appalling to read solemn academic studies of Hitchcock or
von Sternberg by people who seem to have lost sight of the primary
reason for seeing films like *Notorious* or *Morocco* — which is that
they were not intended solemnly, that they were playful and inventive and faintly (often deliberately) absurd. And what's good in
them, what relates them to art, is that playfulness and absence of
solemnity. There is talk now about von Sternberg's technique — his
use of light and décor and detail — and he is, of course, a kitsch
master in these areas, a master of studied artfulness and pretty
excess. Unfortunately, some students take this technique as proof
that his films are works of art, once again, I think, falsifying what
they really respond to — the satisfying romantic glamour of his
very pretty trash. *Morocco* is great trash, and movies are so rarely
great art, that if we cannot appreciate great *trash*, we have very
little reason to be interested in them. The kitsch of an earlier era —
even the best kitsch — does not become art, though it may become
camp. Von Sternberg's movies became camp even while he was
still making them, because as the romantic feeling went out of his
trash — when he became so enamored of his own pretty effects that
he turned his human material into blank, affectless pieces of décor
— his absurd trashy style was all there was. We are now told in
respectable museum publications that in 1932 a movie like *Shanghai Express* 'was completely misunderstood as a mindless adventure'
when indeed it was completely *understood* as a mindless adventure.
And enjoyed as a mindless adventure. It's a peculiar form of movie
madness crossed with academicism, this lowbrowism masquerad-
ing as highbrowism, eating a candy bar and cleaning an 'allegorical
problem of human faith' out of your teeth. If we always wanted
works of complexity and depth we wouldn't be going to movies
about glamorous thieves and seductive women who sing in cheap
cafés, and if we loved *Shanghai Express* it wasn't for its mind but
for the glorious sinfulness of Dietrich informing Clive Brook that,
'It took more than one man to change my name to Shanghai Lily'

and for the villainous Oriental chieftain (Warner Oland!) delivering the classic howler, 'The white woman stays with me.'

If we don't deny the pleasures to be had from certain kinds of trash and accept *The Thomas Crown Affair* as a pretty fair example of entertaining trash, then we may ask if a piece of trash like this has any relationship to art. And I think it does. Steve McQueen gives probably his most glamorous, fashionable performance yet, but even enjoying him as much as I do, I wouldn't call his performance art. It's artful, though, which is exactly what is required in this kind of vehicle. If he had been luckier, if the script had provided what it so embarrassingly lacks, the kind of sophisticated dialogue — the sexy shoptalk — that such writers as Jules Furthman and William Faulkner provided for Bogart, and if the director Norman Jewison had Lubitsch's lightness of touch, McQueen might be acclaimed as a suave, 'polished' artist. Even in this flawed setting, there's a self-awareness in his performance that makes his elegance funny. And Haskell Wexler, the cinematographer, lets go with a whole bag of tricks, flooding the screen with his delight in beauty, shooting all over the place, and sending up the material. And Pablo Ferro's games with the split screen at the beginning are such conscious, clever games designed to draw us in to watch intently what is of no great interest. What gives this trash a lift, what makes it entertaining is clearly that some of those involved, knowing of course that they were working on a silly shallow script and a movie that wasn't about anything of consequence, used the chance to have a good time with it. If the director, Norman Jewison, could have built a movie instead of putting together a patchwork of sequences, *Crown* might have had a chance to be considered a movie in the class and genre of Lubitsch's *Trouble in Paradise*. It doesn't come near that because to transform this kind of kitsch, to make art of it, one needs that unifying grace, that formality and charm that a Lubitsch could sometimes provide. Still, even in this movie we get a few grace notes in McQueen's playfulness, and from Wexler and Ferro. Working on trash, feeling free to play, can loosen up the actors and craftsmen just as seeing trash can liberate the spectator. And as we don't get this playful quality of art much in movies except in trash, we might as well relax and enjoy it freely for what it is. I don't trust anyone who doesn't admit having at some time in his life enjoyed trashy American movies; I don't trust *any* of the tastes of people who were born with such good taste that they didn't need to find their way through trash.

There is a moment in *Children of Paradise* when the rich nobleman (Louis Salou) turns on his mistress, the pearly plebeian Garance (Arletty). He complains that in all their years together he has never had her love, and she replies, 'You've got to leave something for the poor.' We don't ask much from movies, just a little something that we can call our own. Who at some point hasn't set out dutifully for that fine foreign film and then ducked into the nearest piece of American trash? We're not only educated people of taste, we're also common people with common feelings. And our common feelings are not all *bad*. You hoped for some aliveness in that trash that you were pretty sure you wouldn't get from the respected 'art film.' You had long since discovered that you wouldn't get it from certain kinds of American movies, either. The industry now is taking a neo-Victorian tone, priding itself on its (few) 'good, clean' movies — which are always its worst movies because almost nothing can break through the smug surfaces, and even performers' talents become cute and cloying. The lowest action trash is preferable to wholesome family entertainment. When you clean them up, when you make movies respectable, you kill them. The wellspring of their *art*, their greatness, is in not being respectable.

VII

Does trash corrupt? A nutty Puritanism still flourishes in the arts, not just in the schoolteachers' approach of wanting art to be 'worthwhile,' but in the higher reaches of the academic life with those ideologues who denounce us for enjoying trash as if this enjoyment took us away from the really disturbing, angry new art of our time and somehow destroyed us. If we had to *justify* our trivial silly pleasures, we'd have a hard time. How could we possibly *justify* the fun of getting to know some people in movie after movie, like Joan Blondell, the brassy blonde with the heart of gold, or waiting for the virtuous, tiny, tiny-featured heroine to say her line so we could hear the riposte of her tough, wisecracking girlfriend (Iris Adrian was my favorite). Or, when the picture got too monotonous, there would be the song interlude, introduced 'atmospherically' when the cops and crooks were both in the same never-neverland nightclub and everything stopped while a girl sang. Sometimes it would be the most charming thing in the movie, like Dolores Del Rio singing 'You Make Me That Way' in *International Settlement*; sometimes it would drip with maudlin meaning, like 'Oh Give Me Time for Tenderness' in *Dark*

Victory with the dying Bette Davis singing along with the chanteuse. The pleasures of this kind of trash are not intellectually defensible. But why should pleasure need justification? Can one demonstrate that trash desensitizes us, that it prevents people from enjoying something better, that it limits our range of aesthetic response? Nobody I know of has provided such a demonstration. Do even Disney movies or Doris Day movies do us lasting harm? I've never known a person I thought had been harmed by them, though it does seem to me that they affect the tone of a culture, that perhaps — and I don't mean to be facetious — they may poison us collectively though they don't injure us individually. There are women who want to see a world in which everything is pretty and cheerful and in which romance triumphs (*Barefoot in the Park, Any Wednesday*); families who want movies to be an innocuous inspiration, a good example for the children (*The Sound of Music, The Singing Nun*); couples who want the kind of folksy blue humor (*A Guide for the Married Man*) that they still go to Broadway shows for. These people are the reason slick, stale, rotting pictures make money; they're the reason so few pictures are any good. And in that way, this terrible conformist culture does affect us all. It certainly cramps and limits opportunities for artists. But that isn't what generally gets attacked as trash, anyway. I've avoided using the term 'harmless trash' for movies like *The Thomas Crown Affair*, because that would put me on the side of the angels — against 'harmful trash,' and I don't honestly know what that is. It's common for the press to call cheaply made, violent action movies 'brutalizing' but that tells us less about any actual demonstrable effects than about the finicky tastes of the reviewers — who are often highly appreciative of violence in more expensive and 'artistic' settings such as *Petulia*. It's almost a class prejudice, this assumption that crudely made movies, movies without the look of art, are bad for people.

If there's a little art in good trash and sometimes even in poor trash, there may be more trash than is generally recognized in some of the most acclaimed 'art' movies. Such movies as *Petulia* and *2001* may be no more than trash in the latest, up-to-the-minute guises, using 'artistic techniques' to give trash the look of art. The serious art look may be the latest fashion in *expensive trash*. All that 'art' may be what prevents pictures like these from being *enjoyable* trash; they're not honestly crummy, they're very fancy and they take their crummy ideas seriously.

I have rarely seen a more disagreeable, a more dislikable (or a bloodier) movie than *Petulia* and I would guess that its commercial success represents a triumph of publicity — and not the simple kind of just taking ads. It's a very strange movie and people may, of course, like it for all sorts of reasons, but I think many may dislike it as I do and still feel they should be impressed by it; the educated and privileged may now be more susceptible to the mass media than the larger public — they're certainly easier to reach. The publicity about Richard Lester as an artist has been gaining extraordinary momentum ever since *A Hard Day's Night*. A critical success that is also a hit makes the director a genius; he's a magician who made money out of art. The media are in ravenous competition for ever bigger stories, for 'trend' pieces and editorial essays, because once the process starts it's considered news. If Lester is 'making the scene' a magazine that hasn't helped to build him up feels it's been scooped. *Petulia* is the come-dressed-as-the-sick-soul-of-America-party and in the opening sequence the guests arrive — rich victims of highway accidents in their casts and wheel chairs, like the spirit of '76 coming to opening night at the opera. It's science-horror fiction — a garish new world with charity balls at which you're invited to 'Shake for Highway Safety.'

Lester picked San Francisco for his attack on America just as in *How I Won the War* he picked World War II to attack war. That is, it looks like a real frontal attack on war itself if you attack the war that many people consider a just war. But then he concentrated not on the issues of that war but on the class hatreds of British officers and men — who were not engaged in defending London or bombing Germany but in building a cricket pitch in Africa. In *Petulia*, his hate letter to America, he relocates the novel, shifting the locale from Los Angeles to San Francisco, presumably, again, to face the big challenge by showing that even the best the country has to offer is rotten. But then he ducks the challenge he sets for himself by making San Francisco look like Los Angeles. And if he must put carnival barkers in Golden Gate Park and invent Sunday excursions for children to Alcatraz, if he must invent such caricatures of epicene expenditure and commercialism as bizarrely automated motels and dummy television sets, if he must provide his own ugliness and hysteria and lunacy and use filters to destroy the city's beautiful light, if, in short, he must falsify America in order to make it appear hateful, what is it he really hates? He's like a crooked cop framing a suspect with trumped-up evidence. We never find out *why*: he's too interested in making a flashy case to examine what he's doing. And reviewers seem unwilling to ask questions which might expose them to the charge that they're *still* looking for meaning instead of, in the new cant, just reacting to images — such questions as why does the movie keep juxtaposing shots of bloody surgery with shots of rock groups like the Grateful Dead or Big Brother and the Holding Company and shots of the war in Vietnam. What are these little montages supposed to do to us — make us feel that even the hero (a hardworking life-saving surgeon) is implicated in the war and that somehow contemporary popular music is also allied to destruction and death? (I thought only the moralists of the Soviet Union believed that.) The images of *Petulia* don't make valid connections, they're joined together for shock and excitement, and I don't believe in the brilliance of a method which equates hippies, war, surgery, wealth, Southern decadents, bullfights, etc. Lester's mix is almost as fraudulent as *Mondo Cane; Petulia* exploits any shocking material it can throw together to give false importance to a story about Holly Golightly and The Man in the Gray Flannel Suit. The jagged glittering mosaic style of *Petulia* is an armor protecting Lester from an artist's task; this kind of 'style' no longer fools people so much in writing but it knocks them silly in films.

Movie directors in trouble fall back on what they love to call 'personal style' — though how impersonal it often is can be illustrated by *Petulia* — which is not edited in the rhythmic, modulations-of-graphics style associated with Lester (and seen most distinctively in his best-edited, though not necessarily best film, *Help!*) but in the style of the movie surgeon, Anthony Gibbs, who acted as chopper on it, and who gave it the same kind of scissoring which he had used on *The Loneliness of the Long Distance Runner* and in his rescue operation on *Tom Jones*. This is, in much of *Petulia*, the most insanely obvious method of cutting film ever devised; keep the audience jumping with cuts, juxtapose startling images, anything for effectiveness, just make it *brilliant* — with the director taking, apparently, no responsibility for the *implied* connections. (The editing style is derived from Alain Resnais, and though it's a debatable style in his films, he uses it responsibly not just opportunistically.)

Richard Lester, the director of *Petulia*, is a shrill scold in Mod clothes. Consider a sequence like the one in which the beaten-to-a-gruesome-pulp heroine is taken out to an ambulance, to the accompaniment of hippies making stupid, unfeeling remarks. It is embarrassingly reminiscent of the older people's comments about the youthful sub-pre-hippies of *The Knack*. Lester has simply shifted villains. Is he saying that America is so rotten that even our hippies are malignant? I rather suspect he is, but why? Lester has taken a fashionably easy way to attack America, and because of the war in Vietnam some people are willing to accept the bloody montages that make them feel we're all guilty, we're rich, we're violent, we're spoiled, we can't relate to each other, etc. Probably the director who made three celebrations of youth and freedom (*A Hard Day's Night, The Knack* and *Help!*) is now desperate to expand his range and become a 'serious' director, and this is the new look in seriousness.

It's easy to make fun of the familiar ingredients of trash — the kook heroine who steals a tuba (that's not like the best of Carole Lombard but like the worst of Irene Dunne), the vaguely impotent, meaninglessly handsome rotter husband, Richard Chamberlain (back to the rich, spineless weaklings of David Manners), and Joseph Cotten as one more insanely vicious decadent Southerner spewing out villainous lines. (Even Victor Jory in *The Fugitive Kind* wasn't much meaner.) What's terrible is not so much this feeble conventional trash as the director's attempts to turn it all into scintillating art and burning comment; what is really awful is the trash of his ideas and artistic effects.

Is there any art in this obscenely self-important movie? Yes, but in a format like this the few good ideas don't really shine as they do in simpler trash; we have to go through so much unpleasantness and showing-off to get to them. Lester should trust himself more as a director and stop the cinemagician stuff because there's good, tense direction in a few sequences. He got a good performance from George C. Scott and a sequence of post-marital discord between Scott and Shirley Knight that, although overwrought, is not so glaringly over-wrought as the rest of the picture. It begins to suggest something interesting that the picture might have been about. (Shirley Knight should, however, stop fondling her hair like a miser with a golden hoard; it's time for her to get another prop.) And Julie Christie is extraordinary just to look at — lewd and anxious, expressive and empty, brilliantly faceted but with something central missing, almost as if there's no woman inside.

VIII

2001 is a movie that might have been made by the hero of *Blow-Up*, and it's fun to think about Kubrick really doing every dumb thing he wanted to do, building enormous science-fiction sets and equipment, never even bothering to figure out what he was going to do with them. Fellini, too, had gotten carried away with the Erector Set approach to movie-making, but his big science-fiction construction, exposed to view at the end of *8½*, was abandoned. Kubrick never really made his movie either but he doesn't seem to know it. Some people like the American International Pictures stuff because it's rather idiotic and maybe some people love *2001* just because Kubrick did all that stupid stuff, acted out a kind of super sci-fi nut's fantasy. In some ways it's the biggest amateur movie of them all, complete even to the amateur-movie obligatory scene — the director's little daughter (in curls) telling daddy what kind of present she wants.

There was a little pre-title sequence in *You Only Live Twice* with an astronaut out in space that was in a looser, more free style than *2001* — a daring little moment that I think was more fun than all of *2001*. It had an element of the unexpected, of the shock of finding death in space lyrical. Kubrick is carried away by the idea. The secondary title of *Dr Strangelove*, which we took to be satiric, *How I Learned to Stop Worrying and Love the Bomb*, was not, it now appears, altogether satiric for Kubrick. *2001* celebrates the invention of tools of death, as an evolutionary route to a higher order of *non-human* life. Kubrick literally learned to stop worrying and love the bomb; he's become his own butt — the Herman Kahn of extraterrestrial games theory. The ponderous blurry appeal of the picture may be that it takes its stoned audience out of this world to a consoling vision of a graceful world of space, controlled by superior godlike minds, where the hero is reborn as an angelic baby. It has the dreamy somewhere-over-the-rainbow appeal of a new vision of heaven. *2001* is a celebration of cop-out. It says man is just a tiny nothing on the stairway to paradise, something better is coming, and it's all out of your hands anyway. There's an intelligence out there in space controlling your destiny from ape to angel, so just follow the slab. Drop up.

It's a bad, bad sign when a movie director begins to think of himself as a myth-maker, and this limp myth of a grand plan that justifies slaughter and ends with resurrection has been around before. Kubrick's story line — accounting for evolution by an extraterrestrial intelligence — is probably the most gloriously redundant plot of all time. And although his intentions may have been different, *2001* celebrates the *end of man*; those beautiful mushroom clouds at the end of *Strangelove* were no accident. In *2001, A Space Odyssey*, death and

life are all the same: no point is made in the movie of Gary Lockwood's
death — the moment isn't even defined — and the hero doesn't
discover that the hibernating scientists have become corpses. That's
unimportant in a movie about the beauties of resurrection. Trip off to
join the cosmic intelligence and come back a better mind. And as the
trip in the movie is the usual psychedelic light show, the audience
doesn't even have to worry about getting to Jupiter. They can go to
heaven in Cinerama.

It isn't accidental that we don't care if the characters live or die; if
Kubrick has made his people so uninteresting, it is partly because
characters and individual fates just aren't big enough for certain kinds
of big movie directors. Big movie directors become generals in the
arts; and they want subjects to match their new importance. Kubrick
has announced that his next project is *Napoleon* — which, for a movie
director, is the equivalent of Joan of Arc for an actress. Lester's
'savage' comments about affluence and malaise, Kubrick's inspira-
tional banality about how we will become as gods through machinery,
are big-shot show-business deep thinking. This isn't a new show-
business phenomenon; it belongs to the genius tradition of the theatre.
Big entrepreneurs, producers, and directors who stage big spectacular
shows, even designers of large sets have traditionally begun to play
the role of visionaries and thinkers and men with answers. They get
too big for art. Is a work of art possible if pseudoscience and the
technology of movie-making become more important to the 'artist'
than man? This is central to the failure of *2001*. It's a monumentally
unimaginative movie: Kubrick, with his $750,000 centrifuge, and in
love with gigantic hardware and control panels, is the Belasco of
science fiction. The special effects — though straight from the drawing board — are good and big and awesomely, expensively detailed.
There's a little more that's good in the movie, when Kubrick doesn't
take himself too seriously — like the comic moment when the gliding
space vehicles begin their Johann Strauss waltz; that is to say, when
the director shows a bit of a sense of proportion about what he's doing,
and sees things momentarily as comic — when the movie doesn't take
itself with such idiot solemnity. The light-show trip is of no great
distinction; compared to the work of experimental filmmakers like
Jordan Belson, it's third-rate. If big film directors are to get credit for
doing badly what others have been doing brilliantly for years with no
money, just because they've put it on a big screen, then businessmen
are greater than poets and theft is art.

IX

Part of the fun of movies is in seeing 'what everybody's talking about,' and if people are flocking to a movie, or if the press can con us into thinking that they are, then ironically, there is a sense in which we want to see it, even if we suspect we won't enjoy it, because we want to know what's going on. Even if it's the worst inflated pompous trash that is the most talked about (and it usually is) and even if that talk is manufactured, we want to see the movies because so many people fall for whatever is talked about that they make the advertisers' lies true. Movies absorb material from the culture and the other arts so fast that some films that have been widely *sold* become culturally and sociologically important whether they are good movies or not. Movies like *Morgan!* or *Georgy Girl* or *The Graduate* — aesthetically trivial movies which, however, because of the ways some people react to them, enter into the national bloodstream — become cultural and psychological equivalents of watching a political convention, to observe what's going on. And though this has little to do with the art of movies, it has a great deal to do with the appeal of movies.

An analyst tells me that when his patients are not talking about their personal hangups and their immediate problems they talk about the situations and characters in movies like *The Graduate* or *Belle de Jour* and they talk about them with as much personal involvement as about their immediate problems. I have elsewhere suggested that this way of reacting to movies as psychodrama used to be considered a pre-literate way of reacting but that now those considered 'post-literate' are reacting like pre-literates. The high school and college students identifying with Georgy Girl or Dustin Hoffman's Benjamin are not that different from the stenographer who used to live and breathe with the Joan Crawford-working girl and worry about whether that rich boy would really make her happy — and considered her pictures 'great.' They don't see the movie as a movie but as part of the soap opera of their lives. The fan magazines used to encourage this kind of identification; now the *advanced* mass media encourage it, and those who want to sell to youth use the language of 'just let it flow over you.' The person who responds this way does not respond more freely but less freely and less fully than the person who is aware of what is well done and what badly done in a movie, who can accept some things in it and reject others, who uses all his senses in reacting, not just his emotional vulnerabilities.

Still, we care about what other people care about — sometimes because we want to know how far we've gotten from common responses — and if a movie is important to other people we're interested in it because of what it means to them, even if it doesn't mean much to us. The small triumph of *The Graduate* was to have domesticated alienation and the difficulty of communication, by making what Benjamin is alienated from a middle-class comic strip and making it absurdly evident that he has nothing to communicate — which is just what makes him an acceptable hero for the large movie audience. If he said anything or had any ideas, the audience would probably hate him. *The Graduate* isn't a *bad* movie, it's entertaining, though in a fairly slick way (the audience is just about programmed for laughs). What's surprising is that so many people take it so seriously. What's funny about the movie are the laughs on that dumb sincere boy who wants to talk about art in bed when the woman just wants to fornicate. But then the movie begins to pander to youthful narcissism, glorifying his innocence, and making the predatory (and now crazy) woman the villainess. Commercially this works: the inarticulate dull boy becomes a romantic hero for the audience to project into with all those squishy and now conventional feelings of look, his parents don't communicate with him; look, he wants truth not sham, and so on. But the movie betrays itself and its own expertise, sells out its comic moments that click along with the rhythm of a hit Broadway show, to make the oldest movie pitch of them all — asking the audience to identify with the simpleton who is the latest version of the misunderstood teen-ager and the pure-in-heart boy next door. It's almost painful to tell kids who have gone to see *The Graduate* eight times that once was enough for you because you've already seen it eighty times with Charles Ray and Robert Harron and Richard Barthelmess and Richard Cromwell and Charles Farrell. How could you convince them that a movie that sells innocence is a very commercial piece of work when they're so clearly in the market to buy innocence? When *The Graduate* shifts to the tender awakenings of love, it's just the latest version of *David and Lisa*. *The Graduate* only wants to succeed and that's fundamentally what's the matter with it. There is a pause for a laugh after the mention of 'Berkeley' that is an unmistakable sign of hunger for success; this kind of movie-making shifts values, shifts focus, shifts emphasis, shifts everything for a sure-fire response. Mike Nichols's 'gift' is that he lets the audience direct him; this is demagoguery in the arts.

Even the cross-generation fornication is standard for the genre. It goes back to Pauline Frederick in *Smouldering Fires*, and Clara Bow was at it with mama Alice Joyce's boyfriend in *Our Dancing Mothers*, and in the forties it was *Mildred Pierce*. Even the terms are not different: in these movies the seducing adults are customarily sophisticated, worldly, and corrupt, the kids basically innocent, though not so humorless and blank as Benjamin. In its basic attitudes *The Graduate* is corny American; it takes us back to before *The Game of Love* with Edwige Feuillère as the sympathetic older woman and *A Cold Wind in August* with the sympathetic Lola Albright performance.

What's interesting about the success of *The Graduate* is sociological: the revelation of how emotionally accessible modern youth is to the same old manipulation. The recurrence of certain themes in movies suggests that each generation wants romance restated in slightly new terms, and of course it's one of the pleasures of movies as a popular art that they can answer this need. And yet, and yet — one doesn't expect an *educated* generation to be so soft on itself, much softer than the factory workers of the past who didn't go back over and over to the same movies, mooning away in fixation on themselves and thinking this fixation meant movies had suddenly become an art, and *their* art.

X

When you're young the odds are very good that you'll find something to enjoy in almost any movie. But as you grow more experienced, the odds change. I saw a picture a few years ago that was the sixth version of material that wasn't much to start with. Unless you're feebleminded, the odds get worse and worse. We don't go on reading the same kind of manufactured novels — pulp Westerns or detective thrillers, say — all of our lives, and we don't want to go on and on looking at movies about cute heists by comically assorted gangs. The problem with a popular art form is that those who want something more are in a hopeless minority compared with the millions who are always seeing it for the first time, or for the reassurance and gratification of seeing the conventions fulfilled again. Probably a large part of the older audience gives up movies for this reason — simply that they've seen it before. And probably this is why so many of the best movie critics quit. They're wrong when they blame it on the movies going bad; it's the odds becoming so bad, and they can no longer bear the many tedious movies for the few good moments and the tiny shocks of recognition. Some become too tired, too frozen in fatigue, to respond to what *is* new. Others who *do* stay awake may become too demanding for the young who are seeing it all for the first hundred times. The critical task is necessarily comparative, and younger people do not truly know what is new. And despite all the chatter about the media and how smart the young are, they're incredibly naïve about mass culture — perhaps *more* naïve than earlier generations (though I don't know why). Maybe watching all that television hasn't done so much for them as they seem to think; and when I read a young intellectual's appreciation of *Rachel, Rachel* and come to 'the mother's passion for chocolate bars as a superb symbol for the second coming of childhood' I know the writer is still in his first childhood, and I wonder if he's going to come out of it.

One's moviegoing tastes and habits change — I still like in movies what I always liked but now, for example, I really want documentaries. After all the years of stale stupid acted-out stories, with less and less for me in them, I am desperate to know something, desperate for facts, for information, for faces of non-actors and for knowledge of how people live — for revelations, not for the little bits of show-business detail worked up for us by show-business minds who got them from the same movies we're tired ot.

But the big change is in our *habits*. If we make any kind of decent, useful life for ourselves we have less need to run from it to those diminishing pleasures of the movies. When we go to the movies we want something good, something sustained, we don't want to settle for just a bit of something, because we have other things to do. If life at home is more interesting, why go to the movies? And the theatres frequented by true moviegoers — those perennial displaced persons in each city, the loners and the losers — depress us. Listening to them — and they are often more audible than the sound track — as they cheer the cons and jeer the cops, we may still share their disaffection, but it's not enough to keep us interested in cops and robbers. A little nose-thumbing isn't enough. If we've grown up at the movies we know that good work is continuous not with the academic, respectable tradition but with the glimpses of something good in trash, yet we want the subversive gesture carried to the domain of discovery. Trash has given us an appetite for art.

Harper's Magazine, 1969

Raising Kane

Citizen Kane is perhaps the one American talking picture that seems as fresh now as the day it opened. It may seem even fresher. A great deal in the movie that was conventional and almost banal in 1941 is so far in the past as to have been forgotten and become new. The Pop characterizations look modern, and rather better than they did at the time. New audiences may enjoy Orson Welles's theatrical flamboyance even more than earlier generations did, because they're so unfamiliar with the traditions it came out of. When Welles was young — he was twenty-five when the film opened — he used to be accused of 'excessive showmanship,' but the same young audiences who now reject 'theatre' respond innocently and whole-heartedly to the most unabashed tricks of theatre — and of early radio plays — in *Citizen Kane*. At some campus showings, they react so gullibly that when Kane makes a demagogic speech about 'the under-privileged,' stray students will applaud enthusiastically, and a shout of 'Right on!' may be heard. Though the political ironies are not clear to young audiences, and though young audiences don't know much about the subject —William Randolph Hearst, the master jingo journalist, being to them a stock villain, like Joe McCarthy; that is, a villain without the contours of his particular villainy — they neverthe-less respond to the effrontery, the audacity, and the risks. Hearst's career and his power provided a dangerous subject that stimulated and energized all those connected with the picture — they felt they were *doing* something instead of just working on one more cooked-up story that didn't relate to anything that mattered. And to the particular kinds of people who shaped this enterprise the dangers involved made the subject irresistible.

Citizen Kane, the film that, as Truffaut said, is 'probably the one that has started the largest number of filmmakers on their careers,' was not an ordinary assignment. It is one of the few films ever made inside a major studio in the United States *in freedom* — not merely in freedom from interference but freedom from the routine methods of experienced directors. George J. Schaefer, who, with the help of Nelson Rockefeller, had become president of R.K.O. late in 1938, when it was struggling to avert bankruptcy, needed a miracle to save the company, and after the national uproar over Orson Welles's *The War of the Worlds* broadcast Rockefeller apparently thought that Welles — 'the wonder boy' — might come up with one, and urged Schaefer to get him. But Welles, who was committed to the theatre and wasn't especially enthusiastic about making movies, rejected the first offers; he held out until Schaefer offered him complete control over his productions. Then Welles brought out to Hollywood from New York his own production unit — the Mercury Theatre company, a group of actors and associates he could count on — and, because he was inexperienced in movies and was smart and had freedom, he was able to find in Hollywood people who had been waiting all their lives to try out new ideas. So a miracle did come about, though it was not the kind of miracle R.K.O. needed.

Kane does something so well, and with such spirit, that the fullness and completeness of it continue to satisfy us. The formal elements themselves produce elation; we are kept aware of how marvellously worked out the ideas are. It would be high-toned to call this method of keeping the audience aware 'Brechtian,' and it would be wrong. It comes out of a different tradition — the same commercial-comedy tradition that Walter Kerr analyzed so beautifully in his review of the 1969 Broadway revival of *The Front Page*, the 1928 play by Ben Hecht and Charles MacArthur, when he said, 'A play was held to be something of a machine in those days. . . It was a machine for surprising and delighting the audience, regularly, logically, insanely, but accountably. A play was like a watch that laughed.' The mechanics of movies are rarely as entertaining as they are in *Citizen Kane*, as cleverly designed to be the kind of fun that keeps one alert and conscious of the enjoyment of the artifices themselves.

Walter Kerr goes on to describe the second-act entrance prepared for Walter Burns, the scheming, ruthless managing editor of *The Front Page*:

He can't just come on and declare himself. . . He's got to walk into a tough situation in order to be brutally nonchalant, which is what we think is funny about him. The machinery has not only given him and the play the right punctuation, the change of pace that refreshes even as it moves on. It has also covered him, kept him from being obvious while exploiting the one most obvious thing about him. You might say that the machinery has covered itself, perfectly squared itself. We are delighted to have the man on, we are delighted to have him on at this time, we are aware that it is sleight-of-hand that has got him on, and we are as delighted by the sleight-of-hand as by the man.

Citizen Kane is made up of an astonishing number of such bits of technique, and of sequences built to make their points and get their laughs and hit climax just before a fast cut takes us to the next. It is practically a collection of blackout sketches, but blackout sketches arranged to comment on each other, and it was planned that way right in the shooting script.

It is difficult to explain what makes any great work great, and particularly difficult with movies, and maybe more so with *Citizen Kane* than with other great movies, because it isn't a work of special depth or a work of subtle beauty. It is a shallow work, a *shallow* masterpiece. Those who try to account for its stature as a film by claiming it to be profound are simply dodging the problem — or maybe they don't recognize that there is one. Like most of the films of the sound era that are called masterpieces, *Citizen Kane* has reached its audience gradually over the years rather than at the time of release. Yet, unlike the others, it is conceived and acted as entertainment in a popular style (unlike, say, *The Rules of the Game* or *Rashomon* or *Man of Aran*, which one does not think of in crowd-pleasing terms.) Apparently, the easiest thing for people to do when they recognize that something is a work of art is to trot out the proper schoolbook terms for works of art, and there are articles on *Citizen Kane* that call it a tragedy in fugal form and articles that explain that the hero of *Citizen Kane* is time — time being a proper sort of modern hero for an important picture. But to use the conventional schoolbook explanations for greatness, and pretend that it's profound, is to miss what makes it such an American triumph — that it manages to create something aesthetically exciting and durable out of the playfulness of American muckraking satire. *Kane* is closer to comedy than to tragedy, though so overwrought in style as to be almost a Gothic comedy. What might possibly be considered tragic in it has such a Daddy Warbucks quality that if it's tragic at all it's comic-strip tragic. The mystery in *Kane* is largely fake, and the Gothic-thriller atmosphere and the Rosebud gimmickry (though fun) are such obvious penny-dreadful popular theatrics that they're not so very different from the fake mysteries that Hearst's *American Weekly* used to whip up — the haunted castles and the curses fulfilled. *Citizen Kane* is a 'popular' masterpiece — not in terms of actual popularity but in terms of its conceptions and the way it gets its laughs and makes its points. Possibly it was too complexly told to be one of the greatest commercial successes, but we can't really tell whether it might have become even a modest success, because it didn't get a fair chance.

II

Orson Welles brought forth a miracle, but he couldn't get by with it. Though Hearst made some direct attempts to interfere with the film, it wasn't so much what he did that hurt the film commercially as what others feared he might do, to them and to the movie industry. They knew he was contemplating action, so they did the picture in for him; it was as if they decided whom the king might want killed, and, eager to oblige, performed the murder without waiting to be asked. Before *Kane* opened, George J. Schaefer was summoned to New York by Nicholas Schenck, the chairman of the board of Loew's International, the M-G-M affiliate that controlled the distribution of M-G-M pictures. Schaefer had staked just about everything on Welles, and the picture looked like a winner, but now Schenck made Schaefer a cash offer from Louis B. Mayer, the head of production at M-G-M of $842,000 if Schaefer would destroy the negative and all the prints. The picture had actually cost only $686,033; the offer handsomely included a fair amount for the post-production costs.

Mayer's motive may have been partly friendship and loyalty to Hearst, even though Hearst, who had formerly been associated with M-G-M, had, some years earlier, after a dispute with Irving Thalberg, taken his investment out of M-G-M and moved his star, Marion Davies, and his money to Warner Brothers. M-G-M had lost money on a string of costume clinkers starring Miss Davies (*Beverly of Graustark,* et al), and had even lost money on some of her good pictures, but Mayer had got free publicity for M-G-M releases out of the connection with Hearst, and had also got what might be called deep personal satisfaction. In 1929, when Herbert Hoover invited the Mayers to the White House — they were the first 'informal' guests after his inauguration — Hearst's *New York American* gave the visit a full column. Mayer enjoyed fraternizing with Hearst and his eminent guests; photographs show Mayer with Hearst and Lindbergh, Mayer with Hearst and Winston Churchill, Mayer at lunch with Bernard Shaw and Marion Davies — but they never, of course, show Mayer with both Hearst and Miss Davies. Candid cameramen sometimes caught the two together, but Hearst, presumably out of his respect for his wife, did not pose in groups that included Miss Davies. Despite the publicity showered on her in the Hearst papers, the forms were carefully observed. She quietly packed and left for her own house on the rare occasions when Mrs Hearst, who lived in the East, was expected to be in residence at San Simeon. Kane's infatuation for the singer Susan Alexander in the movie was thus a public flaunting of matters that Hearst was careful and considerate about. Because of this, Mayer's longtime friendship for Hearst was probably a lesser factor than the fear that the Hearst press would reveal some sordid stories about the movie moguls and join in one of those recurrent crusades against movie immorality, like the one that had destroyed Fatty Arbuckle's career. The movie industry was frightened of reprisals. (The movie industry is always frightened, and is always proudest of films that celebrate courage.) As one of the trade papers phrased it in those nervous weeks when no one knew whether the picture would be released, 'the industry could ill afford to be made the object of counterattack by the Hearst newspapers.'

There were rumors that Hearst was mounting a general campaign; his legal staff had seen the script, and Louella Parsons, the Hearst movie columnist, who had attended a screening of the film flanked by lawyers, was agitated and had swung into action. The whole industry, it was feared, would take the rap for R.K.O.'s indiscretion, and, according to the trade press at the time (and Schaefer confirms this report), Mayer was not putting up the $842,000 all by himself. It was a joint offer from the top movie magnates, who were combining for common protection. The offer was presented to Schaefer on the ground that it was in the best interests of everybody concerned — which was considered to be the entire, threatened industry — for *Citizen Kane* to be destroyed. Rather astonishingly, Schaefer refused. He didn't confer with his board of directors, because, he says, he had good reason to think they would tell him to accept. He refused even though R.K.O., having few theatres of its own, was dependent on the other companies and he had been warned that the big theatre circuits — controlled by the men who wanted the picture destroyed — would refuse to show it.

Schaefer knew the spot he was in. The premiere had been tentatively set for February 14th at the Radio City Music Hall — usually the showcase for big R.K.O. pictures, because R.K.O. was partly owned by the Rockefellers and the Chase National Bank, who owned the Music Hall. The manager of the theatre had been enthusiastic about the picture. Then, suddenly, the Music Hall turned it down. Schaefer phoned Nelson Rockefeller to find out why, and, he says, 'Rockefeller told me that Louella Parsons had warned him off it, that she had asked him, "How would you like to have the *American Weekly* magazine section run a double-page spread on John D. Rockefeller?" ' According to Schaefer, she had also called David Sarnoff, another large investor in R.K.O., and similarly threatened him. In mid-February, with a minor contract dispute serving as a pretext, the Hearst papers blasted R.K.O. and Schaefer in front-page stories; it was an unmistakable public warning. Schaefer was stranded; he had to scrounge for theatres, and, amid the general fear that Hearst might sue and would almost certainly remove advertising for any houses that showed *Citizen Kane*, he couldn't get bookings. The solution was for R.K.O. to take the risks of any lawsuits, but when the company leased an independent theatre in Los Angeles and refurbished the Palace (then a vaudeville house), which R.K.O. owned, for the New York opening, and did the same for a theatre R.K.O. owned in Chicago, Schaefer had trouble launching an advertising campaign. (Schenck, not surprisingly, owned a piece of the biggest movie-advertising agency.) Even after the early rave reviews and the initial enthusiasm, Schaefer couldn't get bookings except in the theatres that R.K.O. itself owned and in a few small art houses that were willing to take the risk. Eventually, in order to get the picture into theatres, Schaefer threatened to sue Warners', Fox, Paramount, and Loew's on a charge of conspiracy. (There was reason to believe the company heads had promised Hearst they wouldn't show it in their theatres.) Warners' (perhaps afraid of exposure and the troubles with their stockholders that might result from a lawsuit) gave in and booked the picture, and the others followed, halfheartedly — in some cases, theatres paid for the picture but didn't play it.

By then, just about everybody in the industry was scared, or mad, or tired of the whole thing, and though the feared general reprisals against the industry did not take place, R.K.O. was getting bruised. The Hearst papers banned publicity on R.K.O. pictures and dropped an announced serialization of the novel *Kitty Foyle* which had been timed for the release of the R.K.O. film version. Some R.K.O. films didn't get reviewed and others got bad publicity. It was all petty harassment, of a kind that could be blamed on the overzealous Miss Parsons and other Hearst employees, but it was obviously sanctioned by Hearst, and it was steady enough to keep the industry uneasy.

By the time *Citizen Kane* got into Warners' theatres, the picture had acquired such an odd reputation that people seemed to distrust it, and it didn't do very well. It was subsequently withdrawn from circulation, perhaps because of the vicissitudes of R.K.O., and until the late fifties, when it was reissued and began to play in the art houses and to attract a new audience, it was seen only in pirated versions in 16 mm. Even after Mayer had succeeded in destroying the picture commercially, he went on planning vengeance on Schaefer for refusing his offer. Stockholders in R.K.O. began to hear that the company wasn't prospering because Schaefer was anti-Semitic and was therefore having trouble getting proper distribution for R.K.O. pictures. Schaefer says that Mayer wanted to get control of R.K.O. and that the rumor was created to drive down the price of the stock — that Mayer hoped to scare out Floyd Odlum, a major stockholder, and buy his shares. Instead, Odlum, who had opposed Nelson Rockefeller's choice of Schaefer to run the company, bought enough of Sarnoff's stock to have a controlling interest, and by mid-1942 Schaefer was finished at R.K.O. Two weeks after he left, Welles's unit was evicted from its offices on the lot and given a few hours to move out, and the R.K.O. employees who had worked with Welles were punished with degrading assignments on B pictures. Mayer's friendship with Hearst was not ruffled. A few years later, when Mayer left his wife of forty years, he rented Marion Davies's Beverly Hills mansion. Eventually, he was one of Hearst's honorary pallbearers. *Citizen Kane* didn't actually lose money, but in Hollywood bookkeeping it wasn't a big enough moneymaker to balance the scandal.

III

Welles was recently quoted as saying, 'Theatre is a collective experience; cinema is the work of one single person.' This is an extraordinary remark from the man who brought his own Mercury Theatre players to Hollywood (fifteen of them appeared in *Citizen Kane*), and also the Mercury coproducer John Houseman, the Mercury composer Bernard Herrmann, and various assistants, such as Richard Wilson, William Alland, and Richard Barr. He not only brought his whole supportive

group — his family, he called them then — but found people in
Hollywood, such as the cinematographer Gregg Toland, to contribute
their knowledge and gifts to *Citizen Kane*. Orson Welles has done some
marvellous things in his later movies — some great things — and there
is more depth in the somewhat botched *The Magnificent Ambersons*, of
1942 (which also used many of the Mercury players), than in *Citizen
Kane*, but his principal career in the movies has been in adaptation, as it
was earlier on the stage. He has never again worked on a subject with the
immediacy and impact of *Kane*. His later films — even those he has so
painfully struggled to finance out of his earnings as an actor — haven't
been *conceived* in terms of daring modern subjects that excite us, as the
very idea of *Kane* excited us. This particular kind of journalist's sense
of what would be a scandal as well as a great subject, and the ability to
write it, belonged not to Welles but to his now almost forgotten associate
Herman J. Mankiewicz, who wrote the script, and who inadvertently
destroyed the picture's chances. There is a theme that is submerged in
much of *Citizen Kane* but that comes to the surface now and then, and
it's the linking life story of Hearst and of Mankiewicz and of Welles —
the story of how brilliantly gifted men who seem to have everything it
takes to do what they want to do are defeated. It's the story of how heroes
become comedians and con artists.

The Hearst papers ignored Welles — Hearst may have considered
this a fit punishment for an actor — though they attacked him
indirectly with sneak attacks on those associated with him, and
Hearst would frequently activate his secular arm, the American
Legion, against him. But the Hearst papers worked Mankiewicz over
in headlines: they persecuted him so long that he finally appealed to
the American Civil Liberties Union for help. There was some primitive justice in this. Hearst had never met Welles, and, besides,
Welles was a kid, a twenty-five-year-old prodigy (whose daughter
Marion Davies's nephew was bringing up) — hardly the sort of
person one held responsible. But Mankiewicz was a friend of both
Marion Davies and Hearst, and had been a frequent guest at her
beach house and at San Simeon. There, in the great baronial banquet
hall, Hearst liked to seat Mankiewicz on his left, so that Mankiewicz,
with all his worldliness and wit (the Central Park West Voltaire, Ben
Hecht had called him a few years earlier), could entertain the guest
of honor and Hearst wouldn't miss any of it. Mankiewicz betrayed
their hospitality, even though he liked them both. They must have
presented an irresistible target. And so Hearst, the yellow-press lord

who had trained Mankiewicz's generation of reporters to betray *anyone* for a story, became at last the victim of his own style of journalism.

IV

In the first Academy Award ceremony, for 1927–28, Warner Brothers, which had just produced *The Jazz Singer*, was honored for 'Marking an Epoch in Motion Picture History.' If the first decade of talkies — roughly, the thirties — has never been rivalled in wit and exuberance, this is very largely because there was already in Hollywood in the late silent period a nucleus of the best American writers, and they either lured their friends West or were joined by them. Unlike the novelists who were drawn to Hollywood later, most of the best Hollywood writers of the thirties had a shared background; they had been reporters and critics, and they knew each other from their early days on newspapers and magazines.

In his autobiography, Ben Hecht tells of being broke in New York — it was probably the winter of 1926 — and of getting a telegram from Herman Mankiewicz in Hollywood:

> WILL YOU ACCEPT THREE HUNDRED PER WEEK TO WORK FOR PARAMOUNT PICTURES? ALL EXPENSES PAID. THE THREE HUNDRED IS PEANUTS. MILLIONS ARE TO BE GRABBED OUT HERE AND YOUR ONLY COMPETITION IS IDIOTS. DON'T LET THIS GET AROUND.

A newspaper photograph shows Mankiewicz greeting Hecht, 'noted author, dramatist, and former newspaperman,' upon his arrival. After Hecht had begun work at Paramount, he discovered that the studio chief, B.P. Schulberg — who at that time considered writers a waste of money — had been persuaded to hire him by a gambler's ploy: Mankiewicz had offered to tear up his own two-year contract if Hecht failed to write a successful movie. Hecht, that phenomenal fast hack who was to become one of the most prolific of all motion-picture writers (and one of the most frivolously cynical about the results), worked for a week and turned out the script that became Josef von Sternberg's great hit *Underworld*. That script brought Hecht the first Academy Award for an original story, and a few years later he initiated the practice of using Oscars as doorstops. The studio heads knew what they had in Hecht as soon as they read the script, and they showed their gratitude. Hecht has recorded:

> I was given a ten-thousand-dollar check as a bonus for the

week's work, a check which my sponsor Mankiewicz snatched out of my hand as I was bowing my thanks.

'You'll have it back in a week,' Manky said. 'I just want it for a few days to get me out of a little hole.'

He gambled valiantly, tossing a coin in the air with Eddie Cantor and calling heads or tails for a thousand dollars. He lost constantly. He tried to get himself secretly insured behind his good wife Sara's back, planning to hock the policy and thus meet his obligation. This plan collapsed when the insurance-company doctor refused to accept him as a risk.

I finally solved the situation by taking Manky into the Front Office and informing the studio bosses of our joint dilemma. I asked that my talented friend be given a five-hundred-a-week raise. The studio could then deduct this raise from his salary. . .

I left . . . with another full bonus check in my hand; and Manky, with his new raise, became the highest paid writer for Paramount Pictures, Inc.

The bait that brought the writers in was money, but those writers who, like Mankiewicz, helped set the traps had their own reason: conviviality. Mankiewicz's small joke 'Don't let this get around' came from a man who lived for talk, a man who saw moviemaking as too crazy, too profitable, and too *easy* not to share with one's friends. By the early thirties, the writers who lived in Hollywood or commuted there included not only Mankiewicz and Hecht and Charles MacArthur but George S. Kaufman and Marc Connelly, and Nathanael West and his brother-in-law S.J. Perelman, and Preston Sturges, Dorothy Parker, Arthur Kober, Alice Duer Miller, John O'Hara, Donald Ogden Stewart, Samson Raphaelson (the *New York Times* reporter who wrote the play *The Jazz Singer*), Gene Fowler, and Nunnally Johnson, and such already famous playwrights as Philip Barry, S.N. Behrman, Maxwell Anderson, Robert E. Sherwood, and Sidney Howard. Scott Fitzgerald had already been there for his first stretch, in 1927, along with Edwin Justus Mayer, and by 1932 William Faulkner began coming and going, and from time to time Ring Lardner and Moss Hart would turn up. In earlier periods, American writers made a living on newspapers and magazines; in the forties and fifties, they weren't into the academies (or, once they got to college, never left). But in the late twenties and the thirties they went to Hollywood. And though, apparently, they one and all experienced it as prostitution of their talents — joyous prostitution in some cases — and though more than one fell in love with movies and thus suffered not only from personal frustration but from the corruption of the great, still new art, they nonetheless as a group were responsible for that sustained feat of careless magic we call 'thirties comedy.' *Citizen Kane* was, I think, its culmination.

V

Herman J. Mankiewicz, born in New York City in 1897, was the first son of a professor of education, who then took a teaching position in Wilkes-Barre, where his second son, Joseph L. Mankiewicz, was born in 1909, and where the boys and a sister grew up. Herman Mankiewicz graduated from Columbia in 1916, and after a period as managing editor of the *American Jewish Chronicle* he became a flying cadet with the United States Army in 1917 and, in 1918, a private first class with the Fifth Marines, 2nd Division, A.E.F. In 1919 and 1920, he was the director of the American Red Cross News Service in Paris, and after returning to this country to marry a great beauty, Miss Sara Aaronson, of Baltimore, he took his bride overseas with him while he worked as a foreign correspondent in Berlin from 1920 to 1922, doing political reporting for George Seldes on the *Chicago Tribune*. During that time, he also sent pieces on drama and books to the *New York Times* and *Women's Wear*. Hired in Berlin by Isadora Duncan, he became her publicity man for her return to America. At home again, he took a job as a reporter for the *New York World*. He was a gifted, prodigious writer, who contributed to *Vanity Fair*, the *Saturday Evening Post*, and many other magazines, and, while still in his twenties, collaborated with Heywood Broun, Dorothy Parker, Robert E. Sherwood, and others on a revue (*Round the Town*), and collaborated with George S. Kaufman on a play (*The Good Fellow*) and with Marc Connelly on another play (*The Wild Man of Borneo*). From 1923 to 1926, he was at the *Times*, backing up George S. Kaufman in the drama department; while he was there, he also became the first regular theatre critic for *The New Yorker*, writing weekly from June, 1925, until January, 1926, when Walter Wanger offered him a motion-picture contract and he left for Hollywood. The first picture he wrote was the Lon Chaney success *The Road to Mandalay*. In all, he worked on over seventy movies. He went on living and working in Los Angeles until his death, in 1953. He left three children: Don, born in Berlin in 1922, who is a novelist (*Trial*) and a writer for the movies (co-scenarist of *I Want to Live!*) and television ('Marcus Welby, M.D.'); Frank, born in New York in 1924, who became a lawyer, a journalist, a Peace Corps worker, and Robert Kennedy's press assistant, and is now a columnist and television commentator; and Johanna, born in Los Angeles in 1937, who is a journalist (on *Time*) and is married to Peter Davis, the writer-producer of 'The Selling of the Pentagon.'

Told this way, Herman Mankiewicz's career sounds exemplary, but these are just the bare bones of the truth. Even though it would be easy to document this official life of the apparently rising young man with photographs of Mankiewicz in his Berlin days dining with the Chancellor, Mankiewicz in his newspaperman days outside the *Chicago Tribune* with Jack Dempsey, and so on, it would be hard to explain his sudden, early aging and the thickening of his features and the transparently cynical look on his face in later photographs.

It was a lucky thing for Mankiewicz that he got the movie job when he did, because he would never have risen at the *Times*, and though he wrote regularly for *The New Yorker* (and remarked of those of the Algonquin group who didn't, 'The part-time help of wits is no better than the full-time help of half-wits'), *The New Yorker*, despite his pleas for cash, was paying him partly in stock, which wasn't worth much at the time. Mankiewicz drank heavily, and the drinking newspaperman was in the style of the *World* but not in the style of the *Times*. In October, 1925, he was almost fired. The drama critic then was Brooks Atkinson, and the drama editor was George S. Kaufman, with Mankiewicz second in line and Sam Zolotow third. Mankiewicz was sent to cover the performance of Gladys Wallis, who was the wife of the utilities magnate Samuel Insull, as Lady Teazle in *School for Scandal*. Mrs Insull, who had abandoned her theatrical career over a quarter of a century before, was, according to biographers, bored with being a nobody when her husband was such a big somebody. She was fifty-six when she resumed her career, as Lady Teazle, who is meant to be about eighteen. The play had opened in Chicago, where, perhaps astutely, she performed for charity (St Luke's Hospital), and the press had described her as brilliant. The night of the New York opening, Mankiewicz came back to the office drunk, started panning Mrs Insull's performance, and then fell asleep over his typewriter. As Zolotow recalls it, 'Kaufman began to read the review, and it was so venomous he was outraged. That was the only time I ever saw Kaufman lose his temper.' The review wasn't printed. The *Times* suffered the humiliation of running this item on October 23, 1925:

A NEW SCHOOL FOR SCANDAL

The *School for Scandal*, with Mrs Insull as Lady Teazle, was produced at the Little Theatre last night. It will be reviewed in tomorrow's *Times*.

Mankiewicz was in such bad shape that night that Kaufman told Zolotow to call Sara Mankiewicz and have her come get him and take him home. Mrs Mankiewicz recalls that he still had his head down on his typewriter when she arrived, with a friend, to remove him. She says he took it for granted that he was fired, but nevertheless went to work promptly the next day. Zolotow recalls, 'In the morning, Herman came down to the office and asked me to talk to Mr Birchall, the assistant managing editor, on his behalf. Herman had brought a peace offering of a bottle of Scotch and I took it to Birchall. He had a red beard, and he tugged at it and he stabbed the air a few times with his index finger and said, 'Herman is a bad boy, a bad boy.' But he took the bottle and Herman kept his job until he got the movie offer.'

The review — unsigned — that the *Times* printed on October 24, 1925, was a small masterpiece of tact:

> As Lady Teazle, Mrs Insull is as pretty as she is diminutive, with a clear smile and dainty gestures. There is a charming grace in her bearing that makes for excellent deportment. But this Lady Teazle seems much too innocent, too thoroughly the country lass that Joseph terms her, to lend credit to her part in the play.

Scattered through various books, and in the stories that are still told of him in Hollywood, are clues that begin to give one a picture of Herman Mankiewicz, a giant of a man who mongered his own talent, a man who got a head start in the race to 'sell out' to Hollywood. The pay was fantastic. After a month in the movie business, Mankiewicz — though his Broadway shows had not been hits, and though this was in 1926, when movies were still silent — signed a year's contract giving him $400 a week and a bonus of $5,000 for each story that was accepted, with an option for a second year at $500 a week and $7,500 per accepted story, the company guaranteeing to accept at least four stories per year. In other words, his base pay was $40,800 his first year and $56,000 his second; actually, he wrote so many stories that he made much more. By the end of 1927, he was head of Paramount's scenario department, and in January, 1928, there was a newspaper item reporting that he was in New York 'lining up a new set of newspaper feature writers and playwrights to bring to Hollywood,' and that 'most of the newer writers on Paramount's staff who contributed the most successful stories of the past year were selected by "Mank." ' One reason that Herman Mankiewicz is so little known today is, ironically, that he went to Hollywood so early, before he had gained a big enough reputation in the literary and theatrical worlds. Screenwriters don't make names for themselves; the most famous ones are the ones whose names were famous before they went to Hollywood, or who made names later in the theatre or from books, or who, like Preston Sturges, became directors.

Mankiewicz and other *New Yorker* writers in the twenties and the early thirties were very close to the world of theatre; many of them were writing plays, writing about theatre people, reviewing plays. It's not surprising that within a few years the magazine's most celebrated contributors were in Hollywood writing movies. Of the ten friends of the editor Harold Ross who were in the original prospectus as advisory editors, six became screenwriters. When Mankiewicz gave up the drama critic's spot, in 1926, he was replaced by Charles Brackett, and when Brackett headed West, Robert Benchley filled it while commuting, and then followed. Dorothy Parker, the book reviewer Constant Reader, went West, too. Nunnally Johnson, who was to work on over a hundred movies, was a close friend of Harold Ross's and had volunteered to do the movie reviewing in 1926 but had been told that that job was for 'old ladies and fairies.' Others in the group didn't agree: Benchley had written on movies for the old *Life* as early as 1920, and John O'Hara later took time out from screenwriting to become the movie critic for *Newsweek* — where he was to review *Citizen Kane*. The whole group were interested in the theatre and the movies, and they were fast, witty writers, used to regarding their work not as deathless prose but as stories written to order for the market, used also to the newspaperman's pretense of putting a light value on what they did — the 'Look, no hands' attitude. Thus, they were well prepared to become the scenarists and gag writers of the talkies.

VI

The comic muse of the most popular 'daring' late silents was a carefree, wisecracking flapper. Beginning in 1926, Herman Mankiewicz worked on an astounding number of films in that spirit. In 1927 and 1928, he did the titles (the printed dialogue and explanations) for at least twenty-five films that starred Clara Bow, Bebe Daniels, Nancy Carroll, Esther Ralston, George Bancroft, Thomas Meighan, Jack Holt, Richard Dix, Wallace Beery, and other public favorites. He worked on the titles for Jules Furthman's script of *Abie's Irish Rose*, collaborated with Anita

Loos on the wisecracks for *Gentlemen Prefer Blondes*, and did the immensely successful *The Barker* and *The Canary Murder Case*, with William Powell, Louise Brooks, James Hall, and Jean Arthur. By then, sound had come in, and in 1929 he did the script as well as the dialogue for *The Dummy*, with Ruth Chatterton and Fredric March (making his screen début), wrote William Wellman's *The Man I Love*, with Richard Arlen, Pat O'Brien, and Mary Brian, and worked for Josef von Sternberg and many other directors.

Other screenwriters made large contributions, too, but probably none larger than Mankiewicz's at the beginning of the sound era, and if he was at that time one of the highest-paid writers in the world, it was because he wrote the kind of movies that were disapproved of as 'fast' and immoral. His heroes weren't soft-eyed and bucolic; he brought good-humored toughness to the movies, and energy and astringency. And the public responded, because it was eager for modern American subjects. Even those of us who were children at the time loved the fast-moving modern-city stories. The commonplaceness — even tawdriness — of the imagery was such a relief from all that silent 'poetry.' The talkies were a great step down. It's hard to make clear to people who didn't live through the transition how sickly and unpleasant many of those 'artistic' silent pictures were — how you wanted to scrape off all that mist and sentiment.

Almost from the time the motion-picture camera was invented, there had been experiments with sound and attempts at synchronization, and the public was more than ready for talking pictures. Many of the late silents, if one looks at them now, seem to be trying to talk to us, crying out for sound. Despite the legend of paralysis of the medium when sound first came in, there was a burst of inventiveness. In musicals, directors like René Clair and, over here, Ernst Lubitsch and, to a lesser degree, Rouben Mamoulian didn't use sound just for lip synchronization; they played with sound as they had played with images, and they tried to use sound without losing the movement of silents or the daring of silent editing. Some of the early talkies were static and inept; newly imported stage directors literally staged the action, as if the space were stage space, and the technicians had to learn to handle the microphones. But movies didn't suddenly become stagebound because of the microphone. Many of the silents had always been stagebound, for the sufficient reason that they had been adapted from plays — from the war-horses of the repertory, because they had proved their popularity, and from the latest Broadway hits, because the whole country wanted to see them.

The silent adaptations were frequently deadly, not just because of construction based on the classical unities, with all those entrances and exits and that painful emptiness on the screen of plays worked out in terms of absolutely essential characters only, but because everything kept stopping for the explanatory titles and the dialogue titles.

Even in the movies adapted from novels or written directly for the screen, the action rarely went on for long; silents were choked with titles, which were perhaps, on the average, between ten and twenty times as frequent as the interruptions for TV commercials. The printed dialogue was often witty, and often it was essential to an understanding of the action, but it broke up the rhythm of performances and the visual flow, and the titles were generally held for the slowest readers, so that one lost the mood of the film while staring at the dialogue for the third scanning. (It seems to me, thinking back on it, that we were so eager for the movie to go on that we gulped the words down and then were always left with them for what, to our impatience, seemed an eternity, and that the better the movie, the more quickly we tried to absorb and leap past the printed words, and the more frustrating the delays became.) The plain fact that many silent movies were plays without the spoken dialogue, plays deprived of their very substance, was what made the theatre-going audience — and the Broadway crowd of writers — so contemptuous of them. Filmed plays without the actors' voices, and with the deadening delays for the heterogeneous audience to read the dialogue, were an abomination. Many of the journalists and playwrights and wits of the Algonquin Round Table had written perceptively about motion pictures (Alexander Woollcott, who managed to pan some of the greatest films, was an exception); they had, in general, been cynical only about the slop and the silent filmed plays. But though they had been active in the theatre, there had been no real place for them in movies; now, with the introduction of sound, they could bring to the screen the impudence that had given Broadway its flavor in the twenties — and bring it there before the satirical references were out of date. Sound made it possible for them to liberate movies into a new kind of contemporaneity.

VII

There is an elaborate body of theory that treats film as 'the nocturnal voyage into the unconscious,' as Luis Buñuel called it, and for a director such as Buñuel 'the cinema seems to have been invented to express the life of the subconscious.' Some of the greatest work of D.W. Griffith and other masters of the silent film has a magical, fairy-tale appeal, and certainly Surrealists like Buñuel, and other experimental and avant-garde filmmakers as well, have drawn upon this dreamlike vein of film. But these artists were the exceptions; much of the dreamy appeal to the 'subconscious' and to 'universal' or 'primitive' fantasies was an appeal to the most backward, not to say reactionary, elements of illiterate and semiliterate mass society. There was a steady load of calendar-art guck that patronized 'the deserving poor' and idealized 'purity' (i.e., virgin-ity) and 'morality' (i.e., virginity plus charity). And all that is only one kind of movie anyway. Most of the dream theory of film, which takes the audience for passive dreamers, doesn't apply to the way one responded to silent comedies — which, when they were good, kept the audience in a heightened state of consciousness. When we join in laughter, it's as if the lights were on in the theatre. And not just the Mack Sennett comedies and Keaton and Chaplin kept us fully awake but the spirited, bouncy comediennes, like Colleen Moore and Marion Davies, and the romantic comedy 'teams,' and the suave, 'polished' villains, like William Powell. My favorite movies as a child were the Bebe Daniels comedies — I suppose they were the movie equivalent of the series books one reads at that age. During 1927 and 1928, Paramount brought a new one out every few months; Bebe, the athletic madcap, would fence like Douglas Fairbanks, Sr, or she would parody Valentino by kidnapping and taming a man, or she might be a daredevil newsreel camerawoman or a cub reporter.

I did not know until I started to look into the writing of *Citizen Kane* that the man who wrote *Kane* had worked on some of those pictures, too — that Mankiewicz had, in fact, written (alone or with others) about forty of the films I remember best from the twenties and thirties (as well as many I didn't see or don't remember). Mankiewicz didn't work on *every* kind of picture, though. He didn't do Westerns, and once, when a studio attempted to punish him for his customary misbehavior by assigning him to a Rin Tin Tin picture, he turned in a script that began with the craven Rin Tin Tin frightened by a mouse and reached its climax with a house on fire and the dog taking a baby *into* the flames. I had known about Mankiewicz's contribution to *Kane* and a few other films, but I hadn't realized how extensive his career was. I had known that he was the producer of *Million Dollar Legs* (with W.C. Fields and Jack Oakie and Lyda Roberti) and *Laughter* (with Fredric March and Nancy Carroll), but I hadn't known, for example, that he had produced two of the Marx Brothers films that I've always especially liked, the first two made in Hollywood and written directly for the screen — *Monkey Business* and *Horse Feathers* — and part of *Duck Soup* as well. A few years ago, some college students asked me what films I would like to see again just for my own pleasure, and without a second's thought I replied *Duck Soup* and *Million Dollar Legs*, though at that time I had no idea there was any connection between them. Yet surely there is a comic spirit that links them — even the settings, Freedonia and Klopstokia, with Groucho as Prime Minister of one and Fields as President of the other — and now that I have looked into Herman Mankiewicz's career it's apparent that he was a key linking figure in just the kind of movies my friends and I loved best.

When the period of the great silent comedians, with their international audience, was over, a new style of American comedy developed. One couldn't really call a colloquial, skeptical comedy a 'masterpiece,' as one could sometimes call a silent comedy a masterpiece, especially if the talkie looked quite banal and was so topical it felt transient. But I think that many of us enjoyed these comedies more, even though we may not have felt very secure about the aesthetic grounds for our enjoyment. The talking comedies weren't as aesthetically pure as the silents, yet they felt liberating in a way that even great silents didn't. The elements to which we could respond were multiplied; now there were vocal nuances, new kinds of timing, and wonderful new tricks, like the infectious way Claudette Colbert used to break up while listening to someone. It's easy to see why Europeans, who couldn't follow the slang and the jokes and didn't understand the whole satirical frame of reference, should prefer our action films and Westerns. But it's a bad joke on our good jokes that film enthusiasts here often take their cues on the American movie past from Europe, and so they ignore the tradition of comic irreverence and become connoisseurs of the 'visuals' and 'mises en scène' of action pictures, which are usually too silly even to be called reactionary. They're sub-reactionary — the antique melodramas of silent days with noise added — a mass art better suited, one might think, to Fascism, or even feudalism, than to democracy.

There is another reason the American talking comedies, despite their popularity, are so seldom valued highly by film aestheticians. The dream-art kind of film, which lends itself to beautiful visual imagery, is generally the creation of the 'artist' director, while the astringent film is more often directed by a competent, unpretentious craftsman who can be made to look very good by a good script and can be turned into a bum by a bad script. And this competent craftsman may be too worldly and too practical to do the 'imaginative' bits that sometimes helped to make the reputations of 'artist' directors. Ben Hecht said he shuddered at the touches von Sternberg introduced into *Underworld*: 'My head villain, Bull Weed, after robbing a bank, emerged with a suitcase full of money and paused in the crowded street to notice a blind beggar and give him a coin — before making his getaway.' That's exactly the sort of thing that quantities of people react to emotionally as 'deep' and as 'art,' and that many film enthusiasts treasure — the inflated sentimental with a mystical drip. The thirties, though they had their own load of sentimentality, were the hardest-headed period of American movies, and their plainness of style, with its absence of false 'cultural' overtones, has never got its due aesthetically. Film students — and their teachers — often become interested in movies just because they are the kind of people who are emotionally affected by the blind-beggar bits, and they are indifferent by temperament to the emancipation of American movies in the thirties and the role that writers played in it.

I once jotted down the names of some movies that I didn't associate with any celebrated director but that had nevertheless stayed in my memory over the years, because something in them had especially delighted me — such rather obscure movies as *The Moon's Our Home* (Margaret Sullavan and Henry Fonda) and *He Married His Wife* (Nancy Kelly, Joel McCrea, and Mary Boland). When I looked them up, I discovered that Dorothy Parker's name was in the credits of *The Moon's Our Home* and John O'Hara's in the credits of *He Married His Wife*. Other writers worked on those films, too, and perhaps they were the ones who were responsible for what I responded to, but the recurrence of the names of that group of writers, not just on rather obscure remembered films but on almost *all* the films that are generally cited as proof of the vision and style of the most highly acclaimed directors of that period, suggests that the writers — and a particular group of them, at that — may for a brief period, a little more than a decade, have given American talkies their character.

VIII

There is always a time lag in the way movies take over (and broaden and emasculate) material from the other arts — whether it is last season's stage success or the novels of the preceding decade or a style or an idea that has run its course in its original medium. (This does not apply to a man like Jean-Luc Godard, who is not a mass-medium movie director.) In most productions of the big studios, the time lag is enormous. In the thirties, after the great age of musical comedy and burlesque, Hollywood, except for Paramount, was just discovering huge operettas. After the Broadway days of Clifton Webb, Fred Astaire, the Marx Brothers, Fanny Brice, W.C. Fields, and all the rest, M-G-M gave us Nelson Eddy and Jeanette MacDonald, and Universal gave us Deanna Durbin. This is the history of movies. J.D. Salinger has finally come to the screen through his imitators, and Philip Roth's fifties romance arrived at the end of the sixties. It may be that for new ideas to be successful in movies, the way must be prepared by success in other media, and the audience must have grown tired of what it's been getting and be ready for something new. There are always a few people in Hollywood who are considered mad dreamers for trying to do in movies things that have already been done in the other arts. But once one of them breaks through and has a hit, he's called a genius and everybody starts copying him.

The new spirit of the talkies was the twenties moved West in the thirties. George S. Kaufman was writing the Marx Brothers stage shows when he and Mankiewicz worked together at the *Times*; a little later, Kaufman directed the first Broadway production of *The Front Page*. Kaufman's collaborators on Broadway plays in the twenties and the early thirties included Marc Connelly, Edna Ferber, Ring Lardner, Morrie Ryskind, and Moss Hart as well as Mankiewicz — the nucleus of the Algonquin-to-Hollywood group. Nunnally Johnson says that the two most brilliant men he has ever known were George S. Kaufman and Herman Mankiewicz, and that, on the whole, Mankiewicz was the more brilliant of the two. I think that what Mankiewicz did in movies was an offshoot of the gag comedy that Kaufman had initiated on Broadway; Mankiewicz spearheaded the movement of that whole Broadway style of wisecracking, fast-talking, cynical-sentimental entertainment onto the national scene. Kaufman's kind of impersonal, visionless comedy, with its single goal of getting the audience to laugh, led to the degeneration of the Broadway theatre, to its play doctors and gimmickry and scattershot jokes at defenseless targets, and so it would be easy to look down on the movie style that came out of it. But I don't think the results were the same when this type of comedy was transplanted to movies; the only bad long-range consequences were to the writers themselves.

Kaufman fathered a movement that is so unmistakably the bastard child of the arts as to seem fatherless; the gag comedy was perfectly suited to the commercial mass art of the movies, so that it appears to be an almost inevitable development. It suited the low common denominator of the movies even better than it suited the needs of the relatively selective theatre audience, and the basic irresponsibility of this kind of theatre combined with the screenwriters' lack of control over their own writing to produce what one might call the brothel period of American letters. It was a gold rush, and Mankiewicz and his friends had exactly the skills to turn a trick. The journalists' style of working fast and easy and working to order and not caring too much how it was butchered was the best kind of apprenticeship for a Hollywood hack, and they had loved to gather, to joke and play games, to lead the histrionic forms of the glamorous literary life. Now they were gathered in cribs on each studio lot, working in teams side by side, meeting for lunch at the commissary and for dinner at Chasen's, which their old friend and editor Harold Ross had helped finance, and all over town for drinks. They adapted each other's out-of-date plays and novels, and rewrote each other's scripts. Even in their youth in New York, most of them had indulged in what for them proved a vice: they were 'collaborators' — dependent on the fun and companionship of joint authorship, which usually means a shared shallowness. Now they collaborated all over the place and backward in time; they collaborated promiscuously, and within a few years were rewriting the remakes of their own or somebody else's rewrites. Mankiewicz adapted Kaufman and Ferber's *The Royal Family* and *Dinner at Eight*, turned Alice Duer Miller's *Come Out of the Kitchen* into *Honey*, and adapted George Kelly's *The Show-Off* and James Thurber's *My Life and Hard Times* and works by Laurence Stallings and other old friends while Ben Hecht or Preston Sturges or Arthur Kober was working over something of his. They escaped the cold, and they didn't suffer from the Depression. They were a colony — expatriates without leaving the country — and their individual contributions to the scripts that emerged after the various rewrites were almost impossible to assess, because their attitudes were so similar; they made the same kind of jokes, because they had been making them to each other for so long. In Hollywood, they sat around building on to each other's gags, covering up implausibilities and dull spots, throwing new wisecracks on top of jokes they had laughed at in New York. Screenwriting was an extension of what they used to do for fun, and now they got paid for it. They had liked to talk more than to write, and this weakness became their way of life. As far as the official literary culture was concerned, they dropped from sight. To quote a classic bit of dialogue from Budd Schulberg's *The Disenchanted*:

> 'Bane had two hits running on Broadway at the same time. Even Nathan liked 'em. Popular 'n satirical. Like Barry, only better. The critics kept waiting for him to write that great American play.'
> 'What happened to him?'
> 'Hollywood.'

Hollywood destroyed them, but they did wonders for the movies. In New York, they may have valued their own urbanity too highly; faced with the target Hollywood presented, they became cruder and tougher, less tidy, less stylistically elegant, and more iconoclastic, and in the eyes of Hollywood they were slaphappy cynics, they were 'crazies.' They were too talented and too sophisticated to put a high value on what they did, too amused at the spectacle of what they were doing and what they were part of to be respected the way a writer of 'integrity,' like Lillian Hellman, was later to be respected — or, still later, Arthur Miller. Though their style was often flippant and their attitude toward form casual to the point of contempt, they brought movies the subversive gift of sanity. They changed movies by raking the old moralistic muck with derision. Those sickly Graustarkian romances with beautiful, pure high-born girls and pathetic lame girls and dashing princes in love with commoners, and all the Dumas and Sabatini and Blasco-Ibáñez, now had to compete with the freedom and wildness of American comedy. Once American films had their voice and the Algonquin group was turned loose on the scripts, the revolting worship of European aristocracy faded so fast that movie stars even stopped bringing home Georgian princes. In the silents, the heroes were often simpletons. In the talkies, the heroes were to be the men who weren't fooled, who were smart and learned their way around. The new heroes of the screen were created in the image of their authors: they were fast-talking newspaper reporters.

That Walter Burns whose entrance in *The Front Page* Kerr described was based on Walter Howey, who was the city editor of the *Chicago Tribune*, at $8,000 a year, until Hearst lured him away by an offer of $35,000 a year. Howey is generally considered the 'greatest' of all Hearst editors — by those who mean one thing by it, and by

those who mean the other. He edited Hearst's *New York Mirror* at a
time when it *claimed* to be ten percent news and ninety percent
entertainment. The epitome of Hearstian journalism, and a favorite of
Hearst's until the end, he was one of the executors of Hearst's will. At
one time or another, just about all the Hollywood writers had worked
for Walter Howey and/or spent their drinking hours with friends who
did. He was the legend: the classic model of the amoral, irresponsible,
irrepressible newsman who cares about nothing but scoops and circulation. He had lost an eye (supposedly in actual fighting of circulation
wars), and Ben Hecht is quoted as saying you could tell which was the
glass eye because it was the warmer one. Hecht used him again in
Nothing Sacred, as Fredric March's editor — 'a cross between a Ferris
wheel and a werewolf' — and he turns up under other names in other
plays and movies. In a sense, all those newspaper plays and movies
were already about Hearst's kind of corrupt, manic journalism.

The toughest-minded, the most satirical of the thirties pictures
often featured newspaper settings, or, at least, reporters — especially
the 'screwball' comedies, which had some resemblances to later
'black' comedy and current 'freaky' comedy but had a very different
spirit. A newspaper picture meant a contemporary picture in an
American setting, usually a melodrama with crime and political
corruption and suspense and comedy and romance. In 1931, a title like
Five Star Final or *Scandal Sheet* signalled the public that the movie
would be a tough modern talkie, not a tearjerker with sound. Just to
touch a few bases, there was *The Front Page* itself, in 1931, with Pat
O'Brien as the reporter and Adolphe Menjou as Walter Burns; Lee
Tracy as the gossip columnist in *Blessed Event* and as the press agent
in *Bombshell*; Clark Gable as the reporter in *It Happened One Night*;
Paul Muni giving advice to the lovelorn in *Hi, Nellie*; Spencer Tracy
as the editor in *Libeled Lady*; Stuart Erwin as the correspondent in
Viva Villa!; Jean Harlow stealing the affections of a newspaperman
from girl reporter Loretta Young in *Platinum Blonde*; Jean Arthur as
the girl reporter in *Mr Deeds Goes to Town*; a dozen pictures, at least,
with George Bancroft as a Walter Howey-style bullying editor; all
those half-forgotten pictures with reporter 'teams' — Fredric March
and Virginia Bruce, or Joel McCrea and Jean Arthur, or Loretta
Young and Tyrone Power (*Love Is News*); Cary Grant as the editor and
Joan Bennett as the reporter in *Wedding Present*; and then Cary Grant
as Walter Burns in *His Girl Friday*, with Rosalind Russell as the
reporter; and then Cary Grant and James Stewart (who had been a

foreign correspondent in *Next Time We Love*) both involved with a
newsmagazine in *The Philadelphia Story*, in 1940. Which takes us
right up to *Citizen Kane*, the biggest newspaper picture of them all —
the picture that ends with the introduction of the cast and a reprise of
the line 'I think it would be fun to run a newspaper.'

IX

After years of swapping stories about Howey and the other were-
wolves and the crooked, dirty press, Mankiewicz found himself on
story-swapping terms with the power behind it all, Hearst himself.
When he had been in Hollywood only a short time, he met Marion
Davies and Hearst through his friendship with Charles Lederer, a
writer, then in his early twenties, whom Ben Hecht had met and
greatly admired in New York when Lederer was still in his teens.
Lederer, a child prodigy, who had entered college at thirteen, got to
know Mankiewicz, the MacArthurs, Moss Hart, Benchley, and their
friends at about the same time or shortly after he met Hecht, and was
immediately accepted into a group considerably older than he was.
Lederer was Marion Davies's nephew — the son of her sister Reine,
who had been in operetta and musical comedy. In Hollywood,
Charles Lederer's life seems to have revolved around his aunt, whom
he adored. (Many others adored her also, though *Citizen Kane* was to
give the world a different — and false — impression.) She was
childless, and Lederer was very close to her; he spent a great deal of
his time at her various dwelling places, and took his friends to meet
both her and Hearst. The world of letters being small and surprising,
Charles Lederer was among those who worked on the adaptation of
The Front Page to the screen in 1931 and again when it was remade
as *His Girl Friday* in 1940, and, the world being even smaller than
that, Lederer married Orson Welles's ex-wife, Virginia Nicholson
Welles, in 1940, at San Simeon. (She married two prodigies in
succession; the marriage to Welles had lasted five years and produced a daughter.)

Hearst was so fond of Lederer that on the evening of the nuptials he
broke his rule of one cocktail to guests before dinner and no hard
liquor thereafter. A guest who gulped the cocktail down was sometimes able to swindle another, but this is the only occasion that I can
find recorded on which Hearst dropped the rule — a rule that Marion
Davies customarily eased by slipping drinks to desperate guests
before Hearst joined them but that nevertheless made it possible for

Hearst to receive, and see at their best, some of the most talented alcoholics this country has ever produced. Not all writers are attracted to the rich and powerful, but it's a defining characteristic of journalists to be drawn to those who live at the center of power. Even compulsive drinkers like Mankiewicz and Dorothy Parker were so fascinated by the great ménage of Hearst and his consort — and the guest lists of the world-famous — that they managed to stay relatively sober for the evenings at Marion Davies's beach house (Colleen Moore described it as 'the largest house on the beach — and I mean the beach from San Diego to the Canadian border') and the weekends at San Simeon.

If *Kane* has the same love-hate as *The Front Page*, the same joyous infatuation with the antics of the unprincipled press, it's because Mankiewicz, like Hecht and MacArthur, revelled in the complexities of corruption. And Hearst's life was a *spectacle*. For short periods, this was intoxication enough. A man like Hearst seems to embody more history than other people do; in his company a writer may feel that he has been living in the past and on the outskirts and now he's living in the dangerous present, right where the decisions are really made.

Hearst represented a new type of power. He got his first newspaper in 1887, when he was twenty-four, by asking his father for it, and, in the next three decades, when, for the first time, great masses of people became literate, he added more and more papers, until, with his empire of thirty newspapers and fifteen magazines, he was the most powerful journalist and publisher in the world. He had brought the first comic strips to America in 1892, and his battling with Pulitzer a few years later over a cartoon character named the Yellow Kid revived the term 'yellow journalism.' Because there was no tradition of responsibility in this new kind of popular journalism, which was almost a branch of show business, Hearst knew no restraints; perhaps fortunately, he was unguided. Ultimately, he was as purposeless about his power as the craziest of the Roman emperors. His looting of the treasures of the world for his castle at San Simeon symbolized his imperial status. Being at his table was being at court, and the activities of the notables who were invited there were slavishly chronicled in the Hearst papers.

The new social eminence of the Mankiewiczes, who sometimes visited San Simeon for as long as ten days at a time, can be charted from Louella Parsons's columns. By the end of 1928, Louella was announcing Mankiewicz's writing assignments with a big bold headline at the top of the column, and was printing such items as:

One of the few scenario writers in Hollywood who didn't have to unlearn much that he had learned is Herman Mankiewicz. Herman came to Paramount directly from the stage, and naturally he knows the technique just as well as if he hadn't written movies in the interval.

It was worth another item in the same column that Herman Mankiewicz had been observed 'taking his son down Hollywood Boulevard to see the lighted Christmas trees.' In 1931, the Mankiewiczes were so prominent that they were among those who gave Marion Davies a homecoming party at the Hotel Ambassador; the other hosts were Mr and Mrs Irving Thalberg, Mr and Mrs King Vidor, Mr and Mrs Samuel Goldwyn, John Gilbert, Lewis Milestone, Hedda Hopper, and so on. Hedda Hopper, who worked as a movie columnist for a rival newspaper chain but was a close friend of Marion Davies (to whom, it is said, she owed her job), was also an enthusiastic reporter of Mankiewicz's activities during the years when he and his ravishing Sara were part of the Hearst–Davies social set.

When writers begin to see the powerful men operating in terms of available alternatives, while they have been judging them in terms of ideals, they often develop 'personal' admiration for the great bastards whom they have always condemned and still condemn. Hearst was to Mankiewicz, I suspect, what Welles was to be to him a little later — a dangerous new toy. And he needed new toys constantly to keep off the booze. Mankiewicz could control himself at San Simeon in the late twenties and the very early thirties, as, in those days, he could control himself when he was in charge of a movie. Producing the Marx Brothers comedies kept him busy and entertained for a while. With the title of 'supervisor' (a term for the actual working producer, as distinguished from the studio executive whose name might appear above or below the name of the movie), he worked on their pictures from the inception of the ideas through the months of writing and then the shooting. But he got bored easily, and when he started cutting up in the middle of preparing *Duck Soup*, in 1933, he was taken off the picture. When the Marx Brothers left Paramount and went to M-G-M, he joined them again, in the preparation of *A Night at the Opera*, in 1935, and the same thing happened; he was replaced as supervisor by his old boss George S. Kaufman.

His credits began to taper off after 1933, and in 1936 Mankiewicz didn't get a single credit. That year, he published an article called 'On

Approaching Forty,' a brief satirical account of what had happened to him as a writer. It began:

> Right before me, as I write, is a folder in which my wife keeps the blotters from Mr Eschner, the insurance man, Don's first report card, the letter from the income tax people about the gambling loss at Tia Juana, the press photograph of me greeting Helen Kane (on behalf of the studio) at the Pasadena Station and my literary output. There are four separate pieces of this output and they are all excellent. I hope some friend will gather them into a little book after my death. There is plenty of ninety point Marathon in the world, and wide margins can't be hard to find.

He includes those tiny pieces in their entirety, and after one of them — the first three sentences of a short story — he comments:

> I moved to Hollywood soon after I had made this notation and was kept so busy with one thing and another — getting the pool filled, playing the Cadillac and Buick salesmen against each other, only to compromise on a Cadillac and a Buick, after all, and locating the finance company's downtown office — that the first thing I knew, a story, a good deal like the one I had in mind, appeared in the *Saturday Evening Post*, and in *Collier's*, too.

This is the end of his article:

> The fourth note looks rather naked now, all by itself on one desk. It says, simply:
> 'Write piece for *New Yorker* on reaching thirty-fifth birthday. No central idea. Just flit from paragraph to paragraph.'
> People who complain that my work is slipshod would be a little surprised to find that I just am *not* always satisfied with the first thing I put down. I'm changing that thirty-fifth to fortieth right now.

'On Approaching Forty' didn't come out in *The New Yorker*; it appeared in the *Hollywood Reporter*.

Ambivalence was the most common 'literary' emotion of the screenwriters of the thirties, as alienation was to become the most common 'literary' emotion of the screenwriters of the sixties. The thirties writers were ambivalently nostalgic about their youth as reporters, jouralists, critics, or playwrights, and they glorified the hard-drinking, cynical newspaperman. They were ambivalent about Hollywood, which they savaged and satirized whenever possible. Hollywood paid them so much more money than they had ever earned before, and the movies reached so many more people than they had ever reached before, that they were contemptuous of those who hadn't made it on their scale at the same time that they hated themselves for selling out. They had gone to Hollywood as a paid vacation from their playwriting or journalism, and screenwriting became their only writing. The vacation became an extended drunken party, and while they were there in the debris of the long morning after, American letters passed them by. They were never to catch up; nor were American movies ever again to have in their midst a whole school of the richest talents of a generation.

We in the audience didn't have to wake up *afterward* to how good those films of the thirties were; in common with millions of people, I enjoyed them while they were coming out. They were immensely popular. But I did take them for granted. There was such a steady flow of bright comedy that it appeared to be a Hollywood staple, and it didn't occur to me that those films wouldn't go on being made. It didn't occur to me that it required a special gathering of people in a special atmosphere to produce that flow, and that when those people stopped enjoying themselves those pictures couldn't be made. And I guess it didn't occur to older, more experienced people, either, because for decades everybody went on asking why Hollywood wasn't turning out those good, entertaining comedies anymore.

By the end of the thirties, the jokes had soured. The comedies of the forties were heavy and pushy, straining for humor, and the comic impulse was misplaced or lost; they came out of a different atmosphere, a different *feeling*. The comic spirit of the thirties had been happily self-critical about America, the happiness born of the knowledge that in no other country were movies so free to be self-critical. It was the comedy of a country that didn't yet hate itself. Though it wasn't until the sixties that the self-hatred became overt in American life and American movies, it started to show, I think, in the phony, excessive, duplicit use of patriotism by the rich, guilty liberals of Hollywood in the war years.

X

In the forties, a socially conscious film historian said to me, 'You know, Paramount never made a good movie,' and I brought up the names of some Paramount movies — *Easy Living* and *Trouble in Paradise* and lovely trifles like *Midnight* — and, of course, I couldn't make my point, because those movies weren't what was thought of in the forties as a good movie. I knew I wouldn't get anywhere at all if I tried to cite *Million Dollar Legs* or *Mississippi*, or pictures with the Marx Brothers or Mae West; I would be told they weren't even movies. Though Paramount made some elegant comedies in the 'Continental' style, many of the best Paramount pictures were like revues — which was pretty much the style of the Broadway theatre they'd come out of, and was what I liked about them. They entertained you without trying to change your life, yet didn't congratulate you for being a slobbering bag of mush, either. But by the forties these were considered 'escapist entertainment,' and that was supposed to be *bad*. Many of the thirties comedies, especially the Paramount ones, weren't even 'artistic' or 'visual' movies — which is why they look so good on television now. They also sound good, because what that historian thought of as their irresponsibility is so much more modern than the sentimentalities of the war years. What was believed in was implicit in the styles of the heroes and heroines and in the comedy targets; the writers had an almost aristocratic disdain for putting beliefs into words. In the forties, the writers convinced themselves that they believed in everything, and they kept putting it all into so many bad words. It's no wonder the movies had no further use for a Groucho or a Mae West; one can imagine what either of them might have done to those words.

It's common to blame the McCarthyism of the fifties and the removal of blacklisted writers for the terrible, flat writing in American movies of recent years, but the writers might have recovered from McCarthyism (they might even have stood up to it) if they hadn't been destroyed as writers long before. The writing that had given American talkies their special flavor died in the war, killed not in battle but in the politics of Stalinist 'anti-Fascism.' For the writers, Hollywood was just one big crackup, and for most of them it took a political turn. The lost-in-Hollywood generation of writers, trying to clean themselves of guilt for their wasted years and their irresponsibility as *writers*, became political in the worst way — became a special breed of anti-Fascists. The talented writers, the major ones as well as the lightweight yet entertaining ones, went down the same drain as the clods — drawn into it, often, by bored wives, less successful brothers. They became naïvely, hysterically pro-Soviet; they ignored Stalin's actual policies, because they so badly needed to believe in something. They had been so smart, so gifted, and yet they hadn't been able to beat Hollywood's contempt for the writer. (Walter Wanger had put twenty-seven of them to work in groups in succession on the script of Vincent Sheean's *Personal History*.) They lived in the city where Irving Thalberg was enshrined; Thalberg, the saint of M-G-M, had rationalized Mayer's system of putting teams of writers to work simultaneously and in relays on the same project. It had been lunatic before, but Thalberg made it seem mature and responsible to fit writers into an assembly-line method that totally alienated them and took away their last shreds of pride. And most of the Algonquin group had been in Hollywood so long they weren't even famous anymore.

Talented people have rarely had the self-control to flourish in the Hollywood atmosphere of big money and conflicting pressures. The talented — especially those who weren't using their talents to full capacity — have become desperate, impatient, unreliable, self-destructive, and also destructive, and so there has always been some validity in the businessman's argument that he couldn't afford to take chances on 'geniuses.' Thalberg didn't play around with a man like Mankiewicz; after throwing him off *A Night at the Opera*, he didn't use him again.

The writers who had become accustomed to being assembly-line workers were ready to believe it when, in the forties, they were told that, like factory workers, they were 'part of the team on the assembly line' and needed 'that strengthening of the spirit which comes from identity with the labor of others.' Like the producers, The Screen Writers Guild respected discipline and responsibility, but though the businessmen had never been able to organize people of talent — producers like Thalberg just kept discarding them — the union ideologues knew how. The talented rarely become bureaucrats, but the mediocre had put down roots in Hollywood — it doesn't take long in Los Angeles, the only great city that is purely modern, that hasn't even an architectural past in the nineteenth century. In the forties, the talented merged with the untalented and became almost indistinguishable from them, and the mediocre have been writing movies ever since. When the good writers tried to regain their self-respect by becoming political activists in the Stalinist style, it was calamitous to talent; the Algonquin group's own style was lost as their voice blended into the preachy, self-righteous chorus.

The comedy writers who had laughed at cant now learned to write it and were rehabilitated as useful citizens of the community of mediocrity. It was just what the newly political congratulated themselves on — their constructive, uplifting approach — that killed comedy. When they had written frivolously, knowing that they had no control over how their writing would be used, or buried, or rewritten, they may have failed their own gifts and the dreams of their youth, but the work they turned out had human dimensions; they were working at less than full capacity, but they were still honest entertainers. Their humor was the humor of those trapped by human weakness as well as by 'the system,' and this was basic comedy — like the jokes and camaraderie of Army men. But when they became political in that morally superior way of people who are doing something for themselves but pretending it's for others, their self-righteousness was insufferable. They may have told lies in the themes and plots of the thirties comedies, but they didn't take their own lies seriously, they didn't *believe* their own lies, the way they did in the forties. In the forties, the Screen Writers Guild and the Hollywood Writers Mobilization (for wartime morale-building) held conferences at which 'responsible' writers brought the irresponsibles into line. The irresponsibles were told they were part of an army and must 'dedicate their creative abilities to the winning of the war.' And, in case they failed to understand the necessity for didactic, 'positive' humor, there were panels and seminars that analyzed jokes and pointed out which ones might do harm. It was explained to the writers that 'catch-as-catch-can,' 'no-holds-barred' comedy was a thing of the past. 'A very funny line may make blackmarket dealings seem innocent and attractive,' they were told, and 'Respect for officers must be maintained at all times, in any scene, in any situation.'

Show-business people are both giddy and desperately, sincerely intense. When Stalinism was fashionable, movie people became Stalinists, the way they later became witches and warlocks. Apparently, many of the Hollywood Stalinists didn't realize they were taking any risks; they performed propaganda services for the various shifts in Russia's foreign policy and, as long as the needs of American and Russian policy coincided, this took the form of super-patriotism. When the war was over and the Cold War began, history left them stranded, and McCarthy moved in on them. The shame of McCarthyism was not only 'the shame of America' but the shame of a bunch of newly rich people who were eager to advise the world on moral and political matters and who, faced with a test, informed on their friends — and, as Orson Welles put it, not even to save their lives but to save their swimming pools. One might think that whatever they had gained emotionally from their activity they would have lost when they informed on each other, but it doesn't seem to have always worked that way. They didn't change their ideas when they recanted before the House Un-American Activities Committee; they merely gave in and then were restored to themselves. And they often seem to regard it not as their weakness but as their martyrdom. Show-business-Stalinism is basically not political but psychological; it's a fashionable form of hysteria and guilt that is by now not so much pro-Soviet as just abusively anti-American. America is their image of Hell (once again, because of Vietnam, they're in a popular position), and they go on being 'political' in the same way, holding the same faith, and for the same reasons, as in the late thirties and the forties. The restoration there is fairly general. In Hollywood recently, a man who used to be 'involved' told me he wanted to become more active again, and added, 'But, you know, I'm scared. The people who are urging me to do more are the same ones who ratted on me last time.'

Mankiewicz was too well informed politically to become a Communist Partyliner. Because he didn't support this line, he was — and only in part jokingly — considered a 'reactionary' by the activists of the Screen Writers Guild. Yet he went on to write the movie they point to with pride in Hollywood, the movie they all seem to feel demonstrates what *can* be done and what movies should be doing, and it's their all-time favorite because they understand it — and correctly — as a leftist film. Its leftism is, however, the leftism of the twenties and early thirties, before the left became moralistic. There were other expressions of the tough spirit of the thirties that came after the thirties were over. There may be a little of it in the newspaper film of the fifties *Sweet Smell of Success*, but the ambivalence there is harsher, grimmer, more artistically 'serious' than it was in the thirties; there's some in the happy mockery of Hollywood in *Singin' in the Rain*, which takes off from Kaufman and Hart's *Once in a Lifetime*, and in the films of Preston Sturges, who alone somehow managed to stay funny and tart. The only writer of this whole group who became a director with an individual style, Sturges kept American comedy alive singlehanded through the mawkish forties. Maybe he was able to because he was a cynic and so politically baroque that he wasn't torn by doubts and guilts. The political show in Hollywood in the forties was just one more crazy scene to him; he'd grown up rich and eccentric in Europe, the son of that expatriate lady (called Mary in *The Loves of Isadora*) who gave Isadora Duncan the fatal scarf.

But Mankiewicz climaxed an era in *Kane*. He wrote a big movie that is untarnished by sentimentality, and it may be the only big biographical movie ever made in this country of which that can be said. *Kane* is unsanctimonious; it is without scenes of piety, masochism, or remorse, without 'truths' — in that period when the screenwriters were becoming so politically 'responsible' that they were using all the primitive devices to sell their messages, and movies once again became full of blind beggars, and omens of doom, and accidental death as punishment for moral and sexual infractions, and, of course, Maria Ouspenskaya seeing into people's hearts – the crone as guru.

XI

Orson Welles wasn't around when *Citizen Kane* was written, early in 1940. Mankiewicz, hobbling about on a broken leg in a huge cast, was packed off — away from temptation — to Mrs Campbell's Guest Ranch, in Victorville, California, sixty-five miles from Los Angeles, to do the script. He had a nurse and a secretary to watch over him and John Houseman to keep him working, and they all lived there for about three months — in a combination dude ranch and rest home, where liquor was forbidden and unavailable — until the first draft of *Citizen Kane*, called simply and formidably *American*, was completed.

That insurance-company doctor who refused to accept Mankiewicz as a risk back in 1927 had no need to be prophetic. Ben Hecht once described a summer earlier in the twenties when he and his wife and Charles MacArthur were living in a borrowed house near Woodstock, New York, with no money, and Harpo, Groucho, Chico, and Zeppo Marx and their wives, sweethearts, and children came to stay, and then Herman Mankiewicz arrived, carrying two suitcases. 'He had decided to spend his vacation from the *New York Times* drama section with us,' Hecht wrote. 'He had not been allowed to bring any money with him because of Sara's certainty that he would spend it on liquor, and thus impair the influence of country air and sunshine. . . . Herman's larger suitcase contained sixteen bottles of Scotch and nothing else.' A few weeks later, Hecht and MacArthur went in to New York to try to sell a play they'd just written, and encountered Mankiewicz, who, having sent his wife and children out of town to escape the heat, was 'occupying Prince Bibesco's grand suite in the Plaza Hotel while His Highness capered in Long Island.'

Hecht went on, 'We moved in with him, there being no rent to pay. We discovered, while helping Herman to undress the first night, that his torso was bound with yards of adhesive tape. He had slipped while trying to get out of the bathtub and lamed his back. When Herman was asleep, MacArthur and I rolled him on his stomach and with an indelible pencil wrote ardent and obscene love messages on his taping. We signed them Gladys and chuckled over the impending moment in Far Rockaway when Herman would undress before his keen-eyed Sara.'

Not only was Mankiewicz alcoholic and maniacally accident-prone; he was a gambler, constantly in debt. There was a sequence in a thirties movie about a gambling newspaperman that was based on the way the other writers at Paramount used to line up with him when he got his check on Friday afternoon and walk with him to the bank so they could get back some of the money he'd borrowed from them during the week. His old friends say that he would bet from sheer boredom; when he ran out of big sporting events, he would bet on anything — on high-school football games or whether it would rain. He got to the point where he was bored with just betting; he wanted the stakes to be dangerously high. He once explained, 'It's not fun gambling if I lose two thousand and just write a check for it. What's thrilling is to make out a check for fifteen thousand dollars knowing there's not a penny in the bank.' James Thurber referred to him as an 'incurable compulsive gambler.' He described how Mankiewicz went to a psychiatrist to see if anything could be done about it. 'I can't cure you of gambling,' the analyst told him on his last visit, 'but I can tell you why you do it.'

By the late thirties, Mankiewicz had just about run out of studios to get fired from. Scott Fitzgerald described him in those years as 'a ruined man.' His friends would get him jobs and he would lose them — sometimes in spectacular ways that became part of Hollywood legend. Perhaps the best-known is his exit from Columbia Pictures. In his biography of Harry Cohn, who was then the head of the studio, Bob Thomas describes it this way:

The most famous incident in the Columbia dining room concerned an erratic genius named Herman J. Mankiewicz. . . . The freewheeling world of journalism seemed better suited to his temperament than did Hollywood. He possessed two failings that were inimical to the autocratic studio domains: he drank, and he was scornful of his bosses.

These faculties tumbled him from the position of a major screenwriter, and he had difficulty finding jobs. His agent, Charles Feldman, proposed a post at Columbia. Cohn was interested, since he enjoyed hiring bargain talent discarded by the major studios. . . Cohn agreed to employ him at $750 a week.

'I want to make good,' said Mankiewicz when he reported to William Perlberg, then Columbia's executive producer.

'Fine,' said the producer. . . . 'But . . . don't go in the executive dining room. You know what will happen if you tangle with Cohn.'

Mankiewicz concurred. . . . His work habits were exemplary, and he produced many pages a day. But . . . his office was on the third floor, near the door to the executive dining room. As Riskin, Swerling, and other fellow-writers emerged after lunch, he could hear them laughing over wisecracks and jokes that had been told inside. Mankiewicz himself was considered one of Hollywood's premier wits and raconteurs, and he rankled over his banishment.

One day Perlberg entered the dining room and was startled to find Mankiewicz sitting at the end of the table. The writer held a napkin to his mouth and promised, 'I won't say a word.'

When Cohn entered the room, he gave Mankiewicz a warm greeting, then assumed his monarchial position at the head of the table.

Cohn began the conversation: 'Last night I saw the lousiest picture I've seen in years.'

He mentioned the title, and one of the more courageous of his producers spoke up: 'Why, I saw that picture at the Downtown Paramount, and the audience howled over it. Maybe you should have seen it with an audience.'

'That doesn't make any difference,' Cohn replied. 'When I'm alone in a projection room, I have a foolproof device for judging whether a picture is good or bad. If my fanny squirms, it's bad. If my fanny doesn't squirm, it's good. It's as simple as that.'

There was a momentary silence, which was filled by

Mankiewicz at the end of the table: 'Imagine — the whole world wired to Harry Cohn's ass!'

Mankiewicz's attitude toward himself and his work is summed up in one very short, very famous story. A friend who hadn't seen him for a while asked, 'How's Sara?'

Mankiewicz, puzzled: 'Who?'

'Sara. Your wife, Sara.'

'Oh, you mean Poor Sara.'

The only evidence of an instinct for self-preservation in the life of Herman Mankiewicz is his choice of keen-eyed Sara. He was in bad shape by 1939, but Mayer kept him on the payroll — some said so that top people at M-G-M could collect their gambling winnings from him. But Mayer also seems to have had some affection for him, and Sara had become a close friend of Mayer's daughter Irene. Mayer became concerned about Mankiewicz's gambling debts, and, assuming that Mankiewicz was also concerned about them, he concluded that if he got the debts straightened out, Mankiewicz would pull himself together. Mayer called him in and asked him how much money he needed to get financially clear. Mankiewicz came up with the figure of $30,000, and Mayer offered to advance him that sum on a new contract if he would swear a solemn vow never to gamble again. Mankiewicz went through an elaborate ritual of giving Mayer his sacred word, and walked out with the $30,000. The very next day, it is said, Mankiewicz was playing poker on the lot, and he had just raised the stakes to $10,000 when he looked up and saw Mayer standing there. Mankiewicz left the studio and didn't return. A few days after that — early in September of 1939 — Thomas Phipps, a nephew of Lady Astor's, who was also employed as a writer at M-G-M, was driving to New York to court a lady there, and, with nothing better to do, Mankiewicz decided to go along. As Mankiewicz described the trip some months later, in a guest column he wrote, filling in for Hedda Hopper on vacation, it was fairly giddy right from the start. Mankiewicz said that each song on the car radio sent Phipps swooning, because either he had heard it while he was with his lady or he had heard it while he was not with her. On the outskirts of Albuquerque, the car skidded and turned over. Mankiewicz's jocular account included as the climax 'thirty-four weeks in a cast in bed and thirty-two weeks in a brace.' Phipps had a broken collarbone; when it healed, he proceeded on his romantic way to New York. Mankiewicz had a compound fracture of the left leg, which, together with further injuries suffered while the fracture was healing, left him with a limp for the rest of his life.

During the long recuperation — very long, because on his first night out on the town after his cast was removed, he went on crutches to Chasen's, got drunk, slipped and broke more bones, and had to be put in another cast — Mankiewicz, bedridden and in exile from the studios, began to write the Mercury Theatre's 'Campbell Playhouse' radio shows, and the actors often gathered around his bed for story conferences, and even rehearsals. Welles, having come to Hollywood in July to fulfill his contract with Schaefer, had been flying to and from New York for the series; in October he arranged to have the shows originate in Los Angeles, and in November he hired Mankiewicz to write five of them. Welles had met Maniewicz sometime earlier in New York. This is John Houseman's recollection of those events, set down in a letter to Sara Mankiewicz after her husband's death:

> I remember so well the day Orson came back to the theatre from 21, telling me had met this amazingly civilized and charming man. I can just see them there at lunch together — magicians and highbinders at work on each other, vying with each other in wit and savoir-faire and mutual appreciation. Both came away enchanted and convinced that, between them, they were the two most dashing and gallantly intelligent gentlemen in the Western world. And they were not so far wrong! Soon after that I met Herman myself, but I didn't get to know him until . . . he lay in bed at Tower Road, his leg in a monstrous plaster cast . . . and we started to do those peculiar collaborative radio shows in the beginning of our long conspiracy of love and hate for Maestro, the Dog-Faced Boy. Then came *Kane* and Victorville and those enchanted months of inhabiting Mrs Campbell's ranch with our retinue of nurse and secretary and our store of Mickey Finns!

Tower Road was where the Mankiewiczes lived and the Mercury group gathered. The Dog-Faced Boy is, of course, Orson Welles (Cocteau once described him as 'a dog who had broken loose from his chain and gone to sleep on the flower bed'), and the Mickey Finns were a medical concoction that was supposed to make Mankiewicz hate alcohol. It failed. The secretary, Mrs Rita Alexander (she lent her name to the character of Susan Alexander), recalls that during her first week, before Sara Mankiewicz had had a chance to give her a briefing, Mankiewicz persuaded her to take him in to the town of Victorville, where he could get a drink. She withstood his wiles after that. He really wasn't in condition to do much drinking; the broken bones included a hip break, and he was in such poor condition that even eating presented problems. Mrs Alexander recalls spoon-feeding him bicarbonate of soda, and recalls his courtly, formal apologies for the belches that rocked the room.

XII

There are monsters, and there are also sacred monsters; both Welles and Mankiewicz deserve places in the sacred-monster category. Some writers on film — particularly in England — blithely say that Kane wasn't based on Hearst, using as evidence statements that Welles made to the press in early 1941, when he was trying to get the picture released. But those who think Louella Parsons got the *mistaken* idea that the picture was about Hearst don't understand what kind of man the young Welles was. Welles and Mankiewicz wanted to do something startling, something that would cap the invasion of the Martians — which had, after all, panicked only the boobs, and inadvertently at that, though Welles now makes it sound deliberate. This time, he and Mankiewicz *meant* to raise Cain. The pun is surely theirs, and Hearst had walked right into it; he was so fond of a story called *Cain and Mabel*, which he'd bought and produced as a Cosmopolitan Picture back in 1924, that he remade it late in 1936, at Warners', starring Clark Gable and Marion Davies. It had been one of her last pictures before her retirement. Cain and Mabel — it was a perfect description of Hearst and Marion. In 1960, when Welles was interviewed on British television, he said, 'Kane isn't really founded on Hearst in particular.' I suppose he was feeling rather expansive at that moment, and it may have seemed to limit his importance if his Kane had been based on anyone 'in particular.' In the same interview, he said, 'You asked me did Mr Hearst try to stop it. *He* didn't. . . . He was like Kane in that he wouldn't have stooped to such a thing.' This was rather droll, but Welles seemed to mean it. He didn't seem to know much about Hearst anymore; probably he'd forgotten. One may also fairly conclude that Welles, with that grandeur which he seems to have taken over from the theatre into his personal life, was elevating Hearst, lending Hearst some of his own magnitude. More characteristically, however, his grandeur is double-edged, as in this typical statement on Gregg Toland:

> I had a great advantage not only in the real genius of my
> cameraman but in the fact that he, like all men who are masters
> of a craft, told me at the outset that there was nothing about
> camerawork that any intelligent being couldn't learn in half a
> day. And he was right.

Welles was thus telling us that he learned all there was to know about
camerawork in half a day. What, one wonders, was the craft that
Toland needed to master? Welles, like Hearst, and like most very big
men, is capable of some very small gestures. And so was Mankiewicz,
who brought his younger, more stable brother, Joe, out to Hollywood
and helped him get started, but, as soon as Joe had some success,
began behaving atrociously, referring to him as 'my idiot brother.'
   Mankiewicz's ambivalence was generally on a higher level, however. There are many different kinds of senses of humor, and the one
that sometimes comes through Mankiewicz anecdotes is the perverse
soul of Kane himself. There is, for example, the story that Ezra
Goodman tells in *The Fifty Year Decline and Fall of Hollywood*.
Hollywood was not often elegant and correct, but the producer Arthur
Hornblow, Jr, was known for the punctiliousness of his social functions. At a dinner party he gave for Hollywood notables, Herman
Mankiewicz drank too much and threw up on the table. 'A deadly hush
descended over the assembled guests. . . Mankiewicz broke the
silence himself: "It's all right, Arthur; the white wine came up with the
fish." '
   The man who in those circumstances could put his host down was
a fit companion for Welles. They were big eaters, big talkers, big
spenders, big talents; they were not men of what is ordinarily called
'good character.' They were out to get not only Hearst but each other.
The only religious remark that has ever been attributed to Mankiewicz
was recorded on the set of *Citizen Kane*: Welles walked by, and
Mankiewicz muttered, 'There, but for the grace of God, goes God.'

XIII

Herman Mankiewicz didn't — to be exact — write *Citizen Kane*; he
dictated it. The screenwriters may have felt like whores and they
may have been justified in that feeling, but they were certainly well-
paid whores. In New York, they hadn't had secretaries, but the
movie business was mass culture's great joke on talent. The affectation of 'Look, no hands' became the literal truth. Mankiewicz

dictated the script while the nurse watched over him and John House-man stood by in attendance. This was a cut-rate job — Mankiewicz was getting $500 a week for his ghostly labors — but it was still in the royal tradition of screenwriting. Outside the movie business, there has probably never been a writer in the history of the world who got this kind of treatment. There was an urgency about it: Welles and most of the Mercury Theatre company were in Holly-wood doing their weekly radio shows and waiting while this odd little group spent the spring of 1940 in Victorville preparing the script for Orson Welles's début in films.

Welles had come to Hollywood the previous July in a burst of publicity, but his first two film projects hadn't got under way. Within a few months of his arrival, he was being jeered at because nothing had happened. Although his contract with R.K.O. gave him freedom from interference, Schaefer and his legal staff had to approve the project and clear the shooting script and, of course, the budget. It had been agreed that his first project would be Conrad's *Heart of Darkness*, which he had already done as a radio drama. He was to play both Marlow and Kurtz, the two leading roles, and it was reported in the trade press that he was working on the script with John Houseman and Herbert Drake, who was the Mercury's press agent. In the latter part of 1939, Welles brought actors out from New York and shot long test sequences, but the budget looked too high to the poverty-stricken studio, and the production was repeatedly postponed. He decided to do something while he was waiting — something that he could start on right away, to get the Mercury actors on the R.K.O. payroll — and he hit on a spy thriller with a political theme: *The Smiler with the Knife*, from the novel by Nicholas Blake (C. Day-Lewis). Welles adapted the book himself — 'in seven days,' according to the trade press — but this project was abandoned almost at once because of differences with Schaefer over casting. (Welles wanted to use Lucille Ball, then a contract player at R.K.O., in the lead, and Schaefer didn't think she could carry the picture. As the whole world knows, she wound up owning the studio, but Schaefer wasn't necessarily wrong; she never did carry a picture.) There was still hope for *Heart of Darkness* — and a lot of money had already been spent on it — but things seemed to be falling apart for the Mercury group. By the end of 1939, Welles was desperate for a subject that would be acceptable to R.K.O. The movie plans were up in the air, and there was dissension within the Mercury group about staying on in Hollywood with nothing definite in sight to work on. Some of the actors left to take jobs elsewhere, and some were beginning to get film roles — a development that upset Welles, because he wanted them to be 'new faces' in his first film.

A policy meeting was arranged to discuss the failing fortunes of the group and to decide whether to keep them all in Los Angeles or send some of them back to New York. The more or less administrative heads of the Mercury Theatre met for dinner in an upper room at Chasen's. The group included Welles; Houseman, who had founded the Mercury Theatre with him; two all-purpose assistants, Richard Wilson and William Alland; the press agent, Drake; and several others. Houseman argued that the actors should return to New York, but nothing had been settled by the time the coffee and brandy arrived, and then Welles, in a sudden access of rage, shouted that Houseman had always been against him, and he threw the coffee warmers — full of Sterno canned heat — at Houseman. He did not throw them very precisely, it seems; he threw not so much with intent to hit as in Houseman's general direction. Dave Chasen, having been summoned by a waiter, opened the door, and, with the aplomb he had used back in the thirites in vaudeville, when he was the stooge of the comedian Joe Cook, he took one look — a curtain was on fire by them — and closed the door. The men in the room stamped out the fire, and Houseman went home and sent Welles a letter of resignation. The partnership was ended, and a week later Houseman left for New York.

Welles's tantrum and how it ended the partnership that had created the Mercury Theatre was the talk of the actors who gathered around Mankiewicz's bed, and it must have registered on Mankiewicz in a special way: it must have practically thrust on him the recognition of an emotional link between Welles and William Randolph Hearst, whose tantrums had been the stuff of legend among newspapermen for half a century, and whose occasional demonstrations of childishness were the gossip of guests at San Simeon. A week or two after the Chasen's dinner party, Mankiewicz proposed to Welles that they make a 'prismatic' movie about the life of a man seen from several different points of view. Even before he went to work in Hollywood and met Hearst, when he was still at the *New York Times*, Mankiewicz was already caught up in the idea of a movie about Hearst. Marion Fisher, the Mankiewicz baby-sitter, whose family lived in the same Central Park West building, was learning to type in high school and Mankiewicz offered to 'test her typing.' He dictated a screenplay, organized in flashbacks. She recalls that he had barely started on the dictation, which went on for several weeks, when she remarked that it seemed to be about William Randolph Hearst, and he said, 'You're a smart girl.' Mankiewicz couldn't pay her but she and her parents saw about fifty shows on the theatre tickets he gave them, and it was a great year for Broadway — 1925. Although in the intervening years Mankiewicz had often talked to friends about what a movie Hearst's life would make, his first suggestions to Welles for the 'prismatic' movie were Dillinger and, when Welles was cool to that, Aimee. Semple McPherson. Only after Welles had rejected that, too, and after they had discussed the possibilities in the life of Dumas, did he propose Hearst. Mankiewicz must have been stalling and playing games to lead Welles on, because although he was interested in both Dillinger and Aimee Semple McPherson, and subsequently did prepare scripts on them, this movie had to be a starring vehicle for Welles, and what major role could Welles play in the life of either Dillinger or Aimee? From what Mankiewicz told friends at the time, when he sprang the name Hearst, Welles leaped at it.

Welles had grown up hearing stories about Hearst from Dr Maurice Bernstein, who was his guardian after his parents died. Dr Bernstein was a good friend of Ashton Stevens, who had originally been the drama critic on Hearst's flagship paper, the *San Francisco Examiner*, and had gone on to work for Hearst in Chicago. Welles himself was a Hearst-press 'discovery'; it was Ashton Stevens, whom Dr Bernstein got in touch with, who had publicized the nineteen-year-old Orson Welles when he produced *Hamlet* on a vacant second floor in Illinois. But Welles, being a knowledgeable young man, would have known a great deal about Hearst even without this personal connection, for Hearst was the unifying hatred of all liberals and leftists. Welles, with his sense of the dramatic, would have known at once what a sensational idea a movie about Hearst was. Aimee and Dillinger just didn't have the dimensions that Hearst had; Hearst was even right for Welles *physically*. Welles and Mankiewicz must have enjoyed thinking what a scandal a movie about him would make. Mankiewicz didn't need to have misgivings about repercussions, because the risks would all be Welles's. Schaefer had signed Welles up to a widely publicized four-way contract as producer, director, writer, and actor. It was understood that he would take the credit for the script, just as he did for the scripts of the radio plays. His R.K.O. contract stated that 'the screenplay for each picture shall be written by Mr Orson Welles,' and Welles probably took this stipulation as no more than his due — a necessity of his station. He probably accepted the work that others did for him the way modern Presidents accept the work of speech-writers.

The title *American* suggests how Mankiewicz felt about the project. Several years before, in 1933, his friend and drinking companion Preston Sturges had written a big one, an original called *The Power and the Glory*, which, when it was produced, with Spencer Tracy and Colleen Moore in the leading roles, made Tracy a star. *The Power and the Glory* was about a ruthless railroad tycoon who fails in his personal life, and it was told in flashbacks and narration from his funeral. It was an impressive picture, and it was lauded in terms similar to those later used about *Kane*. 'Its subject,' William Troy wrote in the *Nation*, 'is the great American Myth, and its theme is futility.' The ballyhoo included putting a bronze tablet in the New York theatre where it opened to commemorate 'the first motion picture in which narratage was used as a method of telling a dramatic story.' (Hollywood, big on ballyhoo but short on real self-respect, failed to transfer the nitrate negative to safety stock, and modern prints of *The Power and the Glory* are tattered remnants.) Not only is the tycoon treated ambivalently by Sturges but in the boyhood sequence he is injured through his own arrogance, so that he acquires a jagged, lightninglike scar on his hand — the mark of Cain. The idea of the big-businessman as a Cain figure was basic to this genre, which had become popular in the Depression thirties, when many business giants of the twenties were revealed to be swindlers, or, at the very least, ruthless. In another 1933 film, *I Loved a Woman*, a tycoon's mistress sang at the Chicago Opera House. (It was where the tycoons' mistresses did sing in the twenties.) In 1937, Mankiewicz himself had done a trial run on the tycoon theme (with Edward Arnold as a lumber baron) in *John Meade's Woman*. To do Hearst, a much more dangerous man — the only tycoon who was also a demagogue — in a technique similar to Sturges's but from several different points of view would make a really big picture.

But there was a sizable hurdle: How could they get R.K.O. to approve this project? Welles and Mankiewicz went on talking about it for a couple of weeks, while Mankiewicz continued writing the weekly radio shows. When they decided to go ahead and try to slip it over on the studio somehow, Welles still had to find a way to get Mankiewicz to do the writing; the Mercury company couldn't be kept waiting in Los Angeles indefinitely while Mankiewicz wandered loose. Mankiewicz had had to be hauled off to sanatoriums to be dried out too many times for Welles to take chances, and the screenwriters who had worked with Mankiewicz at Metro told too many stories about his losing interest in the scripts he was assigned to and drinking so much during working hours that the other writers would load him into a studio car in midafternoon and have the driver haul him home, where Sara would unload him and put him to bed, and he would sleep it off before dinner and be ready for the night's drinking. He had just injured himself again, in his fall at Chasen's, and his bones were being reset, but soon he would be off on the town once more, despite cast or crutches, and there would be no way to hold him down to work. Welles hit on the scheme of packing Mankiewicz off to the country to recuperate. In early January, 1940, Welles flew to New York, and over lunch at '21' the young magician prevailed on Houseman to return to the Coast and do him and the Mercury one last service by running herd on Mankiewicz; only a month had passed since the fiery scene at Chasen's. (It was to be not the last but the next-to-last collaborative project of Welles and Houseman. A week after *American* was done and the troupe had left Victorville, Houseman and Welles were on bad terms again, but Mankiewicz, who was said to have read every new book by publication date, even when he was in the worst possible shape, told them that they'd be crazy if they didn't buy a new book that was just coming out, and dramatize it. Houseman went to work on it, and as a result Richard Wright's *Native Son* was adapted for the stage and produced so quickly that Welles had it playing in New York by the time *Citizen Kane* opened.)

Both Houseman and Mankiewicz unquestionably had mixed feelings about Welles by the time they found themselves at the guest ranch. Houseman admits that right from the beginning, when Mankiewicz started on the script, they planned to have Welles re-enact his tantrum. It was set for the scene in which Susan leaves Kane (Welles's wife, Virginia, had brought suit for divorce during the month Welles had his tantrum), and Mankiewicz wrote it up rather floridly and with explicit directions, in a passage beginning, 'Kane, in a truly terrible and absolutely silent rage. . .' When it was time to shoot the scene, the various members of the group who had been at Chasen's — or had heard about what happened there, and everybody *had* — encouraged Welles to do what he had done that night. Last year, William Alland, describing the making of the film in an interview printed in the magazine of the Directors Guild of America, said:

There was one scene which stands out above all others in my memory; that was the one in which Orson broke up the roomful of furniture in a rage. Orson never liked himself as an actor. He had the idea that he should have been feeling more, that he intellectualized too much and never achieved the emotion of losing himself in a part.

When he came to the furniture-breaking scene, he set up four cameras, because he obviously couldn't do the scene many times. He did the scene just twice, and each time he threw himself into the action with a fervor I had never seen in him. It was absolutely electric; you felt as if you were in the presence of a man coming apart.

Orson staggered out of the set with his hands bleeding and his face flushed. He almost swooned, yet he was exultant. 'I really felt it,' he exclaimed. 'I really felt it!'

Strangely, that scene didn't have the same power when it appeared on the screen. It might have been how it was cut, or because there hadn't been close-in shots to depict his rage. The scene in the picture was only a mild reflection of what I had witnessed on that movie stage.

Writing that scene into the movie was a cruel trick on Welles, designed to make him squirm. He had been built up so much that he was by then the white hope (as it used to be called) of the theatre. In 1938, even George S. Kaufman and Moss Hart had taken him to be that; they had written one of their worst maudlin 'serious' plays (and a flop) — *The Fabulous Invalid*, a cavalcade-of-the-American-theatre sort of play — and had modelled its hero on Welles. The hero — the leader of a new acting company — made a classic final curtain speech to his actors:

> We haven't got very much money, but we've got youth and, I think, talent. They'll tell you the theatre is dying. I don't believe it. Anything that can bring us together like this, and hold us to this one ideal in spite of everything, isn't going to die. They'll tell you it isn't important, putting makeup on your face and playacting. I don't believe it. It's important to keep alive a thing that can lift men's spirits above the everyday reality of their lives. We mustn't let that die. Remember — you're going to be kicked around, and a lot of the time you're not going to have

enough to eat, but you're going to get one thing in return. The chance to write, and act, say the things you want to say, and do the things you want to do. And I think that's enough.

For the people who did much of the work on Welles's projects, the temptation must have been strong to expose what they considered this savior's feet of clay.

The menagerie at Mrs Campbell's being scarcely a secret, they had many visitors (Welles himself came to dinner once or twice), and several of these visitors, as well as Houseman and Mrs Alexander, describe how Herman Mankiewicz turned out the script that became *Citizen Kane*. Mankiewicz couldn't go anywhere without help; he sat up, in the cast that covered one leg and went up to his middle, and played cribbage with Mrs Alexander during the day, while telling her stories about Hearst and Marion Davies and San Simeon. Then, at night, from about eight-thirty to eleven-thirty or twelve, he dictated, and she would type it out so he could have it the next day. Mrs Alexander recalls that during the first days on the job, when she was fascinated by the romantic significance of 'Rosebud' and asked him how the story would turn out, he said, 'My dear Mrs Alexander, I don't know. I'm making it up as I go along.' Welles was so deeply entangled in the radio shows and other activities and a romance with Dolores Del Rio at the time the script was being prepared that even when he came to dinner at Victorville, it was mainly a social visit; the secretary didn't meet him until after Mankiewicz had finished dictating the long first draft. Welles probably made suggestions in his early conversations with Mankiewicz and since he received copies of the work weekly while it was in progress at Victorville, he may have given advice by phone or letter. Later, he almost certainly made suggestions for cuts that helped Mankiewicz hammer the script into tighter form, and he is known to have made a few changes on the set. But Mrs Alexander, who took the dictation from Mankiewicz, from the first paragraph to the last, and then, when the first draft was completed and they all went back to Los Angeles, did the secretarial work at Mankiewicz's house on the rewriting and the cuts, and who then handled the script at the studio until after the film was shot, says that Welles didn't write (or dictate) one line of the shooting script of *Citizen Kane*.

Toward the end of the period at the ranch, Mankiewicz began to realize that he'd made a very bad financial deal, and that the credit might be more important than he'd anticipated. After talks with Mrs

Alexander and the Mercury people who visited on weekends, he decided he was going to get screen credit, no matter what his bargain with Welles had been. Meanwhile, Houseman, who says that according to his original agreement to go off to the ranch he was supposed to get some kind of credit, discovered once again, and as so many others had, that it wasn't easy to get your name on anything Orson Welles was involved in. Houseman was apparently fed up with arguments, and he says he waived his claim when he saw how determined Welles was; he left for New York and got started on the preparations for *Native Son*. But Mankiewicz was an experienced Hollywood hand and veteran of credit brawls who kept all his drafts and materials, and a man who relished trouble. He had ample proof of his authorship, and he took his evidence to the Screen Writers Guild and raised so much hell that Welles was forced to split the credit and take second place in the listing.

At the time the movie came out, Mankiewicz's contribution to the film was generally known. The screen credit was to Herman J. Mankiewicz and Orson Welles. The *Hollywood Reporter* simplified the credit to 'Written by Herman Mankiewicz'; Burns Mantle, in his newspaper column, referred to Mankiewicz's having written it; and, of course, Ben Hecht explained to the readers of *PM*, 'This movie was not written by Orson Welles. It is the work of Herman J. Mankiewicz.' In that period, it was well known that if the producer of a film wanted a screenplay credit it was almost impossible to prevent him from getting it. So many producers took a writing credit as a *droit du seigneur* for a few consultations or suggestions that the Screen Writers Guild later instituted a rule calling for compulsory arbitration whenever a producer sought a credit. Under the present rules of the Guild, Welles's name would probably not have appeared. And so it was by an awful fluke of justice that when Academy Awards night came, and Welles should have got the awards he deserved as director and actor, the award he got (the only Academy Award he has ever got) was as co-author of the Best Original Screenplay.*

XIV

The Mercury group wasn't surprised at Welles's taking a script credit; they'd had experience with this foible of his. Very early in his life as

---

* Shortly after this article appeared, Welles was voted a special Academy Award for 'superlative artistry and versatility in the creation of motion pictures.'

a prodigy, Welles seems to have fallen into the trap that has caught so many lesser men — believing his own publicity, believing that he really was the whole creative works, producer-director-writer-actor. Because he *could* do all these things, he imagined that he *did* do them. (A Profile of him that appeared in *The New Yorker* two years before *Citizen Kane* was made said that 'outside the theatre . . . Welles is exactly twenty-three years old.') In the days before the Mercury Theatre's weekly radio shows got a sponsor, it was considered a good publicity technique to build up public identification with Welles's name, so he was credited with just about everything, and was named on the air as the writer of the Mercury shows. Probably no one but Welles believed it. He had written some of the shows when the program first started, and had also worked on some with Houseman, but soon he had become much too busy even to collaborate; for a while Houseman wrote them, and then they were farmed out. By the time of *The War of the Worlds* broadcast, on Halloween, 1928, Welles wasn't doing any of the writing. He was so busy with his various other activities that he didn't always direct the rehearsals himself, either — William Alland or Richard Wilson or one of the other Mercury assistants did it. Welles might not come in until the last day, but somehow, all agree, he would pull the show together 'with a magic touch.' Yet when the Martian broadcast became accidentally famous, Welles seemed to forget that Howard Koch had written it. (In all the furor over the broadcast, with front-page stories everywhere, the name of the author of the radio play wasn't mentioned.) Koch had been writing the shows for some time. He lasted for six months, writing about twenty-five shows altogether — working six and a half days a week, and frantically, on each one, he says, with no more than half a day off to see his family. The weekly broadcasts were a 'studio presentation' until after *The War of the Worlds* (Campbell's Soup picked them up then), and Koch, a young writer, who was to make his name with the film *The Letter* in 1940 and win an Academy Award for his share in the script of the 1942 *Casablanca*, was writing them for $75 apiece. Koch's understanding of the agreement was that Welles would get the writing credit on the air for publicity purposes but that Koch would have any later benefit, and the copyright was in Koch's name. (He says that it was, however, Welles's idea that he do the Martian show in the form of radio bulletins.) Some years later, when C.B.S. did a program about the broadcast and the panic it had caused, the network re-created parts of the original broadcast and paid Koch

$300 for the use of his material. Welles sued C.B.S. for $375,000, claiming that he was the author and that the material had been used without his permission. He lost, of course, but he may still think he wrote it. (He frequently indicates as much in interviews and on television.)

'Foible' is the word that Welles's former associates tend to apply to his assertions of authorship. Welles could do so many different things in those days that it must have seemed almost accidental when he didn't do things he claimed to. Directors, in the theatre and in movies, are by function (and often by character, or, at least, disposition) cavalier toward other people's work, and Welles was so much more talented and magnetic than most directors — and so much younger, too — that people he robbed of credit went on working with him for years, as Koch went on writing more of the radio programs after Welles failed to mention him during the national publicity about the panic. Welles was dedicated to the company, and he was exciting to work with, so the company stuck together, working for love, and even a little bit more money (Koch was raised to $125 a show) when they got a sponsor and, also as a result of *The War of the Worlds* broadcast, the movie contract that took them to Hollywood.

If there was ever a young man who didn't need unearned credits, it was Orson Welles, yet though he was already too big, he must have felt he needed to dazzle the world. Welles was hated in Hollywood long before he'd made a movie; he was hated almost upon his arrival. From time to time, Hollywood used to work up considerable puerile resentment against 'outsiders' who dared to make movies. The scope of Welles's reputation seems to have infuriated Hollywood; it was a cultural reproach from the East, and the Hollywood people tried to protect themselves by closing ranks and making Welles a butt of their humor. Gene Lockhart composed a stupid, nasty ditty called 'Little Orson Annie,' which was sung at Hollywood parties; the name stuck and was used by the columnists, though Hedda Hopper supported him and suggested that Hollywood reserve judgment, and Louella Parsons, on December 31st, selected him as 'the most discussed personality to come to the films in 1939.' Yet for Welles, with his beard (he was growing it for the Shakespearean production he intended to stage as soon as he could pick up his Hollywood loot), to be ensconced in the Mary Pickford–Buddy Rogers estate, right next door to Shirley Temple, was too much for Hollywood. Welles became the victim of practical jokers. One night when he was dining at Chasen's, an actor cut off his tie with a table knife. Not all the jokes were so Freudian, but they were mostly ugly. Welles had come with an unprecedented contract. Probably the old Hollywoodians not only expected him to fall on his face but hoped he would, so that their mediocrity and prosperity would be vindicated. But Welles was the braggart who makes good. And, despite their resentment, they *were* dazzled by *Citizen Kane*.

XV

The picture got a thunderous reception, even in the Hollywood press. In recent years, the rumor has spread that *Citizen Kane* opened to bad reviews — presumably on the theory that it was so far ahead of its time that it wasn't understood — and this is now recorded in many film histories. But it was very well understood by the press (who would understand a newspaper picture better?), and it got smashing reviews. It isn't, after all, a difficult picture. In some ways, it was probably better understood then than it is now, and, as far as I can determine, it was more highly praised by the American press than any other movie in history. The New York opening of *Citizen Kane*, which had been scheduled for February 14, 1941, finally took place on May 1st, and a week later it opened in Los Angeles. In January, Hedda Hopper had 'doubted' whether the picture would ever be released, and some of the trade press had predicted that it wouldn't be. Possibly it wouldn't have been except for the screenings that Welles arranged and the publicity that he got.

The whole industry was already involved in the picture. Although technically Welles had the right of final cut, the editor, Robert Wise, was instructed by the studio, with Welles's consent, to take a print to New York in January. Wise ran it for the heads of all the major companies and their lawyers, and for six weeks he and his then assistant, Mark Robson, who was on the Coast, fussed over the movie, making tiny, nervous changes — mostly a word here or there — that the executives and lawyers hoped would render the picture less objectionable to Hearst. Meanwhile, Schaefer had engaged Time, Inc's legal specialist on invasion-of-privacy suits; the lawyer instructed Schaefer that if he made one small cut in the film, no one could win such a suit. The dangerous section was a bit of dialogue by Raymond, the butler, suggesting that the old man was senile. Schaefer says he had no difficulty persuading Welles to agree to the cut. However, at the beginning of March, Hearst sent for Walter Howey, and no one was sure what they might be poking into. 'Nor are private lives to be overlooked,' Hedda Hopper predicted; and her predictions were the same as threats. Hearst's maneuvers were in the true Kane spirit: In January, Hedda Hopper had warned that 'the refugee situation would be looked into,' which meant that there would be pressure for a legal review of whether various imported stars and directors should be allowed to remain in the country, and the industry would be attacked for employing foreigners; that is, refugees from Hitler. Three days after the press previews, the Hearst newspapers, the American Legion, the Veterans of Foreign Wars, and other patriotic organizations went into action to rid radio of 'subversives.' The 'subversives' they were after were William Saroyan, Maxwell Anderson, Marc Connelly, Robert E. Sherwood, Stephen Vincent Benét, Paul Green, Sherwood Anderson, and James Boyd, who were involved with Welles in a series of C.B.S. radio plays on the general theme of freedom, which, although it had been encouraged by the Justice Department, was now condemned as un-American and as tending to promote Communism. Before *Citizen Kane* was released, *PM* reported that Hearst photographers were following Welles 'in G-man style,' trying to get something on him, while *Variety* reported 'persistent inquiries at the draft board as to why Welles hadn't been drafted.' It was along about this time that Hearst himself saw the picture. Schaefer says, 'Hearst personally sent to me at the studio and asked to see a print, and we let him have it. This was before it opened. There was no response, no comment. Orson knew this.' Welles may have feared that Schaefer would buckle unless he squeezed him from the other side, or, as Schaefer claims, it may have been Welles's way of getting more publicity, but, for whatever reason, Welles began to issue threats: he gave R.K.O. the deadline of March 30th for releasing the picture or facing a lawsuit. On March 11th, Welles called a press conference to alert the press to the danger that the film might be suppressed, and gave out this statement:

> I believe that the public is entitled to see *Citizen Kane*. For me to stand by while this picture was being suppressed would constitute a breach of faith with the public on my part as producer. I have at this moment sufficient financial backing to buy *Citizen Kane* from R.K.O. and to release it myself. Under my contract with R.K.O. I have the right to demand that the picture be released and to bring legal action to force its release. R.K.O. must release *Citizen Kane*. If it does not do so immedi-

ately, I have instructed my attorney to commence proceedings.

I have been advised that strong pressure is being brought to bear in certain quarters to cause the withdrawal of my picture *Citizen Kane* because of an alleged resemblance between incidents in the picture and incidents in the life of Mr William Randolph Hearst.

Any such attempts at suppression would involve a serious interference with freedom of speech and with the integrity of the moving picture industry as the foremost medium of artistic expression in the country.

There is nothing in the facts to warrant the situation that has arisen. *Citizen Kane* was not intended to have nor has it any reference to Mr Hearst or to any other living person. No statement to the contrary has ever been authorized by me. *Citizen Kane* is the story of a wholly fictitious character.

The script for *Citizen Kane* was scrutinized and approved by both R.K.O. Radio Pictures and the Hays office. No one in those organizations nor anyone associated with me in the production of the picture believed that it represented anything but psychological analysis of an imaginary individual. I regret exceedingly that anyone should interpret *Citizen Kane* to have a bearing upon any living person, or should impugn the artistic purposes of its producers.

Several of the magazines responded to his plea for the pressure of publicity by reviewing the picture before it opened, obviously with the intention of helping to get it released. A review in *Time* on March 17, 1941, began:

As in some grotesque fable, it appeared last week that Hollywood was about to turn upon and destroy its greatest creation.

It continued:

To most of the several hundred people who have seen the film at private showings, *Citizen Kane* is the most sensational product of the U.S. movie industry. It has found important new techniques in picture-making and story telling. . . It is as psychiatrically sound as a fine novel. . . . It is a work of art created by grown people for grown people.

In *Newsweek*, also on March 17, 1941, John O'Hara began his review with:

> It is with exceeding regret that your faithful bystander reports that he has just seen a picture which he thinks must be the best picture he ever saw.
>
> With no less regret he reports that he has just seen the best actor in the history of action.
>
> Name of picture: *Citizen Kane.*
>
> Name of actor: Orson Welles.
>
> Reason for regret: you, my dear, may never seen the picture.
>
> I saw *Citizen Kane* the other night. I am told that my name was crossed off a list of persons who were invited to look at the picture, my name being crossed off because some big shot remembered I had been a newspaperman. So, for the first time in my life, I indignantly denied I was a newspaperman. Nevertheless, I had to be snuck into the showing of *Citizen Kane* under a phony name. That's what's going on about this wonderful picture. Intrigue.
>
> Why intrigue? Well, because. A few obsequious and/or bulbous middle-aged ladies think the picture ought not to be shown, owing to the fact that the picture is rumored to have something to do with a certain publisher, who, for the first time in his life, or maybe the second, shall be nameless. That the nameless publisher might be astute enough to realize that for the first time in his rowdy life he had been made a human being did not worry the loyal ladies. Sycophancy of that kind, like curtseying, is deliberate. The ladies merely wait for a chance to show they can still do it, even if it means cracking a femur. This time I think they may have cracked off more than they can chew. I hope.

Along the way, O'Hara said such things as:

> My intention is to make you want to see the picture; if possible, to make you wonder why you are not seeing what I think is as good a picture as was ever made. . . . And aside from what it does not lack, *Citizen Kane* has Orson Welles. It is traditional that if you are a great artist, no one gives a damn about you while you're still alive. Welles has had plenty of that. He got a tag put to his name through the Mars thing, just as Scott Fitzgerald, who wrote better than any man in our time, got a

Jazz Age tag put to his name. I say, if you plan to have any grandchildren to see and to bore, see Orson Welles so that you can bore your grandchildren with some honesty. There never has been a better actor than Orson Welles. I just got finished saying there never has been a better actor than Orson Welles, and I don't want any of your lip.

Do yourself a favor. Go to your neighborhood exhibitor and ask him why he isn't showing *Citizen Kane*.

The same day — March 17, 1941 — *Life*, which was to run several more features on the movie in the following months, came out with four pages of pictures and a review:

> Few movies have ever come from Hollywood with such powerful narrative, such original technique, such exciting photography. Director Welles and Cameraman Gregg Toland do brilliantly with a camera everything Hollywood has always said you couldn't do. They shoot into bright lights, they shoot into the dark and against low ceilings, till every scene comes with the impact of something never seen before. Even the sound track is new. And for narrative Welles has tapped a segment of life fearfully skirted by the U.S. cinema: the swift and brutal biography of a power-mad newspaper tycoon, a man of twisted greatness who buys or bullies his way into everything but friends' love and his nation's respect. To a film industry floundering in a rut, *Citizen Kane* offers enough new channels to explore for five years to come.

Hearst must have known he would be in for a bad time if the picture should be withheld; the Luce magazines — *Time* and *Life* — had always been eager to embarrass him, and certainly wouldn't let the subject drop. (The financial backing that Welles said he had to buy the picture was probably from Henry Luce.) One surmises that Hearst decided not to try to block its release — though the petty harrassment of R.K.O. and others involved went on, like a reflex to a blow.

Here is a representative selection from the reviews:

Variety: A film possessing the sure dollar mark.

Times (Bosley Crowther): Suppression of this film would have been a crime. . . . *Citizen Kane* is far and away the most surprising and cinematically exciting motion picture to be seen here in many a moon. . . . It comes close to being the most sensational film ever made in Hollywod.

Herald Tribune (Howard Barnes): A young man named Orson Welles has shaken the medium wide-awake with his magnificent film, *Citizen Kane*. His biography of an American dynast is not only a great picture; it is something of a revolutionary screen achievement. . . . From any standpoint *Citizen Kane* is truly a great motion picture.

Post (Archer Winsten): It goes without saying this is the picture that wins the majority of 1941's movie prizes in a walk, for it is inconceivable that another will come along to challenge it. . . . Orson Welles with this one film establishes himself as the most exciting director now working. . . . Technically the result marks a new epoch.

PM (Cecelia Ager): Before *Citizen Kane*, it's as if the motion picture was a slumbering monster, a mighty force stupidly sleeping, lying there sleek, torpid, complacent — awaiting a fierce young man to come kick it to life, to rouse it, shake it, awaken it to its potentialities, to show it what it's got. Seeing it, it's as if you never really saw a movie before: no movie has ever grabbed you, pummelled you, socked you on the button with the vitality, the accuracy, the impact, the professional aim, that this one does.

Esquire (Gilbert Seldes): Welles has shown Hollywood how to make movies. . . . He has made the movies young again, by filling them with life.

Cue (Jesse Zunser): It is an astounding experience to watch Orson Welles, 25-year-old Boy Genius of the Western World, in the process of creating on the screen one of the awesome products of her fertile imagination. You come away limp, much as if you had turned into Broadway and suddenly beheld Niagara Falls towering behind the Paramount Building, the Matterhorn looming over Bryant Park, and the Grand Canyon yawning down the middle of Times Square.

Hollywood Reporter: A great motion picture. . . . A few steps ahead of anything that has been made in pictures before.

Chicago Journal of Commerce (Claudia Cassidy): Anyone who has eyes in his head and ears to hear with will enjoy *Citizen Kane* for the unleashed power of its stature on the screen.

Even Kate Cameron, in the *Daily News*, gave it four stars, and on Sunday, May 4th, Bosley Crowther (though he had some second thoughts of his own) wrote in the *Times*, 'The returns are in from most of the local journalistic precincts and Orson Welles' *Citizen Kane* has been overwhelmingly selected as one of the great (if not the greatest) motion pictures of all time. . .' The *Film Daily* said, 'Welles can prepare his mantel for a couple of Oscars.'

XVI

Had it not been for the delays and the nervous atmosphere that made the picture *seem* unpopular and so *become* unpopular, it might have swept the Academy Awards. It had taken the New York Film Critics Award with ease, but early in 1942, when the 1941 Academy Awards were given, the picture had the aroma of box-office failure — an aroma that frightens off awards in Hollywood. The picture had been nominated in nine categories, and at the ceremony, each time the title or Orson Welles's name was read, there were hisses and loud boos. The prize for the Original Screenplay was perhaps partly a love gesture to Herman Mankiewicz, one of their own; the film community had closed ranks against Orson Welles.

While the picture was being shot, Welles, like a good showman, had done his best to preserve the element of surprise, and he had been smart about keeping a tight, closed set. He didn't want interference from anybody, and even though the R.K.O. executives had read the script, when one of them 'dropped in' once to see what was going on, Welles coolly called a halt in the shooting, and the Mercury players went outside and played baseball until he left. There were visitors, of course. Invitations to attend the first official day of shooting were sent to the press, and Welles was simply careful about what he shot that day. And the crew didn't go out to play baseball when Louella Parsons visited the set a few weeks later; they were just very careful, so that even though she had heard rumors that the picture was about Hearst, everything looked so innocent and Welles denied the rumors so disarmingly that she went on giving him an enthusiastic press. (She later described his outfoxing her on this occasion as 'one of the classic double crosses of Hollywood.') But

Mankiewicz with his 'Don't let this get around,' was practically incapable of keeping a secret. He was so proud of his script that he lent a copy to Charles Lederer. In some crazily naïve way, Mankiewicz seems to have imagined that Lederer would be pleased by how good it was. But Lederer, apparently, was deeply upset and took the script to his aunt and Hearst. It went from them to Hearst's lawyers (who marked various passages) before it was returned to Mankiewicz, and thus Hearst and his associates were alerted early to the content of the film. It was probably as a result of Mankiewicz's idiotic indiscretion that the various forces were set in motion that resulted in the cancellation of the première at the Radio City Music Hall, the commercial failure of *Citizen Kane*, and the subsequent failure of Orson Welles. This was how, even before the film was finished, Hearst's minions were in action, and how there was time for Mayer and his people to set about their attempt to suppress the film, and, having failed in that, to destroy it commercially.

In the aftermath of the pressures, and of the disappointing returns on the film, the members of the Academy could feel very courageous about the writing award. Mankiewicz had become a foolhardy hero in taking on Hearst; *Kane* was Mankiewicz's finest moment. They wanted him to have a prize; he deserved it and he needed it. Hollywood loves the luxury of show-business sentimentality, and Hollywood loves a comeback. The members of the Academy destroyed Orson Welles that night, but they probably felt good because their hearts had gone out to crazy, reckless Mank, their own resident loser-genius, the has-been who was washed up in the big studios, who was so far down he had been reduced to writing Welles's radio shows. At the beginning of the thirites, he had been earning $4,000 a week; at the end of the thirites, he was a ghost. What they couldn't know was that *Kane* was Welles's finest moment, too; the reason they couldn't know it was that their failure to back him that night was the turning point. Welles had made *Citizen Kane* at twenty-five, and he seemed to have the world before him. They'd had time to get used to Mank's self-destructiveness, and he'd been down on his luck so long he was easy to love; besides, they admired the pranks that had got him thrown out of one studio after another. Welles was self-destructive in a style they weren't yet accustomed to.

One may speculate that if the members of the Academy had supported Welles and voted *Citizen Kane* Best Picture of the Year, if they had backed the nation's press and their own honest judgment, the picture might have got into the big theatrical showcases despite the pressures against it. If they had, *Kane* might have made money, and things might have gone differently for Welles — and for American movies. The Academy had plenty of sentiment but not enough guts. And so Orson Welles peaked early. Later, as his situation changed and his fortunes sank and *Kane* became the golden opportunity of his youth, his one great chance of freedom to accomplish something, then, when he looked back, he may really have needed to believe what he was quoted as saying in France: 'Le seul film que j'aie jamais écrit du premier du dernier mot et pu mener à bien est *Citizen Kane*.' The literal translation is 'The only film that I ever wrote from first word to last and was able to bring to a successful issue is *Citizen Kane*,' but I think that what it means is 'The picture came out well.' What else can it mean when one considers the contributions of Mankiewicz and Toland and all the rest? Men cheated of their due are notoriously given to claiming more than their due. The Academy members had made their token gesture to *Citizen Kane* with the screenplay award. They failed what they believed in; they gave in to the scandal and to the business pressures. They couldn't yet know how much guilt they *should* feel: guilt that by their failure to support *Citizen Kane* at this crucial time — the last chance to make *Kane* a financial success — they had started the downward spiral of Orson Welles, who was to become perhaps the greatest loser in Hollywood history.

XVII

Like D.W. Griffith, Orson Welles came into the movies in order to make money so that he could continue in the theatre, and, like Griffith, he discovered that movies were the medium in which he could do what he had barely dreamed of doing in the theatre. Soon — even before he started on *Citizen Kane* — Welles was desperate for money to make movies. It took guile to get *Kane* approved. Robert Wise, whom the head of the R.K.O. editing department had assigned to the picture because he was close to Welles's age, says, 'Orson sneaked the project onto R.K.O. He told the studio that he was merely shooting tests.' Sets were built, and shooting began on June 29, 1940; the 'test shots' were fully produced. The Mercury actors and associates were there anyway, most of them under personal contract to Welles, as Mankiewicz was. But Dorothy Comingore, not a member of the Mercury Theatre but a Hollywood bit player (who,

as Linda Winters, had worked in Westerns and with the Three
Stooges and in Blondie and Charlie Chan pictures), says that she
lived on unemployment checks of $18 a week while she 'tested for
one month' for the role of Susan Alexander. She adds, 'All these
tests were incorporated into the film; they were never retaken.' After
a month, with the studio buzzing about how brilliant the footage was,
the movie was practically a *fait accompli*, and Welles was able to
bulldoze Schaefer into approving the project. All the people who
were already at work on *Citizen Kane* — the cameraman, the grips,
the composer, the assistants, and the actors — met at Herman
Mankiewicz's house for breakfast, and Welles announced that the
picture had been approved and could formally begin. They officially
started on July 30, 1940, and they finished 'principal photography'
eighty-two shooting days later, on October 23, 1940, even though
Welles — almost as accident-prone as Mankiewicz — broke his
ankle during the scene when he ran down the stairs from Susan's
room while yelling that he'd get Boss Gettys.

Yet it took more than guile to function in the motion-picture
business at that time. It helped to be mercenary, of course, but what
really counted then was not to care *too* much about your work. After
Citizen Kane, the contract that gave Welles the right of final cut was
cancelled, so he did not have control of *The Magnificent Ambersons*,
and it was shortened and mangled. The industry was suspicious of
him, and not just because of the scandal of *Kane*, and the general fear
of Hearst, and *Kane*'s unsatisfactory financial returns. Alva Johnston
described the Hollywood attitude toward Welles in an article in the
Saturday Evening Post in 1942, the year after *Kane* came out:

> Big agents soon lost interest in the boy genius. They learned that
> he wasn't interested in money. Welles became known as a
> dangerous Red because, when his first picture project was
> shelved after the studio had wasted a good deal of money on it,
> he offered to make another picture for nothing.
>
> Genius got a bad name on account of Welles. It was brought
> into complete disrepute by Saroyan. The gifted Armenian came
> to Hollywood with a small agent and insisted on working
> without a salary, leaving it to M-G-M to set a value on his
> services after his work was completed. He said, 'I'll trust the
> studio.' The $10,000,000-a-year agency business is wholly
> based on the motto 'Don't trust the studio.' Since the Welles and

Saroyan affairs, it has been practically impossible to interest a big agent in an intellectual giant.

When you write straight reporting about the motion-picture business, you're writing satire. Motion-picture executives prefer to do business with men whose values they understand. It's very easy for these executives — businessmen running an art — to begin to fancy that they are creative artists themselves, because they are indeed very much like the 'artists' who work for them, because the 'artists' who work for them are, or have become, businessmen. Those who aren't businessmen are the Hollywood unreliables — the ones whom, it is always explained to you, the studios can't hire, because they're crazy. As soon as movies became Welles's passion, and he was willing to work on any terms, he was finished in the big studios — they didn't trust him. And so, somehow, Welles aged before he matured — and not just physically. He went from child prodigy to defeated old man, though today, at fiftyfive, he is younger by a decade or two than most of the big American directors.

In later years, Welles, a brilliant talker, was to give many interviews, and as his power in the studios diminished, his role in past movies grew larger. Sometimes it seems that his only power is over the interviewers who believe him. He is a masterful subject. The new generation of film historians have their own version of 'Look, no hands': they tape-record interviews. Young interviewers, particularly, don't bother to check the statements of their subjects — they seem to regard that as outside their province — and thus leave the impression that the self-aggrandizing stories they record are history. And so, as the years go on, if one trusts what appears in print, Welles wrote not only *Kane* but just about everything halfway good in any picture he ever acted in, and in interviews he's beginning to have directed anything good in them, too. Directors are now the most interviewed group of people since the stars in the forties, and they have told the same stories so many times that not only they believe them, whether they're true or false, but everybody is beginning to.

The worship of the director is cyclical — Welles or Fellini is probably adored no more than von Stroheim or von Sternberg or De Mille was in his heyday — but such worship generally doesn't help in sorting out what went into the making of good pictures and bad pictures. The directors try to please the interviewers by telling them the anecdotes that have got a good response before. The anecdotes are sometimes charming and superficial, like the famous one — now taken for motion-picture history — about how Howard Hawks supposedly discovered that *The Front Page* would be better if a girl played the reporter Hildy, and thus transformed the play into *His Girl Friday* in 1940. ('I was going to prove to somebody that *The Front Page* had the finest modern dialogue that had been written, and I asked a girl to read Hildy's part and I read the editor, and I stopped and said, "Hell, it's better between a girl and a man than between two men." ') Now, a charming story is not nothing. Still, this is nothing but a charming and superficial story. *His Girl Friday* turned out joyously, but if such an accident did cause Hawks to see how easy it was to alter the play, he still must have done it rather cynically, in order to make it conform to the box-office patterns then current. By the mid-thirties — after the surprise success of *It Happened One Night* — the new independent, wisecracking girl was very popular, especially in a whole cycle of newspaper pictures with rival girl and boy reporters. Newspaper pictures were now 'romantic comedies,' and, just as the movies about lady fliers were almost all based on Amelia Earhart, the criminal-mouthpiece movies on William Fallon, and the gossip-column movies on Walter Winchell, the movies about girl reporters were almost all based on the most highly publicized girl reporter — Hearst's Adela Rogers St Johns. Everybody had already been stealing from and unofficially adapting *The Front Page* in the 'wacky' romantic newspaper comedies, and one of these rewrites, *Wedding Present*, in 1936 (by Adela Rogers St Johns's then son-in-law Paul Gallico), had tough editor (Cary Grant) and smart girl reporter (Joan Bennett) with square fiancé (Conrad Nagel). This was the mold that *The Front Page* was then squeezed into to become *His Girl Friday*, with Cary Grant, Rosalind Russell, and Ralph Bellamy (already a favorite square from *The Awful Truth*) in the same roles, and Rosalind Russell was so obviously playing Adela Rogers St Johns that she was dressed in an imitation of the St Johns girl-reporter striped suit.

Some things that students now, seeing films out of the context of the cycles they were part of, may take to be brilliant inventions were fairly standard; in fact, the public at the time was so familiar with the conventions of the popular comedies that the clichés were frequently spoofed within the pictures. But today, because of the problems peculiar to writing the history of modern mass-art forms, and because of the jumbled circumstances in which movies survive, with knowledge of them acquired in haphazard fashion from television, and from screenings here and there, film enthusiasts find it simpler to explain movies in terms of the genius-artist-director, the school-book hero — the man who did it all. Those who admire *Citizen Kane*, which is constructed to present different perspectives on a man's life, seem naïvely willing to accept Welles's view of its making; namely, that it is his sole creation.

Howard Hawks must wonder what the admiration of the young is worth when he learns from them that he invented overlapping dialogue in *His Girl Friday*, since it means that they have never bothered to look at the text of the original Hecht and MacArthur play. Welles, too, has been said to have invented overlapping dialogue, and just about everything else in *Kane*. But unearned praise is insulting, and a burden; Welles sometimes says, 'I drag my myth around with me.' His true achievements are heavy enough to weigh him down. Welles is a great figure in motion-picture history: he directed what is almost universally acclaimed as the greatest American film of the sound era; he might have become the greatest all-around American director of that era; and in his inability to realize all his artistic potentialities he is the greatest symbolic figure in American film history since Griffith.

XVIII

In the past few years, I have heard two famous 'artist' directors, after showings of their early films, explain how it happened that in the screen credits there was someone else listed for the script. It seems there was this poor guy on the lot who needed a credit desperately, and the company asked the director if he'd give the stumblebum a break; the incompetent turned in some material, but the director couldn't use any of it. Some listeners must swallow this, because in the latest incense-burning book on Josef von Sternberg the screen credits are simply ignored, and he, rather than Ben Hecht, is listed as the author of *Underworld*. Herman J. Mankiewicz has been similarly dropped from one film after another. The directors' generosity to those poor credit-hungry guys seems to have cutoff points in time (the directors' creative roles get bigger when the writers are dead) and in space (when the directors are interviewed abroad). Orson Welles, however, didn't need time or distance; he omitted any mention of his writer right from the start. (This custom is now being followed by many directors.) In later years, when he has been specifically asked by interviewers whether Mankiewicz wrote the scenario for *Citizen Kane*, he has had a set reply. 'Everything concerning Rosebud belongs to him,' he has said. Rosebud is what was most frequently criticized in the movie, and Gilbert Seldes, in one of the most solid and intelligent reviews of *Kane* (in *Esquire*), called it 'a phony' and 'the only bit of stale stuff in the picture.' Welles himself has said, 'The Rosebud gimmick is what I like least about the movie. It's a gimmick, really, and rather dollar-book Freud.'

Welles may have been goaded into malice; he had probably never come up against a man so well equipped to deal with him as Mankiewicz. Welles, who used to tell stories about how when he was seventeen he became a *torero* in Seville and entered several *corridas* and was billed on the posters as 'The American,' may have got a few welts, starting with Mankiewicz's original title — *American*. When Welles read the script, he must certainly have recognized what he was caught in. There's no doubt that Welles — the fabulous Orson Welles — wasn't accustomed to sharing credit. However, his persistent lack of generosity toward Mankiewicz started at the time the movie came out, and it may have its basis in a very specific grievance. Mankiewicz may have outsmarted Welles on the credits more than once. Nunnally Johnson says that while *Citizen Kane* was being shot, Mankiewicz told him that he had received an offer of a ten-thousand-dollar bonus from Welles (through Welles's 'chums') to hold to the original understanding and keep his name off the picture. Mankiewicz said that Welles had been brooding over the credits, that he could see how beautiful they would be: 'Produced by Orson Welles. Directed by Orson Welles. Starring Orson Welles.' It was perfect until he got to 'Herman J. Mankiewicz' in the writing credit, which spoiled everything. Mankiewicz said he was tempted by Welles's offer. As usual, he needed money, and, besides, he was fearful of what would happen when the picture came out — he might be blackballed forever. William Randolph Hearst, like Stalin, was known to be fairly Byzantine in his punishments. At the same time, Mankiewicz knew that *Citizen Kane* was his best work, and he was proud of it. He told Johnson that he went to Ben Hecht with his dilemma, and that Hecht, as prompt with advice as with scripts, said, 'Take the ten grand and double-cross the son of a bitch.'

I asked Nunnally Johnson if he thought Mankiewicz's story was true, and Mankiewicz actually had got the offer and had taken Hecht's advice. Johnson replied, 'I like to believe he did.' It's not unlikely. Mankiewicz wrote the first draft in about three months and tightened and polished it into the final shooting script of *Citizen Kane* in a few more weeks, and he probably didn't get more than eight or nine thousand dollars for the whole job; according to the costs sheets for the movie, the screenplay cost was $34,195.24, which wasn't much, even for that day, and the figure probably includes the salary and expenses of John Houseman and the others at Victorville. Mankiewicz may easily have felt he deserved an extra ten thousand. 'An Irish bum,' Johnson calls him — and if that makes him sound lovable, the operative word is still 'bum.' If Mankiewicz made up the story he told Johnson — and he was probably capable of such juicy slander — this kind of invention may be a clue to why Welles tries to turn the credit into blame. And if Mankiewicz did get the offer, did take the money, and did double-cross Welles, this might equally well explain why Welles doesn't want Mankiewicz to get any honor.

But Welles needed Mankiewicz. Since sound came in, almost every time an actor has scored in a role and become a 'star,' it has been because the role provided a realistic base for contradictory elements. Welles has never been able to write this kind of vehicle for himself. *Kane* may be a study of egotism and a movie about money and love, but it isn't just another movie about a rich man who isn't loved; it's a scandalously unauthorized, muckraking biography of a man who was still alive and — though past his peak influence — still powerful, so it conveyed shock and danger, and it drew its strength from its reverberations in the life of the period. Mankiewicz brought to the film the force of journalism. The thirties had been full of movie biographies of tycoons and robber barons, and some, like *The Power and the Glory*, were complexly told, but even Preston Sturges, as if in awe of the material, had taken a solemn, almost lachrymose approach to the money-doesn't-bring-happiness theme. Mankiewicz did it better: the prismatic technique turned into a masterly juggling act. There's an almost palpable sense of enjoyment in the script itself; Mankiewicz was skillful at making his points through comedy, and frequently it's higher, blacker comedy than was customary in the thirties pictures. Welles is a different kind of writer — theatrical and Gothic, not journalistic, and not *organized*. His later thrillers are portentous, sensational in a void, entertaining thrillers, often, but *mere* thrillers.

Lacking the realistic base and the beautifully engineered structure that Mankiewicz provided, Welles has never again been able to release that charming, wicked rapport with the audience that he brought to *Kane* both as actor and as director (or has been able to release it only in distorted form, in self-satire and self-humiliation). He has brought many qualities to film — and there was perhaps a new, mellowed vitality in his work in the flawed *Falstaff* of a few years ago — but he has brought no more great original characters. In his movies, he can create an atmosphere but not a base. And without that the spirit that makes Kane so likeable a bastard is missing. Kane, that mass of living contradictions, was conceived by Mankiewicz, an atheist who was proud of his kosher home, a man who was ambivalent about *both* Hearst and Welles.

However, things that get printed often enough begin to seep into the general consciousness of the past, so there is a widespread impression that Welles wrote *Citizen Kane*. And even if one hadn't heard that he wrote it, and despite the presence in the film of so many elements and interests that are unreleated to Welles's other work (mundane activities and social content are not his forte), Kane and Welles are identified in our minds. This is not only a tribute to Welles as an actor but a backhanded tribute to Mankiewicz who wrote the role for Welles the actor and wrote Welles the capricious, talented, domineering prodigy into the role, combining Welles's personality and character traits with Hearst's life in publishing and politics and acquisition.

If one asks how it is that Herman J. Mankiewicz, who wrote the film that many people think is the greatest film they've ever seen, is almost unknown, the answer must surely be not just that he died too soon but that he outsmarted himself. As a result of his wicked sense of humor in drawing upon Welles's character for Kane's, his own authorship was obscured. Sensing the unity of Kane and Welles, audiences assume that Kane is Welles's creation, that Welles is playing 'the role he was born to play,' while film scholars, seeing the material from Welles's life in the movie, interpret the film as Welles working out autobiographical themes. It is commonplace in theatre talk to say that Olivier *is* Archie Rice or Olivier *is* Macbeth without assuming that the actor has conceived the role, but in movies we don't see other actors in the same role (except in remakes, which are usually very different in style), and film is so vivid and the actor so large and so close that it is a common primitive response to assume that the actor invented his lines. In this case, the primitive response is combined with the circumstances that Welles's name had been heavily featured for years, that the role was a new creation, that the movie audience's image of Welles was set by this overpowering role, in which they saw him for the first time, and that not only was the role partly based on him but he began to live up to it. Herman Mankiewicz died, and his share faded from knowledge, but Welles carries on in a baronial style that always reminds us of Kane. Kane seems an emanation of Welles, and if Mankiewicz didn't take the ten thousand, he might just as well have, because he helped stamp Welles all over the film.

XIX

James Agee, who didn't begin reviewing until later in 1941, wrote several years afterward that Welles had been 'fatuously overrated as a "genius," ' and that he himself, annoyed by all the talk, had for a while underrated him. At the time the film was released, the most perceptive movie critic in the United States was Otis Ferguson (an early volunteer and early casualty in the Second World War), on *The New Republic*. Ferguson saw more clearly than anybody else what was specifically good and bad in *Kane*, and though he was wrong, I think, in maintaining that unobtrusive technique is the only good technique, he did perceive that *Citizen Kane* challenged this concept.

One of the games that film students sometimes play is to judge a director on whether you have the illusion that the people on the screen will go on doing what they're doing after the camera leaves them. Directors are rated by how much time you think elapsed before the actors grabbed their coats or ordered a sandwich. The longer the time, the more of a film man the director is said to be; when a director is stage-oriented, you can practically see the actors walking off the set. This game doesn't help in judging a film's content, but it's a fairly reliable test of a director's film technique; one could call it a test of movie believability. However, it isn't applicable to *Citizen Kane*. You're perfectly well aware that the people won't go on doing what they're doing — that they have, indeed, completed their actions on the screen. *Kane* depends not on naturalistic believability but on our enjoyment of the very fact that those actions *are* completed, and that they all fit into place. This bravura is, I think, the picture's only true originality, and it wasn't an intentional challenge to the concept of unobtrusive technique but was (mainly) the result of Welles's discovery of — and his delight in — the fun of making movies.

The best American directors in the thirties had been developing an unpretentious American naturalism; modern subjects and the advent of sound had freed them from the heavy dead hand of Germanic stage lighting and design. And so Ferguson was dismayed to see this all come back, and it *was* depressing that the critics who had always fallen for the synthetic serious were bowing and scraping and calling the picture 'deep' and 'realistic.' Probably so many people called it realistic because the social satire made contact with what they felt about Hearst and the country; when they used the term, they were referring to the content rather than the style. But it was the 'retrogressive' style that upset Ferguson — because it was when Orson Welles, an 'artist' director, joined the toughness and cynicism and the verbal skills of the thirties to that incomparable, faintly absurd, wonderfully overblown style of his that people said 'art.' Where Ferguson went wrong was in not recognizing one crucial element: that the unconcealed — even flaunted — pleasure that Welles took in all that claptrap made it new.

And it has kept it new. Even a number of those who worked on *Kane*, such as Houseman and Dorothy Gomingore, have observed that the film seems to improve with the years. At the time, I got more simple, frivolous pleasure from Preston Sturges's *The Lady Eve*, which had come out a few months earlier, and I found more excitement in John Huston's *The Maltese Falcon*, which came out a few months later. At the time (I was twenty-one), I enjoyed *Kane* for the performances and the wit, but I was very conscious of how shallow the iconoclasm was. I don't think I was wrong, exactly, but now the movie seems marvellous to me. It's an *exuberant* shallow iconoclasm, and that youthful zest for shock and for the Expressionist theatricality seems to transform the shallowness. Now the movie sums up and preserves a period, and the youthful iconoclasm is preserved in all its freshness — even the freshness of its callowness. Now that the political theme (in its specific form, that is) is part of the past, the naïveté and obviousness fade, and what remains is a great American archetype and a popular legend — and so it has a strength that makes the artificially created comic world of a movie like *The Lady Eve* disappear by comparison. *Citizen Kane* has such energy it drives the viewer along. Though Mankiewicz provided the basic apparatus for it, that magical exuberance which fused the whole scandalous enterprise was Welles's. Works of art are enjoyed for different reasons in different periods; it may even be one of the defining characteristics of a lasting work of art that it yields up different qualities for admiration at different times. Welles's 'magic,' his extraordinary pleasure in playacting and illusion and in impressing an audience — what seems so charming about the movie now — was what seemed silly to me then. It was bouncy Pop Gothic in a period when the term 'comic strip' applied to works of art was still a term of abuse. Now Welles's discovery of movie-making — and the boyishness and excitement of that discovery — is preserved in *Kane* the way the snow scene is preserved in the glass ball.

Seeing the movie again recently, I liked the way it looked; now that the style no longer boded a return to the aestheticism of sets and the rigidly arranged figures of the German silents, I could enjoy it without misgivings. In the thirties, Jean Renoir had been using deep focus (that is, keeping the middle range and the background as clear as the foreground) in a naturalistic way. The light seemed (and often was) 'natural.' You looked at a scene, and the drama that you saw going on in it was just part of that scene, and so you had the sense of discovering it for yourself, of seeing drama in the midst of life. This was a tremendous relief from the usual studio lighting, which forced your attention to the dramatic action in the frame, blurred the rest, and rarely gave you a chance to feel that the action was part of anything larger or anything continuous. In Welles's far more extreme use of deep focus, and in his arrangement of the actors in the compositions, he swung back to the most coercive use of artificial, theatrical lighting. He used light like a spotlight on the stage, darkening or blacking out the irrelevant. He used deep focus not for a naturalistic effect but for the startling dramatic effect of having crucial action going on in the background (as when Kane appears in a distant doorway). The difference between Renoir's style and Welles's style seems almost literally the difference between day and night. Welles didn't have (nor did he, at that time, need) the kind of freedom Renoir needed and couldn't get in Hollywood — the freedom to shoot outside the studio and to depart from the script and improvise. *Kane* is a studio-made film — much of it was shot in that large room at R.K.O. where, a few years earlier, Ginger Rogers and Fred Astaire had danced their big numbers. However, Welles had the freedom to try out new solutions to technical problems, and he made his theatrical technique work spectacularly. Probably it was the first time in American movies that Expressionism had ever worked for comic and satiric effects (except in bits of some of the early spoof horror films), and probably it would have been impossible to tell the *Kane* story another way without spending a fortune on crowds and set construction. Welles's method is a triumph of ingenuity in that the pinpoints of light in the darkness conceal the absence of detailed sets (a chair or two and a huge fireplace, and one thinks one is seeing a great room), and the almost treacherously brilliant use of sound conceals the absence of crowds. We see Susan at the *deserted* cabaret; we see her from the back on the opera-house stage and we imagine that she is facing an audience; we get a sense of crowds at the political rally without seeing them. It was Welles's experience both in the theatre and in radio that enabled him to produce a huge historical film on a shoestring; he produced the *illusion* of a huge historical film.

But, seeing *Kane* now, I winced, as I did the first time, at the empty virtuosity of the shot near the beginning when Kane, dying, drops the glass ball and we see the nurse's entrance reflected in the glass. I noticed once again, though without being bothered by it this time, either, that there was no one in the room to hear the dying Kane say 'Rosebud.' I was much more disturbed by little picky defects, like the obtrusive shot up to the bridge before the reporter goes into the hospital. What is strange about reseeing a movie that one reacted to fairly intensely many years ago is that one may respond exactly the same way to so many details and *be aware* each time of having responded that way before. I was disappointed once again by the clumsily staged 'cute' meeting of Kane and Susan, which seemed to belong to a routine comedy, and I thought the early scenes with Susan were weak not just because while listening to her dull, sentimental singing Welles is in a passive position and so can't animate the scenes but — and mainly — because the man of simple pleasures who would find a dumb girl deeply appealing does not tie in with the personality projected by Orson Welles. (And as Welles doesn't project any sexual interest in either Kane's first wife, Emily, or in Susan, his second wife, we don't know how to interpret Susan's claim that he just likes her voice.) Most of the newspaper-office scenes looked as clumsily staged as ever, and the first appearance of Bernstein, Kane's business manager, arriving with a load of furniture, was still confusing. (He seems to be a junk dealer — probably because an earlier scene in *American* introducing him was eliminated.) I disliked again the attempt to wring humor out of the sputtering confusion of Carter, the old Dickensian editor. It's a scene like the ones Mankiewicz helped prepare for the Marx Brothers, but what was probably intended to make fun of a stuffed shirt turned into making fun of a helpless old man trying to keep his dignity, which is mean and barbarous. I still thought Susan became too thin a conception, and more shrill and shrewish than necessary, and, as Emily, Ruth Warrick was all pursed lips — a stereotype of refinement. I was still uncomfortable during the visit to Jed Leland in the hospital; Leland's character throughout is dependent on Joseph Cotten's obvious charm, and the sentimental-old-codger bit in this sequence is really a disgrace. The sequence plays all too well at a low conventional level — pulling out easy stops. I still didn't see the function of the sequence about Kane's being broke and losing control of his empire, since nothing followed from it. (I subsequently discovered that things weren't going well on the set at one point, and Welles decided to go back to this scene, which had been in an earlier draft and had then been eliminated. What it coordinated with was, unfortunately, not restored.) This sequence also has the most grating, bad line in the movie, when Kane says, 'You know, Mr Bernstein, if I hadn't been very rich, I might have been a really great man.'

What's still surprising is how well a novice movie director handled so many of the standard thirties tricks and caricatures — the device of the alternative newspaper headlines, for example, and the stock explosive, handwaving Italian opera coach (well played by Fortunio Bonanova). The engineering — the way the sequences are prepared for and commented on by preceding sequences, the way the five accounts tie together to tell the story — seems as ingenious as ever; though one is aware that the narrators are telling things they couldn't have witnessed, one accepts this as part of the convention. The cutting (which a reading of the script reveals to have been carried out almost exactly as it was planned) is elegantly precise, and some sequences have a good, sphomoric musical-comedy buoyancy.

What had changed for me — what I had once enjoyed but now found almost mysteriously *beautiful* — was Orson Welles's performance. An additional quality that old movies acquire is that people can be seen as they once were. It is a pleasure we can't get in theatre; we can only hear and read descriptions of past fabulous performances. But here in *Kane* is the young Welles, and he seems almost embarrassed to be exposed as so young. Perhaps he *was* embarrassed, and that's why he so often hid in extravagant roles and behind those old-man false faces. He seems unsure of himself as the young Kane, and there's something very engaging (and surprisingly *human*) about Welles unsure of himself; he's a big, overgrown, heavy boy, and rather sheepish, one suspects, at being seen as he is. Many years later, Welles remarked, 'Like most performers, I naturally prefer a live audience to that lie-detector full of celluloid.' Maybe his spoiled-baby face was just too nearly perfect for the role, and he knew it, and knew the hostile humor that lay behind Mankiewicz's putting so much of him in the role of Hearst the braggart self-publicist and making Kane so infantile. That statement of principles that Jed sends back to Kane and that Kane then tears up must surely refer to the principles behind the co-founding of the Mercury Theatre by Welles and Houseman. Lines like Susan's 'You're not a professional magician are you?' may have made Welles flinch. And it wasn't just the writer who played games on him. There's the scene of Welles eating in the newspaper office, which was obviously caught by the camera crew, and which, to be 'a good sport,' he had to use. Welles is one of the most self-conscious of actors — it's part of his rapport with the audience — and this is what is so nakedly revealed in this role, in which he's playing a young man his own age and he's insecure (and with some reason) about what's coming through. Something of the young, unmasked man is revealed in these scenes — to be closed off forever after.

Welles picks up assurance and flair as Kane in his thirties, and he's also good when Kane is just a little older and jowly. I think there's no doubt that he's more sure of himself when he's playing this somewhat older Kane, and this is the Kane we remember best from the first viewing — the brash, confident Kane of the pre-election-disaster period. He's so fully — classically — American a showoff one almost regrets the change of title. But when I saw the movie again it was the younger Kane who stayed with me — as if I had been looking through a photograph album and had come upon a group of pictures of an old friend, long dead, as he had been when I first met him. I had almost forgotten Welles in his youth, and here he is, smiling, eager, looking forward to the magnificent career that everyone exepcted him to have.

XX

Just as Welles suggested the radio-bulletin approach to the H.G. Wells landing-of-the-Martians material to Howard Koch, he may very well have suggested the 'March of Time' summary of Hearst's career in his early talks with Mankiewicz. Welles had worked as an actor for the 'March of Time' radio program in 1934 and 1935, and he had worked steadily as a narrator and radio actor (his most famous role was the lead in the popular weekly mystery show 'The Shadow') until he went to Hollywood. The 'March of Time' is exactly the kind of idea the young Welles *would* have suggested. It's the sort of technique that was being used in the experimental theatre of the late thirties — when the Federal Theatre Project (in which

Welles and Houseman had worked together) staged the documentary series 'The Living Newspaper,' and when members of the Group Theatre and other actors were performing anti-Fascist political cabaret. The imitation 'March of Time' was not a new device, even in movies; it had already been used, though humorlessly, to convey the fact that a theme was current, part of 'today's news,' and to provide background information — as in *Confessions of a Nazi Spy*, of 1939. What was needed to transform that device and make it the basis for the memorable parody in *Citizen Kane* was not only Welles's experience and not only his 'touch' but the great sense of mischief that he and Mankiewicz shared. The smug manner of the 'March of Time' was already a joke to many people; when I was a student at Berkeley in the late thirties, there was always laughter in the theatres when the 'March of Time' came on, with its racy neo-conservatism and its ritual pomposity — with that impersonal tone, as if God above were narrating. There was an element of unconscious self-parody in the important tone of the 'March of Time,' as in all the Luce enterprises, and, in his script, Mankiewicz pushed it further. He used consciously those elements which part of the public already found funny, bringing into a mass medium what was already a subject for satire among the knowledgeable.

Mankiewicz's 'On Approaching Forty' had not appeared in *The New Yorker*, but a few weeks after it was printed in 1936, Wolcott Gibbs, who was to take Mankiewicz's old chair as *The New Yorker* drama critic (and who was the first occupant of that chair not to emigrate to Hollywood), published the celebrated Profile 'Time — Fortune — Life — Luce,' which was written in mock Timese ('Backward ran sentences until reeled the mind,' and so on, concluding with 'Where it all will end, knows God!'), and this was probably not merely the spur to Mankiewicz but the competition. Mankiewicz's pastiche was fully worked out in the first long draft of the script, the processed prose and epigrams already honed to perfection ('For forty years appeared in Kane newsprint no public issue on which Kane papers took no stand. No public man whom Kane himself did not support or denounce — often support, then denounce'). And even on paper — without Welles's realization of the plan — the section is good enough to invite the comparison that I suspect Mankiewicz sought with the Gibbs parody. (Mankiewicz's widow keeps the Oscar statuette for *Citizen Kane* on the mantel, along with the latest *Who's Who in America* with the marker set at her sons' listings, and on the shelf next to the mantel are the bound volumes of *The New Yorker* in which her husband's reviews appeared.)

Part of the fun of the 'March of Time' parody for the audiences back in 1941 was that, of course, we kept *recognizing* things about Hearst in it, and its daring meant great suspense about what was to follow in the picture. But Mankiewicz tried to do more with this parody than is completely evident either in the final script or in the film itself. He tried to use the 'March of Time' as a historical framing device to close one era and open the next, with Hearstian journalism giving way to the new Luce empire. In the movie, it seems a structural gimmick — though a very cleverly *used* gimmick, which is enjoyable in itself. In Mankiewicz's original conception, in the long first-draft *American*, which ran three hundred and twenty-five pages, that device is more clearly integral to the theme. In Mankiewicz's conception, the Hearst-Kane empire is doomed: Kane's own death is being 'sent' to the world by the filmed 'March of Time' (called 'News on the March' in the movie), which means the end of the newspaper business as Hearst knew it. The funny thing is that Mankiewicz, in commenting on Hearst's lack of vision, overestimated Luce's vision. After Luce took news coverage from newspapers into newsmagazines, he moved into photo-journalism and then into news documentaries, but he didn't follow through on what he had started, and he failed to get into television production. Now, after *his* death, the Luce organization is trying to get back into film activities.

In Mankiewicz's original conception, the historical line of succession was laid out as in a chronicle play. Hearst supplanted the old-style quiet upper-class journalism with his penny-dreadful treatment of crime and sex and disasters, his attacks on the rich, his phony lawsuits against the big corporations that he called 'predators,' his screaming patriotism, his faked photographs, and his exploitation of superstition, plus puzzles, comics, contests, sheet music, and medical quackery. His youthful dedication to the cause of the common people declined into the cheap chauvinism that infected everything and helped to turn the readers into a political mob. The irony built into the structure was that his own demise should be treated in the new, lofty style of Luce.

And it was in terms of this framework that the elements of admiration in the ambivalent portrait of Kane made sense. Hearst represented a colorful kind of journalism that was already going out. Mankiewicz was summing up the era of *The Front Page* at the end of it, and was treating it right at its source in the American system that made it possible for a rich boy to inherit the power to control public opinion as his own personal plaything. *American* (and, to a lesser degree, *Citizen Kane*) was a there-were-giants-in-those-days valedictory to the old-style big scoundrels. The word had been used straight by Mrs Fremont Older in 1936 when she published the authorized biography, *William Randolph Hearst, American*. 'American' was Hearst's shibboleth; his Sunday magazine section was the *American Weekly*, and he had been changing his newspaper titles to include the word 'American' whenever possible ever since Senator Henry Cabot Lodge accused him of being un-American in those days after the McKinley assassination when Hearst was hanged in effigy. Hearst's attacks on McKinley as 'the most despised and hated creature in the hemisphere' had culminated in an editorial that said 'Killing must be done' shortly before it was. When the storm died down, Hearst became super-American. For Mankiewicz, Hearst's Americanism was the refuge of a scoundrel, though by no means his last refuge; *that*, in the first draft, was clearly blackmail. What the title was meant to signify was indicated by Kane in the 'News on the March' segment when he said, 'I am, have been, and will be only one thing — an American.' That was pure flag-waving Pop before we had a name for it: 'American' as it was used by the American Legion and the Daughters of the American Revolution. In addition, Mankiewicz may have wanted to score off his movie friends who since the middle thirties — the period of the Popular Front — had also been draping themselves in the flag. In that period, the Communist left had become insistent about its Americanism, in its rather embarrassing effort to tout American democracy, which it had called 'imperialism' until the U.S.S.R. sought the United States as an ally against Hitler. In the later title, 'Citizen' is similarly ironic: Hearst, the offspring of an economic baron, and himself a press lord and the master of San Simeon, was a 'citizen' the way Louis XIV at Versailles was a citizen. And joining the word to 'Kane' (Cain) made its own point.

Both the parodistic use of Timese and the facelessness of Luce's company men served a historical purpose in the first script. But *American* was much too long and inclusive and loose, and much too ambitious, and Mankiewicz rapidly cut it down (copies of these gradually shorter drafts were saved) until it reached the hundred and fifty-six pages of the final shooting script — which still made for a then unusually long picture, of a hundred and nineteen minutes. In the trimming, dialogue that was crucial to the original dramatic conception of the Hearst–Luce succession was cut. (In terms of the final conception, though, it's perfectly clear why.) This deleted exchange between Thompson, the investigating reporter for the Rawlston (Luce) organization, and Raymond, Kane's butler, makes the point about the line of succession from Hearst to Luce all too explicit:

THOMPSON: Well, if you get around to your memoirs — don't forget, Mr Rawlston wants to be sure of getting first chance. We pay awful well for long excerpts.
RAYMOND: Maybe he'd like to buy the excerpts of what Mr Kane said about him.
THOMPSON: Huh?
RAYMOND: He thought Rawlston would break his neck sooner or later. He gave that weekly magazine of yours three years.
THOMPSOM: (*Smugly*) He made a bit of a mistake.
RAYMOND: He made a lot of mistakes.

Welles, who did such memorable casting in the rest of the movie, used a number of his own faceless executive assistants in the vapid roles of the Luce men. They are the performers in *Citizen Kane* that nobody remembers, and they didn't go on to become actors. William Alland, whose voice was fine as the voice of 'News on the March' but who was a vacuum as Thompson, the reporter, became a producer and investment broker; another of Welles's assistants, Richard Wilson, who also played a reporter, is now a director (*Three in the Attic*); still another, Richard Barr, is the well-known New York theatrical producer. Among the 'News on the March' men, there were some bit players who did have potential faces (Alan Ladd was one of them), but they weren't presented as personalities. Nevertheless, in a movie as verbally explicit as *Citizen Kane* the faceless idea doesn't really come across. You probably don't get the intention behind it in *Kane* unless you start thinking about the unusual feebleness of the scenes with the 'News on the March' people and about the fact that though Thompson is a principal in the movie in terms of how much he appears, there isn't a shred of characterization in his lines or in his performance; he is such a shadowy presence that you may even have a hard time remembering whether you ever saw his face, though this movie introduced to the screen a large group of performers who made strong, astonishing distinct impressions, sometimes in very brief roles. Perhaps the acting and the group movement of the faceless men needed to be more stylized, the dialogue more satirical; as it was done, it's just dull rather than purposefully blank. Welles probably thought it didn't matter how bad these actors were, because they should be colorless anyway; after R.K.O. gave him the go-ahead on the project, he didn't reshoot the test scene he had made of the projection-room sequence. But the movie misses on the attitudes *behind* Luce's new journalism. It's true that for the practitioners of Timese impersonality becomes their personal style and reporters become bureaucrats, but there's also a particular aura of programmed self-importance and of awareness of power — the ambitiousness of colorless people.

Among the minor absurdities of the script is that the 'News on the March' men never think of sending a cameraman along with the inquiring reporter, though Gable had just played a newsreel camera-man in *Too Hot to Handle*, in 1938, and though in *The Philadelphia Story*, which had opened on Broadway in 1939, and which Mankiewicz's brother Joe produced for the screen in 1940, while *Kane* was being shot, the magazine team, also obviously from Luce, includes a photographer. There's something rather pathetic — al-most as if *Kane* were a Grade B movie that didn't have a big enough budget for a few extra players — about that one lonely sleuthing reporter travelling around the country while a big organization de-lays the release of an important newsreel documentary on the head of a rival news chain. Maybe Mankiewicz, despite his attempt to place Hearst historically through the 'March of Time' framework, still thought in terms of the older journalism and of all the gimmicky movies about detective-reporters. And Mankiewicz was by tempera-ment a reckless, colorful newspaperman. That deleted material about the Luce organization's wanting Raymond's memoirs, with Raymond's teaser 'He made a lot of mistakes,' is part of an elaborate series of scandalous subplots, closely paralleling scandals in Hearst's life, that were cut out in the final script. In the movie, Susan says to Thompson, 'Look, if you're smart, you'll get in touch with Raymond. He's the butler. You'll learn a lot from him. He knows where all the bodies are buried.' It's an odd, cryptic speech. In the first draft, Raymond *literally* knew where the bodies were buried: Mankiewicz had dished up a nasty version of the scandal sometimes referred to as the Strange Death of Thomas Ince. Even with this kind of material cut down to the barest allusions, Mankiewicz, in *Citizen Kane*, treated the material of Hearst's life in Hearstian yellow-journalism style.

XXI

Welles is right, of course, about Rosebud — it *is* dollar-book Freud. But it is such a primitive kind of Freudianism that, like some of the movie derivations from Freud later in the forties — in *The Seventh Veil*, for instance — it hardly seems Freudian at all now. Looking for 'the secret' of a famous man's last words is about as phony as the blind-beggar-for-luck bit, yet it does 'work' for some poeple; they go for the idea that Rosebud represents lost maternal bliss and somehow symbolizes Kane's loss of the power to love or be loved. The one significant change from Hearst's life — Kane's separation from his parents — seems to be used to explain Kane, though there is an explicit disavowal of any such intention toward the end. Someone says to Thompson, 'If you could have found out what Rosebud meant, I bet that would've explained everything.' Thompson replies, 'No, I don't think so. No. Mr Kane was a man who got everything he wanted, and then lost it. Maybe Rosebud was something he couldn't get or something he lost. Anyway, it wouldn't have explained anything. I don't think any word can explain a man's life. No. I guess Rosebud is just a piece in a jigsaw puzzle, a missing piece.'

Nevertheless, the structure of the picture — searching for the solution to a mystery — and the exaggerated style make it appear that Rosebud *is* the key to Kane's life, and the public responds to what is presented dramatically, not to the reservations of the moviemakers. Rosebud has become part of popular culture, and people remember it who have forgotten just about everything else in *Citizen Kane*; the jokes started a week before the movie opened, with a child's sled marked 'Rosebud' dragged onstage in the first act of *Native Son*, and a couple of years ago, in *Peanuts*, Snoopy walked in the snow pulling a sled and Charlie Brown said, 'Rosebud?' The Rosebud of Rosebud is as banal as Rosebud itself. It seems that as a child Herman Mankiewicz had had a sled, which may or may not have carried the label 'Rosebud' (his family doesn't remember); he was dramatically parted from the sled, but he once had a bicycle that was stolen, and he mourned that all his life. He simply put the emotion of the one onto the other.

Though Rosebud was in the long first draft, it didn't carry the same weight there, because the newspaper business itself undermined Kane's idealism. In that draft, Kane, like Hearst, in order to reach the masses he thought he wanted to serve and protect, built circulation by turning the newspapers into pulp magazines, and, in order to stay in business and expand, squeezed nonadvertisers. The long script went as far as to show that, in the process of becoming one of the mighty, Kane–Hearst, like Louis B. Mayer and so many other tycoons, developed close ties to the underworld. Mankiewicz was trying to give a comprehensive view of the contradictions that emerge when an idealist attempts to succeed in business and politics. Fragments of this are left, but their meaning is no longer clear. For example, the point of the sequence of Kane's buying up the staff of the *Chronicle*, the paper that was outselling his *Inquirer* by featuring crime and sex, was that the *Chronicle*'s staff would change him by deflecting him from an idealistic course (and Jed tries to point this out to Bernstein), but as it appears in the film it almost seems that in buying the *Chronicle*'s staff Kane is corrupting *them*.

It is just a fragment, too, that Kane's first wife, Emily, is the niece of the President of the United States. Hearst's only wife, Millicent, the daughter of a vaudeville hoofer, was a teen-age member of a group called The Merry Maidens when he met her. Emily was probably made the niece of the President in order to link Kane with the rich and to make a breach in the marriage when Kane was held responsible for the assassination of the President (as Hearst was accused of having incited the death of President McKinley).

In the condensation, the whole direction was, for commercial reasons, away from the newspaper business that dominated the early script, and, for obvious reasons, away from factual resemblances to Hearst's life. This was generally accomplished by making things funny. For example, Hearst had actually been cheated out of the office of mayor of New York by fraud at the polls, and this incident was included in *American*. In *Citizen Kane* it became, instead, a joke: when Kane loses the election for governor, the Kane papers automatically claim 'FRAUD AT POLLS.' This version is, of course, a quick way of dramatizing the spirit of yellow journalism, and it's useful and comic, but the tendency of this change, as of many others, was, whether deliberately or unconsciously, to make things easier for the audience by playing down material on how wealth and the power it buys can also buy the love of the voters. Hearst (the son of a senator whose money had got him into the Senate) did buy his way into public office; as a young man, he was twice elected to Congress, and he had tried to get the Democratic nomination for President just before he decided to run for mayor of New York. The movie flatters the audience by saying that Kane couldn't buy the people's love — that he 'was never granted elective office by the voters of his country.'

Actually, it wasn't the voters but crooked politicians who defeated Hearst. When the Tammany boss Charles F. Murphy refused to help Hearst get the Democratic nomination for mayor, he ran as an independent, campaigning against the corrupt Tammany 'boodlers,' and he printed a cartoon of Murphy in prison stripes. Kane gave Boss Jim Gettys this treatment. Murphy was so deeply wounded by the cartoon that he arranged for Hearst's ballots to be stolen, and, it is said, even managed to rig the recount. That reckless cartoon was the turning point in Hearst's political career. The movie gives Gettys a different revenge; namely, exposing Kane's 'love nest' — which was something that also happened to Hearst, but on another occasion, long after he had abandoned his political ambitions, when his *Los Angeles Examiner* was attacking the *Los Angeles Times*, and the *Times* used his own tactics against him by bringing up his 'double life' and his 'love nest' with Marion Davies. The movie ultimately plays the same game. *Citizen Kane* becomes a movie about the private life of a public figure — the scandals and tidbits and splashy sensations that the Hearst press always preferred to issues. The assumption of the movie was much like that of the yellow press: that the mass audience wasn't interested in issues, that all it wanted was to get 'behind the scenes' and find out the dirt.

XXII

As the newspaper business and the political maneuvering were pared away, the personal material took on the weight and the shape of the solution to a mystery. Even so, if the movie had been directed in a more matter-of-fact, naturalistic style, Thompson's explanation that Rosebud was just a piece in a jigsaw puzzle would have seemed quite sensible. Instead, Welles's heavily theatrical style overemphasized the psychological explanation to such a point that when we finally glimpse the name on the sled we in the audience are made to feel hat we're in on a big secret — a revelation that the world missed out on. However, Rosebud is so cleverly worked into the structure that, like the entrance that Hecht and MacArthur prepared for Walter Burns, it is enjoyable as beautiful tomfoolery even while we are conscious of it as 'commercial' mechanics. I think what makes Welles's directorial style so satisfying in this movie is that we are constantly aware of the mechanics — that the pleasure *Kane* gives doesn't come from illusion but comes from our enjoyment of the dexterity of the illusionists and the working of the machinery. *Kane*, too, is a clock that laughs. *Citizen Kane* is a film made by a very young man of enormous spirit; he took the Mankiewicz material and he played with it, he turned it into a magic show. It is Welles's distinctive quality as a movie director — I think it is his genius — that he never hides his cleverness, that he makes it possible for us not only to enjoy what he does but to share his enjoyment in doing it. Welles's showmanship is right there on the surface, just as it was when, as a stage director, he set *Julius Caesar* among the Nazis, and set *Macbeth* in Haiti with a black cast and, during the banquet scene, blasted the audience with a recording of the 'Blue Danube Waltz' — an effect that Kubrick was to echo (perhaps unknowingly?) in *2001*. There is something childlike — and great, too — about his pleasure in the magic of theatre and movies. No other director in the history of movies has been so open in his delight, so eager to share with us the game of pretending, and Welles's silly pretense of having done everything himself is just another part of the game.

Welles's magic as a director (at this time) was that he could put his finger right on the dramatic fun of each scene. Mankiewicz had built the scenes to end at ironic, dramatic high points, and Welles probably had a more innocently brazen sense of melodramatic timing than any other movie director. Welles also had a special magic beyond this: he could give *élan* to scenes that were confused in intention, so that the movie seems to go from dramatic highlight to highlight without lagging in between. There doesn't appear to be any waste material in *Kane*, because he charges right through the weak spots as if they were bright, and he almost convinces you (or *does* convince you) that they're shining jewels. Perhaps these different kinds of magic can be suggested by two examples. There's the famous sequence in which Kane's first marriage is summarized by a series of breakfasts, with overlapping dialogue. The method was not new, and it's used here on a standard marriage joke, but the joke is a basic good joke, and the method is honestly used to sum up as speedily as possible the banality of what goes wrong with the marriage. This sequence is adroit, and Welles brings out the fun in the material, but there's no *special* Wellesian magic in it — except, perhaps, in his own acting. But in the cutting from the sequence of Kane's first meeting with Susan (where the writing supplies almost no clue to why he's drawn to this particular twerp of a girl beyond his finding her relaxing) to the political rally, Welles's special talent comes into play. Welles directs the individual scenes with such flourish and such *enjoyment of flourish* that the audience reacts as if the leap into the rally were clever and funny and logical, too, although the connection between the scenes isn't established until later, when Boss Jim Gettys uses Susan to wreck Kane's political career. As a director, Welles is so ebullient that we go along with the way he wants us to feel; we're happy to let him 'put it over on us.' Given the subject of Hearst and the witty script, the effect is of complicity, of a shared knowingness between Welles and the audience about what the movie is about. Kane's big smile at the rally seals the pact between him and us. Until Kane's later years, Welles, in the role, has an almost total empathy with the audience. It's the same kind of empathy we're likely to feel for smart kids who grin at us when they're showing off in the school play. It's a beautiful kind of emotional nakedness — ingenuously exposing the sheer love of playacting — that most actors lose long before they become 'professional.' If an older actor — even a very good one — had played the role, faking youth for the young Kane the way Edward Arnold, say, sometimes faked it, I think the picture might have been routine. Some people used to say that Welles might be a great director but he was a bad actor, and his performances wrecked his pictures. I think just the opposite — that his directing style is such an emanation of his adolescent love of theatre that his films lack a vital unifying element when he's not in them or when he plays only a small part in them. He needs to be at the center. *The Magnificent Ambersons* is a work of feeling and imagination and of obvious effort — and the milieu is much closer to Welles's own background than the milieu of *Kane* is — but Welles isn't in it, and it's too bland. It feels empty, uninhabited. Without Orson Welles's physical presence — the pudgy, big prodigy who incarnates egotism — *Citizen Kane* might (as Otis Ferguson suggested) have disintegrated into vignettes. We feel that he's making it all happen. Like the actor-managers of the old theatre, he's the man onstage running the show, pulling it all together.

XXIII

Mankiewicz's script, though nominally an 'original' — and in the best sense original — was in large part an adaptation of the material (much of it published) of Hearst's life. Hearst's life was so full of knavery and perversity that Mankiewicz simply sorted out the plums. Mankiewicz had been a reporter on the *New York World*, the Pulitzer paper, where Hearst himself had worked for a time before he persuaded his father to give him the *San Francisco Examiner*. When Hearst got the *Examiner*, he changed it in imitation of the *World*, and then expanded to New York, where he bought a paper and started raiding and decimating the *World*'s staff. One of his favorite tactics was to hire away men he didn't actually want at double or treble what Pulitzer was paying them, then fire them, leaving them stranded (a tactic memorialized in *The Front Page* when Walter Burns hires and fires the poetic reporter Bensinger). Kane's business practices are so closely patterned on Hearst's that in reading about Hearst one seems to be reading the script. Descriptions — like the one in the *Atlantic Monthly* in 1931 — of how Hearst cynically bought away the whole of Pulitzer's Sunday staff might be descriptions of Kane's maneuver. In 1935, *Fortune* described Hearst's warehouse in the Bronx in terms that might have been the specifications for the warehouse in the film, and by 1938 even the *Reader's Digest* was reprinting, from the *Saturday Evening Post*, a description of Hearst's empire in phrases that might be part of the script:

> All his life, Mr Hearst bought, bought, bought — whatever touched his fancy. He purchased newspapers, Egyptian mummies, a California mountain range, herds of Tibetan yaks. He picked up a Spanish abbey, had it knocked down, crated, shipped to New York, and never has seen it since.
>
> To his shares in the Homestake, largest gold producer in the United States, his Peruvian copper mines, his 900,000 acre Mexican cattle ranch, and his other inherited properties, he added 28 daily newspapers, 14 magazines here and in England, eight radio stations, wire services, a Hollywood producing unit, a newsreel, a castle in Wales, and one of the world's largest collection of objects d'art, gathered at a toll of $40,000,000.

Kane's dialogue is often almost Hearst verbatim; in the margin of the script that Mankiewicz lent to Charles Lederer one of Hearst's lawyers annotated Kane's speech beginning, 'Young man, there'll be no war. I have talked with the responsible leaders,' with the words 'This happens to be the gist of an authentic interview with WRH — occasion, his last trip from Europe.' Some of the dialogue was legendary long before the movie was made. When Hearst was spending a fortune in his circulation war with Pulitzer, someone told his mother that Willie was losing money at the rate of a million dollars a year, and she equably replied, 'Is he? Then he will only last about thirty years.' This is no more than slightly transposed in the film, though it's really milked:

THATCHER: Tell me, honestly, my boy, don't you think it's rather unwise to continue this philanthropic enterprise . . . this 'Inquirer' that is costing you a million dollars a year?

KANE: You're right, Mr Thatcher. I did lose a million dollars this year. I expect to lose a million dollars next year. You know, Mr Thatcher, at the rate of a million dollars a year . . . I'll have to close this place in sixty years.

(To audiences in 1941, Thatcher, appearing at the congressional-committee hearing, was obviously J.P. Morgan the younger, and the Thatcher Library was, of course, the Pierpont Morgan Library.)

Mankiewicz could hardly improve on the most famous of all Hearst stories, so he merely touched it up a trifle. According to many accounts, Hearst, trying to foment war with Spain, had sent Richard Harding Davis to Havana to write about the Spanish atrocities and Frederic Remington to sketch them. Remington grew restless there and sent Hearst a telegram:

EVERYTHING IS QUIET, THERE IS NO TROUBLE HERE. THERE WILL BE NO WAR. I WISH TO RETURN — REMINGTON

Hearst replied:

PLEASE REMAIN. YOU FURNISH THE PICTURES AND I'LL FURNISH THE WAR — W.R. HEARST

In the movie, Bernstein reads Kane a telegram from a reporter named Wheeler:

GIRLS DELIGHTFUL IN CUBA, STOP. COULD SEND YOU PROSE POEMS ABOUT SCENERY BUT DON'T FEEL RIGHT SPENDING YOUR MONEY, STOP. THERE IS NO WAR IN CUBA. SIGNED WHEELER.

And Bernstein asks, 'Any answer?'
  Kane replies:

DEAR WHEELER, YOU PROVIDE THE PROSE POEMS, I'LL PROVIDE THE WAR.

These stories were so well known at the time of the movie's release that in the picture spread on the movie in *Life* (with captions in the very style that Mankiewicz had parodied in his 'New on the March') the magazine — unconsciously, no doubt — returned to the Hearst original, and flubbed even that:

Kane buys a newspaper in New York and sets out to be a great
social reformer. But even at 25 he is unscrupulous and wangles
the U.S. into war by fake news dispatches. To a cartoonist in
Cuba he wires: 'You get the pictures and I'll make the war.'

One passage of dialogue that is bad because it sounds slanted to make
an ideological point is almost a straight steal (and that's probably why
Mankiewicz didn't realize how fraudulent it would sound), and was
especially familiar because John Dos Passos had quoted it in *U.S.A.*,
in his section on Hearst, 'Poor Little Rich Boy.' (That title might be
the theme of the movie.) Dos Passos quotes Hearst's answer to fellow-
millionaires who thought he was a traitor to his class:

> You know I believe in property, and you know where I stand on
> personal fortunes, but isn't it better that I should represent in this
> country the dissatisfied than have somebody else do it who
> might not have the same real property relations that I may have?

Hearst apparently did say it, but even though it's made more conversational in the movie, it's unconvincing — it sounds like left-wing
paranoia.

> KANE: I'll let you in on another little secret, Mr Thatcher. I
> think I'm the man to do it. You see, I have money and property.
> If I don't look after the interests of the underprivileged maybe
> somebody else will . . . maybe somebody without any money or
> property.

Despite the fake childhood events, Kane's life story follows Hearst's
much more closely than most movie biographies follow acknowledged and named subjects. Kane is burned in effigy, as Hearst was,
and there is even a reference to Kane's expulsion from Harvard; one
of the best-known stories in America was how young Willie Hearst
had been expelled from Harvard after sending each of his instructors
a chamber pot with the recipient's name handsomely lettered on the
inside bottom. Even many of the subsidiary characters are replicas of
Hearst's associates. For example, Bernstein (given the name of Welles's
old guardian) is obviously Solomon S. Carvalho, the business manager of Pulitzer's *World*, whom Hearst hired away, and who became
the watchdog of the *Journal*'s exchequer and Hearst's devoted business manager. There was no special significance in the use of
Mankiewicz's secretary's last name for Susan Alexander, or in nam-

ing Jed Leland for Leland Hayward (Mankiewicz's agent, whose wife, Margaret Sullavan, spent a weekend visiting at Victorville), just as there was no significance in the fact that the actor Whitford Kane had been part of the nucleus of the Mercury Theatre, but the use of the name Bernstein for Kane's devoted, uncritical friend had some significance in relation not only to Welles but to Hearst, and it was Mankiewicz's way of giving Hearst points (he did it in the breakfast scene when Emily is snobbish about Bernstein) because, whatever else Hearst was, he was not a snob or an anti-Semite. (For one thing, Marion's brother-in-law — Charles Lederer's father — was Jewish.) No doubt Mankiewicz also meant to give Kane points when he had him finish Jed's negative review of Susan's singing in the same negative spirit — which was more than George S. Kaufman had done for Mankiewicz's review back at the *New York Times*. This episode is perversely entertaining but not convincing. *Kane* used so much of Hearst's already legendary life that for liberals it was like a new kind of folk art; we knew all this about Hearst from books and magazines but gasped when we saw it on the big movie screen, and so defiantly — almost contemptuously — undisguised.

The departure from Hearst's life represented by Susan Alexander's opera career, which is a composite of the loves and scandals of several Chicago tycoons, didn't weaken the attack on Hearst — it strengthened it. Attaching the other scandals to him made him seem the epitome of the powerful and spoiled, and thus stand for them all. Opera — which used to be called 'grand opera' — was a ritual target of American comedy. It was an easier target for the public to respond to than Hearst's own folly — motion pictures — because the public already connected opera with wealth and temperament, tycoons in opera hats and women in jewels, imported prima donnas, and all the affectations of 'culture.' It was a world the movie public didn't share, and it was already absurd in American movies — the way valets and effete English butlers and the high-toned Americans putting on airs who kept them were absurd. George S. Kaufman and Morrie Ryskind had worked opera over in two of the Marx Brothers pictures; Mankiewicz had been taken off *A Night at the Opera*, but what he and Welles — with the assistance of Bernard Herrmann — did to opera in *Citizen Kane* was in almost exactly the same style, and as funny.

Mankiewicz was working overseas for the *Chicago Tribune* when Harold McCormick and his wife, Edith Rockefeller McCormick, were divorced, in 1921. The McCormicks had been the leading patrons of

opera in Chicago; they had made up the Chicago Opera Company's
deficits, which were awe-inspiring during the time the company was
under the management of Mary Garden (she chose to be called the
'directa'), rising to a million dollars one great, lavish season. After the
divorce, McCormick married Ganna Walska, the preeminent tempera-
mental mediocre soprano of her day. Mankiewicz combined this
scandal with a far more widely publicized event that occurred a few
years later, replacing Hearst and Cosmopolitan Pictures with Samuel
Insull and his building of the Chicago Civic Opera House. Insull didn't
build the opera house for his wife (dainty little Gladys Wallis didn't
sing), but there was a story to it, and it was the biggest opera story of
the decade. After the McCormick–Rockefeller divorce, their joint
largesse to opera ended, and the deficits were a big problem. Insull,
'the Czar of Commonwealth Edison,' who also loved opera (and
dallied with divas), wanted to put it on a self-supporting business
basis. He concluded that if an opera house should be built in a
skyscraper, the rental of the upper regions would eventually cover the
opera's deficits. The building was started in 1928; it had forty-five
stories, with the opera company occupying the first six, and with
Insull's office-lair on top. The structure was known as 'Insull's
throne,' and it cost twenty million dollars. The opening of the new
opera house was scheduled for November 4, 1929; six days before, on
October 29th, the stock market crashed. The opening took place during
the panic, with plain-clothesmen and eight detective-bureau squads
guarding the bejewelled patrons against robbers, rioters, and the
mobsters who more or less ran the city. (The former Mrs McCormick
attended, wearing, according to one newspaper report, 'her gorgeous
diamond necklace, almost an inch wide and reaching practically to her
waist'; Mrs Insull wore pearls and 'a wide diamond bracelet.')
Mankiewicz must have placed the episode of the opera house in
Chicago in order to give it roots — to make it connect with what the
public already knew about Chicago and robber barons and opera.
(Chicago was big on opera; it was there that the infant Orson Welles
played Madame Butterfly's love child.) Insull's opera house never
really had a chance to prove or disprove his financial theories. Mary
Garden quit after one year there, calling it 'that long black hole,' and
in 1932, when Insull's mammoth interlocking directorate of power
plants collapsed and he fled to Greece, the opera house was closed.
Insull was extradited, and in the mid-thirties he stood trial for fraud
and embezzlement; he died two years before *Citizen Kane* was written.

The fretful banality of Susan Alexander is clearly derived from Mankiewicz's hated old adversary Mrs Insull — notorious for her 'discordant twitter' and her petty dissatisfaction with everything. The Insulls had been called the least popular couple who had ever lived in Chicago, and there was ample evidence that they hadn't even liked each other. Opera and the Insulls provided cover for Mankiewicz and Welles. George J. Schaefer, who is quite open about this, says that when he couldn't get an opening for *Kane*, because the theatres were frightened off by the stories in the Hearst press about injunctions and lawsuits, he went to see Hearst's lawyers in Los Angeles and took the position that Kane could be Insull. No one was expected to be fooled; it was simply a legal maneuver.

There was also an actual (and malicious) scrap of Hearst's past in the opera idea in the first draft. As Mankiewicz planned it, Susan was to make her début in Massenet's *Thaïs*. As a very young man, Hearst had been briefly engaged to the San Francisco singer Sybil Sanderson. In order to break the engagement, Miss Sanderson's parents had sent her to study in Paris, where she became well known in opera and as the 'constant companion' of Massenet, who wrote *Thaïs* for her. But to use *Thaïs* would have cost a fee, so Bernard Herrmann wrote choice excerpts for a fake French-Oriental opera — *Salammbô*. (Dorothy Comingore did her own singing in the movie except for the opera-house sequence; that was dubbed by a professional singer who deliberately sang badly.) The Kane amalgam may also contain a dab or two from the lives of other magnates, such as Frank Munsey and Pulitzer, and more than a dab from the life of Jules Brulatour, who got his start in business by selling Eastman Kodak film. Hope Hampton, his blond protégée and later his wife, had a career even more ridiculous than Susan Alexander's. After she failed as a movie actress, Brulatour financed her career at the Chicago Opera Company at the end of the twenties, and then, using his power to extend credit to movie companies for film stock, he pushed the near-bankrupt Universal to star her in a 1937 disaster, in which she sang eight songs.

The only other major addition to Hearst's actual history comes near the beginning of the movie. The latter days of Susan Alexander as a tawdry-looking drunken singer at El Rancho in Atlantic City, where she is billed as 'Susan Alexander Kane' — which tells us at once that she is so poor an entertainer that she must resort to this cheap attempt to exploit her connection with Kane — may have been lifted from the frayed end of Evelyn Nesbit's life. After her divorce from Harry K.

Thaw — the rich socialite who murdered Stanford White on her account — she drifted down to appearing in honky-tonks, and was periodically denounced in the press for 'capitalizing her shame.'

XXIV

Dorothy Comingore says, 'When I read for Orson, Herman was in the room, with a broken leg and a crutch, and Orson turned to him and said, "What do you think?' and Herman said, 'Yes, she looks precisely like the image of a kitten we've been looking for." '

The handling of Susan Alexander is a classic of duplicity. By diversifying the material and combining several careers, Mankiewicz could protect himself. He could claim that Susan wasn't meant to be Marion Davies — that she was nothing at all like Marion, whom he called a darling and a minx. He could point out that Marion wasn't a singer and that Hearst had never built an opera house for her — and it was true, she wasn't and he hadn't, but she was an actress and he did run Cosmopolitan Pictures for her. Right at the beginning of the movie, Kane was said to be the greatest newspaper tycoon of this or any other generation, so he was obviously Hearst; Xanadu was transparently San Simeon; and Susan's fake stardom and the role she played in Kane's life spelled Marion Davies to practically everybody in the Western world. And even though Mankiewicz *liked* Marion Davies, he was the same Mankiewicz who couldn't resist the disastrous 'Imagine — the whole world wired to Harry Cohn's ass!' He skewered her with certain identifying details that were just too good to resist, such as her love of jigsaw puzzles. They were a feature of San Simeon; the puzzles, which sometimes took two weeks to complete, were set out on tables in the salon, and the guests would work at them before lunch. And when Kane destroys Susan's room in a rage after she leaves him, he turns up a hidden bottle of booze, which was a vicious touch, coming from Mankiewicz, who had often been the beneficiary of Marion's secret cache. He provided bits that had a special *frisson* for those in the know.

One can sometimes hurt one's enemies, but that's nothing compared to what one can do to one's friends. Marion Davies, living in the style of the royal courtesans with a man who couldn't marry her without messes and scandal (his wife, Millicent, had become a Catholic, and she had also given him five sons), was an easy target. Hearst and Louella Parsons had set her up for it, and she became the victim of *Citizen Kane*. In her best roles, Marion Davies was a spunky, funny, beautiful girl, and that's apparently what she *was* and why Hearst adored her. But, in his adoration, he insisted that the Hearst press overpublicize her and overpraise her constantly, and the public in general got wise. A typical Davies film would open with the theatre ventilating system pouring attar of roses at the audience, or the theatre would be specially redecorated, sometimes featuring posters that famous popular artists had done of her in the costumes of the picture. Charity functions of which she was the queen would be splashed all over the society pages, and the movie would be reviewed under eight-column headlines. In the news section, Mayor Hylan of New York would be saying, '*When Knighthood Was in Flower* is unquestionably the greatest picture I have ever seen. . . . No person can afford to miss this great screen masterpiece,' or '*Little Old New York* is unquestion-ably the greatest screen epic I have ever looked upon, and Marion Davies is the most versatile screen star ever cast in any part. The wide range of her stellar acting is something to marvel at. . . . Every man, woman and child in New York City ought to see this splendid picture. . . . I must pay my tribute to the geniuses in all lines who created such a masterpiece.'

When the toadying and praise were already sickening, Hearst fell for one of the dumbest smart con tricks of all time: A movie reviewer named Louella O. Parsons, working for the *New York Telegraph* for $110 a week, wrote a column saying that although Marion Davies's movies were properly publicized, the star herself wasn't publicized *enough*. Hearst fell for it and hired Parsons at $250 a week, and she began her profitable lifework of praising (and destroying) Marion Davies. Some of Davies's costume spectacles weren't bad — and she was generally charming in them — but the pictures didn't have to be bad for all the corrupt drumbeaters to turn the public's stomach. Other actresses were pushed to stardom and were accepted. (The flapper heroine Colleen Moore was Walter Howey's niece, and she was started on her career when she was fifteen. D.W. Griffith owed Howey a favor for getting *The Birth of a Nation* and *Intolerance* past the Chicago censors, and her movie contract was the payoff. She says that many of the Griffith stars were 'payoffs.') Marion Davies had more talent than most of the reigning queens, but Hearst and Louella were too ostentatious, and they never let up. There was a steady march of headlines ('Marion Davies' Greatest Film Opens Tonight'); there were too many charity balls. The public can swallow just so much: her seventy-five-thousand-dollar fourteen-room mobile 'bungalow' on the M-G-M lot, O.K.; the special carpet for alighting, no. Her pictures had to be forced on exhibitors, and Hearst spent so much on them that even when they did well, the cost frequently couldn't be recovered. One of his biographers reports a friend's saying to Hearst, 'There's money in the movies,' and Hearst's replying, 'Yes. Mine.'

Marion Davies was born in 1897, and, as a teen-ager, went right from the convent to the musical-comedy stage, where she put in two years as a dancer before Ziegfeld 'glorified' her in the 'Ziegfeld Follies of 1916.' That was where William Randolph Hearst, already in his mid-fifties, spotted her. It is said, and may even be true, that he attended the 'Follies' every night for eight weeks, buying two tickets — one for himself and the other for his hat — just 'to gaze upon her.' It is almost certainly true that from then 'to the day of his death,' as Adela Rogers St Johns put it, 'he wanted to know every minute where she was.' Marion Davies entered movies in 1917, with *Runaway Romany*, which she also wrote, and then she began that really strange, unparalleled movie career. She had starred in about fifty pictures by the time she retired, in 1937 — all under Hearst's aegis, and under his close personal supervision. (Leading men were afraid to kiss her; Hearst was always watching.) The pictures were all expensively produced, and most of them were financial failures. Marion Davies was a mimic and a parodist and a very original sort of comedienne, but though Hearst liked her to make him laugh at home, he wanted her to be a romantic maiden in the movies, and — what was irreconcilable with her talent — dignified. Like Susan, she was tutored, and he spent incredible sums on movies that would be the perfect setting for her. He appears to have been sincerely infatuated with her in old-fashioned, sentimental, ladylike roles; he loved to see her in ruffles on garden swings. But actresses didn't become public favorites in roles like those, and even if they could get by with them sometimes, they needed startling changes of pace to stay in public favor, and Hearst wouldn't let Marion Davies do anything 'sordid.'

To judge by what those who worked with her have said, she was thoroughly unpretentious and was depressed by Hearst's taste in roles for her. She finally broke out of the costume cycle in the late twenties and did some funny pictures: *The Red Mill* (which Fatty Arbuckle, whom Hearst the moralizer had helped ruin, directed, under his new, satirical pseudonym, Will B. Goodrich), *The Fair Coed*, my childhood favorite *The Patsy*, and others. But even when she played in a slapstick parody of Gloria Swanson's career (*Show*

People, in 1928), Hearst wouldn't let her do a custard-pie sequence, despite her own pleas and those of the director, King Vidor, and the writer, Laurence Stallings. (King Vidor has described the conference that Louis B. Mayer called so that Vidor could make his case to Hearst for the plot necessity of the pie. 'Presently, the great man rose and in a high-pitched voice said, "King's right. But I'm right, too — because I'm not going to let Marion be hit in the face with a pie." ') She wanted to play Sadie Thompson in *Rain*, but he wouldn't hear of it, and the role went to Gloria Swanson (and made her a star all over again). When Marion Davies should have been playing hard-boiled, good-hearted blondes, Hearst's idea of a role for her was Elizabeth Barrett Browning in *The Barretts of Wimpole Street*, and when Thalberg reserved that one for *his* lady, Norma Shearer, Hearst, in 1934, indignantly left M-G-M and took his money and his 'Cosmopolitan Pictures' label over to Warner Brothers. (The editors of his newspapers were instructed never again to mention Norma Shearer in print.) It was a long blighted career for an actress who might very well have become a big star on her own, and she finally recognized that with Hearst's help it was hopeless. By the time *Citizen Kane* came out, she had been in retirement for four years, but the sickening publicity had gone grinding on relentlessly, and, among the audiences at *Kane*, probably even those who remembered her as the charming, giddy comedienne of the late twenties no longer trusted their memories.

Mankiewicz, catering to the public, gave it the empty, stupid, no-talent blonde it wanted — the 'confidential' backstairs view of the great gracious lady featured in the Hearst press. It was, though perhaps partly inadvertently, a much worse betrayal than if he'd made Susan more like Davies, because movie audiences assumed that Davies was a pathetic whiner like Susan Alexander, and Marion Davies was nailed to the cross of harmless stupidity and nothingness, which in high places is the worst joke of all.

XXV

Right from the start of movies, it was a convention that the rich were vulgarly acquisitive but were lonely and miserable and incapable of giving or receiving love. As a mass medium, movies have always soothed and consoled the public with the theme that the rich can buy everything except what counts — love. (The convention remains, having absorbed the *Dolce Vita* variation that the rich use each other sexually because they are incapable of love.) It was consistent with this popular view of the emptiness of the lives of the rich to make Susan Alexander a cartoon character; the movie reduces Hearst's love affair to an infatuation for a silly, ordinary nothing of a girl, as if everything in his life were synthetic, his passion vacuous, and the object of it a cipher. What happened in Hearst's life was far more interesting: he took a beautiful, warm-hearted girl and made her the best-known kept woman in America and the butt of an infinity of dirty jokes, and he did it out of love and the blindness of love.

Citizen Kane, however, employs the simplification, so convenient to melodrama, that there is a unity between a man's private life and his public one. This simplification has enabled ambitious bad writers to make reputations as thinkers, and in the movies of the forties it was given a superficial plausibility by popular Freudianism. Hideous character defects traceable to childhood traumas explained just about anything the authors disapproved of. Mankiewicz certainly knew better, but as a screenwriter he dealt in ideas that had popular appeal. Hearst was a notorious anti-union, pro-Nazi Redbaiter, so Kane must have a miserable, deformed childhood. He must be *wrecked* in infancy. It was a movie convention going back to silents that when you did a bio or a thesis picture you started with the principal characters as children and showed them to be miniature versions of their later characters. This convention almost invariably pleased audiences, because it also demonstrated the magic of movies — the kids so extraordinarily resembled the adult actors they would turn into. And it wasn't just makeup — they really did, having been searched out for that resemblance. (This is *possible* in theatre, but it's rarely feasible.) That rather old-fashioned view of the predestination of character from childhood needed only a small injection of popular Freudianism to pass for new, and if you tucked in a trauma, you took care of the motivation for the later events. Since nothing very bad had happened to Hearst, Mankiewicz drew upon Little Orson Annie. He *orphaned* Kane, and used that to explain Hearst's career. (And, as Welles directed it, there's more real emotion and pain in the childhood separation sequence than in all the rest of the movie.)

Thus Kane was emotionally stunted. Offering personal emptiness as the explanation of Hearst's career really doesn't do much but feed the complacency of those liberals who are eager to believe that conservatives are 'sick' (which is also how conservatives tend to see liberals). Liberals were willing to see this hollow-man explanation of

Hearst as something much deeper than a cliché of popular melodrama, though the film's explaining his attempts to win public office and his empire-building and his art collecting by the childhood loss of maternal love is as unilluminating as the conservative conceit that Marx was a revolutionary because he hated his father. The point of the film becomes the cliché irony that although Hearst has everything materially, he has nothing humanly.

Quite by chance, I saw William Randolph Hearst once, when I was about nineteen. It was Father's Day, which sometimes falls on my birthday, and my escort bumped me into him on the dance floor. I can't remember whether it was at the Palace Hotel in San Francisco or at the St Francis, and I can't remember the year, though it was probably 1938. But I remember Hearst in almost terrifying detail, with the kind of memory I generally have only for movies. He was dinner-dancing, just like us, except that his table was a large one. He was seated with Marion Davies and his sons with their wives or dates; obviously, it was a kind of family celebration. I had read the then current *Hearst, Lord of San Simeon* and Ferdinand Lundberg's *Imperial Hearst*, and probably almost everything else that was available about him, and I remember thinking, as I watched him, of Charles A. Beard's preface to the Lundberg book — that deliberately cruel premature 'Farewell to William Randolph Hearst,' with its tone of 'He will depart loved by few and respected by none whose respect is worthy of respect. . . None will be proud to do honor to his memory,' and so on. You don't expect to bump into a man on the dance floor after you've been reading that sort of thing about him. It was like stumbling onto Caligula, and Hearst looked like a Roman emperor mixing with the commoners on a night out. He was a huge man — six feet four or five — and he was old and heavy, and he moved slowly about the dance floor with *her*. He seemed like some prehistoric monster gliding among the couples, quietly majestic, towering over everyone; he had little, odd eyes, like a whale's, and they looked pulled down, sinking into his cheeks. Maybe I had just never seen anybody so massive and dignified and old *dancing*, and maybe it was that plus who he was, but I've never seen anyone else who seemed to incarnate power and solemnity as he did; he was frightening and he was impressive, almost as if he were wearing ceremonial robes of office. When he danced with Marion Davies, he was indifferent to everything else. They looked isolated and entranced together; this slow, huge dinosaur clung to the frowzy-looking aging blonde in what seemed to be a ritual performance. Joined together, they were as alone as the young dancing couple in the sky with diamonds in *Yellow Submarine*. Maybe they *were* that couple a few decades later, for they had an extraordinary romance — one that lasted thirty-two years — and they certainly had the diamonds (or *had* had them). He seemed unbelievably old to me that night, when he was probably about seventy-five; they were still together when he died, in 1951, at the age of eighty-eight.

The private pattern that was devised as a correlative (and possible explanation) of Hearst's public role was false. Hearst didn't have any (recorded) early traumas, Marion Davies did have talent, and they were an extraordinarily devoted pair; far from leaving him, when he faced bankruptcy she gave him her money and jewels and real estate, and even borrowed money to enable him to keep his newspapers. He was well loved, and *still* he was a dangerous demagogue. And, despite what Charles A. Beard said and what Dos Passos said, and despite the way Mankiewicz presented him in *Citizen Kane*, and all the rest, Hearst and his consort were hardly lonely, with all those writers around, and movie stars and directors, and Shaw, and Winston Churchill, and weekend parties with Marion Davies spiking teetotaller Calvin Coolidge's fruit punch (though only with liquor that came from fruit). Even Mrs Luce came; the pictures of Hearst on the walls at Time-Life might show him as an octopus, but who could resist an invitation? Nor did Hearst lose his attraction or his friends after he lost his *big* money. After San Simeon was stripped of its silver treasures, which were sold at auction in the thirties, the regal-party weekends were finished, but he still entertained, if less lavishly, at his smaller houses. Dos Passos played the same game as *Citizen Kane* when he wrote of Hearst 'amid the relaxing adulations of screenstars, admen, screenwriters, publicitymen, columnists, millionaire editors' — suggesting that Hearst was surrounded by third-raters and sycophantic hirelings. But the lists and the photographs of Hearst's guests tell another story. He had the one great, dazzling court of the first half of the twentieth century, and the statesmen and kings, the queens and duchesses at his table were as authentic as the writers and wits and great movie stars and directors. When one considers who even those screenwriters were, it's not surprising that Hearst wanted their company. Harold Ross must have wondered what drew his old friends there, for he came, too, escorted by Robert Benchley.

It is both a limitation and *in the nature of the appeal* of popular art that it constructs false, easy patterns. Like the blind-beggar-for-luck, *Kane* has a primitive appeal that is implicit in the conception. It tells the audience that fate or destiny or God or childhood trauma has already taken revenge on the wicked — that if the rich man had a good time he has suffered remorse, or, better still, that he hasn't really enjoyed himself at all. Before Mankiewicz began writing the script, he talked about what a great love story it would be — but who would buy tickets for a movie about a rich, powerful tycoon who also found true love? In popular art, riches and power destroy people, and so the secret of Kane is that he longs for the simple pleasures of his childhood before wealth tore him away from his mother — he longs for what is available to the mass audience.

XXVI

Even when Hearst's speeches, or facsimiles of them, were used in *Kane*, their character was transformed. If one looks at his actual remarks on property and then at Mankiewicz's adaptation of them, one can see how. Hearst's remarks are tight and slightly oblique, and it takes one an instant to realize what he's saying. Mankiewicz makes them easier to grasp (and rather florid) but kills some of their almost sinister double edge by making them consciously flip. He turns them into a joke. And when Mankiewicz didn't make the speeches flip, Welles's delivery did. When you hear Kane dictate the telegram to Cuba, you don't really think for a minute that it's *acted* on. And so the movie becomes a comic strip about Hearst, without much resonance, and certainly without much tragic resonance. Hearst, who compared himself to an elephant, *looked* like a great man. I don't think he actually was great in any sense, but he was *extraordinary*, and his power and wealth, plus his enormous size, made him a phenomenally commanding presence. Mankiewicz, like Dos Passos, may have believed that Hearst fell from greatness, or (as I suspect) Mankiewicz may have liked the facile dramatic possibilities of that approach. But he couldn't carry it out. He couldn't write the character as a tragic fallen hero, because he couldn't resist making him funny. Mankiewicz had been hacking out popular comedies and melodramas for too long to write drama; one does not *dictate* tragedy to a stenotypist. He automatically, because of his own temperament and his writing habits, turned out a bitchy satirical melodrama. Inside the three hundred and twenty-five pages of his long, ambitious first draft was the crowd-pleasing material waiting to be carved out. When one reads the long version, it's obvious what must go; if I had been doing the cutting I might have cut just about the same material. *And yet* that fat to be cut away is everything that tends to make it a political and historical drama, and what is left is the private scandals of a poor little rich boy. The scandals in the long draft — some of it, set in Italy during Kane's youth, startlingly like material that came to the screen twenty years later in *La Dolce Vita* — served a purpose beyond crowd pleasing: to show what a powerful man could cover up and get away with. Yet this, of course, went out, for reasons similar to the ones that kept Kane, unlike Hearst, from winning elected office — to reassure the public that the rich *don't* get away with it.

Welles now has a lumbering grace and a gliding, whalelike motion not unlike Hearst's, but when he played the role he became stiff and crusty as the older Kane, and something went blank in the aging process — not just because the makeup was erratic and waxy (especially in the bald-headed scenes, such as the one in the picnic tent) but because the character lost his connection with business and politics and became a fancy theatrical notion, an Expressionist puppet. Also, there are times when the magic of movies fails. The camera comes so close that it can reveal too much: Kane as an old man was an actor trying to look old, and Welles had as yet only a schoolboy's perception of how age weighs one down. On a popular level, however, his limitations worked to his advantage; they tied in with the myth of the soulless rich.

The conceptions are basically *kitsch*; basically, *Kane* is popular melodrama — Freud plus scandal, a comic strip about Hearst. Yet, partly because of the resonance of what was left of the historical context, partly because of the juiciness of Welles's young talent and of the varied gifts and personalities others brought to the film, partly because of the daring of the attack on the most powerful and dangerous press lord known to that time, the picture has great richness and flair: its *kitsch* redeemed. I would argue that this is what is remarkable about movies — that shallow conceptions in one area can be offset by elements playing against them or altering them or affecting the texture. If a movie is good, there is a general tendency to believe that everything in it was conceived and worked out according to a beautiful master plan, or that it is the result of the creative imagination of the director, but in movies things rarely happen that way — even more rarely than they do in opera or the theatre. There are so many variables; imagine how different the whole feeling of *Kane* would be if the film had been shot in a naturalistic style, or even if it had been made at M-G-M instead of at R.K.O. Extraordinary movies are the result of the 'right' people's getting together on the 'right' project at the 'right' time — in their lives and in history. I don't mean to suggest that a good movie is just a mess that happens to work (although there have been such cases) — only that a good movie is not always the result of a single artistic intelligence. It can be the result of a fortunate collaboration, of cross-fertilizing accidents. And I would argue that what redeems movies in general, what makes them so much easier to take than other arts, is that many talents in interaction in a work can produce something more enjoyable than one talent that is not of the highest. Because of the collaborative nature of most movies, masterpieces are rare, and even masterpieces may, like *Kane*, be full of flaws, but the interaction frequently results in special pleasures and surprises.

XXVII

The director should be in control not because he is the sole creative intelligence but because only if he is in control can he liberate and utilize the talents of his co-workers, who languish (as directors do) in studio-factory productions. The best interpretation to put on it when a director says that a movie is totally his is not that he did it all himself but that he wasn't interfered with, that he made the choices and the ultimate decisions, that the whole thing isn't an unhappy compromise for which no one is responsible; not that he was the sole creator but almost the reverse — that he was free to use all the best ideas offered him.

Welles had a vitalizing, spellbinding talent; he was the man who brought out the best in others and knew how to use it. What keeps *Citizen Kane* alive is that Welles wasn't prevented (as so many directors are) from trying things out. He was young and *open*, and, as the members of that crew tell it — and they remember it very well, because it was the only time it ever happened for many of them — they could always talk to him and make suggestions, as long as they didn't make the suggestions publicly. Most big-studio movies were made in such a restrictive way that the crews were hostile and bored and the atmosphere was oppressive. The worst aspect of the factory system was that almost everyone worked beneath his capacity. Working on *Kane*, in an atmosphere of freedom, the designers and technicians came forth with ideas they'd been bottling up for years; they were all in on the creative process. Welles was so eager to try out new ideas that even the tough, hardened studio craftsmen were caught up by his spirit, just as his co-workers in the theatre and in radio had been. *Citizen Kane* is not a great work that suddenly burst out of a young prodigy's head. There are such works in the arts (though few, if any, in movies), but this is not one of them. It is a superb example of collaboration; everyone connected with it seems to have had the time of his life because he was able to contribute something.

Welles had just the right background for the sound era. He used sound not just as an inexpensive method of creating the illusion of halls and crowds but to create an American environment. He knew how to convey the way people feel about each other by the way they sound; he knew how they sounded in different rooms, in different situations. The directors who had been most imaginative in the use of sound in the early talkies were not Americans, and when they worked in America, as Ernst Lubitsch did, they didn't have the ear for American life that Welles had. And the good American movie directors in that period (men like Howard Hawks and John Ford and William Wellman) didn't have the background in theatre or — that key element — the background in radio. Hawks handled the dialogue expertly in *His Girl Friday*, but the other sounds are not much more imaginative than those in a first-rate stage production. When Welles came to Hollywood, at the age of twenty-four, his previous movie experience had not been on a professional level, but he already knew more about the dramatic possibilities of sound than most veteran directors, and the sound engineers responded to his inventiveness by giving him extraordinary new effects. At every point along the way, the studio craftsmen tried something out. Nearly all the thirty-five members of the R.K.O. special-effects department worked on *Kane*; roughly eighty percent of the film was not merely printed but re-printed, in order to add trick effects and blend in painted sets and bits of stock footage. The view up from Susan singing on the opera stage to the stagehands high above on the catwalk, as one of them puts two fingers to his nose — which looks like a tilt (or vertical pan) — is actually made up of three shots, the middle one a miniature. When the camera seems to pass through a rooftop skylight into the El Rancho night club where Susan works, the sign, the rooftop, and the skylight are miniatures, with a flash of lightning to conceal the cut to the full-scale interior. The craftsmen were so ingenious about giving Welles the effects he wanted that even now audiences aren't aware of how cheaply made *Citizen Kane* was.

In the case of the cinematographer, Gregg Toland, the contribution goes far beyond suggestions and technical solutions. I think he not only provided much of the visual style of *Citizen Kane* but was responsible for affecting the conception, and even for introducing a few elements that are not in the script. It's always a little risky to assign credit for ideas in movies; somebody is bound to turn up a film that used whatever it is — a detail, a device, a technique — earlier. The most one can hope for, generally, is to catch on to a few late links in the chain. It was clear that *Kane* had visual links to James Wong Howe's cinematography in *Transatlantic* (Howe, coincidentally, had also shot *The Power and the Glory*), but I had always been puzzled by the fact that *Kane* seemed to draw not only on the Expressionist theatrical style of Welles's stage productions but on the German Expressionist and Gothic movies of the silent period. In *Kane*, as in the German silents, depth was used like stage depth, and attention was frequently moved from one figure to another within a fixed frame by essentially the same techniques as on the stage — by the actors' moving into light or by a shift of the light to other actors (rather than by the fluid camera of a Renoir, which follows the actors, or the fragmentation and quick cutting of the early Russians). There were frames in *Kane* that seemed so close to the exaggerations in German films like *Pandora's Box* and *The Last Laugh* and *Secrets of a Soul* that I wondered what Welles was talking about when he said he had prepared for *Kane* by running John Ford's *Stagecoach* forty times. Even allowing for the hyperbole of the forty times, why should Orson Welles have studied *Stagecoach* and come up with a film that looked more like *The Cabinet of Dr Caligari*? I wondered if there might be a link between Gregg Toland and the German tradition, though most of Toland's other films didn't suggest much German influence. When I looked up his credits as a cameraman, the name *Mad Love* rang a bell; I closed my eyes and visualized it, and there was the Gothic atmosphere, and the huge, dark rooms with lighted figures, and Peter Lorre, bald, with a spoiled-baby face, looking astoundingly like a miniature Orson Welles.

Mad Love, made in Hollywood in 1935, was a dismal, static horror movie — an American version of a German film directed by the same man who had directed *The Cabinet of Dr Caligari*. The American remake, remarkable only for its photography, was directed by Karl

Freund, who had been head cinematographer at Ufa, in Germany. He had worked with such great directors as Fritz Lang and F.W. Murnau and G.W. Pabst, and, by his technical innovations, had helped create their styles; he had shot many of the German silent classics (*The Last Laugh, Variety, Metropolis, Tartuffe*). I recently looked at a print of *Mad Love*, and the resemblances to *Citizen Kane* are even greater than my memories of it suggested. Not only is the large room with the fireplace at Xanadu similar to Lorre's domain as a mad doctor, with similar lighting and similar placement of figures, but Kane's appearance and makeup in some sequences might be a facsimile of Lorre's. Lorre, who had come out of the German theatre and German films, played in a stylized manner that is visually imitated in *Kane*. And, amusingly, that screeching white cockatoo, which isn't in the script of *Kane*, but appeared out of nowhere in the movie to provide an extra 'touch,' is a regular member of Lorre's household.

Gregg Toland was the 'hottest' photographer in Hollywood at the time he called Welles and asked to work with him; in March he had won the Academy Award for *Wuthering Heights*, and his other recent credits included *The Grapes of Wrath* and the film in which he had experimented with deep focus, *The Long Voyage Home*. He brought along his own four-man camera crew, who had recently celebrated their fifteenth year of working together. This picture was made with love; the year before his death, in 1948, Toland said that he had wanted to work with Welles because he was miserable and felt like a whore when he was on run-of-the-mill assignments, and that 'photographing *Citizen Kane* was the most exciting professional adventure of my career.' I surmise that part of the adventure was his finding a way to use and develop what the great Karl Freund had taught him.

Like the German cinematographers in the silent period, Toland took a more active role than the usual Hollywood cinematographer. For some years, whenever it was possible, he had been supervising the set construction of his films, so that he could plan the lighting. He probably responded to Welles's penchant for tales of terror and his desire for a portentous, mythic look, and since Welles didn't have enough financing for full-scale sets and was more than willing to try the unconventional, Toland suggested many of the Expressionist solutions. When a director is new to films, he is, of course, extremely dependent on his camerman, and he is particularly so if he is also the star of the film, and is thus in front of the camera. Toland was a disciplined man, and those who worked on the set say he was a steadying influence on Welles; it is generally agreed that the two planned and discussed every shot together. With Welles, Toland was free to make suggestions that went beyond lighting techniques. Seeing Welles's facial resemblance to the tiny Lorre — even to the bulging eyes and the dimpled, sad expression — Toland probably suggested the makeup and the doll-like, jerky use of the body for Kane in his rage and as a lonely old man, and, having enjoyed the flamboyant photographic effect of the cockatoo in *Mad Love*, suggested that, too. When Toland provided Welles with the silent-picture setups that had been moribund under Karl Freund's direction, Welles used them in a childlike spirit that made them playful and witty. There's nothing static or Germanic in Welles's *direction*, but he had such unifying energy that just a couple of years ago an eminent movie critic cited the cockatoo in *Citizen Kane* as 'an unforced metaphor arising naturally out of the action.'

It's the Gothic atmosphere, partly derived from Toland's work on *Mad Love*, that inflates *Citizen Kane* and puts it in a different tradition from the newspaper comedies and the big bios of the thirties. *Citizen Kane* is, in some ways, a freak of art. Toland, although he used deep focus again later, reverted to a more conventional look for the films following *Kane*, directed by men who rejected technique 'for its own sake,' but he had passed on Freund's techniques to Welles. The dark, Gothic horror style, with looming figures, and with vast interiors that suggested castles rather than houses, formed the basis for much of Welles's later visual style. It suited Welles; it was the visual equivalent of The Shadow's voice — a gigantic echo chamber. Welles, too big for ordinary roles, too overpowering for normal characters, is stylized by nature — is by nature an Expressionist actor.

XXVIII

Two years after the release of *Citizen Kane*, when Herman Mankiewicz had become respectable — his career had taken a leap after *Kane*, and he had had several major credits later in 1941, and had just won another Academy nomination, for his work on *Pride of the Yankees* — he stumbled right into Hearst's waiting arms. He managed to have an accident that involved so many of the elements of his life that it sounds like a made-up surreal joke. Though some of his other calamities are lost in an alcoholic fog — people remember only the bandages and Mankiewicz's stories about how he got them, and maybe even he didn't always know the facts — this one is all too well documented.

Driving home after a few drinks at Romanoff's, he was only a block and a half from his house when he hit a tiny car right at the gates of the Marion Davies residence. And it wasn't just any little car he hit; it was one driven by Lee Gershwin — Ira Gershwin's wife, Lenore, a woman Mankiewicz had known for years. He had adapted the Gershwins' musical *Girl Crazy* to the screen in 1932, and he had known the Gershwins before that, in the twenties, in New York; they were part of the same group. It was a gruesomely comic accident: Hearst was living on the grounds of the Marion Davies estate at the time, in that bungalow that Marion had used at M-G-M and then at Warners, and he was conferring with the publisher of his *New York Journal-American* when he heard the crash. Hearst sent the publisher down to investigate, and as soon as the man reported who was involved, Hearst went into action. Lee Gershwin had had two passengers — her secretary, who wasn't hurt, and her laundress, whom she was taking home, and who just got a bump. Mrs Gershwin herself wasn't badly hurt, though she had a head injury that required some stitches. It was a minor accident, but Mankiewicz was taken to the police station, and he apparently behaved noisily and badly there. When he got home, a few hours later, his wife, Sara, sobered him up, and, having ascertained that Lee Gershwin had been treated at the hospital and had already been discharged, she sent him over to the Gershwins' with a couple of dozen roses. Marc Connelly, who was at the Gershwins' that night, says that when Mankiewicz arrived the house was full of reporters, and Ira Gershwin was serving them drinks and trying to keep things affable. Mankiewicz went upstairs to see Lee, who was lying in bed with her head bandaged. Amiable madman that he was, he noticed a painting on the bedroom wall, and his first remark was that he had a picture by the same artist. He apparently didn't have any idea that he was in serious trouble.

Hearst's persistent vindictiveness was one of his least attractive traits. Mankiewicz was charged with a felony, and the minor accident became a major front-page story in the Hearst papers across the country for four successive days, with headlines more appropriate to a declaration of war. It became the excuse for another Hearst campaign against the orgies and dissolute lives of the movie colony, and Hearst dragged it on for months. By then, the Hearst press was on its way to becoming the crank press, and Hearst had so many enemies that Mankiewicz had many friends. When Mankiewicz appealed to the American Civil Liberties Union, there had already been stories in

Time, Newsweek, Variety, and elsewhere pointing out that the persecution in the Hearst papers was a reprisal for his having written the script of *Citizen Kane*. Mankiewicz, however, had to stand trial on a felony charge. And although he got through the mess of the trial all right, the hounding by the Hearst papers took its toll, and his reputation was permanently damaged.

In a letter to Harold Ross after the trial, Mankiewicz asked to write a Profile of Hearst that Ross was considering. 'Honestly,' he wrote, 'I know more about Hearst than any other man alive. (There are a couple of deaders before their time who knew more, I think.) I studied his career like a scholar before I wrote *Citizen Kane*.' And then, in a paragraph that suggests his admiration, despite everything, for both Hearst and Welles, he wrote, 'Shortly after I had been dragged from the obscurity of the police blotter and — a middle-aged, flat-footed, stylish-stout scenario writer — been promoted by the International News Service into Gary Grant, who, with a tank, had just drunkenly ploughed into a baby carriage occupied by the Dionne quintuplets, the Duchess of Kent, Mrs Franklin D. Roosevelt (the President's wife), and the favorite niece of the Pope, with retouched art combining the more unflattering features of Goering and Dillinger, I happened to be discussing Our Hero with Orson. With the fair-mindedness that I have always recognized as my outstanding trait, I said to Orson that, despite this and that, Mr Hearst was, in many ways, a great man. He was, and is, said Orson, a horse's ass, no more nor less, who has been wrong, without exception, on everything he's ever touched. For instance, for fifty years, said Orson, Hearst did nothing but scream about the Yellow Peril, and then he gave up his seat and hopped off two months before Pearl Harbor.'

XXIX

In 1947, Ferdinand Lundberg sued Orson Welles, Herman J. Mankiewicz, and R.K.O. Radio Pictures, Inc, for two hundred and fifty thousand dollars for copyright infringement, charging that *Citizen Kane* had plagiarized his book *Imperial Hearst*. On the face of it, the suit looked ridiculous. No doubt (as Houseman admits) Mankiewicz had drawn upon everything available about Hearst, in addition to his own knowledge, and no doubt the Lundberg book, which brought a great deal of Hearst material together and printed some things that had not been printed before, was especially useful, but John Dos Passos might have sued on similar grounds, since material that was in *U.S.A.*

was also in the movie, and so might dozens of magazine writers. Hearst himself might have sued, on the basis that he hadn't been credited with the dialogue. The defense would obviously be that the material was in the public domain, and the suit looked like the usual nuisance-value suit that Hollywood is plagued by — especially since Lundberg offered to settle for a flat payment of $18,000. But R.K.O. had become one of Howard Hughes's toys in the late forties, and a crew of expensive lawyers was hired. When the suit came to trial, in 1950, Welles was out of the country; he had given his testimony earlier, in the form of a deposition taken before the American vice-consul at Casablanca, Morocco. This deposition is a curious document, full of pontification and evasion and some bluffing so outrageous that one wonders whether the legal stenographer was able to keep a straight face. *Citizen Kane* had already begun to take over and change the public image of Hearst; Hearst and Kane had become inseparable, as Welles and Kane were, but Welles possibly didn't really know in detail — or, more likely, simply didn't remember — how close the movie was to Hearst's life. He seemed more concerned with continuing the old pretense that the movie was not about Hearst than with refuting Lundberg's charge of plagiarism, and his attempts to explain specific incidents in the movie as if their relationship to Hearst were a mere coincidence are fairly funny. He stated that 'I have done no research into the life of William Randolph Hearst at any time,' and that 'in writing the screenplay of *Citizen Kane* I drew entirely upon my own observations of life,' and then was helpless to explain how there were so many episodes from Hearst's life in the movie. When he was cornered with specific details, such as the picture of Jim Gettys in prison clothes, he gave up and said, 'The dialogue for the scene in question was written in its first and second draftings exclusively by my colleague Mr Mankiewicz. I worked on the third draft.' When he was read a long list of events in the film that parallel Hearst's life as it is recorded in *Imperial Hearst*, he tried to use the Insull cover story and came up with the surprising information that the film dealt 'quite as fully with the world of grand opera as with the world of newspaper publishing.'

Mankiewicz, in a preparatory statement, freely admitted that many of the incidents and details came from Hearst's life but said that he knew them from personal acquaintance and from a lifetime of reading. He was called to testify at the trial, and John Houseman was called as a witness to Mankiewicz's labor on the script. Mankiewicz was indignant that anyone could suggest that a man of his knowledge would need to crib, and he paraded his credentials. It was pointed out that John Gunther had said Mankiewicz made better sense than all the politicans and diplomats put together, and that he was widely known to have a passionate interest in contemporary history, particularly as it related to power, and to have an enormous library. And, of course, he had known Hearst in the years of his full imperial glory, and his friends knew of his absorption in everything to do with Hearst. According to Houseman, he and Mankiewicz thought they were both brilliant in court; they treated the whole suit as an insult, and enjoyed themselves so much while testifying that they spent the time between appearances on the stand congratulating each other. Mankiewicz, in a final gesture of contempt for the charge, brought an inventory of his library and tossed it to the R.K.O. lawyers to demonstrate the width and depth of his culture. It was an inventory that Sara had prepared some years before, when (during a stretch of hard times) they had rented out their house on Tower Road; no one had bothered to look at the inventory — not even the R.K.O. attorneys before they put it into evidence. But Lundberg's lawyers did; they turned to 'L,' and there, neatly listed under 'Lundberg,' were three copies of *Imperial Hearst*. During Mankiewicz's long recuperation, his friends had sent him many books, and since his friends knew of his admiration for many sides of the man he called 'the outstanding whirling pagoda of our times,' he had been showered with copies of this particular book. The inventory apparently made quite an impression in court, and the tide turned. The jury had been cordial to Mankiewicz's explanation of how it was that he knew details that were in the Lundberg book and were unpublished elsewhere, but now the width and depth of his culture became suspect. After thirty days, the trial resulted in a hung jury, and rather than go through another trial, R.K.O. settled for $15,000 — and also paid an estimated couple of hundred thousand dollars in lawyers' fees and court costs.

Mankiewicz went on writing scripts, but his work in the middle and late forties is not in the same spirit as *Kane*. It's rather embarrassing to look at his later credits, because they are yea-saying movies — decrepit 'family pictures' like *The Enchanted Cottage*. The booze and the accidents finally added up, and he declined into the forties sentimental slop. He tried to rise above it. He wrote the script he had proposed earlier on Aimee Semple McPherson, and he started the one on Dillinger, but he had squandered his health as well as his talents. I have read the

McPherson script; it is called *Woman of the Rock*, and it's a tired, persevering-to-the-end, burned-out script. He uses a bit of newspaper atmosphere, and Jed again, this time as a reporter, and relies on a flashback structure from Aimee's death to her childhood; there are 'modern' touches — a semi-lesbian lady who manages the evangelist, for instance — and the script comes to life whenever he introduces sophisticated characters, but he can't write simple people, and even the central character is out of his best range. The one device that is interesting is the heroine's love of bright scarves, starting in childhood with one her father gives her and ending with one that strangles her when it catches on a car wheel, but this is stolen from Isadora Duncan's death, and to give the death of one world-famous lady to another is depressingly poverty-stricken. Mankiewicz's character hadn't changed. He had written friends that he bore the scars of his mistake with Charlie Lederer, but just as he had lent the script of *Kane* to Lederer, Marion Davies's nephew, he proudly showed *Woman of the Rock* to Aimee Semple McPherson's daughter, Roberta Semple, and that ended the project. His behavior probably wasn't deliberately self-destructive as much as it was a form of innocence inside the worldly, cynical man — I visualize him as so *pleased* with what he was doing that he wanted to share his delight with others. I haven't read the unfinished Dillinger; the title, *As the Twig Is Bent,* tells too hoary much.

In his drama column in *The New Yorker* in 1925, Mankiewicz parodied those who thought the Marx Brothers had invented all their own material in *The Cocoanuts* and who failed to recognize George S. Kaufman's contribution. It has been Mankiewicz's fate to be totally ignored in the books on the Marx Brothers movies; though his name is large in the original ads, and though Groucho Marx and Harry Ruby and S.J. Perelman all confirm the fact that he functioned as the producer of *Monkey Business* and *Horse Feathers*, the last reference I can find to this in print is in *Who's Who in America* for 1953, the year of his death. Many of the thirties movies he wrote are popular on television and at college showings, but when they have been discussed in film books his name has never, to my knowledge, appeared. He is never mentioned in connection with *Duck Soup*, though Groucho confirms the fact that he worked on it. He is now all but ignored even in many accounts of *Citizen Kane*. By the fifties, his brother Joe — with *A Letter to Three Wives* and *All About Eve* — had become the famous wit in Hollywood, and there wasn't room for two Mankiewiczes in movie history; Herman became a parentheses in the listings for Joe.

XXX

Welles has offered his semi-defiant apologia for his own notoriously self-destructive conduct in the form of the old fable that he tells as Arkadin in *Confidential Report*, of 1955 — an 'original screenplay' that, from internal evidence, he may very well have written. A scorpion wants to get across a lake and asks a frog to carry him on his back. The frog obliges, but midway the scorpion stings him. As they both sink, the frog asks the scorpion why he did it, pointing out that now he, too, will die, and the scorpion answers, 'I know, but I can't help it; it's my character.' The fable is inserted conspicuously, as a personal statement, almost as if it were a confession, and it's a bad story for a man to use as a parable of his life, since it's a disclaimer of responsibility. It's as if Welles believed in predestination and were saying that he was helpless. Yet Welles's characterization of himself seems rather odd. Whom, after all, has he fatally stung? He was the catalyst for the only moments of triumph that most of his associates ever achieved.

Every time someone in the theatre or in movies breaks through and does something good, people expect the moon of him and hold it against him personally when he doesn't deliver it. That windy speech Kaufman and Hart gave their hero in *The Fabulous Invalid* indicates the enormous burden of people's hopes that Welles carried. He has a long history of disappointing people. In the *Saturday Evening Post* of January 20, 1940, Alva Johnston and Fred Smith wrote:

> Orson was an old war horse in the infant prodigy line by the time he was ten. He had already seen eight years' service as a child genius. . . . Some of the oldest acquaintances of Welles have been disappointed in his career. They see the twenty-four-year-old boy of today as a mere shadow of the two-year-old man they used to know.

A decade after *Citizen Kane,* the gibes were no longer so good-natured; the terms 'wonder boy' and 'boy genius' were thrown in Welles's face. When Welles was only thirty-six, the normally gracious Walter Kerr referred to him as 'an international joke, and possibly the youngest living has-been.' Welles had the special problems of fame without commercial success. Because of the moderate financial returns on *Kane*, he lost the freedom to control his own productions; after *Kane*, he never had complete control of a movie in America. And he lost the collaborative partnerships that he needed.

For whatever reasons, neither Mankiewicz nor Houseman nor Toland ever worked on another Welles movie. He had been advertised as a one-man show; it was not altogether his own fault when he became one. He was alone, trying to be 'Orson Welles,' though 'Orson Welles' had stood for the activities of a group. But he needed the family to hold him together on a project and to take over for him when his energies became scattered. With them, he was a prodigy of accomplishments; without them, he flew apart, became disorderly. Welles lost his magic touch, and as his films began to be diffuse he acquired the reputation of being an intellectual, difficult-to-understand artist. When he appears on television to recite from Shakespeare or the Bible, he is introduced as if he were the epitome of the highbrow; it's television's more polite way of cutting off his necktie.

The Mercury players had scored their separate successes in *Kane*, and they went on to conventional careers; they had hoped to revolutionize theatre and films, and they became part of the industry. Turn on the TV and there they are, dispersed, each in old movies or his new series or his reruns. Away from Welles and each other, they were neither revolutionaries nor great originals, and so Welles became a scapegoat — the man who 'let everyone down.' He has lived all his life in a cloud of failure because he hasn't lived up to what was unrealistically expected of him. No one has ever been able to do what was expected of Welles — to create a new radical theatre and to make one movie masterpiece after another — but Welles's 'figurehead' publicity had snowballed to the point where all his actual and considerable achievements looked puny compared to what his destiny was supposed to be. In a less confused world, his glory would be greater than his guilt.

The New Yorker, 1971

On the Future of Movies

Sometime during the last year, a number of the most devoted moviegoers stopped going to the movies. I say 'a number' because I have no idea how many are actually involved, but I keep meeting people — typically, men in their late twenties and early thirties — who say, 'You know, I just don't have the impulse to go to a movie anymore,' or 'There aren't any movies anymore, are there?' The interest in pictures has left these people almost overnight; they turned off as suddenly as they'd turned on, and, since they no longer care to go, they feel that there's nothing to see. It was no accident that the Americans walked off with most of the top awards at Cannes this year. Right now, American movies — not the big hits but many of the movies that Hollywood considers failures — are probably the best in the world. No country rivals us in the diversity of skilled, talented filmmakers, but there are few lines for the sorts of films that young audiences were queuing up for a couple of years ago. They talked fervently then about how they loved movies; now they feel there can't be anything good going on, even at the movies.

Whatever their individual qualities, such films as *Bonnie and Clyde, The Graduate, Easy Rider, Five Easy Pieces, Joe, M.A.S.H., Little Big Man, Midnight Cowboy,* and *They Shoot Horses, Don't They?* all helped to form the counterculture. The young, anti-draft, anti-Vietnam audiences that were 'the film generation' might go to some of the same pictures that the older audience did, but not to those only. They were willing to give something fresh a chance, and they went to movies that weren't certified hits. They made modest — sometimes large — successes of pictures that had new, different perceptions. A movie like the tentative, fumbling *Alice's Restaurant* would probably be a flop now, because student audiences are no longer willing to look for feelings, to accept something suggestive and elliptical and go with the mood. Students accept the elliptical on records — the Joni Mitchell 'Court and Spark,' say, and some of the more offbeat Carly Simon cuts — but not in movies. The subdued, fine-drawn *McCabe & Mrs Miller*, which came out in 1971, managed to break even, but the soft-colored *Thieves Like Us*, the latest film by the same director, Robert Altman, has been seen by almost nobody. Those who might be expected to identify with Jeff Bridges in *The Last American Hero* are going to see Clint Eastwood in *Magnum Force* instead. They're going to the kind of slam-bang pictures that succeed with illiterate audiences in 'underdeveloped' countries who are starved for entertainment. The almost voluptuously obsessive *Mean Streets* — a film that one might have thought would be talked about endlessly — passed through college towns without causing a stir. The new generations of high-school and college students are going to movies that you can't talk about afterward — movies that are completely consumed in the theatre.

There is no way to estimate the full effect of Vietnam and Watergate on popular culture, but earlier films were predicated on an implied system of values which is gone now, except in the corrupt, vigilante form of a *Dirty Harry* or a *Walking Tall*. Almost all the current hits are jokes on the past, and especially on old films — a mixture of nostalgia and parody, laid on with a trowel. The pictures reach back in time, spoofing the past, jabbing at it. Nobody understands what contemporary heroes or heroines should be, or how they should relate to each other, and it's safer not to risk the box-office embarrassment of seriousness.

For many years, some of us alarmists have been saying things like 'Suppose people get used to constant visceral excitement — will they still respond to the work of artists?' Maybe, owing partly to the national self-devaluation and partly to the stepped-up power of advertising, what we feared has come about. It's hardly surprising: how can people who have just been pummeled and deafened by *The French Connection* be expected to respond to a quiet picture? If, still groggy, they should stumble in to see George Segal in Irvin Kershner's *Loving* the next night, they'd think there was nothing going on in it, because it didn't tighten the screws on them. *The Rules of the Game* might seem like a hole in the screen. When *The Getaway* is double-billed with *Mean Streets*, it's no wonder that some people walk out on *Mean Streets*. Audiences like movies that do all the work for them — just as in the old days, and with an arm-twisting rubdown besides. College students don't appear to feel insulted (what's left to insult us?); they don't mind being banged over the head — the louder the better. They seem to enjoy seeing the performers whacked around, too; sloppy knockabout farce is the newest smash, and knockabout horror isn't far behind. People go for the obvious, the broad, the movies that don't ask them to feel anything. If a movie is a hit, that means practically guaranteed sensations — and sensations without feeling.

I often come out of a movie now feeling wiped out, desolate — and often it's a movie that the audience around me has reacted to noisily, as if it were having a high, great time — and I think I feel that way because of the nihilism in the atmosphere. It isn't intentional or philosophical nihilism; it's the kind one sometimes feels at a porn show — the way everything is turned to dung, oneself included. A couple of years ago, I went with another film critic, a young man, to see a hard-core movie in the Broadway area, and there was a live stage show with it. A young black girl — she looked about seventeen but must have been older — did a strip and then danced naked. The theater was small, and the girl's eyes, full at hatred, kept raking the customers' faces. I was the only other woman there, and each time her eyes came toward me, I had to look down; finally, I couldn't look up at all. The young critic and I sat in misery, unable to leave, since that would look like a put-down of her performance. We had to take the contempt with which she hid her sense of being degraded, and we shared in her degradation, too. Hits like *The Exorcist* give most of the audience just what it wants and expects, the way hard-core porn does. The hits have something in common: blatancy. They are films that *deliver*. They're debauches — their subject might almost be mindlessness and futurelessness. People in the audience want to laugh, and at pictures like *Enter the Dragon* and *Andy Warhol's Frankenstein* and *The Three Musketeers* and *Blazing Saddles* they're laughing at pandemonium and accepting it as the comic truth.

The counterculture films made corruption seem inevitable and hence something you learn to live with; the next step was seeing it as slapstick comedy and learning to enjoy it. For the fatalistic, case-hardened audience, absurdism has become the only acceptable point of view — a new complacency. In *The Three Musketeers*, Richard Lester keeps his actors at a distance and scales the characters down to subnormal size; they're letching, carousing buffoons who don't care about anything but blood sport. The film isn't politically or socially abrasive; it's just 'for fun.' At showings of *Chinatown*, the audience squeals with pleasure when Faye Dunaway reveals her incest. The success of *Chinatown* — with its beautifully structured script and draggy, overdeliberate direction — represents something dialecti- cally new: nostalgia (for the thirties) openly turned to rot, and the *celebration* of rot. Robert Towne's script had ended with the detective (Jack Nicholson) realizing what horrors the Dunaway character had been through, and, after she killed her incentuous father, helping her daughter get to Mexico. But Roman Polanski seals the picture with his gargoyle grin; now evil runs rampant. The picture is compelling, but coldly, suffocatingly compelling. Polanski keeps so much of it in closeup that there's no air, no freedom to breathe; you don't care who is hurt, since everything is blighted. Life is a blood-red maze. Polanski may leave the story muddy and opaque, but he shoves the rot at you, and large numbers of people seem to find it juicy. Audiences now appear to accept as view of themselves what in the movies of the past six or seven years counterculture audiences jeered at Americans for being — cynical materialists who cared for nothing but their own greed and lust. The nihilistic, coarse-grained movies are telling us that nothing matters to us, that we're all a bad joke.

It's becoming tough for a movie that isn't a big media-created event to find an audience, no matter how good it is. And if a movie has been turned into an event, it doesn't have to be good; an event — such as *Papillon* — draws an audience simply because it's an event. You don't expect Mount Rushmore to be a work of art, but if you're anywhere near it you have to go; *Papillon* is a movie Mount Rushmore, though it features only two heads. People no longer go to a picture just for itself, and ticket-buyers certainly aren't looking for the movie equivalent of 'a good read.' They want to be battered, to be knocked out — they want to get wrecked. They want what 'everybody's talking about,' and even if they don't like the picture — and some people didn't really care for *A Touch of Class*, and some detested *The Three Musketeers*, and many don't like *Blazing Saddles*, either — they don't feel out of it. Increasingly, though, I've noticed that those who don't enjoy a big event-film feel out of it in another way. They wonder if there's something they're not getting — if the fault is theirs.

The public can't really be said to have rejected a film like *Payday*, since the public never heard of it. If you don't know what a movie is and it plays at a theatre near you, you barely register it. *Payday* may not come at all; when the event strategy really works, as it has of late, the hits and the routine action films and horror films are all that get to most towns. And if a film turns up that hasn't had a big campaign, people assume it's a dog; you risk associating yourself with failure if you go to see Jon Voight in *Conrack* or Blythe Danner in the messed-up but still affecting *Lovin' Molly*. When other values are rickety, the fact that something is selling gives it a primacy, and its detractors seem like spoilsports. The person who holds out against an event looks a loser: the minority is a fool. People are cynical about advertising, of course, but their cynicism is so all-inclusive now that they're indifferent, and so they're more susceptible to advertising than ever. If nothing matters anyway, why not just go where the crowd goes? That's a high in itself.

There are a few exceptions, but in general it can be said that the public no longer discovers movies, the public no longer makes a picture a hit. If the advertising for a movie doesn't build up an overwhelming desire to be part of the event, people just don't go. They don't listen to their own instincts, they don't listen to the critics — they listen to the advertising. Or, to put it more precisely, they do listen to their instincts, but their instincts are now controlled by advertising. It seeps through everything — talk shows, game shows, magazine and newspaper stories. Museums organize retrospectives of a movie director's work to coordinate with the opening of his latest film, and publish monographs paid for by the movie companies. College editors travel at a movie company's expense to see its big new film and to meet the director, and directors preview their new pictures at colleges. The public-relations event becomes part of the national consciousness. You don't hear anybody say, 'I saw the most wonderful movie you never heard of'; when you hear people talking, it's about the same blasted movie that everybody's going to — the one that's flooding the media. Yet even the worst cynics still like to think that 'word of mouth' makes hits. And the executives who set up the machinery of manipulation love to believe that the public — the public that's sitting stone-dead in front of its TV sets — spontaneously discovered their wonderful movie. If it's a winner, they say it's the people's choice. But, in the TV age, when people say they're going to see *Walking Tall* because they've 'heard' it's terrific, that rarely means a friend has told them; it means they've picked up signals from the atmosphere. It means *Walking Tall* has been plugged so much that every cell in a person's body tells him he's got to see it. Nobody ever says that it was the advertising that made him vote for a particular candidate, yet there is considerable evidence that in recent decades the presidential candidates who spent the most money always won. They were the people's choice. Advertising is a form of psychological warfare that in popular culture, as in politics, is becoming harder to fight with aboveboard weapons. It's becoming damned near invincible.

The ludicrous *Mame* or the limp, benumbed *The Great Gatsby* may not make as much money as the producing companies hoped for, but these pictures don't fail abjectly, either. They're hits. If Hollywood executives still believe in word of mouth, it's because the words come out of their own mouths.

The businessmen have always been in control of film production; now advertising puts them, finally, on top of public reaction as well. They can transcend the content and the quality of a film by advertising. The new blatancy represents the triumph — for the moment, at least — of the businessmen's taste and the businessmen's ethic. Traditionally, movies were thought linked to dreams and illusions, and to pleasures that went way beyond satisfaction. Now the big ones are stridently illusionless, for a public determined not to be taken in. Audiences have become 'realists' in the manner of businessmen who congratulate themselves for being realists: they believe only in what gives immediate gratification. It's got to be right there — tangible, direct, basic, in their laps. The movie executives were shaken for a few years; they didn't understand what made a film a counterculture hit. They're happy to be back on firm ground with *The Sting*. Harmless, inoffensive. Plenty of plot but no meanings. Not even any sex to worry about.

Much — perhaps most — of the students' and educated moviegoers' unresponsiveness to recent fine work can be traced to the decisions of the movie companies about what will sell and what won't. With their overweening campaign budgets for *The Great Gatsby* and *Chinatown*, the Paramount executives didn't even take a full-page ad in the *Times* to announce that *The Conversation* had won the Grand Prize at Cannes. They didn't *plan* on *The Conversation* being a success, and nothing now is going to make them help it become one. *Gatsby* and *Chinatown* were their pictures, but *The Conversation* was Francis Ford Coppola's and they're incensed at his being in a position (after directing *The Godfather*) to do what he wanted to do; they're *hurt* that he flouts their authority, working out of San Francisco instead of Los

Angeles. And they don't really have any respect for *The Conversation*, because it's an idea film. It's the story of a compulsive loner (Gene Hackman), a wizard at electronic surveillance who is so afraid others will spy on him that he empties his life; he's a cipher — a cipher in torment. There's nothing to discover about him, and *still* he's in terror of being bugged. (Hackman is a superlative actor, but his peculiarity, his limitation, like Ralph Richardson's when he was younger, is his quality of anonymity: just what is right for this role.) *The Conversation* is driven by an inner logic. It's a little thin, because the logic is the working out of one character's obsession, but it's a buggy movie that can get to you so that when it's over you really feel you're being bugged. Maybe the reason the promotion people didn't try to exploit the Watergate tie-in was that they suspected the picture might also be saying something about movie companies. If a film isn't promoted, it's often because something about it — the idea itself, or the director's obstinate determination to make it — needles the bosses.

Executives show a gambler's ardor in arranging the financing of a picture. Sometimes they buy into one when it's finished or almost finished, in what appears to be the absolute conviction that it's a winner. But almost any straw in the wind can make them lose confidence. They'll try out a tricky, subtle movie on a Friday-night preview audience that has come to see *Walking Tall* or John Wayne in *McQ* and decide that the movie has no public appeal. They pull away from what they fear will be a failure; within the fiefdom of their company they don't want to be associated with a risky venture. They all snuggle deep into the company's hits; a picture like *The Sting* becomes a soft fur collar that they caress themselves with. The company that has *The Sting* doesn't worry about a real sendoff for *The Sugarland Express*: where are the big stars? The company with *The Exorcist* doesn't give much thought to a campaign for *Mean Streets*: some of the executives don't find it 'satisfying,' so they're sure the public won't. The movie companies used to give all their pictures a chance, but now they'll put two or three million, or even five, into selling something they consider surefire, and a token — a pittance — into the others. And when an unpublicized picture fails they can always cover their tracks by blaming the director. 'There was nothing we could do for it,' the executives in charge of advertising always say, and once they have doomed a picture, who can prove them wrong?

What isn't generally understood is that the top men don't want to be proved wrong and the lower-echelon executives have a jobholder's interest in proving their bosses right. For all the publicity the companies get from giving a picture 'a second chance' — never really having given it a first — I can think of only one or two cases when they honestly did provide a fresh chance, and there's a whole morgueful of movies that were killed despite indications of public response; for example, Gillo Pontecorvo's only picture after *The Battle of Algiers* — *Burn!*, starring Marlon Brando, which came and went so fast that hardly anybody knows it exists.

If the company men don't like a picture, or are nervous about its chances, or just resent the director's wanting to do something he cares about (instead of taking the big assignments they believe in), they do minimal advertising, telling him, 'Let's wait for the reviews,' or 'We'll see how the reviewers like it,' and then, even if the reviews are great, they say, 'But the picture isn't doing business. Why should we throw away money on it?' And if he mentions the reviews, they say, 'Listen, the critics have never meant anything. You know that. Why waste money? If people don't want to go, you can't force them to buy tickets.'

There's a natural war in Hollywood between the businessmen and the artists. It's based on drives that may go deeper than politics or religion: on the need for status, and warring dreams. The entrepreneur class in the arts is a relatively late social development; there were impressarios earlier, but it was roughly a hundred years ago, when the arts began to be commercialized for a large audience, that the mass-culture middleman was born. He functions as a book publisher, as a theatrical producer, as a concert manager, as a rock promoter, but the middleman in the movie world is probably more filled with hatred for the artists he traffics in than the middleman in any other area. The movie entrepreneur is even more of a self-made man than the others; he came out of nowhere. He has to raise — and risk — more money, and he stands to gain more. In a field with no traditions, he is more of a gambler and less of an aesthete than entrepreneurs in the other arts. He's a street fighter, his specialty low cunning. Even if he's a second- or third-generation movie executive with a college education, or a Harvard-educated lawyer turned agent turned producer, he's learned to be a street fighter if he wasn't born to it, and he has the same hatred of the artist. The artist, with his expressive needs — the artist, who, by definition, cares about something besides money — denigrates the only talent that the entrepreneur has: raising money. Nobody respects the entrepreneur's dream of glory, and nobody respects his singular talent — least of all the artist who needs him, and is often at his mercy.

The entrepreneur has no class, no status; and, whether he was a scrambling junk dealer or a scheming agent or a poor little rich boy who managed to survive his mogul father's ruthless bullying, he knows that. A director or an actor doesn't even have to be an artist — only to identify himself as an artist — to get the cachet, while the moneyman is likely to be treated as a moneygrubbing clown. Some few — Joe Levine, and Sam Goldwyn before him — have been able to make celebrities of themselves by acquiring a comic status, the status of a shrewd, amusing vulgarian. In no other field is the entrepreneur so naked a status-seeker. Underlings are kept busy arranging awards and medals and honorary degrees for the producer, whose name looms so large in the ads that the public — and often the producer himself — comes to think he actually made the pictures. Ross Hunter, Robert Radnitz, even Hal Wallis in recent years hardly have room in their advertising for the writers' and directors' names. The packagers offer themselves as the stars, and in many cases their pictures fail because they insist on employing nonentity directors who don't assert any authority.

The hatred of the moneyman for the ungovernable artist is based on a degradation that isn't far from that stripper's hatred of the audience — furious resentment of the privileged people who, as he sees it, have never had to stoop to do the things he has done. As in Mordecai Richler's exultant novel *The Apprenticeship of Duddy Kravitz* (which really enables one to understand what makes Sammy run), and the teeming, energetic Canadian film based on it, the entrepreneur is, typically, a man who has always been treated like dirt. And even after he's fought his way up, finagling like crazy every step of the way, a profligate director with the world at his feet may not only threaten that solvency but still treat him like dirt, as in Peter Viertel's thinly disguised account, in the novel *White Hunter, Black Heart*, of the relations of John Huston and Sam Spiegel during the making of *The African Queen*. There are few directors who feel such disdain, fewer still who would express it so nakedly, but the moneymen keep looking for signs of it: they tap phones, they turn employees into sneaks and spies — all to get proof of the disloyalty of those ingrate artists. It doesn't help if the artists like the tough bosses personally — if they prize the unconcealed wiliness or the manic, rude drive. In Richler's later novel *St Urbain's Horseman*, the now rich Duddy Kravitz appears as a minor character. When someone assures Duddy that his blond actress wife loves him, Duddy is exasperated: 'What are you talking, she loves me? Who in the hell could love Duddy Kravitz?' Duddy's view of himself doesn't leave much of a basis for friendship, and any affection the artist may feel disintegrates as soon as the businessman uses his power to control the artist's work. The artist's crime is caring less for profits than for what he wants to do; that caring is an insult and a threat. The war of the businessmen against the artists is the war of the powerful against the powerless, based on the hatred of those who can't for those who can, and in return the hatred of those who can for those who won't let them.

The producers' complaint about the hothead director who puts up a fight to try something different is 'He's self-destructive. He's irresponsible. You can't do business with him.' And they make him suffer for it. The artists in Hollywood are objects of ridicule because they're trying to work as artists. When a gifted director is broke and needs to work, the producers stick him on a project that is compromised from the start, and then the picture is one more failure to be held against him. They frustrate him at every turn because he doesn't respect them, and he is humiliated by men he doesn't even respect. The producers feel secure with the directors and actors who don't have ideas of their own, who will take jobs because they need to work and don't really care what they do. Those are the ones the producers call 'artists with discipline.'

An actor or a director can become an 'artist with discipline' when he has a huge box-office hit, and his reputation for discipline will soar if, like Paul Newman or Robert Redford, he has a string of hits. Actually, to the moneymen discipline means success plus a belief in success. Coppola isn't called disciplined, despite the success of *The Godfather*, because he wants to work on his own projects (such as *The Conversation*), but George Roy Hill (*Butch Cassidy and the Sundance Kid, Slaughterhouse Five, The Sting*) is disciplined, because he believes in big-name, big-star projects. Peter Yates (*Bullitt, John and Mary*) is considered a man you can do business with, despite a flop like *Murphy's War* and the far from successful *The Hot Rock* and *The Friends of Eddie Coyle*; his flops aren't held against him, because he believes in the same kind of projects that the moneymen do and he doesn't try to do anything *special* with those projects. His latest, *For*

Pete's Sake, probably won't bring in much of a bundle, but it's a model of Hollywood 'discipline.'

Peter Yates's lack of distinction, like the veteran Richard Fleischer's, is a proof of trustworthiness. The moneymen want a director who won't surprise them. They're scared of a man like Altman, because they just don't know what he'll do on a picture; they can't trust him to make it resemble the latest big hit. They want solid imitations, pictures that reek of money spent and money to come, pictures that look safe — like those Biblical epics that came rumbling off the assembly lines in the fifties. Twentieth Century-Fox and Warner Brothers are jointly producing a burning-skyscraper picture, *The Towering Inferno*, with Steve McQueen, Paul Newman, William Holden, Jennifer Jones, Robert Wagner, Fred Astaire, Richard Chamberlain, and other assorted big names. It's Grand Hotel in flames at last. Universal, for starters, has signed up Anne Bancroft and George C. Scott for *The Hindenburg,* described as 'a multilayered drama with a gallery of international characters.' In other words, Grand Hotel in flames in the sky. Every couple of years, the American movie public is said to crave something. Now it's calamity, and already the wave of apocalyptic movies — which aren't even here yet — is being analyzed in terms of our necrophilia. The studio heads are setting up disaster epics like kids reaching hand over hand up a baseball bat — all because of the success of *The Poseidon Adventure*, which probably had about as much to do with a public interest in apocalypse as Agatha Christie's *Ten Little Indians* had. I doubt whether there's a single one of the directors mounting these disaster specials — becoming commanders-in-chief in an idiot war — who wouldn't infinitely rather be working on something else. By the time the public is gorged with disasters and the epics begin to flop, the studio heads will have fastened on another get-rich-quick gimmick (pirate capers are said to be on the agenda), and the people who work for them will lose a few more years of what might have been their creative lives. The producers gamble on the public's wanting more of whatever is a hit, and since they *all* gamble on that, the public is always quickly surfeited, but the failures of the flaccid would-be hits never anger the producers the way the failures of the films that someone really fought for do. The producers want those films to fail; they often make them fail. A Sam Peckinpah film, an Altman film, a Kershner film — the executives get pleasure out of seeing those films fail. It's a *punishment* of the artist.

Since all the businessmen's energy goes into strategy and manipulation, they can outfox the artists damn near every time; that's really the business they're in. Their right of 'final cut' — one of the great symbolic terms in moviemaking — gives them the chance to chop up the film of a director who has angered them by doing it his own way; they'll mutilate the picture trying to remove the complexities he battled to put in. They love to play God with other people's creations. Movie after movie is mangled, usually by executives' last-minute guesses about what the public wants. When they've finished, they frequently can't do anything with the pictures but throw them away. That's their final godlike act — an act easy for them to live with, because they always have the director to blame. To them, the artist is the outsider; he's not a member of the family, to be protected. A few years ago, when word was out in the industry that Brando didn't mean anything at the box office, the produced David Merrick fired him from a picture; I asked an executive connected with the production what Brando had done. 'Nothing,' he said. 'Brando was working hard, and he was cooperative with everyone. But he suggested some ways to improve the script; they were good suggestions — the script was a mess. But legally that was interference, and Merrick could fire Brando and collect on the insurance.' 'But why?' I persisted. He shrugged at my ignorance. 'What could make David Merrick bigger than firing Marlon Brando?' he said.

The star can be defined by what the producer says of him: 'If he wants to burn down the studio, I'll hand him the match.' That was said, I think, of Jerry Lewis, but it applies to such Hollywood figures as Frank Sinatra and, of course, Clint Eastwood and Robert Redford and Steve McQueen. What it means is very simple: the producers will hand them a match because the producers are banking the money. The producer is saying, 'He can degrade me as long as I get mine out of it.' And underneath that he's saying, 'But wait until he has to come to me for something.' The producers hate Brando for refusing to settle down and go for the money; they love-hate McQueen and Redford and Eastwood. They need them; they court them. And, yes, they can make a deal with them, but only on the star's terms, and the producers are never allowed to forget it. If the chance ever comes, they'll make the star pay for that.

The country has never been as star crazy as it is right now; there aren't very many movie stars, but the phenomenon of stardom operates in television, in radio, in literature, in the academic world, in politics, in the women's movement. (The black movement hasn't been getting much publicity recently, because it lacks stars.) Yet one can watch a few TV 'roasts' — those ugly-jolly orgies of mock insults and real insults and odious sentimental disclaimers in which celebrities are fêted — without becoming aware of the sense of betrayal that is just under the surface? The best performer at the roast is obviously the one who dares to be the most malicious, and the person honored is forced to be a good sport while others 'kid' him, letting out their aggression while he tries to laugh. And then they embrace him and say they didn't mean it. The roast is the show-business form of Shirley Jackson's lottery. It's a public display of the anger and self-hatred of those caught in the system, a ritual gathering of sellouts hitting each other with bladders and pretending it doesn't hurt. And that's how they feel when they're *at the top*. Their contempt for the audience, like the stripper's, is probably what makes it possible for them to keep going. They begin to believe that Las Vegas is all there is. The roast is a metaphor for the truth of the business; that's why it has become impossible for the Academy Awards presentation to have any style or dignity. The members of the Hollywood community can't control their self-destructive impulses any longer; they can't resist humiliating themselves before the whole world. 'If that's what people want,' the performers say, 'I'll give it to them.' Essentially, they're all playing to Duddy Kravitz. He's the man backing the international motion-picture roast.

A reviewer who pans a producer's picture is just one more person telling him he has no taste. When the reviewers praise movies that are allowed to die, the moneyman's brute instincts are confirmed, and the reviewers' impotence gives him joy. 'Why must we sit back and allow the critics to determine if a film is acceptable as a consumer product?' Frank Yablans, the president of Paramount, asked this June. He was speaking to some two hundred people who work in television, explaining to them that word of mouth, which can defeat downbeat reviews, will be Paramount's target. A reviewer speaks out once, or maybe twice. The advertisers are an invisible force pounding at the public day after day. Unfavorable reviews are almost never powerful enough to undo the saturation publicity. Besides, curiosity about an event like *The Exorcist* is a big factor; as the woman quoted in *Variety* said, 'I want to see what everybody is throwing up about.'

People often make analogies between the world of live theater and the world of movies, and raise the question 'Don't movie critics have too much power?' But in movies it's the businessmen who have the power. A reviewer's words can't be heard above the din unless they're amplified in the ads — which usually means reduced to a short, exclamatory quote and repeated incessantly. But that's only if the reviewer provided a quote for a picture that the company 'has high hopes for'; if it's a picture that the company has lost interest in, there will be a few halfhearted ads, with apathetically selected quotes. Raves from even the dozen most influential papers and magazines can't make a success of *Mean Streets* if the company doesn't construct a campaign around those raves. The public indifference is a result of something that starts at the top of the movie company and filters down. Five years ago — even two years ago — a handful of reviewers could help persuade people to give a small or unheralded film a chance, but not now. The reviewers spoke to that audience which has lost the impulse to go to movies. The demise of 'the film generation' means a sharp break with the past, since there won't be anything like that mass of youth — the Second World War babies reaching maturity — again. Because of its styles of hair and dress and manner, it was an identifiable generation; the members tuned in together for the last time at *American Graffiti* — that pop-comics view of their own adolescence, before they became the counterculture. Now the links are mostly broken and they're the aging young, tuned out.

The younger audience — high-school and college students — grew up with the rating system. As kids, they couldn't escape to the movies, the way their parents did, and so movies weren't an important part of their lives (though television was). When *they* say they love movies, they mean the old movies that they're just discovering, and the new hits. Even the sub-teens want the events; they were born into sixties cynicism and saturation advertising. They've never known anything but the noise and the frantic atmosphere; they think it's a cop-out if a movie cuts away from mayhem and doesn't show them the gore. They loved *Jesus Christ Superstar* (a masochistic revel for eight-year-olds), and they're eager to be part of *The Sting* and *Blazing Saddles*. They're saturated.

The students now who discover movies in college and want to get into film production have a different outlook from the young counterculture filmmakers of the sixties. They're not interested in getting into movie work in order to change movies; they just want to get into movie work. A young film student expressed anger to me about Elia Kazan, who had given a lecture at his university. Kazan had said that the studios wouldn't finance the subjects he was interested in, and offered him projects he couldn't face doing. The student, without a shade of sympathy for those caught in this basic Hollywood trap, said, 'How can we listen to him? We would do anything to break in, and he says he's turning down projects!' Students have little interest in why a person refuses to direct the forty-sixth dope-heist picture or a romp about sprightly, beguiling swindlers; they don't care to hear some director say that he turned down *The Exorcist*. A hit makes a director a hero. A critic who speaks at a college now is almost certain to be asked such questions as 'How many times do you see a movie before writing your critique?' and 'Do you take notes?' The students are really asking, 'How do you do it? How did you get to be a film critic?' They sometimes used to ask, 'What do you think of Academy Awards?' — a question that was a sure laugh-getter from an audience that anticipated a tart rejoinder. Now they ask, 'What [or who] do you think will win the Oscars this year?' And they really want to know the answer. Celebrity and success are so big on campus that the Academy Awards are discussed as if they were a perfectly respectable academic issue.

Stardom is success made manifest, success in human form, and, naturally, the yes-sayers are, in general, the biggest stars. College students are impressed and contemptuous at the same time. Can one imagine any picture so reactionary or vile that it would diminish Clint Eastwood's standing at a university? Even a reputation for corruption — for being willing to do anything for money — increases a star's stature, and the money gained gives him power and standing that are admired in a way the no-sayer's intransigence isn't, especially if his intransigence puts him out of the scene. There is nothing a star can do now that would really disgrace him. 'Celebrity' has destroyed the concept of disgrace: scandal creates celebrity, and public misbehavior enhances it. Maybe *The Sting* is such a whopping hit because it's really a celebration of celebrity and stardom; it's not about anything but the golden yes-yes images of Redford and Newman. It doesn't need sex; it's got the true modern sex appeal — success.

In Los Angeles this spring, busloads of high-school students were brought in to listen to a Best-Sellers Panel composed of Helen Gurley Brown, Garson Kanin, Jacqueline Susann, and William Friedkin on the subject of how it feels to sell fifteen million books or to gross a hundred and twenty-five million dollars on a movie. From all accounts, there were no impolite questions, and no one made a rude noise when Kanin (*Tracy and Hepburn*) said, 'We have to recognize that the public is smarter than we are. As individuals, one by one, perhaps no. But when that thousand-headed monster sits out there in the auditorium or sits reading your book of fiction, suddenly that mass audience is what the late Moss Hart called "an idiot genius." ' This conceit of the successful — their absolute conviction that the crap that is sold is magically superior to the work that didn't sell — is the basis for the entrepreneurs' self-righteousness. The public has nothing to gain from believing this (and everything to lose), and yet the public swallows it.

The businessmen's confidence has taken a leap; business is better than it has been in several years, and they've got the artists where they want them. They're sure they're on the right track, because the public likes what they like. It's no longer just a Harry Cohn who could be said to have the world wired to his ass; the world is wired to all their asses. The hits are not uniformly terrible, and in themselves they don't pose any great threat. But if this is all that people want from movies — if even educated people and people of taste and some sensibility settle for the nihilistic brassiness of the hits — there's no audience for new work. In the past ten years, filmmaking has attracted some of the most inspired college students — the aces and prodigies who in previous eras would have headed into poetry or architecture or painting or playwriting. There they are, poised and ready to take off, and there is no place for them to take off to except the same old Hollywood vise — tighter now, perfected. And there are the high-fliers who have been locked out all along — the dozens of artist-filmmakers who work in film not as a collaborative storytelling medium but as a highly individual art form, more closely related to the graphic arts than to Hollywood. Some of them, such as Ed Emshwiller, with his great trip film *Relativity*, and Jordan Belson, who has made flawless abstract visionary shorts, have already reached new peaks of film art; others, such as John Schofill, who works at scarily intense psychosexual imagery, may. Right now, there is no way for their work to reach movie theaters and no way for them to heat up and fertilize feature filmmaking, which needs renewal. Everything is ready for an age of great movies, except the entrepreneurs and the public.

Movies could easily go the way of the theater — and faster, since the moneymen have no aesthetic commitment whatever. And probably there'd be less lamentation for movies than for live theater. Because, of course, there's television. But it's not the same medium. And though if you don't read a book when it comes out you can read it a year later, if you don't see a movie when it comes out, and wait to see it a year later on television, you're not seeing what you could have seen in the theatre. (Nor do you see that movie if you wait to see it in a college, or at a film society in a cheap, grainy 16 mm reduction.) What's lost on television is the visual beauty, the spatial sense, the fusion of image and sound — everything that makes movies an art form. And movies made directly for television almost never have these qualities; one talks of TV movies in terms of pace and impact and tension, and occasionally — with the prestige ones — subject and performances, but who talks of television movies in terms of beauty? Movies made for TV, or movies made for a big screen and shown on TV, are reduced to just what the businessmen believe in — the bare bones of entertainment. There is something spurious about the very term 'a movie made for TV,' because what you make for TV is a TV program.

Television as we have it isn't an art form — it's a piece of furniture that is good for a few things. There's a problem of dimensions: no matter what people say, the screen is too small, and that's why the thing TV does best is a closeup of a person being asked a direct question — because both you and that person know that it operates like a lie detector. For perhaps most Americans, TV is an appliance, not to be used selectively but to be turned on — there's always something to watch. If a hundred million people see a movie in two showings on TV, that doesn't mean what it would if a hundred million people saw it in theaters. Sure, forty-two million people saw *The Autobiography of Miss Jane Pittman*, but they saw it sandwiched between two other shows. TV stars with audiences larger than the world has ever before known are eager to appear in a real movie — which, even if a hit, will be seen by only a handful, relatively speaking (until it, too, winds up on TV) — because they know that on TV they're part of the furniture. On TV they're mundane, they're reduced to the routinely, boringly tolerable. There's an aesthetic element in the phrase 'larger than life,' and the artists working in the movie medium instinctively take that into consideration. What is on the big screen has an aesthetic clarity denied to the box; when you're watching a movie in a theater, you don't need a voice telling you what you have just seen.

There have been some few subjects filmed for TV which nobody would finance for theaters, because it's generally understood that people won't pay to see a film on a subject like that of *I Heard the Owl Call My Name* or *Jane Pittman* or *The Execution of Private Slovik*. But a few TV shows with social themes shouldn't become the occasion for big headlines in the press about how television 'has been growing bolder.' Bold is just what these shows aren't; even when they're made as well as possible, they're mincingly careful. And they're not a key to new opportunities on TV so much as a key to the constriction of opportunities for moviemakers: moviemakers can't get backing for pictures with social themes — or with any real themes at all. Probably it's true that people wouldn't pay to see the films on social themes which they'll watch on television, but that's because those subjects are treated in the sober, limited TV manner. We have no way of knowing how the public might respond if a hugely talented filmmaker with adequate resources and a campaign to back him took on a large social theme. Nobody has had the chance in decades.

Television represents what happens to a medium when the artists have no power and the businessmen are in full, unquestioned control. People's TV expectations are so low and so routinized that *Brian's Song* can pass for an event, and a pitifully predictable problem play like *Tell Me Where It Hurts*, in which Maureen Stapleton plays a middle-aged housewife who joins a women's-lib group and has her consciousness raised, is received by the press as if it marked a significant advance. And what sort of opportunities does *normal* television offer for the development of talent? Here are the words of Brandon Stoddard, A.B.C.'s vice-president in charge of motion pictures for television:

> I am interested in emotional jeopardy, not physical jeopardy. I want the viewer to really care about the people and to feel something when it is over. . . . I have nothing against exploitative material if it is done right, and the way to do it right is to translate it into human drama rather than gimmicks. I don't want to know about the two Vampires in the casino in Las Vegas. I want to know about the man they are attacking and how it will affect his life. . . . We are looking everywhere for story ideas and even calling colleges to get some new blood into this.

Movies as an art form won't die and go to the heaven of television. If they die, they'll be truly dead. Even if the shift in the audience toward the crude and insensitive is only a temporary derangement, it could be sufficient to destroy movies. The good recent films — all together — can't possibly lose as much money as a single clinker like *Star!* or *Camelot*, but even if each one of them should manage to break even, and some of them to show a small or moderate profit, the businessmen will still see them as failures. The businessmen don't collect medals for moderate profits; they get their medals for box-office killers, and they don't want pictures by people who reject their values. When they tell a director, 'Listen, what you call crap is what the public wants,' it's not just an objective comment; they want the public to want this crap, and they've made stark sure it will. Since they've cold-decked public opinion, since they promote and sell only what they like, when they say, 'That's what the public wants,' it's the truth.

Nathanael West got it upside down. The locusts aren't those poor bastards from Oklahoma who want to touch a movie star and die in the sun; the locusts run the studios, and it's they who, in West's metaphor, will burn Los Angeles — they'll hand *everybody* a match. It's the smart empty people — not the dull-eyed but the beady-eyed — who are whipping up the orgiastic possibilities in irrational violence. We all know in advance that the forthcoming movie version of West's apocalyptic novel won't distance us, as the novel did, so that we recoil from the destructive potential in a numbed, envious crowd, but will, *of course*, seize the opportunity to turn audiences on to the excitement of a mob with murder in its heart.

It's the carnivore locusts at the top who tear the artists apart, but the writers and directors have often (unwittingly) aided them. Writers, who assume an ideal reader when they 'do their own writing,' accept the moguls' view of the public when they work for the movies. Not that they necessarily write down — probably most scenarists write as well as they can, considering the limitations imposed on them — but that they begin to subscribe to the moguls' attitudes, which are endemic in Hollywood, and so they come to believe in the necessity for those limitations. They don't assume an ideal viewer — they assume a hollow-eyed, empty-souled, know-nothing hick.

And, in some crazy, vindictive way — as if the masses were their enemy — certain writers and directors enjoy satirizing the rootless, uncultured Americans. John Schlesinger in *Midnight Cowboy*, Tony Richardson in *The Loved One*, Antonioni in *Zabriskie Point* — liberals all, but aesthetes first — spin a new baroque out of the grotesqueness of American bad taste. They lose their socially conscious moorings when they treat American culture, just as American liberals and leftists from the East lose them in the West. Nathanael West — and what a misnomer he chose for himself — must have recognized that he was caught in an ideological bind in *The Day of the Locust*. In the middle of his apocalyptic climax, when the hollow-eyed people are gathering, he carefully exempts himself from the political criticism by having his hero, Tod, observe, 'He could see very few people who looked tough, nor could he see any working men. The crowd was made up of the lower middle classes.' That handy, safe target of the left — 'the lower middle classes.' But, a few lines farther on, Tod describes the people and contradicts himself: 'All their lives they had slaved at some kind of dull, heavy labor, behind desks and counters, in the fields and at tedious machines of all sorts, saving their pennies and dreaming of the leisure that would be theirs when they had enough.' It's nonsense to think that working people don't get debased, and only the 'lower middle classes' are susceptible to the deadening effects of mass culture, but if one makes this false split between the workers and the riffraff it's one hell of a lot easier to take movie money. Generations of screenwriters played the same game that West did, trying to convince themselves that they weren't doing any damage to anyone who really counted. The movie audience became a huge subhuman abstraction to them; it was a faceless joke, and they weren't accountable to it. In modern Hollywood, where most of the writing and directing are for TV, that is now the attitude toward the television audience.

Perhaps no work of art is possible without belief in the audience — the kind of belief that has nothing to do with facts and figures about what people actually buy or enjoy but comes out of the individual artist's absolute conviction that only the best he can do is fit to be offered to others. It's what makes a director insist on a retake even when he knows he's going to be penalized for it; it's what makes young dancers drop from exhaustion; it's what made Caruso burst his throat. You have to believe in the audience, and believe that your peak effort just barely makes you worthy of it. That's implicit when an artist says he does it 'because he has to,' and even when he says he does it 'just for himself.' An artist's sense of honor is founded on the honor due others. Honor in the arts — and in show business, too — is giving of one's utmost, even if the audience does not appear to know the difference, even if the audience shows every sign of preferring something easy, cheap, and synthetic. The audience one must believe in is the great audience: the audience one was part of as a child, when one first began to respond to great work — the audience one is still part of. As soon as an artist ceases to see himself as part of the audience — when he begins to believe that what matters is to satisfy the jerk audience out there — he stops being an artist. He becomes a businessman, marketing a commodity — his talent, himself.

Probably the last big movie hits that were also works of genuine talent — that is, of people going the whole length — were *The Godfather* and *Cabaret*, but surely Coppola has already learned from the handling of *The Conversation* that the big boys play the game on their own terms. Even the very biggest hits provide only a feeling of power, an illusion of freedom. You get what you want up to a certain point, and then you're done in. The artists have got to break out of this humiliating, suicidal struggle with the entrepreneurs.

There's only one way: They've got to help each other. It's a matter not of the lunatics' taking over the asylum (how the businessmen love to say that each time an artist tries to wrest control of his work away from them) but of the artists' abandoning the asylum to the lunatics who are the keepers. Before the mass market and the entrepreneurs, people in show business weren't spoiled children — gypsies, yes, but not infants. It is the movie companies that have infantilized them. In the days of the studio system, with its long-term contracts, the stars were encouraged, even pushed, to live like the French dauphins; they showed off the gaudiest, most expensive playthings, and studio publicists worked to create the very image that was used as proof that the artists were indulged. (The vulgar excesses were always attributed to the infantile artists, but the studio heads, those paternal figures who made the decisions for them, lived even higher, and that wasn't taken as a sign of mindless irresponsibility.) Artists in all the arts are made to feel helpless, because they don't know what to do with their gifts, and many believe the image of themselves that businessman create. They begin to think that they can't do anything unless they sign themselves away, and when offered the opportunity they're scared not to take it. Edward G. Robinson wrote that when he was a young stage actor he made a picture for Irving Thalberg, and Thalberg offered him a three-year, million-dollar contract; he was to work exclusively for M-G-M and be built into a star. Robinson countered with the proposition that he

work at M-G-M for six months a year and have the other six months
free to work on the stage, but, as he described it, 'Thalberg compromised on nothing; he sat there, stern and immovable — the
godhead. . . . His eyes showed me that an actor was beneath contempt.' Robinson turned the offer down, left the office, and vomited.
And Thalberg, the courtly, refined Thalberg, most admired of all the
moguls — he was even *thin* — never forgave Robinson for the
rejection and never used him in another picture. Yes, they groomed
you for stardom, but only if you were theirs — their pet. There's so
much bathetic bull about the old days — so many TV hosts have
said, 'Mr Capra, why don't you make another one of your wonderful
pictures for us?' — that people may actually begin to believe they're
being deprived of something great. On TV, people talk about the big
old producers as if they really had the magic, knew the secret of how
to do it. It's like remembering Captain Kidd as someone who was
particularly knowledgeable about the properties of gold and silver.
Professional sentimentalists have forgotten — or don't care — that
most of the moguls' big 'personally supervised' projects were overblown bores. If one looks at the lists of pictures they put their stars
in, it's apparent that the stars were buried in garbage up to their
necks and only rarely got a chance to climb out and act. The moguls
usually fought and despised the people who brought in the hits — the
people who didn't want to be owned. Preston Sturges had only four
years in his lifetime when he could do the pictures he wanted to; 'a
comic opera,' he called the battle with the producers long after he
had been beaten down. When the director Tay Garnett, who had just
brought in a big Jean Harlow hit for Thalberg, declined to direct her
next picture, because he felt she was miscast, Thalberg simply termi-
nated Garnett's contract. (She *was* miscast, and the picture failed.)
Thalberg had fired Erich von Stroheim and Mauritz Stiller and
replaced them with functionaries when he was still a boy — a boy
wonder.

Now that the studios don't keep stables of indentured stars, they
don't even groom young talent; they corrupt and destroy the gifted
actors and directors much faster. Performers who are thought to have
money in them are sought by all the bosses at the same time; overused
and trashed, James Coburn, Sandy Dennis, Tony Randall, Eva Marie
Saint are stars one year and gone the next. Yet the agents and
entrepreneurs claim that the artists can't think straight and can't do
anything without them. The stars are often convinced by the agent or

adviser or accountant who says, 'You need me. I'll take care of everything for you,' though people don't say that unless they get something out of it. Could the artists do *worse* on their own than *For Pete's Sake*?

Pampered children can go rotten; the young Off Broadway actor who was dedicated to his work can in the space of a few years become the star who says that honestly he loves the script a talented young director wants him for, and he would really like to do it, but he can't *afford* to do a small movie, because his price now is a million dollars a picture. The million-dollar-a-picture star can be more corrupt and worse to deal with than any producer, because he usually operates behind the cover of his agent or his manager. The agent represents the truth about this star: the deal has become more important to him than the picture. He has become his own Dudy Kravitz.

There's no way for movies to be saved from premature senility unless the artists finally abandon the whole crooked system of Hollywood bookkeeping, with its kited budgets and trick percentages. Most directors are signed up for only one picture now, but after the deal is made the director gets the full de-luxe ritual: fancy hotels, first-class travel, expense money to maintain cool, silky blond groupies for traveling companions. The directors are like calves being fattened — all on the budget of the picture. The thieving, high-salaried executives and their entourage of whores and underlings are also traveling and living it up on that same budget; that's how a picture that cost $1,200,000 comes in on the books at $3,000,000, and why the director who has a percentage of the profits doesn't get any.

It isn't impossible to raise money outside the industry to make a movie — the studios themselves finance some of their biggest pictures with tax-shelter money (*Gatsby*, in part) — but even those who raise independent financing and make a picture cheaply (*Mean Streets* was brought in for $380,000, plus $200,000 deferred costs, *Payday* for $767,000) are stuck for a way to distribute it and fall victim to the dream of a big Hollywood win. So they sell their pictures to 'the majors' to exhibit, and watch helplessly as the films die or the swindled profits disappear. And they are beggars again. Brian De Palma's *Greetings* was made for $20,000, plus $23,000 in deferred costs in 1968; back in the fifties, Irvin Kershner made *Stakeout on Dope Street* for $30,000, plus $8,000 in deferred costs. If there had been an artists' co-op to distribute the films, the directors might have been able to use the profits to continue working, instead of pouring energy into planning films that they could never finance, and seeing the films they did make get sliced to ribbons.

If the directors started one distribution company, or even several (they could certainly get backing), they might have to spend time on business problems, but, with any luck, much less time on dealmaking sessions: those traumatic meetings at which the businessmen air their grievances while the artists anxiously vulgarize the projects they're submitting, hoping to make them sound commercial enough. If they have a book they want to film or if they try to get development money for a story idea, the lack of enthusiasm is deadly. One director says, 'You look at them and you give up. And if, after a year or two years, they finally give you the go-ahead, then they cut you down to a twenty-five-day shooting schedule and *dare* you to make a picture.' Right now, all but a handful of Hollywood directors spend most of their time preparing projects that they never get to shoot. They work on scripts with writers, piling up successions of drafts, and if they still can't please the producers and get a deal, the properties are finally abandoned or turned over to other directors, who start the process all over again, with new writers. One could outline a history of modern Hollywood by following the passage of one such project — the French novel *Choice Cuts*, say, which more than a dozen of the best writers and close to a dozen of the best directors have worked on: script after script in insane succession, and the waltz still goes on, each person in turn thinking that he's got a deal and his version will be made. The directors spend their lives not in learning their craft and not in doing anything useful to them as human beings but in fighting a battle they keep losing. The business problems of controlling their own distribution should be minor compared to what they go through now — the abuse from the self-pitying bosses, the indignity, the paralysis. And if the directors had to think out how their movies should be presented to the public — what the basis for the advertising campaign should be — this mightn't be so bad for them. If they had to worry about what a movie was going to mean to people and why anybody should come to see it, they might be saved from too much folly. A fatal difference between the 'high' arts and the popular, or mass-culture, arts has been that in one the artist's mistakes are his own, while in the other the mistakes are largely the businessmen's. The artist can grow making his own mistakes; he decays carrying out the businessmen's decisions — working on large, custom-made versions of the soulless entertainment on TV.

Privately, almost every one of the directors whose work I admire tells the same ugly, bitter story, yet they live in such fear of those spiteful, spying bosses that they don't dare even talk to each other. Hollywood is a small, ingrown community where people live in terror that 'word will get back.' They inhabit a paranoia-inducing company town, and within it they imagine the bosses to have more power in the outside world than they actually do. If such talents as Sam Peckinpah, Paul Mazursky, Martin Scorsese, Coppola, Kershner, Altman, De Palma, Woody Allen, Frederick Wiseman, Lamont Johnson, John Korty, Steven Spielberg, Michael Crichton, and even some of the older directors, such as Kazan and Fred Zinnemann, joined together to distribute their own films, they'd be able to work on the projects they really want to work on, and they'd get most of the writers and performers and craftsmen they want, too. The main obstacles are not in the actual world. It's not impossible to buck the majors and to book movies into theaters, and it's not really hard to publicize movies; the media are almost obscenely eager for movie news, and the businessmen, who know only one way to advertise a film — by heavy bombardment — often kill interest in an unusual picture by halfheartedly trying to sell it as if it were the kind of routine action show they wanted it to be.

There's no way of knowing whether a new audience can be found; it's a matter of picking up the pieces, and it may be too late. But if the directors started talking to each other, they'd realize that they're all in the same rapidly sinking boat, and there'd be a chance for them to reach out and try to connect with a new audience. If they don't, they'll never test themselves as artists and they'll never know whether an audience could have been found for the work they want to do.

The artists have to break out of their own fearful, star-struck heads; the system that's destroying them is able to destroy them only as long as they believe in it and want to win within it — only as long as they're psychologically dependent on it. But the one kind of winning that is still possible in those terms is to be a winner like William Friedkin or George Roy Hill. The system works for those who don't have needs or aspirations that are in conflict with it; but for the others — and they're the ones who are making *movies* — the system doesn't work anymore, and it's not going to.

The New Yorker, 1974

The Man from Dream City
Cary Grant

You can be had, Mae West said to Cary Grant in *She Done Him Wrong*, which opened in January, 1933, and that was what the women stars of most of his greatest hits were saying to him for thirty years, as he backed away — but not too far. One after another, the great ladies courted him — Irene Dunne in *The Awful Truth* and *My Favorite Wife*, Katharine Hepburn in *Bringing Up Baby* and *Holiday*, Jean Arthur and Rita Hayworth in *Only Angels Have Wings*, Ingrid Bergman in *Notorious*, Grace Kelly in *To Catch a Thief*, Eva Marie Saint in *North by Northwest*, Audrey Hepburn in *Charade*. Willing but not forward, Cary Grant must be the most publicly seduced male the world has known, yet he has never become a public joke — not even when Tony Curtis parodied him in *Some Like It Hot*, encouraging Marilyn Monroe to rape. The little bit of shyness and reserve in Grant is pure box-office gold, and being the pursued doesn't make him seem weak or passively soft. It makes him glamorous — and, since he is not as available as other men, far more desirable.

Cary Grant is the male love object. Men want to be as lucky and enviable as he is — they want to be like him. And women imagine landing him. Like Robert Redford, he's sexiest in pictures in which the woman is the aggressor and all the film's erotic energy is concentrated on him, as it was in *Notorious*: Ingrid Bergman practically ravished him while he was trying to conduct a phone conversation. Redford has never been so radiantly glamorous as in *The Way We Were*, when we saw him through Barbra Streisand's infatuated eyes. But in *The Great Gatsby*, when Redford needed to do for Mia Farrow what Streisand had done for him, he couldn't transcend his immaculate self-absorption. If he had looked at her with desire, everything else about the movie might have been forgiven. Cary Grant would not have failed; yearning for an idealized love was not beyond his resources. It may even be part of his essence: in the sleekly confected *The Philadelphia Story*, he brought conviction to the dim role of the blue blood standing by Katharine Hepburn and waiting on the sidelines. He expressed the very sort of desperate constancy that Redford failed to express. Grant's marital farces with Irene Dunne probably wouldn't have been as effective as they were if he hadn't suggested a bedevilled constancy in the midst of the confusion. The heroine who chases him knows that deep down he wants to be caught only by her. He draws women to him by making them feel he needs them, yet the last thing he'd do would be to come right out and say it. In *Only Angels Have Wings*, Jean Arthur half falls apart waiting for him to make a move; in *His Girl Friday*, he's unabashed about everything in the world except why he doesn't want Rosalind Russell to go off with Ralph Bellamy. He isn't weak, yet something in him makes him hold back — and that something (a slight uncertainty? the fear of a commitment? a mixture of ardor and idealism?) makes him more exciting.

The romantic male stars aren't necessarily sexually aggressive. Henry Fonda wasn't; neither was James Stewart, or, later, Marcello Mastroianni. The foursquare Clark Gable, with his bold, open challenge to women, was more the exception than the rule, and Gable wasn't romantic, like Grant. Gable got down to brass tacks; his advances were basic, his unspoken question was 'Well, sister, what do you say?' If she said no, she was failing what might almost be nature's test. She'd become overcivilized, afraid of her instincts — afraid of being a woman. There was a violent, primal appeal in Gable's sex scenes: it was all out front — in the way he looked at her, man to woman. Cary Grant doesn't challenge a woman that way. (When he tried, as the frontiersman in *The Howards of Virginia*, he looked thick and stupid.) With Gable, sex is inevitable: What is there but sex? Basically, he thinks women are good for only one thing. Grant is interested in the qualities of a particular woman — her sappy expression, her non sequiturs, the way her voice bobbles. She isn't going to be pushed to the wall as soon as she's alone with him. With Grant, the social, urban man, there are infinite possibilities for mutual entertainment. They might dance the night away or stroll or go to a carnival — and nothing sexual would happen unless she wanted it to. Grant doesn't assert his male supremacy; in the climax of a picture he doesn't triumph by his fists and brawn — or even by outwitting anybody. He isn't a conqueror, like Gable. But he's a winner. The game, however, is an artful dodge. He gets the blithe, funny girl by maneuvering her into going after him. He's a fairy-tale hero, but she has to pass through the trials: She has to trim her cold or pompous adversaries; she has to dispel his fog. In picture after picture, he seems to give up his resistance at the end, as if to say, What's the use of fighting?

Many men must have wanted to be Clark Gable and look straight at a woman with a faint smirk and lifted, questioning eyebrows. What man doesn't — at some level — want to feel supremely confident and earthy and irresistible? But a few steps up the dreamy social ladder there's the more subtle fantasy of worldly grace — of being so gallant and gentlemanly and charming that every woman longs to be your date. And at that deluxe level men want to be Cary Grant. Men as far apart as John F. Kennedy and Lucky Luciano thought that he should star in their life story. Who but Cary Grant could be a fantasy self-image for a President and a gangster chief? Who else could demonstrate that sophistication didn't have to be a sign of weakness — that it could be the polished, fun-loving style of those who were basically tough? Cary Grant has said that even he wanted to be Cary Grant.

And for women, if the roof leaks, or the car stalls, or you don't know how to get the super to keep his paws off you, you may long for a Clark Gable to take charge, but when you think of going out, Cary Grant is your dream date — not sexless but sex with civilized grace, sex with mystery. He's the man of the big city, triumphantly sun-tanned. Sitting out there in Los Angeles, the expatriate New York writers projected onto him their fantasies of Eastern connoissseurship with suavity. How could the heroine ever consider marrying a rich rube from Oklahoma and leaving Cary Grant and the night spots? Los Angeles itself has never recovered from the inferiority complex that its movies nourished, and every moviegoing kid in America felt that the people in New York were smarter, livelier, and better-looking than anyone in his home town. The audience didn't become hostile; it took the contempt as earned. There were no Cary Grants in the sticks. He and his counterparts were to be found only in the imaginary cities of the movies. When you look at him, you take for granted expensive tailors, international travel, and the best that life has to offer. Women see a man they could have fun with. Clark Gable is an intensely realistic sexual presence; you don't fool around with Gable. But with Grant there are no pressures, no demands; he's the sky that women aspire to. When he and a woman are together, they can laugh at each other and at themselves. He's a slapstick Prince Charming.

Mae West's raucous invitation to him — 'Why don't you come up sometime and see me?' — was echoed thirty years later by Audrey Hepburn in *Charade*: 'Won't you come in for a minute? I don't bite, you know, unless it's called for.' And then, purringly, 'Do you know what's wrong with you? Nothing.' That might be a summary of Cary Grant, the finest romantic comedian of his era: there's nothing the matter with him. Many of the male actors who entered movies when sound came in showed remarkable powers of endurance — James Cagney, Bing Crosby, Charles Boyer, Fred Astaire — but they didn't remain heroes. Spencer Tracy didn't, either; he became paternal and judicious. Henry Fonda and James Stewart turned into folksy elder statesmen, sagacious but desexed. Cary Grant has had the longest romantic reign in the short history of movies. He might be cast as an arrogant rich boy, an unscrupulous cynic, or a selfish diplomat, but there was nothing sullen or self-centered in his acting. Grant never got star-stuck on himself; he never seemed to be saying, Look at me. The most obvious characteristic of his acting is the absence of narcissism — the outgoingness to the audience.

Cary Grant was a knockout in his dapper young days as a Paramount leading man to such suffering sinners as Sylvia Sidney, Carole Lombard, Tallulah Bankhead, Marlene Dietrich, Nancy Carroll. He appeared with this batch in 1932; Paramount threw him into seven pictures in his first year. In some two dozen roles in four years, he was a passable imitation of Noël Coward or Jack Buchanan, though not as brittle as Coward or as ingratiatingly silly as Buchanan. He played a celebrated javelin thrower in *This Is the Night*, a rotten rich roué in *Sinners in the Sun*, the husband of a diva in *Enter Madam* and of another diva in *When You're in Love*. He was a flier who went blind in *Wings in the Dark*; he wore a dinky mustache and was captured by the Kurds in *The Last Outpost*; he used a black bullwhip on the villainous Jack La Rue in *The Woman Accused*. But that's all a blur. He didn't have a strong enough personality to impose himself on viewers, and most people don't remember Cary Grant for those roles, or even much for his tall-dark-and-handsome stints with Mae West. He might never have become a star if it had not been for the sudden onset of screwball comedy in 1934 — the year when *The Thin Man* and *Twentieth Century* and *It Happened One Night* changed American movies. His performances in screwball comedies — particularly *The Awful Truth*, in 1937, his twenty-ninth picture — turned him into the comedian-hero that people think of as Cary Grant. He was resplendent before but characterless, even a trace languid — a slightly wilted sheik. He was Mae West's classiest and best leading man, but he did more for her in *She Done Him Wrong* and *I'm No Angel* than she did for him. She brought out his passivity, and a quality of refinement in him which made her physical aggression seem a playful gambit. (With tough men opposite her, she was less charming, more crude.) Sizing him up with her satyr's eyes and deciding he was a prize catch, she raised our estimate of him. Yet Grant still had that pretty-boy killer look; he was too good-looking to be on the level. And although he was outrageously attractive with Mae West, he was vaguely ill at ease; his face muscles betrayed him, and he looked a little fleshy. He didn't yet know how the camera should see him; he didn't focus his eyes on her the way he learned to use his eyes later. No doubt he felt absurd in his soulful, cow-eyed leading-man roles, and tried to conceal it; when he had nothing to do in a scene, he stood lunged forward as if hoping to catch a ball. He became Cary Grant when he learned to project his feelings of absurdity through his characters and to make a style out of their feeling silly. Once he realized that each movement could be stylized for humor, the eyepopping, the cocked head, the forward lunge, and the slightly ungainly stride became as certain as the pen strokes of a master cartoonist. The new element of romantic slapstick in the mid-thirties comedies — the teasing role reversals and shifts of mood — loosened him up and brought him to life. At last, he could do on the screen what he had been trained to do, and a rambunctious, springy side of his nature came out. Less 'Continental' and more physical, he became funny and at the same time sexy. He was no longer effete; the booming voice had vitality.

It was in 1935, when the director George Cukor cast him as a loud-mouthed product of the British slums — a con man and strolling player — in the Katharine Hepburn picture *Sylvia Scarlett*, that Grant's boisterous energy first broke through. He was so brashly likable that viewers felt vaguely discomfited at the end when Brian Aherne (who had given an insufferably egotistic performance) wound up with Hepburn. Grant, on loan from Paramount to R.K.O., doesn't play the leading-man role, yet his con man is so loose and virile that he has more life than anything else in the picture. Grant seemed to be enjoying himself on the screen in a way he never had before. Cukor said that Grant suddenly 'felt the ground under his feet.' Instead of hiding in his role, as usual, he expanded and gave his scenes momentum. *Sylvia Scarlett* was a box-office failure, but Grant knew now what he could play, and a year later, free to pick his own projects, he appeared in *Topper* and his fan mail jumped from two hundred letters a week to fourteen hundred. A few months after that, he got into his full stride with *The Awful Truth*.

What makes Grant such an uncannily romantic comedian is that with the heroine he's different from the way he is with everybody else; you sense an affinity between them. In *The Awful Truth*, he's a hearty, sociable businessman when he's with other people, but when he's with Irene Dunne you feel the tenderness that he conceals from others. The conventional bedroom-farce plot (filmed twice before) is about a couple who still love each other but have a tiff and file for divorce; during the period of the interlocutory decree, the husband has visiting rights to see their dog, and this cunning device enables Grant to hang around, romping affectionately with the dog while showing his (unstated) longing for his wife. Grant is a comic master at throwaway lines, and he turns them into a dialogue, as if he were talking to himself. The husband can't quite straighten out his marriage, yet every muttered, throwaway word expresses how badly he wants to. Grant's work with Irene Dunne in *The Awful Truth* is the most gifted stooging imaginable. She was betrayed by the costume designer: she's shrilly dressed. And though she is often funny, she overdoes the coy gurgles, and that bright, toothy smile of hers — she shows both rows of teeth, prettily held together — can make one want to slug her. The ancestor of Julie Andrews, Irene Dunne has a bad habit of condescending to anything oddball her character does — signalling the audience that she's really a lady playacting. But Grant stabilizes her and provides the believability. He's forceful and extroverted, yet he underplays so gently that his restraint enables her to get by with her affections. Grant uses his intense physical awareness to make the scenes play, and never to make himself look good at the expense of someone else — not even when he could waltz away with the show. He performs the gags with great gusto, but he never lets us forget that the character is behaving like an oaf because he doesn't want to lose his wife, and that he's trying to protect his raw places.

Henry Fonda played roles similar to Grant's, and it isn't hard to imagine Fonda as the husband in *The Awful Truth* or as the paleontologist hero of *Bringing Up Baby*, but Fonda would have been more of a hayseed, and lighter-weight. And if Grant had played Fonda's role in *The Lady Eve* Grant wouldn't have been the perfect, pratfalling innocent that Fonda was: Fonda, with his saintly bumpkin's apologetic smile and his double-jointed gait, could play bashful stupes more convincingly than any other romantic star. However, it's part of the audience's pleasure in Grant that he isn't a green kid — he's a muscular, full-bodied man making a fool of himself. There were other gifted urbane *farceurs*. The best of them, William Powell, with his skeptical, tolerant equanimity, was supremely likable; he got the most out of each blink and each twitch of his lips, and he had amazing dimples, which he could invoke without even smiling. But Powell and the others didn't have romantic ardor hidden inside their jokes. And although there were other fine romantic actors, such as Charles Boyer, their love scenes often turned mooshy, while Grant's had the redemming zest of farce.

Perfection in drawing-room comedy was almost certainly Grant's dream of glory (it appears to have remained so), but he had, as a young vaudeville comedian, acquired the skills that were to turn him into an idol for all social classes. Drawing-room-comedy stars — no matter how artful — don't become that kind of idol. When we in the audience began to sense the pleasure he took in low comedy, we accepted him as one of us. Ray Milland, Melvyn Douglas, and Robert Young acted the screwball-comedy heroes proficiently, but the roles didn't release anything in their own natures — didn't liberate and complete them, the way farce completed Grant. Afterward, even when he played straight romantic parts the freedom and strength stayed with him. And never left him: he gave some embarrassed, awful performances when he was miscast, but he was never less than a star. He might still parade in the tuxedos and tails of his dashing-young-idiot days, but he was a buoyant, lusty performer. The assurance he gained in slapstick turned him into the smoothie he had aspired to be. He brought elegance to low comedy, and low comedy gave him the corky common-man touch that made him a great star. Grant was English, so Hollywood thought he sounded educated and was just right for rich playboys, but he didn't speak in the gentlemanly tones that American moviegoers think of as British; he was a Cockney. In the early sixties, when he was offered the role of Henry Higgins in the big movie version of *My Fair Lady*, he laughed at the idea. 'The way I talk *now*,' he said, 'is the way Eliza talked at the beginning.' Cary Grant's romantic elegance is wrapped around the resilient, tough core of a mutt, and Americans dream of thoroughbreds while identifying with mutts. So do moviegoers the world over. The greatest movie stars have not been highborn; they have been strong-willed (often deprived) kids who came to embody their own dreams, and the public's.

Archibald Alexander Leach, born in Bristol on January 18, 1904, was the only child of Elias James Leach and Elsie Kingdom Leach, their firstborn son having died in infancy. Elias Leach was tall, and in photographs he seems almost reprehensibly handsome, with a cavalier's mustache, soft, flashing dark eyes, and a faintly melancholy look of resignation. He is said to have been convivial and fond of singing — a temperament his wife definitely did not share. There wasn't much they did share. He came, probably, from a Jewish background, but went along with his wife's Anglicanism. He couldn't live up to her middle-class expectations, however. Elias Leach pressed men's suits in a garment factory, and although he worked hard in the first years of the marriage, he never rose far or made much of a living. Mrs Leach pampered their protesting child, keeping him in baby dresses, and then in short pants and long curls. A domineering woman with an early history of mental instability, she was married to a pants-presser but she wanted her son to be a cultured, piano-playing little gentleman. The parents were miserable together, and the boy was caught in the middle. When Archie was nine, he returned home from school one day to find that his mother was missing; he was led to think she had gone to a local seaside resort, and it was a long time before he learned that she had broken down and been taken to an institution. In a series of autobiographical articles published in the *Ladies' Home Journal* in 1963, he wrote, 'I was not to see my mother again for more than twenty years, by which time my name was changed and I was a full-grown man living in America, thousands of miles away in California. I was known to most people of the world by sight and by name, yet not to my mother.'

After Mrs Leach's removal, Leach and his son took up quarters in the same building as Leach's mother, but the boy was left pretty much on his own, fixing meals for himself most of the week, and trying to live up to his absent mother's hopes for him. He went to Boy Scout meetings, studied hard, and won a school scholarship: he planned to try for a further scholarship, which would take him to college, but found out that even with a scholarship college would be too expensive. From early childhood, he had been going to the children's

Saturday movie matinées, and he later said that the sessions with Chaplin, Ford Sterling and the Keystone Cops, Fatty Arbuckle, Mack Swain, John Bunny and Flora Finch, and Broncho Billy Anderson were the high point of his week. When his mother was still at home, he had a party (the only children's party he remembers attending) that featured a candle-powered magic lantern with comic slides, to which he added his own joking commentary. His first contact with music hall came quite by chance. At school, he liked chemistry, and he sometimes hung around the lab on rainy days; the assistant science teacher was an electrician, who had installed the lighting system at the Bristol Hippodrome, and one Saturday matinée he took Archie, just turned thirteen, backstage.

It was probably the only free atmosphere the boy had ever experienced. He wrote later that backstage, in a 'dazzling land of smiling, jostling people,' he *knew*. 'What other life could there *be* but that of an actor? . . . They were classless, cheerful, and carefree.' He was lonely enough and had enough hustle to start going to the Hippodrome, and another theatre, the Empire, in the early evenings, making himself useful; he helped with the lights, ran errands, and began to pick up the show-business vernacular. When he learned that Bob Pender, a former Drury Lane clown, had a troupe of young knockabout comedians that suffered attrition each time a boy came of military age, he wrote, in the guise of his father, asking that Archibald be taken for training. Pender replied offering an interview and enclosing the railway fare to Norwich, and Archie ran away from home to become an apprentice. He was so tall that Pender accepted him, not realizing that he wasn't yet fourteen — the legal age for leaving school. It took a few days before Leach noticed that his son was gone. Earlier that year, Archie had taken a spill on an icy playground and broken an upper front tooth. Rather than tell his father, he had gone to a dental school and had the remainder of the tooth pulled out. His other teeth had closed together over the gap (giving him his characteristic upper-lip-pulled-down, tough-urchin grin) without his father's ever noticing. But, whatever Leach's failings, he appears to have meant well, and when it registered with him that the boy had run off, he tracked him down and brought him back. He might as well have saved himself the effort. Having given up his dream of college, Archie no longer cared about school, and he concentrated on acrobatics, so he'd be in shape to rejoin Pender as soon as he could. It was soon. Just after he turned fourteen, he and another boy attempted to explore the girls' lavatories, and he was expelled from school. Three days later, with his father's consent, he was a member of Pender's troupe. Only three months passed before he returned to Bristol in triumph — on the stage at the Empire, his old schoolmates in the audience.

Archie Leach found his vocation early and stuck to it. He studied dancing, tumbling, stilt-walking, and pantomime, and performed constantly in provincial towns and cities and in the London vaudeville houses. In the Christmas season, the troupe appeared in the traditional entertainments for children — slapstick musical-comedy versions of such stories as 'Cinderella' and 'Puss in Boots.' Living dormitory-style, exercising and rehearsing, Archie had left his parents' class-ridden world behind. Once he'd joined up with Pender, he never lived with his father again, and he lost track of him over the years. The music-hall theatre became his world; he has said that at each theatre, when he wasn't onstage, he was watching and studying the other acts from the wings. In July, 1920, when Pender selected a group of eight boys for an engagement in New York City, the sixteen-year-old Archie was among them. They sailed on the S.S. *Olympic*, which was also carrying the celebrated honeymooners Douglas Fairbanks, Sr, and Mary Pickford. More than forty years later, Cary Grant described his reaction to Fairbanks: 'Once even I found myself being photographed with Mr Fairbanks during a game of shuffleboard. As I stood beside him, I tried with shy, inadequate words to tell him of my adulation. He was a splendidly trained athlete and acrobat, affable and warmed by success and well-being. A gentleman in the true sense of the word. . . . It suddenly dawns on me as this is being written that I've doggedly striven to keep tanned ever since, only because of a desire to emulate his healthful appearance.' He and Fairbanks had much in common: shattered, messy childhoods, and fathers who drifted away and turned to drink. It appears that they were both part Jewish but were raised as Christians; and they both used acrobatics in their careers — though Fairbanks, a narrowly limited actor but a fine acrobat, was a passionate devotee, while Grant used acrobatics only as a means of getting into theatrical life. And, though they represented different eras, they were loved by the public in similar ways — for their strapping health and high spirits, for being *on* and giving out whenever they were in front of an audience, for grinning with pleasure at their own good luck. Grant's later marriage to Barbara Hutton —

Babs, the golden girl, 'the richest girl in the world' — had a fairy-tale resemblance to the Fairbanks–Pickford nuptials.

In New York City, the Bob Pender boys were a great success at the Hippodrome, which was considered the world's largest theatre. After the engagement was over, they got booked in the major Eastern cities and wound up back in New York at the top — the Palace. When the American tour ended, in 1922, and it was time to go home, Archie Leach and several of the other boys decided to stay. He had four solid years of performing behind him, but he had never actually been in a play, and though he'd been singing on the stage, he'd never spoken dialogue. The Pender troupe had been big time, but on his own he wasn't even small time — he had no act. In the first summer of job-hunting in New York, his savings went and he ate into the return fare Pender had given him for an emergency retreat. He must, however, have been an incredible charmer (it isn't hard to imagine), because, although he was only eighteen, he was invited to fill in at dinner parties, where he sat among the wealthy and famous — on one occasion, he was delegated to be the escort of the great soprano Lucrezia Bori. By day, after he finally landed work, he was a stilt-walker on the boardwalk at Coney Island, advertising Steeplechase Park. (It was many years before his status in life was commensurate with the regard people had for him.) In the fall, he shared quarters with a young Australian, who later became known as the costume designer Orry-Kelly; in those days, Kelly made and tried to sell hand-painted neckties, and Archie Leach peddled them along Sixth Avenue and in Greenwich Village. Around the same time, Leach and other ex-members of the Pender troupe got together in the new Hippodrome show, and joined up with some Americans and organized a vaudeville act. After trying it out in small towns in the East, they played the lesser vaudeville circuits through Canada and back across the country from California to New York. In 1924, having saved enough money to go their separate ways, the boys disbanded, some of them returning to England, Archie Leach to job-hunting in New York again.

He worked in juggling acts, and with unicycle riders, and with dancers; he was the audience plant with a mind-reading act. As a straight man for comics, he got one-night stands at churches and lodges, and brief engagements in the stage shows that movie theatres used to put on before the film. As his timing improved and he became more experienced, he got more bookings; he says that eventually he played 'practically every small town in America.' Then, when he was working in New York, a friend who was a musical-comedy juvenile suggested that instead of going on with his vaudeville career he should try to get into Broadway musical comedy, and introduced him to Reggie Hammerstein, who took him to his uncle, the producer Arthur Hammerstein. At the end of 1927, Archie Leach appeared in the role of an Australian — the second male lead — in the Otto Harbach–Oscar Hammerstein II show *Golden Dawn*, which opened the new Hammerstein's Theatre and ran there until the late spring. He'd got onto Broadway, all right — and Broadway was then in its frivolous heyday — but he hadn't got into musical comedy. It was operetta he was caught in, and, having signed a contract with the Hammersteins, that's where he stayed. Marilyn Miller wanted him as a replacement for Jack Donahue, her leading man in the Ziegfeld hit *Rosalie*, but Arthur Hammerstein and Ziegfeld were enemies, and instead (despite his pleas) his contract was turned over to the Shuberts — for three full years of operetta.

Archie Leach's first Shubert show was *Boom Boom*, a 1929 hit, starring Jeanette MacDonald. (*The New Yorker*'s reviewer, Charles Brackett, wrote that '*Boom Boom* can teach one more about despair than the most expert philosopher.') During its run, he and Jeanette MacDonald were both tested at Paramount's Astoria studio. She was immediately signed up to be the bubbly Maurice Chevalier's petulant, coy co-star in Ernst Lubitsch's *The Love Parade*; he was rejected, because he had a thick neck and bowlegs. Had he been signed as a singing star, he might have been stuck in a Mountie's hat, like Nelson Eddy. He did become a singing star on the stage. He played a leading role in a lavish and, apparently, admirable version of *Die Fledermaus* called *A Wonderful Night*, but it opened on October 31, 1929, two days after the stock-market crash, and it crashed too; for months it was performed to near-empty houses. In the summer of 1931, the Shuberts sent him to St Louis for the open-air Municipal Opera season, where he was a great success in such shows as *Irene, Rio Rita, Countess Maritza, The Three Musketeers*, and the Broadway casualty *A Wonderful Night*. After that, he got a temporary release from the Shuberts and appeared on Broadway in the role of Cary Lockwood, supporting Fay Wray (who was already a popular movie actress) in *Nikki*, a musical play by her husband, John Monk Saunders, which flopped.

In 1931, Leach also appeared in *Singapore Sue*, a ten-minute movie short, starring Anna Chang, that Casey Robinson made for Paramount in Astoria; Leach, Millard Mitchell, and two other actors played

American sailors in an Oriental café. Leach is striking; he grabs the screen — but not pleasantly, and he does have a huge neck. He's rather gross in general — heavy-featured, and with a wide, false smile. His curly-lipped sailor is excessively handsome — overripe, like the voluptuous young Victor Mature. Some of the early-thirties Hollywood publicity photographs of Grant are like that, too; the images have the pop overeagerness one often sees in graduation and wedding poses in photographers' shop windows. Self-consciousness and bad makeup must have overcome him on that first bout with the movie camera, because photographs of him in his stage performances show a far more refined handsomeness, and the Leach of *Singapore Sue* doesn't fit the image of him in accounts by his contemporaries.

Although Leach didn't appear in the smart shows, he was something of a figure in the New York smart set, and he was known to the Algonquin group in that period when the theatrical and literary worlds were one. Some people considered him an intellectual and a powerhouse talent of the future. Moss Hart later described him as disconsolate in those years; Hart and Leach were among a group of dreamers talking of changing the theatre (the circle also included Edward Chodorov and Preston Sturges) who met daily in Rudley's Restaurant at Forty-first Street and Broadway. It was a hang-out where one got leads about possible jobs, and many performers frequented the place — Jeanette MacDonald, George Murphy, Humphrey Bogart. But Archie Leach was the only actor who was a regular at the Rudley rebels' table. The Anzac role he'd played in *Golden Dawn* must have clung to him, or perhaps, since he never talked much about his background, some of the others mistook his Cockney for an Australian accent, because they called him Kangaroo, and sometimes Boomerang. 'He was never a very open fellow,' Chodorov says, 'but he was earnest and we liked him.' 'Intellectual' was probably the wrong word for Leach. They talked; he listened. He doesn't appear to have been much of a reader (except later on, during his marriage to Betsy Drake, when he became immersed in the literature of hypnotism and the occult), but there's no indication that anyone ever doubted his native intelligence. It's a wide-awake intelligence, though this may not be apparent from his public remarks of the sixties, which had a wholesome Rotarian tone he adopted during LSD treatments with a medical guru. In his youth, Leach like to hang around people who were gifted and highly educated; always looking for ways to improve himself, he probably hoped that their knowledge would rub off on him. But there must have been more to it than that; he must have looked up to the brilliant young Rudley's group because the theatre he worked in didn't fully satisfy his mind. Uneducated outside the theatre, he was eager for spiritual leadership — for wisdom. In Hollywood, he was to sit at the feet of Clifford Odets, the leading wisdom merchant of the theatrical left (the sagacity was what marred Odets's plays). And during his many years of LSD sessions he was euphoric about how the drug had enabled him to relax his conscious controls and reach his subconscious, thus making him a better man — less selfish, fit at last for marriage, and so on. Obviously, he felt that he'd found a scientific route to wisdom.

When *Nikki* closed, on October 31, 1931, Leach decided to take a 'vacation,' and set out with a composer friend to drive to Los Angeles. He knew what he was after; many of the people he'd been working with were already in the movies. He had the situation cooled: he'd been earning from three hundred dollars to four hundred and fifty dollars a week for several years, and the Shuberts were eager to employ him if he returned. He had barely arrived in Hollywood when he was taken to a small dinner party at the home of B.P. Schulberg, the head of Paramount, who invited him to make a test. (*Singapore Sue* had not yet been released), and after seeing it Schulberg offered him a contract. The studio executives wanted his name changed, and his friends Fay Wray and John Monk Saunders suggested that he use 'Cary Lockwood.' He proposed it when he went back to discuss the contract, but he was told that 'Lockwood' was a little long. Someone went down a list of names and stopped at 'Grant.' He nodded, they nodded, and the contract went into effect on December 7th. He wasn't ever 'discovered.' Movies were simply the next step.

If Archie Leach's upward progress seems a familiar saga, it is familiar in the rags-to-riches mode of a tycoon or a statesman. What is missing from his steady climb to fame is tension. He became a performer in an era in which learning to entertain the public was a trade; he worked at his trade, progressed, and rose to the top. He has probably never had the sort of doubts about acting which have plagued so many later performers, and he didn't agonize over choices, as actors of his stature do now. A young actor now generally feels that he is an artist only when he uses his technique for personal expression and for something he believes in. And so he has a problem that Archie Leach never faced:

When actors became artists in the modern sense, they also became sellouts. They began to feel emasculated when they played formula roles that depended on technique only, and they had to fight themselves to retain their belief in the audience, which often preferred what they did when they sold out. They were up against all the temptations, corruptions, and conflicts that writers and composers and painters had long been wrestling with. Commerce is a bind for actors now in a way it never was for Archie Leach; art for him was always a trade.

He was unusually long-sighted about his career, and prodigiously disciplined, and so he got into a position in which he didn't have to take any guff from anybody. The Hammersteins had sold him to the Shuberts when he wanted to go to Ziegfeld; and to get movie roles he had to commit himself to a five-year contract with Paramount. But that was the last time he let others have the power to tell him what to do. He was twenty-seven when he signed the contract — at a starting salary of four hundred and fifty dollars a week. Paramount didn't know what it had. It used him as a second-string Gary Cooper, putting him in the pictures Cooper was too busy for — or, even worse, in imitations of roles that Cooper had just scored in. In between, Paramount lent him out to other studios and collected the fees. He was no more than a pawn in these deals. M-G-M requested him for one of the top roles in *Mutiny on the Bounty*, a role he desperately wanted, but Paramount refused, and Franchot Tone won the part. A little later, Paramount lent him to M-G-M to support Jean Harlow in the piddling *Suzy*.

When the contract ended, in February, 1937, Cary Grant, just turned thirty-three, was raring to go. He never signed another exclusive contract with a studio; he selected his scripts and his directors, and this is probably what saved him from turning into a depressingly sentimental figure, like the later, tired Gary Cooper, or a drudge, like the big M-G-M stars. It was in his first year on his own, free of studio orders, that he became a true star. In comedy, Cary Grant just might be the greatest straight man in the business, and his specialty is to apply his aplomb as a straight man to romance.

The 'lunatic' thirties comedies that made him a star are still enjoyed, but their rationale has dropped from sight. In essence, they turned love and marriage into vaudeville acts and changed the movie heroine from sweet clinging vine into vaudeville partner. Starting in 1934, when things were still bad but Roosevelt and the New Deal had created an upswing spirit, the happy screwball comedies were entertainment for a country that had weathered the worst of the Depression and was beginning to feel hopeful. Yet people had been shaken up. The new comedies suggested an element of lunacy and confusion in the world; the heroes and heroines rolled with the punches and laughed at disasters. Love became slightly surreal; it became stylized — lovers talked back to each other, and fast. Comedy became the new romance, and trading wisecracks was the new courtship rite. The cheerful, wacked-out heroes and heroines had abandoned sanity; they were a little crazy, and that's what they liked in each other. They were like the wise-cracking soldiers in service comedies: if you were swapping quips, you were alive — you hadn't gone under. The jokes were a national form of gallantry — humor for survival. Actual lunatics in these movies became enjoyable eccentrics, endearing nuts who often made better sense than anybody else (or at least as much sense), while the butts of screwball humor were the prigs and phonies, the conventional go-getters, the stick-in-the-mud conformists. Ralph Bellamy, the classic loser and opposite number to Cary Grant in *The Awful Truth* and again in *His Girl Friday*, still thought in the strict, stuffed-shirt terms of the Babbitty past. The word 'square' wasn't yet in slang use, but that's the part Bellamy played — the man who didn't get the joke. Obliging and available, always around when you didn't want him (there was really no time when you did), he was the man to be jilted.

The comedies celebrated a change in values. In the movies of the twenties and the early thirties, girls who chased after riches and luxury learned the error of their ways, but after 1934 sin wasn't the big movie theme it had been. Adultery was no longer tragic; the unashamed, wisecracking gold diggers saw to that. Glenda Farrell, one of the toughest and most honestly predatory of the millionaire-hunters, put it this way in *Gold Diggers of 1937*: 'It's so hard to be good under the capitalistic system.' Impudence became a virtue. Earlier, the sweet, archly virginal heroine had often had a breezy, good-hearted confidante; now the roles were reversed, and the lively, resilient heroine might have an innocent kid sister or a naïve little friend from her home town who needed looking after. What man in the Depression years would welcome a darling, dependent girl? Maybe the hero's shy buddy, but not the hero. He looked for the girl with verve; often she was so high and buoyant she could bounce right over trouble without noticing it. It was Carole Lombard's good-hearted giddiness that made her lovable, Jean

Arthur's flightiness, Myrna Loy's blithe imperviousness — and in *Bringing Up Baby*, Katharine Hepburn was so light-headed, so out of it, that she was unbeatable. The mistreated, masochistic women who had been moping through the confessional movies, pining for the men who had ruined them and looking tenderly at their father-less offspring, either faded (like Ann Harding, Ruth Chatterton, and Helen Hayes) or changed their styles (like Constance Bennett in *Topper*, Lombard in *Twentieth Century*, and, of course, Claudette Colbert in *It Happened One Night* and Irene Dunne in *Theodora Goes Wild* and *The Awful Truth*). The stars came down to earth in the middle and late thirties — and became ever bigger stars. Marlene Dietrich, who had turned into a lolling mannequin, reemerged as the battling floozy of *Destry Rides Again*. Just as in the late sixties some of the performers loosened up and became hip, thirties per-formers such as Joel McCrea and Fredric March became lighter-toned, gabby, and flip. An actor who changes from serious to comic roles doesn't have problems with the audience (the audi-ence loves seeing actors shed their dignity, which has generally become a threadbare pose long before it's shed); it's the change from comic to serious that may confound the audience's expecta-tions.

The speed and stylization of screwball humor were like a stunt, and some of the biggest directors of the thirties had come out of two-reel comedy and had the right training. Leo McCarey, who directed *The Awful Truth*, had directed the Marx Brothers in *Duck Soup* and, before that, Laurel & Hardy comedies for Hal Roach. George Stevens, who directed Grant in *Gunga Din*, was also a Hal Roach alumnus — cameraman on Laurel & Hardy and Harry Langdon shorts, and then a Roach director. *Topper*, with its sunny hocus-pocus and Grant as a debonair ghost, was actually a Hal Roach production; it was consid-ered Roach's most ambitious project. Movies in the thirties were still close to their beginnings. Wesley Ruggles, who directed Grant in *I'm No Angel*, had been one of Mack Sennett's Keystone Cops; Howard Hawks, who directed Grant in several of his best thirties films, had started as a director by writing and directing two comedy shorts. The directors had graduated from slapstick when sound came in and Hollywood took over Broadway's plays, but after a few years all that talk without much action was becoming wearying.

The screwball movies brought back the slapstick tradition of vaude-ville with the two-reelers, and blended it into those brittle Broadway comedies. When it was joined to a marital farce or a slightly daring society romance, slapstick no longer seemed like kid stuff: it was no longer innocent and was no longer regarded as 'low' comedy. The screwball movies pleased people of all ages. (The faithful adaptations of stage plays had often been a little tepid for children.) And the directors, who had come out of a Hollywood in which improvising and building gags were part of the fun of moviemaking, went back — partly, at least — to that way of working. No longer so script-bound, movies regained some of the creative energy and exuberance — and the joy in horseplay, too — that had been lost in the early years of talkies. The new freedom can be seen even in small ways, in trivia. Grant's screwball comedies are full of cross-references, and gags from one are repeated or continued in another. In *The Awful Truth*, Irene Dunne, trying to do in her (almost) ex-husband — Grant — refers to him as Jerry the Nipper; in *Bringing Up Baby*, Hepburn, pretending to be a gun moll, tells the town constable that Grant is the notorious Jerry the Nipper. And the same dog trots through the pictures, as Mr Smith in *The Awful Truth*, as George in *Bringing Up Baby* (and as Mr Atlas in *Topper Takes a Trip* and Asta in the *Thin Man* movies). That dog was a great actor: he appeared to adore each master in turn.

Once Grant's Paramount contract ended, there seemed no stopping him. As long as the screwball-comedy period lasted, he was king. After *The Awful Truth*, in 1937, he did two pictures with Katharine Hepburn in 1938 — *Bringing Up Baby* and *Holiday*. It was a true mating — they had the same high-energy level, the same physical absorption in acting. In 1939 he did *Gunga Din* and *Only Angels Have Wings*, and in 1940 *His Girl Friday, My Favorite Wife* and *The Philadelphia Story*.

During those peak years — 1937 to 1940 — he proved himself in romantic melodrama, high comedy, and low farce. He does uproarious mugging in the knockabout jamboree *Gunga Din* — a moviemakers' prank, like *Beat the Devil*. Ben Hecht and Charles MacArthur stole the adolescent boys' fantasy atmosphere from *Lives of a Bengal Lancer*, then took the plot from their own *The Front Page*, mixed it with a slapstick *The Three Musketeers*, and set it in a Hollywood Kipling India. Douglas Fairbanks, Jr, plays the Hildy Johnson role — he plans to leave the British Army to get married and go into the tea business — and Victor McLaglen, in the Walter Burns role, and Grant, as the Cockney bruiser Archibald Cutter, scheme to

310 ──────────────────────────────── Raising Kane

get him to re-enlist. When the three comrades fight off their enemies, they're like three Fairbankses flying through the air. Grant looks so great in his helmet in the bright sunshine and seems to be having such a marvellous time that he becomes the picture's romantic center, and his affection for the worshipful Gunga Din (Sam Jaffe) becomes the love story. The picture is both a stirring, beautifully photographed satiric colonial-adventure story and a walloping vaudeville show. Grant's grimaces and cries when Annie the elephant tries to follow him and Sam Jaffe onto a rope bridge over a chasm are his broadest clowning. (The scene is right out of Laurel & Hardy.) And he's never been more of a burlesque comic than when he arrives at the gold temple of the religious cult of thugs and whinnies with greedy delight at the very moment he's being shot at. The thug guru is shaven-headed Eduardo Ciannelli (the original Diamond Louis of *The Front Page*), who wears a loincloth and chants 'Kill! Kill! Kill for the love of Kali!' Perhaps because the picture winds up with a bit of pop magic — an eye-moistening, Kiplingesque tribute to Gunga Din, shown in Heaven in the British Army uniform he longed to wear — the press treated it rather severely, and George Stevens, the director, was a little apologetic about it. He may have got in over his head. He had replaced Howard Hawks as director, and when he added his Stan Laurel specialties to the heroic flourishes Hawks had prepared, and after the various rewrite men (William Faulkner and Joel Sayre were among them) built on to the gags, the result was a great, bounding piece of camp. Grant has always claimed that he doesn't like to exert himself, and that his ideal role would be a silent man in a wheelchair, but his performance here tells a different story. (All his performances tell a different story.) The following year, when Grant played Walter Burns in *His Girl Friday* (this time an acknowledged remake of *The Front Page*, and, with Charles Lederer's additions, a spastic explosion of dialogue), he raised mugging to a joyful art. Grant obviously loves the comedy of monomaniac egotism: Walter Burns's callousness and unscrupulousness are expressed in some of the best farce lines ever written in this country, and Grant hits those lines with a smack. He uses the same stiff-neck, cocked-head stance that he did in *Gunga Din*: it's his position for all-out, unsubtle farce. He snorts and whoops. His Walter Burns is a strong-arm performance, defiantly self-centered and funny.

When Grant was reunited with Irene Dunne in *My Favorite Wife*, they had another box-office smash, but his playing wasn't as fresh as in *The Awful Truth*. This marital farce was really moldy (it was based on Tennyson's *Enoch Arden*, filmed at least a dozen times, starting in 1908), and Grant's performance as the rattled husband is a matter of comic bewilderment and skittish double takes. The presence in the cast of his close friend Randolph Scott (they shared a house for several years) as the rival for Irene Dunne's affections may have interfered with his concentration; he doesn't provide an underlayer of conviction. He's expert but lightweight, and the role and the bustling plot don't bring anything new out of him.

The Hollywood comedy era was just about over by then. The screwball comedies, in particular, had become strained and witless; the spoiled, headstrong runaway heiresses and the top-hatted playboy cutups had begun to pall on the public, and third-rate directors who had no feeling for slapstick though it was enough to have players giggling and falling over the furniture. Right from the start, screwball comedy was infected by the germ of commercial hypocrisy. The fun-loving rich, with their glistening clothes, whitewall tires, mansions in the country, and sleek Art Deco apartments, exalted a carefree contempt for material values. The heroes and heroines rarely had any visible means of support, but they lived high, and in movie after movie their indifference to such mundane matters as food and rent became a self-admiring attitude — the attitude that is still touted in *Travels with My Aunt* and *Mame*. Like Mame, the unconventional heroines of the thirties were beloved by their servants. Irene Dunne in white fox and a trailing evening gown would kick her satin train impatiently to tell us that it was not money but love and laughter that mattered. The costume designers often went in for sprightly effects: Irene Dunne and Katharine Hepburn would be put into pixie hats that clung on the side of the head, dipping over one eye, while on top there were pagodas that shot up six or seven inches to a peak. All too often, the villains were stuffy society people or social climbers (as in *Mame*), and the heroes and heroines just too incorrigibly happy-go-lucky. Love seemed to mean making a fool of yourself. The froth hung heavy on many a screwball comedy, and as the pictures got worse and the Cary Grant parts began to be played by Lee Bowman and David Niven the public got fed up. The movement had already run down before the war started. In the forties, there were still some screwball comedies, but they were antic and shrill, except for a few strays: some of the Tracy–Hepburn pictures, and the comedies in which Preston Sturges reinvented slapstick in a more organic form — creating an image of Americans as a people who never stopped explaining themselves while balling up whatever they were trying to do.

Though he remained a top box-office star, Cary Grant fell on evil days. After 1940, he didn't seem to have any place to go — there were no longer Cary Grant pictures. Instead, he acted in pictures that nobody could have been right for — abominations like the 1942 anti-Nazi romantic comedy *Once Upon a Honeymoon*, in which he was an American newsman in Warsaw trying to rescue the American stripper Ginger Rogers from her Nazi husband (Walter Slezak). From the first frame, it was as clammily contrived as anything that Paramount had shoved him into, and in one pathetically insensitive sequence Grant and Rogers are mistaken for Jews and held in a concentration camp. His performance is frequently atrocious: he twinkles with condescending affection when the nitwit stripper develops a political consciousness and helps a Jewish hotel maid escape from danger. Mostly, he acted in stock situation comedies — comedies with no comic roots, like *The Bachelor and the Bobby-Soxer* (1947), in which Myrna Loy is a judge who works out a deal. Grant, a philandering artist, will go to jail unless he dates her schoolgirl sister (Shirley Temple) until the teen-ager's crush on him wears off. Escorting Shirley Temple — wearing his shirt open and acting like an adolescent — Cary Grant is degradingly unfunny. There's no core of plausibility in his role. Grant doesn't have the eyes of a Don Juan, or the temperament. When Grant is accused of being a skirt-chaser, it seems like some kind of mistake.

In the thirties, Grant would sometimes appear in a role, such as the despondent husband of a mercenary, coldhearted woman (Kay Francis) in the 1939 *In Name Only*, that suggested that he had unexplored dimensions. They remained unexplored. In 1941, when he departed from comedy, it was in just the sort of sincere tearjerker that Hollywood was always proudest of — *Penny Serenade*, with Irene Dunne again. The unrealistic casting of this inert, horribly pristine film is the trick: the appeal to the audience is that these two glamorous stars play an ordinary couple and suffer the calamities that do in fact happen to ordinary people. When tragedy strikes Cary Grant and Irene Dunne, it hurts the audience in a special way — *Penny Serenade* is a sweet-and-sour pacifier. Grant, who got an Academy Award nomination, could hardly have been better. Using his dark eyes and his sensuous, clouded handsomeness as a romantic mask, he gave his role a defensive, not quite forthright quality, and he brought out everything that it was possible to bring out of his warmed-over lines, weighing them perfectly, so that they almost seemed felt.

Nearly all Grant's seventy-two films have a certain amount of class and are well above the Hollywood average, but most of them, when you come right down to it, are not really very good. Grant could glide through a picture in a way that leaves one indifferent, as in the role of a quaint guardian angel named Dudley in the bland, musty Goldwyn production *The Bishop's Wife* (1947), and he could be the standard put-upon male of burbling comedy, as in *Every Girl Should Be Married* (1948) and the pitifully punk *Room for One More* (1952) — the nice-nice pictures he made with Betsy Drake, who in 1949 became his third wife. He could be fairly persuasive in astute, reflective parts, as in the Richard Brooks thriller *Crisis* (1950), in which he plays a brain surgeon forced to operate on a Latin-American dictator (José Ferrer). He's a seasoned performer here, though his energy level isn't as high as in the true Grant roles and he's a little cold, staring absently when he means to indicate serious thought. What's missing is probably that his own sense of humor isn't allowed to come through; generally when he isn't playing a man who laughs easily he isn't all there.

He was able to keep his independence because he had a good head for business. Within a short time of leaving Paramount, he could command a hundred and fifty thousand dollars a picture, and that was only the beginning. Later, he formed partnerships and produced his pictures through his own corporations — Grandon, Granart, Granley, and Granox. He didn't do what stars like Kirk Douglas did when they gained control over their productions: he didn't appear in Westerns, for the virtually guaranteed market. He was too self-aware for that; he was a lonely holdout in the period when even Frank Sinatra turned cowpoke. From the thirties on, Grant looked for comedies that would be mass-oriented versions of the Noël Coward and Philip Barry and Frederick Lonsdale drawing-room and boudoir farces that Broadway theatregoers admired in the twenties. And so he settled for Sidney Sheldon (*The Bachelor and the Bobby-Soxer, Dream Wife*), or Stanley Shapiro (*Operation Petticoat, That Touch of Mink*), or Norman Panama and Melvin Frank (*Mr Blandings Builds His Dream House*), or for Melville Shavelson and Jack Rose (*Room for One More, Houseboat*). He sought the best material and got the second-rate and synthetic, because good writers wouldn't (and couldn't) write that way anymore.

His taste didn't change, but he didn't do the real thing — not even the real Lonsdale. His friends say he believes that the world doesn't understand fine language. With *People Will Talk* and *The Talk of the Town*, he was probably reaching toward Shaw. He got the loquacity without the wit.

Considering that he selected his roles, these choices indicate one of the traps of stardom. When actors are young, they're eager for great roles, but when they become stars they generally become fearful that the public won't accept them in something different. They look for roles that seem a little more worthwhile than the general run. With one exception — *None but the Lonely Heart* — Cary Grant appeared to be content throughout his career to bring savoir-faire to pratfalls, romantic misunderstandings, and narrow escapes. It seems reasonable to assume that he attained something so close to the highest aspirations of his youth that, as far as acting was concerned, he had no other goals — and no conflicts. Moss Hart said that Archie Leach's gloom vanished when he became Cary Grant.

The only trace of gloom in Grant's movies is in *None but the Lonely Heart*, which he made in association with Clifford Odets (as writer and director) in 1944. The film was an ironic interlude in Grant's career, coming, as it did, between the cloying whimsey of *Once Upon a Time*, in which he was a Broadway sharpie exploiting a boy who had a pet dancing caterpillar, and *Night and Day*, the ten-ton Cole Porter musical bio, in which he skittered about as a youthful Yalie before facing life with stoic courage and inscrutable psychic hangups. In *None but the Lonely Heart*, set in the East End of London, he plays Ernie Mott, a young Cockney — a restless drifter who lacks the will to leave the ghetto for good. Ernie grew up in oppressive poverty, but he wants to make life better for his mother, who runs a grubby antiques and secondhand-furniture shop. Made at Grant's instigation (he acquired the rights of the book), the film was a gesture toward the ideas he shared with the other dissidents at Rudley's, and, even more, a gesture toward his own roots — toward the grimness of his life before he apprenticed himself to the theatre. His mother was released from confinement in 1933 (that same year, his father died of 'extreme toxicity'), and he established a surprisingly close relationship with her. Eccentric but hardy and self-sufficient, she had a whole new life after that twenty-year incarceration. She lived into her mid-nineties, and until she was in her late eighties she did all her own shopping and housework, and occupied her days with antiquing — driving fierce bargains when she spotted something she wanted. Grant has described her as 'extremely good company.' He wrote that 'sometimes we laugh together until tears come into our eyes.' In the thirties, he went to England several times a year to see her, and he took the socialite beauty Virginia Cherrill (Chaplin's leading lady in *City Lights*) to meet his mother before they were married, in London, in 1934 — his first marriage, which was dissolved the following year. The outbreak of the Second World War must have brought his English past even closer to him; he was still a British subject, and in 1939 he became involved in activities to aid the British. Later, when the United States was in the war, he went on trips to entertain the troops and on bond-selling tours. (In one routine, he played straight man to Bert Lahr.) In June, 1942, less than two weeks before his marriage to Barbara Hutton, he legally changed his name and became an American citizen.

Grant's old name had long been a joke — to the public and to him. He had named his pet Sealyham Archibald, and when the dog ran away from his Los Angeles home (it is said that the dog ran out the door while Grant was carrying Virginia Cherrill over the threshold), he took large ads in the papers giving the dog's name. In *Gunga Din*, when Grant, as the soldier Cutter, received an invitation to a regimental ball, he reads the salutation aloud — 'Arch-i-bald Cutter' — chewing the syllables and savoring their preposterousness. As the editor in *His Girl Friday*, when Grant is threatened with prison by the major and the sheriff, he yammers out, 'The last man to say that to me was Archie Leach, just a week before he cut his throat.'

Yet when he played Ernie Mott in *None but the Lonely Heart* he became Archie Leach again; even the names are similar. *None but the Lonely Heart* was the first movie Clifford Odets had ever directed, and although the original material was not his but a best-selling novel by Richard Llewellyn, Odets gave it the rich melancholy of his best plays. Too much of it, however: the dirgelike, mournful, fogged-up atmosphere seemed fake and stagy. Odets worked up each scene (almost as one develops scenes in the theatre) and didn't get them to flow thematically, but he went all out. He brought off some hard-earned effects with an élan that recalled Orson Welles's first films, and there were unexpected crosscurrents. (Ernie's girl, played by June Duprez, was plaintive and distressed, and turned out not to be Ernie's girl at all.) It was an extraordinary début film, and it is an indication of the movie industry's attitude

toward talent that Odets got only one other chance to direct —
fifteen years later (*The Story on Page One*, in 1959). The complicated texture of *None but the Lonely Heart* made a pervasive,
long-lasting impression. What can one remember of such Grant
films as *Room for One More* or *Dream Wife* or *Kiss Them for Me* or
Houseboat? But from *None but the Lonely Heart* one retains June
Duprez's puzzlingly perverse face and voice; a scene of Grant and a
buddy (Barry Fitzgerald) drunk in a tunnel, letting out their voices
and teasing their echoes; and — especially — Grant and Ethel
Barrymore together. She played his mother, and her great, heavy
eyes matched up with his. In her screen roles, this statuesque, handsome woman usually substituted presence and charm and hokum for
performance; she wasn't tedious, like her brother Lionel, but she was
a hollow technician. Not this time, though. In a few scenes, she and
Grant touched off emotions in each other which neither of them ever
showed on the screen again. When Ernie, who has become a petty
racketeer, is told that his mother has been arrested for trafficking in
stolen goods, he has an instant's disbelief: 'They got her inside, you
mean — pinched?' Grant says that line with more fervor than any
other line he ever delivered. And there are viewers who still — after
three decades — recall the timbre of Ethel Barrymore's voice in the
prison hospital when she cries, 'Disgraced you, Son.'

Grant is not as vivid in the memory as Ethel Barrymore is. Of the
profusion of themes in the film, the deeply troubled bond of love
between the mother and the son must have been a strong factor in his
original decision to buy the book. Yet he didn't fully express what
had attracted him to the material. His performance was finer than one
might have expected, considering that in all his years on the stage
he'd never actually done a play without music, and that he couldn't
use the confident technique that made him such a dynamo in screen
comedy, or the straightforward, subdued acting he depended on in
the war film *Destination Tokyo*. Grant was always desperately uncomfortable when he played anyone who wasn't close to his own
age, and though he may have felt like the Ernie of the novel (a
dreamy nineteen-year-old, an unformed artist-intellectual), as an
actor he was too set in his ways. The slight stylization of his comic
technique — the deadpan primed to react, the fencer's awareness of
the camera, all the self-protective skills he'd acquired — worked
against him when he needed to be expressive. Cary Grant acts from
the outside; he's the wrong kind of actor to play a disharmonious

character, a precursor of the fifties rebel-hero. Grant isn't totally on the surface; there's a mystery in him — he has an almost stricken look, a memory of suffering — but he's not the modern kind of actor who taps his unconscious in his acting. Part of his charm is·that his angers are all externally provoked; there are no internal pressures in him that need worry us, no rage or rebelliousness to churn us up. If he reacts with exasperation or a glowering look, we know everything there is to know about his reaction. When we watch Brando, the dramatic stage is *in* him, and the external aggressions against him are the occasions for us to see the conflicts within; the traditional actor's distance and his perfect clarity are gone. Life seemed simpler with Cary Grant's pre-Freudian, pre-psychological acting-as-entertaining. But he couldn't split Ernie Mott apart effectively, and he couldn't hold him together, either. And — it was nobody's fault — one reason Ernie wasn't as vivid a character as needed to be was that it was Cary Grant trying to be grubby Ernie Mott. A movie star like Cary Grant carries his movie past with him. He becomes the sum of his most successful roles, and he has only to appear for our good will to be extended to him. We smile when we see him, we laugh before he does anything; it makes us happy just to look at him. And so in *None but the Lonely Heart*, in the role that was closest to Grant's own buried feelings — the only character he ever played that he is known to have consciously identified with — he seemed somewhat miscast.

It's impossible to estimate how much this failure meant to him, but more than a year passed before he plunged into the inanities of *Night and Day* — the only year since he had entered movies in which he made no pictures, and a bad year in other ways, too, since his marriage to Barbara Hutton broke up. However, Cary Grant appears to be a profoundly practical man; after the disappointing box-office returns from *None but the Lonely Heart* (he did get an Academy Award nomination for it, but the award was given to Bing Crosby for *Going My Way*), he never tried anything except Cary Grant roles. As far as one can judge, he never looked back. He remained a lifelong friend of Clifford Odets; he was proud to be accepted by Odets, and Odets was proud that the handsome, tanned idol was there at his feet. But Odets's passion no longer fired Cary Grant to make business decisions. When Odets was trying to set up picture deals and needed him as a star, he didn't return the calls. This didn't spoil their friendship — they had both been living in Los Angeles a long time.

No doubt Grant was big enough at the box office to have kept going indefinitely, surviving fables about caterpillars, and even such mournful mistakes as hauling a cannon through the Napoleonic period of *The Pride and the Passion*. But if Alfred Hitchcock, who had worked with him earlier on *Suspicion*, hadn't rescued him with *Notorious*, in 1946, and again, in 1955, with *To Catch a Thief* (a flimsy script but with a show-off role for him) and in 1959 with *North by Northwest*, and if Grant hadn't appeared in the Stanley Donen film *Charade* in 1963, his development as an actor would have essentially been over in 1940, when he was only thirty-six. In all four of those romantic suspense comedies, Grant played the glamorous, worldly figure that 'Cary Grant' had come to mean: he was cast as Cary Grant, and he gave a performance as Cary Grant. It was his one creation, and it had become the only role for him to play — the only role, finally, he *could* play.

Had he made different choices, had he taken more risks like *None but the Lonely Heart*, he might eventually have won acceptance as an actor with a wide range. He might have become a great actor; he had the intensity, and the command of an audience's attention. But how can one tell? One thinks of Cary Grant in such a set way it's difficult even to speculate about his capacities. Yet, considering his wealth and his unusually independent situation, it's apparent that if he was constricted, it wasn't just Hollywood's doing but his own. Working within the framework of commercial movies, James Mason, who at one time also seemed a highly specialized star, moved on from romantic starring roles to a series of deeper character portraits. However, Mason had to move away from the sexual center of his movies to do it, and it's doubtful if Grant would have sacrificed — or even endangered — the type of stardom he had won. His bargaining power was probably more important to him than his development as an actor; he *was* a tycoon. Whatever his reasons were, they're concealed now by his brisk businessman's manner. He doesn't seem to know or to care whether his pictures were good or bad; he says that if they did well at the box office, that's all that matters to him, and this doesn't appear to be an affectation. He made a gigantic profit on the gagged-up *Operation Petticoat*, which he produced in 1959; his friends say that he makes no distinction between that and *Notorious*.

Cary Grant always looks as if he'd just come from a workout in a miracle gym. And it's easy for audiences to forget about his stinkers (they're not held against him), because he himself isn't very different in them from the way he is when he has a strong director and a script with some drive. It's his sameness that general audiences respond to; they may weary of him, but still he's a guaranteed product. (It's the pictures that aren't.) And if he didn't grow as an actor, he certainly perfected 'Cary Grant.' One does not necessarily admire an icon, as one admires, say, Laurence Olivier, but it can be a wonderful object of contemplation. (If Olivier had patented the brand of adorable spoiled-boy charm he exhibited on the stage in *No Time for Comedy*, he might have had a career much like Grant's — and, indeed, in *Sleuth* Olivier played the sort of role which would then have been all that could be expected of him.)

As a movie star, Grant is so much a man of the city that he couldn't play a rural hero or a noble, rugged man of action, and so much a modern man that he couldn't appear in a costume or period picture without looking obstreperous — as if he felt he was being made a fool of. In *The Howards of Virginia*, it wasn't just the hot-blooded fighter-lover role that threw him, it was also wearing a Revolutionary uniform and a tricornered hat, with his hair in a chignon; he waddled through the picture like a bowlegged duck. The thought of him in Biblical sackcloth or in a Roman toga or some Egyptian getup is grisly-funny. And he's inconceivable in most of the modern urban films: how could Cary Grant play a silent stud or a two-fisted supercop? Grant never quite created another character — not even in the limited sense that screen stars sometimes do, using their own bodies and personalities as the base for imaginative creations. There are no Fred C. Dobbses or Sam Spades in his career. It's doubtful if he could even play a biographical character without being robbed of his essence. As Cole Porter, he wanders around in *Night and Day* looking politely oblivious; he's afraid to cut loose and be himself, yet he's too constrained to suggest anything resembling Cole Porter, so the hero seems to have a sickly, joyless nature. Composing song after song, his Cole Porter appears to have less music in his soul than any other living creature. Grant relaxes a little just once, while singing 'You're the Top' with Ginny Simms.

He sings quite often in movies — as in *The Awful Truth*, when he parodies Ralph Bellamy's version of 'Home on the Range,' or in *Suzy*, in which he does the number that is included in *That's Entertainment*, and he replaced Bing Crosby as the Mock Turtle in the 1933 *Alice in Wonderland*, and sang 'Beautiful Soup' — but he played an actual singing role in only one movie, early in his career: the disarmingly frilly 1934 *Kiss and Make Up*, one of Paramount's many imitations of the Lubitsch musical-comedy style. A sense of fun breaks through when he shows off his vaudeville skills — a confident, full-hearted exhibitionism. He frequently plays the piano in movies — happily and enthusiastically — and he does off the screen, too. For the past decade, since the breakup of his fourth marriage — to Dyan Cannon — following the birth of a daughter (his first child), he's been in retirement from the screen, but he's been active as an executive with Fabergé, whose president, George Barrie, used to play the saxophone for a living (Barrie composed the title song for *A Touch of Class*, produced by Brut, a subsidiary of Fabergé); they sometimes have jam sessions after board meetings, with Grant playing piano or organ. It's a corporate business right out of a thirties Cary Grant movie: in *Kiss and Make Up*, he actually ran a swank beauty salon. Grant belongs to the tradition of the success-worshipping immigrant boy who works his way to the top, but with a difference: the success he believes in is in the international high style of the worldly, fun-loving men he played — he's got Rolls-Royces stashed away in key cities. He has lived up to his screen image, and then some; welcome everywhere, more sought after than the Duke of Windsor was, in his seventies he's glitteringly — almost foolishly — hale.

Grant has had an apparently wide range of roles, but only apparently. Even in the era when he became a star, his sexual attraction worked only with a certain type of co-star — usually playing a high-strung, scatterbrained heroine, dizzy but not dumb. He would have been a disaster opposite Joan Crawford. With her gash smile, thick-syrup voice, and enormous tension, she required a roughneck titan like Gable to smite her; she would have turned Cary Grant into Woody Allen. A typical fan-magazine quote from Joan Crawford in her big-box-office youth was 'Whatever we feel toward the man of the moment, it is he who is our very life and soul.' It hardly matters whether Crawford herself was the author of those sentiments; that was the kind of woman she represented on the screen. It's easy to visualize Cary Grant's panic at the thought of being somebody's 'very life and soul.' He wanted to have a good time with a girl. It was always implicit that she had something going on her own; she was a free lance. She wasn't going to weigh him down — not like Crawford, who was all character armor and exorbitant needs. Crawford actually intended to take over the man of the moment's life and soul; that was what love meant in her pictures, and why she was so effective with skinny, refined, rich-hero types, like Robert Mongomery and Franchot Tone, whom she could scoop up. She gave the same intensity to everything she did; she inspired awe. But Grant didn't want to be carried away — nobody scoops up Cary Grant — and he didn't want an electrical powerhouse. (He's unthinkable with Bette Davis.) Once Grant became a star, there was a civilized equality in his sex partnerships, though his co-star had to be not only a pal but an ardent pal. When he appeared with Myrna Loy, they were pleasant together, but they didn't really strike sparks. Loy isn't particularly vulnerable, and she isn't dominant, either; she's so cool and airy she doesn't take the initiative, and since he doesn't either (except perfunctorily), nothing happens. They're too much alike — both lightly self-deprecating, both faintly reserved and aloof.

In dramatic roles, the women stars of the thirties and forties could sometimes triumph over mediocre material. This has been one of the saving aspects of the movie medium: Garbo could project so much more than a role required that we responded to her own emotional nature. Her uniquely spiritual eroticism turned men into willing slaves, and she was often at her best with rather passive men — frequently asexual or unisexual or homosexual (though not meant to be in the course of the films). Garbo's love transcended sex; her sensuality transcended sex. She played opposite Clark Gable once, and the collision, though heated, didn't quite work; his macho directness — and opacity — reduced her from passionate goddess to passionate woman. And Garbo seemed to lose her soul when she played mere women — that's why she was finished when the audience had had enough of goddesses. But for a time in the late twenties and early thirites, when she leaned back on a couch and exposed her throat, the whole audience could dream away — heterosexual men as much as the homosexuals (whom she was, indeed, generally seducing in her movies). Something similar operated, to a lesser extent, with Katharine Hepburn. In the thirties, she was frequently most effective with the kind of juveniles who were called boys: they were male versions of sensitive waifs, all cheekbone. She was effective, but there wasn't much sexual tension in those movies. And, despite the camaraderie and marvellous byplay of her later series with Spencer Tracy, she lost some of her charge when she acted with him. She was humanized but maybe also a little subjugated, and when we saw her through his eyes there seemed to be something the matter with her — she was too high-strung, had too much temperament. Tracy was stodgily heterosexual. She was more exciting with Cary Grant, who had a faint ambiguity and didn't want her to be more like ordinary women: Katharine Hepburn was a one-of-a-kind entertainment, and he could enjoy the show. The element of Broadway conventionality that mars *The Philadelphia Story* is in the way she's set up for a fall — as a snow maiden and a phony. Grant is cast as an élitist variation of the later Spencer Tracy characters.

Cary Grant could bring out the sexuality of his co-stars in comedies. Ingrid Bergman, a powerful presence on the screen, and with a deep, emotional voice (her voice is a big part of her romantic appeal in *Casablanca*), is a trifle heavy-spirited for comedy. She was never again as sexy as in that famous scene in *Notorious* when she just keeps advancing on Grant; you feel that she's so far gone on him that she can't wait any longer — and it's funny. Although Grant is a perfectionist on the set, some of his directors say that he wrecks certain scenes because he won't do fully articulated passages of dialogue. He wants always to be searching for how he feels; he wants to waffle charmingly. This may be a pain to a scenarist or a director, but in his own terms Grant knows what he's doing. He's the greatest sexual stooge the screen has ever known: his side steps and delighted stares turn his co-stars into comic goddesses. Nobody else has ever been able to do that.

When the sexual psychology of a comedy was right for Grant, he could be sensational, but if it was wrong and his energy still came pouring out, he could be terrible. In Frank Capra's *Arsenic and Old Lace* (made in 1941 but not released until 1944, because, by contract, it couldn't open until the Broadway production closed) he's more painful to watch than a normally bad actor — like, say, Robert Cummings — would be, because our affection for Grant enters into our discomfort. As it was originally written, the Mortimer Brewster role — an acerbic theatre critic being pursued by his aggressive, nononsense fiancée — wouldn't have been bad for Grant, but the Capra film sweetened the critic and turned the fiancée into a cuddly, innocuous little dear (Priscilla Lane). Capra called Grant Hollywood's greatest *farceur*, but the role was shaped as if for Fred MacMurray, and Grant was pushed into frenzied overreacting — prolonging his stupefied double takes, stretching out his whinny. Sometime after the whopping success of *It Happened One Night*, Frank Capra had lost his instinct for sex scenes, and his comedies became almost obscenely neuter, with clean, friendly old grandpas presiding over blandly retarded families. Capra's hick jollity was not the atmosphere for Cary

Grant, and he was turned into a manic enuch in *Arsenic and Old Lace*.

In drag scenes — even in his best movies — Grant also loses his grace. He is never so butch — so beefy and clumsy a he-man — as in his female impersonations or in scenes involving a clothes switch. In *Bringing Up Baby*, Katharine Hepburn takes his suit away, and he has nothing to wear but a flouncy fur-trimmed negligee. When Hepburn's aunt (May Robson) arrives and demands crossly, querulously, 'Why are you wearing a robe?' Grant, exasperated, answers 'Because I just went gay all of a sudden.' It doesn't work: he goes completely out of character. Burt Lancaster was deliriously, unself-consciously funny in a long drag sequence in *The Crimson Pirate* (a parody adventure picture roughly comparable to *Gunga Din*); he turned himself into a scrambled cartoon of a woman, as Harry Ritz had done in *On the Avenue*. That's what Tony Curtis and Jack Lemmon did in *Some Like It Hot* — only they did it by yielding to their feminine disguises and becoming their own versions of gorgeous, desirable girls. Bert Remsen does it that way in *California Split*, anxiously seeing himself as a gracious lady of quality. But Grant doesn't yield to cartooning femininity or to enjoying it; he doesn't play a woman, he threatens to — flirting with the idea and giggling over it. His sequence in a skirt and a horsehair wig in the stupid, humiliating *I Was a Male War Bride* was a fizzle. He made himself brusque and clumsy to call attention to how inappropriate the women's clothes were on him — as if he needed to prove he was a big, burly guy.

The beautifully tailored clothes that seem now to be almost an intrinsic part of the Cary Grant persona came very late in his career. Decked out in the pinstripes, wide lapels, and bulky shoulders of the early forties, Grant, with his thick, shiny black hair, often suggested a race-track tout or a hood. He was a snappy dresser, and when he was playing Ivy League gentlemen, his clothes were often kingpin flashy, in the George Raft manner. Happy and hearty, he looked terrific in those noisy clothes; he wore baggy pants in *Only Angels Have Wings* and was still a sexual magnet. But sometimes his slouch hats and floppy, loose-draped jackets seemed to dominate the actor inside. His strutting appearance was distracting, like a gaudy stage set. As he got older, however, he and his slim-line clothes developed such an ideal one-to-one love affair that people could grin appreciatively in the sheer pleasure of observing the union. In *North by Northwest*, the lean-fitting suit he wore through so many perils seemed the skin of his character; and in *Charade*, when for the sake of a dim joke about drip-dry he got under the shower with his suit on, he lost the skin of his character — even though that character was 'Cary Grant.'

It's a peerless creation, the 'Cary Grant' of the later triumphs — *Notorious, To Catch a Thief, North by Northwest* and *Charade*. Without a trace of narcissism, he appears as a man women are drawn to — a worldly, sophisticated man who has become more attractive with the years. And Grant really had got better looking. The sensual lusciousness was burned off: age purified him (as it has purified Paul Newman). His acting was purified, too; it became more economical. When he was young, he had been able to do lovely fluff like *Topper* without being too elfin, or getting smirky, like Ray Milland, or becoming a brittle, too bright gentleman, like Franchot Tone. But he'd done more that his share of arch mugging — lowering his eyebrows and pulling his head back as if something funny were going on in front of him when nothing was. Now the excess energy was pared away; his performances were simple and understated and seamlessly smooth. In *Charade*, he gives an amazingly calm performance; he knows how much his presence does for him and how little he needs to do. His romantic glamour, which had reached a high peak in 1939 in *Only Angels Have Wings*, wasn't lost; his glamour was now a matter of his resonances from the past, and he wore it like a mantle.

Some stars (Kirk Douglas, for one) don't realize that as they get older, if they continue to play the same sort of parts, they no longer need to use big, bold strokes; they risk self-caricature when they show their old flash, and they're a bit of a joke when they try to demonstrate that they're as good as they ever were. But if you pare down their styles and let our memories and imaginations fill in from the past, they can seem masters. Sitting in an airport V.I.P. lounge a few years ago, Anthony Quinn looked up from the TV set on which he was watching *To Catch a Thief* and said, 'That's the actor I always wanted to be' — which is fairly funny, not only because Quinn and Grant are such contrasting types but because Quinn has never learned the first thing from Cary Grant. He's never understood that he needs to dry out a little. Some actors are almost insultingly robust. If you should ask Anthony Quinn 'Do you know how to dance?' he would cry 'Do I know how to dance?' and he'd answer the question with his whole body — and you'd probably wind up sorry that you'd asked. Cary Grant might twirl a couple of fingers, or perhaps he'd execute an intricate, quick step and make us long for more. Unlike the macho actors who as they got older became more strident about their virility, puffing their big, flabby chests in an effort to make themselves look even larger, Grant, with his sexual diffidence, quietly became less physical — and more assured. He doesn't wear out his welcome: when he has a good role, we never get enough of him. Not only is his reserve his greatest romantic resource — it is the resource that enables him to age gracefully.

What the directors and writers of those four suspense films understood was that Cary Grant could no longer play an ordinary man — he had to be what he had become to the audience. In box-office terms, he might get by with playing opposite Doris Day in *That Touch of Mink*, but he was interchangeable with Rock Hudson in this sort of picture, and the role was a little demeaning — it didn't take cognizance of his grace or of the authority that enduring stardom confers. The special charm of *Notorious*, of the piffle *To Catch a Thief*, and of *North by Northwest* and *Charade* is that they give him his due. He is, after all, an immortal — an ideal of sophistication forever. He spins high in the sky, like Fred Astaire and Ginger Rogers. He may not be able to do much, but what he can do no one else has ever done so well, and because of his civilized nonaggressiveness and his witty acceptance of his own foolishness we see ourselves idealized in him. He's self-aware in a charming, non-egotistic way that appeals to the very people we'd want to appeal to. Even when he plays Cockneys, he isn't English or foreign to us — or American, either, exactly. Some stars lose their nationality, especially if their voices are distinctive. Ronald Colman, with his familiar cultivated, rhythmic singsong, seemed no more British, really, than the American Douglas Fairbanks, Jr; they were both 'dashing' men of the world. Ingrid Bergman doesn't sound Swedish to us but sounds simply like Ingrid Bergman. Cary Grant became stateless early: he was always Cary Grant. Making love to him, the heroines of the later movies are all aware that he's a legendary presence, that they're trying to seduce a legend. 'How do you shave in there?' Audrey Hepburn asks bemusedly in *Charade*, putting her finger up to the cleft in his chin. Her character in the movie is to be smitten by him and to dote on him. Actually, he had begun to show his age by that time (1963); it was obvious that he was being lighted very carefully and kept in threequarter shots, and that his face was rounder and a little puffy. And although lampblack may have shielded the neck, one could tell that it was being shielded. But we saw him on Audrey Hepburn's terms: Cary Grant at his most elegant. He didn't need the show-stopping handsomeness of his youth; his style, though it was based on his handsomeness, had transcended it.

Everyone likes the idea of Cary Grant. Everyone thinks of him affectionately, because he embodies what seems a happier time — a time when we had a simpler relationship to a performer. We could admire him for his timing and nonchalance; we didn't expect emotional revelations from Cary Grant. We were used to his keeping his distance — which, if we cared to, we could close in idle fantasy. He appeared before us in his radiantly shallow perfection, and that was all we wanted of him. He was the Dufy of acting — shallow but in a good way, shallow without trying to be deep. We didn't want depth from him; we asked only that he be handsome and silky and make us laugh.

Cary Grant's bravado — his wonderful sense of pleasure in performance, which we respond to and share in — is a pride in craft. His confident timing is linked to a sense of movies as popular entertainment: he wants to please the public. He became a 'polished,' 'finished' performer in a tradition that has long since atrophied. The suave, accomplished actors were usually poor boys who went into a trade and trained themselves to become perfect gentlemen. They're the ones who seem to have 'class.' Cary Grant achieved Mrs Leach's ideal, and it turned out to be the whole world's ideal.

The New Yorker, 1975

Why are Movies so Bad?
Or, the Numbers

The movies have been so rank the last couple of years that when I see people lining up to buy tickets I sometimes think that the movies aren't drawing an audience — they're inheriting an audience. People just want to go to a movie. They're stung repeatedly, yet their desire for a good movie — for *any* movie — is so strong that all over the country they keep lining up. 'There's one God for all creation, but there must be a separate God for the movies,' a producer said. 'How else can you explain their survival?' An atmosphere of hope develops before a big picture's release, and even after your friends tell you how bad it is, you can't quite believe it until you see for yourself. The lines (and the grosses) tell us only that people are going to the movies — not that they're having a good time. Financially, the industry is healthy, so among the people at the top there seems to be little recognition of what miserable shape movies are in. They think the grosses are proof that people are happy with what they're getting, just as TV executives think that the programs with the highest ratings are what TV viewers want, rather than what they settle for. (A number of the new movie executives come from TV.) These new executives don't necessarily see many movies themselves, and they rarely go to a theatre. If for the last couple of years Hollywood couldn't seem to do anything right, it isn't that it was just a stretch of bad luck — it's the result of recent developments within the industry. And in all probability it will get worse, not better. There have been few recent American movies worth lining up for — last year there was chiefly *The Black Stallion*, and this year there is *The Empire Strikes Back*. The first was made under the aegis of Francis Ford Coppola; the second was financed by George Lucas, using his profits from *Star Wars* as a guarantee to obtain bank loans. One can say with fair confidence that neither *The Black Stallion* nor *The Empire Strikes Back* could have been made with such care for visual richness and imagination if it had been done under studio control. Even small films on traditional subjects are difficult to get financed at a studio if there are no parts for stars in them; Peter Yates, the director of *Breaking Away* — a graceful, unpredictable comedy that pleases and satisfies audiences — took the project to one studio after another for almost six years before he could get the backing for it.

There are direct results when conglomerates take over movie companies. At first, the heads of the conglomerates may be drawn into the movie business for the status implications — the opportunity to associate with world-famous celebrities. Some other conglomerate heads may be drawn in for the girls, but for them, too, a new social life beckons, and as they become socially involved, people with great names approach them as equals, and it gets them crazy. Famous stars and producers and writers and directors tell them about offers they've had from other studios and about ideas that they have for pictures, and the conglomerate heads become indignant that the studios they control aren't in on these wonderful projects. The next day, they're on the phone raising hell with their studio bosses. Very soon, they're likely to be summoning directors and suggesting material to them, talking to actors, and telling the company executives what projects should be developed. How bad are the taste and judgment of the conglomerate heads? Very bad. They haven't grown up in a show-business milieu — they don't have the background, the instincts, the information of those who have lived and sweated movies for many years. (Neither do most of the current studio bosses.) The conglomerate heads may be business geniuses, but as far as movies are concerned they have virgin instincts; ideas that are new to them and take them by storm may have failed grotesquely dozens of times. But they feel that they are creative people — how else could they have made so much money and be in a position to advise artists what to do? Who is to tell them no? Within a very short time, they are in fact, though not in title, running the studio. They turn up compliant executives who will settle for the title and not fight for the authority or for their own tastes — if, in fact, they have any. The conglomerate heads find these compliant executives among lawyers and agents, among lawyer-agents, among television executives, and in the lower echelons of the companies they've taken over. Generally, these executives reserve all their enthusiasm for movies that have made money; those are the only movies they like. When a director or a writer talks to them and tries to suggest the kind of picture he has in mind by using a comparison, they may stare at him blankly. They are usually law-school or business-school graduates; they have no frame of reference. Worse, they have no shame about not knowing anything about movies. From their point of view, such knowledge is not essential to their work. Their talent is being able to anticipate their superiors' opinions; in meetings, they show a sixth sense for guessing what the most powerful person in the room wants to hear. And if they ever guess wrong, they know how to shift gears without a tremor. So the movie companies wind up with top production executives whose interest in movies rarely extends beyond the immediate selling possibilities; they could be selling neckties just as well as movies, except that they are drawn to glamour and power.

This does not prevent these executives from being universally treated as creative giants. If a studio considers eighty projects, and eventually twenty of them (the least risky) go into production, and two of them become runaway hits (or even one of them), the studio's top executive will be a hero to his company and the media, and will soon be quoted in the *Los Angeles Times* and *The New York Times* talking about his secret for picking winners — his intuitive understanding, developed from his childhood experiences, that people want a strong, upbeat narrative, that they want to cheer the hero and hiss the villain. When *Alien* opened 'big,' Alan Ladd, Jr, president of the pictures division of Twentieth Century-Fox, was regarded as a demigod; it's the same way that Fred Silverman was a demigod. It has nothing to do with quality, only with the numbers. (Ladd and his team weren't admired for the small pictures they took chances on and the artists they stuck by.) The media now echo the kind of thinking that goes on in Hollywood, and spread it wide. Movie critics on TV discuss the relative grosses of the new releases; the grosses at this point relative to previous hits; which pictures will pass the others in a few weeks. It's like the Olympics — which will be the winners?

There are a lot of reasons that movies have been so bad during the last couple of years and probably won't be any better for the next couple of years. One big reason is that rotten pictures are making money — not necessarily wild amounts (though a few are), but sizable amounts. So if studio heads want nothing more than to make money and grab power, there is no reason for them to make better ones. Turning out better pictures might actually jeopardize their position. Originally, the studios were controlled by theatre chains — the chains opened the studios in order to have a source of supply. But the studios and the theatre chains were separated by a Supreme Court order in 1948 and subsequent lower-court rulings; after that, the studios, operating without the protection of theatres committed in advance to play their product, resorted to 'blind bidding' and other maneuvers in order to reduce the risk on their films. It's only in the last few years that the studios have found a new kind of protection. They have discovered that they can get much more from the sale of movies to television than they had been getting, and that they can negotiate presale agreements with the networks for guaranteed amounts before they commit themselves to a production. Licensing fees to the networks now run between $3,000,000 and $4,000,000 for an average picture, and the studios negotiate in advance not only for network showings and later TV syndication (about $1,500,000 for an average picture), and for pay television (between $1,000,000 and $1,500,000), but for cable TV, the airlines, cassettes, and overseas television. And, of course, they still sell to foreign distributors and to exhibitors here, and much of that money is also committed in advance — sometimes even paid in advance. So if a film is budgeted at $8,500,000, the studio may have $14,000,000 guaranteed and — theoretically, at least — show a profit before shooting starts, even if $4,000,000 is allowed for marketing and advertising. And the studio still has the possibility of a big box-office hit and *really* big money. If a picture is a large-scale adventure story or has superstars, the licensing fee to the networks alone may be between $15,000,000 and $25,000,000, and the total advance guarantees may come to almost double the budget. Financially, the only danger in an arrangement like this is that if the film goes seriously over budget the studio can still lose money. That's why directors who have the reputation of always coming in on schedule are in steady demand even if they've had a long line of box-office failures and their work is consistently mediocre, and why directors who are perfectionists are shunned as if they were lepers — unless, like Hal Ashby, they've had some recent hits.

The studios no longer make movies primarily to attract and please moviegoers; they make movies in such a way as to get as much as possible from the prearranged and anticipated deals. Every picture (allowing for a few exceptions) is cast and planned in terms of those deals. Though the studio is very happy when it has a box-office hit, it isn't terribly concerned about the people who buy tickets and come out grumbling. They don't grumble very loudly anyway, because even the lumpiest pictures are generally an improvement over television; at least, they're always bigger. TV accustoms people to not expecting much, and because of the new prearranged deals they're not getting very much. There is a quid pro quo for a big advance sale to television and theatres: the project must be from a fat, dumb best-seller about an international jewel heist or a sky-jacking that involves a planeload of the rich and famous, or be a thinly disguised show-business biography of someone who came to an appallingly wretched end, or have an easily paraphrasable theme — preferably something that can be done justice to in a sentence and brings to mind the hits of the past. How else could you entice buyers? Certainly not with something unfamiliar, original. They feel safe with big-star packages, with chase thrillers, with known ingredients. For a big overseas sale, you must have 'international' stars — performers who are known all over, such as Sophia Loren, Richard Burton, Candice Bergen, Roger Moore, Clint Eastwood, Burt Reynolds, Alain Delon, Charles Bronson, Steve McQueen. And you should probably avoid complexities: much of the new overseas audience is subliterate. For a big advance sale to world-wide television, a movie should also be innocuous: it shouldn't raise any hackles, either by strong language or by a controversial theme. And there must be stars, though not necessarily movie stars. It has recently been discovered that even many Americans are actually more interested in TV personalities than in movie ones, and may be roused from their TV-viewing to go see a film with John Denver or John Ritter. In countries where American TV series have become popular, our TV stars may be better known that our movie stars (especially the ones who appear infrequently). A 1979 Canadian film, *Running*, starring Michael Douglas, who has appeared in a TV series and was featured in *The China Syndrome*, cost $4,200,000; by the time it was completed, the various rights to it had been sold for over $6,000,000. The lawyer-financier who set up the production of *Foolin' Around*, which stars Gary Busey, said he would not have made the picture without the television insurance of a supporting cast that included Tony Randall, Cloris Leachman, and Eddie Albert. Nobody needs to have heard of these independently packaged pictures for them to be profitable, and, in some cases, if it were not contractually necessary to open the film in theatres in order to give it legitimacy as a movie, it would be cheaper not to, because the marketing and advertising costs may outstrip the box-office revenue (unless that, too, was guaranteed). On productions like these, the backers don't suffer the gamblers' anxieties that were part of film business in the fifties and sixties, and even in the early seventies. Of course, these backers don't experience the gamblers' highs, either. Movie executives now study the television Q ratings, which measure the public's familiarity with performers, and a performer with a high rating (which he attains if he's been in a long-running series or on a daytime quiz show) is offered plum movie roles — even if this means that the script will have to be completely rewritten for his narrow range or bland personality.

There is an even grimmer side to all this: because the studios have discovered how to take the risk out of moviemaking, they don't want to make any movies that they can't protect themselves on. Production and advertising costs have gone so high that there is genuine nervous panic about risky projects. If an executive finances what looks like a perfectly safe, stale piece of material and packs it with stars, and the production costs skyrocket way beyond the guarantees and the picture loses many millions, *he* won't be blamed for it — he was playing the game by the same rules as everybody else. If, however, he takes a gamble on a small project that can't be sold in advance — something that a gifted director really wants to do, with a subtle, not easily summarized theme and no big names in the cast — and it loses just a little money, his neck is on the block. So to the executives a good script is a script that attracts a star, and they will make their deals and set the full machinery of a big production in motion and schedule the picture's release dates, even though the script problems have never been worked out and everyone (even the director) secretly knows that the film will be a confused mess, an embarrassment.

Another new factor makes a risky project still riskier; if a movie doesn't have an easily paraphrasable theme or big stars it's hard to sell via a thirty-second TV commercial. (The networks pay a lot for movies, but they get much of it back directly from the movie industry, which increasingly relies on TV commercials to sell a film.) It's even hard for the studio advertising departments to figure out a campaign for newspapers and magazines. And so, faced with something unusual or original, the studio head generally says, 'I don't know how to market it, and if I don't know how to market it, it will lose money.' The new breed of studio head is not likely to say, 'It's something I feel we should take a chance on. Let's see if there's somebody who might be able to figure out how to market it.' Just about the only picture the studios made last year that the executives took a financial risk on was *Breaking Away*. And despite the fact that it cost what is now a pittance ($2,400,000) and received an Academy Award Best Picture nomination, Twentieth Century-Fox didn't give it a big theatrical re-release (the standard procedure for a nominated film) but sold it to NBC for immediate showing, for $5,000,000. So a couple of weeks after the Awards ceremony, just when many people had finally heard of *Breaking Away* and might have gone to a theatre to see it, it appeared, trashed in the usual manner, on television. The studio couldn't be sure how much more money might come in from box offices and grabbed a sure thing. In order to accept the NBC offer, the studio even bypassed pay TV, where the picture could have been seen uncut. It was almost as if *Breaking Away* were being punished for not having stars and not having got a big advance TV sale. And the price was almost insulting: last year, Fox licensed *The Sound of Music* to NBC for $21,500,000, and licensed *Alien* to ABC for $12,000,000, with escalator clauses that could take the figure up to $15,000,000; Columbia licensed *Kramer vs Kramer* to ABC for nearly $20,000,000, and United Artists got $20,000,000 for *Rocky II* from CBS. But then how do you summarize in a sentence the appeal of a calm, evenhanded film about fathers and sons, town boys and college boys, and growing up — a modest classic that never states its themes, that stirs the emotions by indirection, by the smallest of actions and the smallest exchanges of dialogue?

If a writer-director conceives a script for a fiery young actor — K, a young man with star potential who has not yet had a role that brought him to the consciousness of the public — and shapes the central character to bring out K's volatility and ardor, he is likely to be told by the studio head, 'K doesn't do anything to me.' That rules out K, even if the studio head has never seen K act (and chances are he wouldn't remember him if he had). The studio head doesn't care if K could become a star in this part; he wants R, because he can get a $4,000,000 network sale with the impassive, logy R, a Robert Wagner type who was featured in a mini-series. And if the point is pressed, the studio head may cut off discussion with some variation of 'I must know what I'm doing, or I wouldn't be in this job.' If he is feeling expansive, he may go on with 'I won't say that you can't make a good film with K, and some people — some critics and your friends — will like it. But a good picture to me is a successful picture — one that will make money.' If the writer-director still persists, it's taken as a sign of stupidity. A finer-grained executive — one of the rare ones who loves movies — may put it to him this way: 'I like K, I like you, I like the script. But I can't recommend it. It's an expensive picture, and the subject matter makes it a long shot. And if I back too many long shots that don't come in, I'm out on my ass.' That's the distillation of executive timidity, and maybe it's better to get it from the coarser man: you can have the pleasure of hating him — you aren't made to sympathize with his plight. Since all the major studios basically play by the same rules, the writer-director will wind up with a picture that is crucially miscast and has a vacuum at its center. By the time it is released and falls by the wayside, and he is publicly humiliated, K, disgusted at not having got the part, may have accepted a dumb role in a TV series and become a hot new TV personality, whom all the movie studios are propositioning.

Chances are that even if the writer-director had been allowed to use K, he would have been completely enraged and demoralized by the time he started shooting, because the negotiating process can stretch on for years, and anyone who wants to make a movie is treated as a hustler and an adversary. 'Studios!' said Billy Wilder, paraphrasing an old complaint about women. 'You can't make pictures with 'em, and you can't make pictures without 'em.' Everybody in the movie business has the power to say no, and the least secure executives protect themselves by saying no to just about anything that comes their way. Only those at the very top can say yes, and they protect themselves, too. They postpone decisions because they're fearful, and also because they don't mind keeping someone dangling while his creative excitement dries up and all the motor drive goes out of his proposal. They don't mind keeping people waiting, because it makes them feel more powerful. I'm describing trends; of course, there are exceptions — those who are known (and sometimes revered) for quick decisions, like David Picker in his United Artists days, and Daniel Melnick in his brief stints at M-G-M and Columbia, and David Begelman at Columbia and now at M-G-M But most of the ones who could say yes don't; they consider it and string you along. (Hollywood is the only place where you can die of encouragement.) For the supplicant, it's a matter of weeks, months, years, waiting for meetings at which he can beg permission to do what he was, at the start, eager to do. And even when he's got a meeting, he has to catch the executive's attention and try to keep it; in general the higher the executive, the more cruelly short his attention span. (They're television babies. Thirty seconds is a long time to them.) In this atmosphere of bureaucratic indifference or contempt, things aren't really decided — they just happen, along bureaucratic lines. (Generally, it's only if a picture is a hit that executives talk about having given it the go-ahead. They all angle for credit in the media.) During the long wait, the director has lost the cinematographer he wanted and half the performers; in order to get the necessary approvals, he has agreed to actors he knows are wrong, and he has pared down the script to cut costs, chopping out the scenes that once meant the most to him but that he knows he can't get in the tight, ten-week shooting schedule he has been forced to accept. And then, at the last minute, a few days before shooting is to start, the studio is likely to slice the budget further — and he's down to a nine-week schedule, which means trimming the camera moves that were half the reason he'd been eager to work on the idea in the first place. Is it any wonder if the picture that comes out has a sour spirit?

It may just barely come out anyway. If there's an executive shakeup during production or after the film is completed (and shakeups take place every few months), the new studio head has nothing to gain if the film succeeds (he can't take credit for initiating it); he may find it to his strategic advantage for the film to fail. The executives — bed-hoppers, who go from one berth to another — have no particular loyalty to the studio, and there isn't the lower-echelon executive stability to launch a film initiated during the old regime with the same care as one initiated during the new regime. It all depends on the signals that come from the top.

If a big star and a big director show interest in a project, the executives will go along for a $14,000,000 or $15,000,000 budget even if, by the nature of the material, the picture should be small. And so what might have been a charming light entertainment that millions of people all over the world would enjoy is inflated, rewritten to enlarge the star's part, and overscaled. It makes money in advance and sends people out of theatres complaining and depressed. Often, when people leave theatres now they're bewildered by the anxious nervous construction of the film — by the feeling it gives them of having been pieced together out of parts that don't fit. Movies have gone to hell and amateurism. A third of the pictures being made by Hollywood this year are in the hands of first-time directors, who will receive almost no guidance or help. They're thrown right into a pressure-cooker situation, where any delay is costly. They may have come out of sitcoms, and their dialogue will sound forced, as if it were all recorded in a large, empty cave; they may have come out of nowhere and have never worked with actors before. Even if a director is highly experienced, he probably has certain characteristic weaknesses, such as a tendency to lose track of the story, or an ineptness with women characters; he's going to need watching. But who knows that, or cares enough to try to protect the picture? The executives may have hired the director after 'looking at his work' — that is, running off every other reel of one of his films. They are busy people. Network executives who are offered a completed movie commonly save time by looking at a fifteen-minute selection from it — a précis of its highlights — which has been specially prepared for them. God forbid that they should have to sit through the whole thing.

What isn't generally understood is how much talent and hard work are wasted — enough, maybe, to supply the world with true entertainment. A writer who is commissioned to adapt a book and turns in a crackerjack script, acclaimed by the studio executives, who call him a genius, then stands helplessly by as the studio submits it to the ritual lists of the stars and the directors whom they can get the biggest guarantees on. And as, one by one, the stars and directors who aren't right for the project anyway take months to read it and turn it down, the executives' confidence in the script drains away. If a star expresses tentative interest, contingent on a complete rewrite they will throw out the snappy script and authorize a new script by a sodden writer who has just had a fluke hit, and when the star decides to do something else anyway, they will have a new script written for a different star, and another and another, until no one can remember why there was ever any interest in the project. It may be shelved then, but so much money has already gone into it that in a couple of years some canny producer will think it should be brought back to life and reworked to fit a hot new teenager from television — who eventually will decide not to do it, and so on. To put it simply: A good script is a script to which Robert Redford has committed himself. A bad script is a script which Redford has turned down. A script that 'needs work' is a script about which Redford has yet to make up his mind. It is possible to run a studio with this formula; it is even possible to run a studio *profitably* with this formula. But this world of realpolitik that has replaced moviemaking has nothing to do with moviemaking. It's not just that the decisions made by the executives might have been made by anyone off the street — it's that the pictures themselves seem to have been made by anyone off the street.

The executives are a managerial class with no real stake in the studio; they didn't build it, it's not part of them, and they're moving on — into a bigger job at another studio, or into independent production (where there's more money), or to form their own companies. The executives just try to hold things together for the short period that they're going to be around; there isn't even an elementary regard for the conservation of talent. And, as in any chaotic bureaucracy, the personalities and goals of those at the top set the tone for all the day-to-day decisions; the top executives' apathy about the quality of movies infects the studio right down the line. The younger executives who are pushing their way up don't want to waste their time considering scripts that may not attract a star. For them, too, a good picture is a picture that makes money, and so after *The China Syndrome* clicked at box offices, they could be heard talking about what a wonderful craftsman its director, James Bridges, was, and after *The Amityville Horror*, with its unbelievably clunky script, by Sandor Stern, showed big grosses, they wanted to sign up Stern as a writer-director. At the bottom as at the top, the executives want to score; they want a hit, not just for the money but for the personal pleasure of the kill.

Part of what has deranged American life in this past decade is the change in book publishing and in magazines and newspapers and in the movies as they have passed out of the control of those whose lives were bound up in them and into the control of conglomerates, financiers, and managers who treat them as ordinary commodities. This isn't a reversible process; even if there were Supreme Court rulings that split some of these holdings from the conglomerates, the traditions that developed inside many of those businesses have been ruptured. And the continuity is gone. In earlier eras, when a writer made a book agreement with a publisher, he expected to be working with the people he signed up with; now those people may be replaced the next day, or the whole firm may be bought up and turned into a sub-division of a textbook-publishing house or a leisure-activities company. The new people in the job aren't going to worry about guiding a writer slowly; they're not going to think about the book after this one. They want bestsellers. Their job is to find them or manufacture them. And just as the studios have been hiring writers to work on screenplays, they are now beginning to hire writers to work on novels, which the publishers, with the help of studio money, will then attempt to promote to bestsellerdom at the same time that they are being made into movies. The writer Avery Corman has suggested 'the horrifying prospect of a novelist being fired from his own book.' It won't horrify the people who are commissioning these new books — pre-novelizations.

There are certain kinds of business in which the public interest is more of a factor than it is in the manufacture of neckties. Book publishing, magazines and newspapers, movies and television and live theatre — these are businesses, of course, but traditionally the people who work in them have felt privileged (by birth or ability or talent or luck, or by a combination of those factors). That has been true not only of the actors and journalists but of the entrepreneurs and the managers. There have always been a few businessmen in these fields who had the sensibility of artists (without the talent or the drive); if they had a good critical sense and a generous nature, they were appreciators of artists and didn't resent them. And so they became great producers in the theatre and movies, or great book and magazine editors. Contemporary variants of these people insist on being celebrity-artists themselves, and right now they all seem to be writing and directing movies.

In movies, the balance between art and business has always been precarious, with business outweighing art, but the business was, at least, in the hands of businessmen who loved movies. As popular entertainment, movies need something of what the vulgarian moguls had — zest, a belief in their own instincts, a sentimental dedication to producing pictures that would make their country proud of their contribution, a respect for quality, and the biggest thing: a willingness to take chances. The cool managerial sharks don't have that; neither do the academics. But the vulgarians also did more than their share of damage, and they're gone forever anyway. They were part of a different America. They were, more often than not, men who paid only lip service to high ideals, while gouging everyone for profits. The big change in the country is reflected in the fact that people in the movie business no longer feel it necessary to talk about principles at all. They operate on the same assumptions as the newspapers that make heroes of the executives who have a hit and don't raise questions about its quality.

When the numbers game takes over a country, artists who work in a popular medium, such as the movies, lose their bearings fast. There's a pecking order in filmmaking, and the director is at the top — he's the authority figure. A man who was never particularly attractive to women now finds that he's the padrone: everyone is waiting on his word, and women are his for the nod. The constant, unlimited opportunities for sex can be insidious; so is the limitless flattery of college students who turn directors into gurus. Directors are easily seduced. They mainline admiration. Recently, a screenwriter now directing his first picture was talking about his inability to find a producer who would take some of the burden off him; he said he needed a clone — someone who would know what was in his mind and be able to handle a million details for him. But anyone observing this writer-director would know that he needs a real producer, and for a much more important reason: to provide the sense of judgment he has already lost. Nobody really controls a production now; the director is on his own, even if he's insecure, careless, or nuts. There has always been a megalomaniac potential in moviemaking, and in this period of stupor, when values have been so thoroughly undermined that even the finest directors and the ones with the most freedom aren't sure what they want to do, they often become obsessive and grandiloquent — like mad royalty. Perpetually dissatisfied with the footage they're compulsively piling up, they keep shooting — adding rooms to the palace. megalomania and art become the same thing to them. But the disorder isn't just in their heads, and a lot of people around them are deeply impressed by megalomania. What our directors need most of all, probably, is a sense of purpose and a subject that they can think their way through. Filmmakers want big themes, and where are the kinds of themes that they would fight the studios to express? It's no accident that the two best recent American movies are both fantasy fairy tales — childish in the fullest, deepest sense. Working inside a magical structure, Carroll Ballard in *The Black Stallion* and Irvin Kershner in *The Empire Strikes Back* didn't have to deal with the modern world; they were free to use the medium luxuriantly, without guilt. You can feel the love of moviemaking — almost a revelry in moviemaking — in their films, as you can also in Walter Hill's *The Long Riders*, despite its narrative weaknesses and a slight remoteness. But we don't go to the movies just for great fairy tales and myths of the old West; we also hope for something that connects directly with where we are. Part of the widespread anticipation of *Apocalypse Now* was, I think, our readiness for a visionary, climactic, summing-up movie. We felt that the terrible rehash of pop culture couldn't go on, mustn't go on — that something new was needed. Coppola must have felt that, too, but he couldn't supply it. His film was posited on great thoughts arriving at the end — a confrontation and a revelation. And when they weren't there, people slunk out of the theatres, or tried to comfort themselves with chatter about the psychedelic imagery. Trying to say something big, Coppola got tied up in a big knot of American self-hatred and guilt, and what the picture boiled down to was: White man — he devil. Since then, I think, people have expected less of movies and have been willing to settle for less. Some have even been willing to settle for *Kramer vs Kramer* and other pictures that seem to be made for an audience of over-age flower children. These pictures express the belief that if a man cares about anything besides being at home with the kids, he's corrupt. Parenting ennobles Dustin Hoffman and makes him a better person in every way, while in *The Seduction of Joe Tynan* we can see that Alan Alda is a weak, corruptible fellow because he wants to be President of the United States more than he wants to stay at home communing with his daughter about her adolescent miseries. Pictures like these should all end with the fathers and the children sitting at home watching TV together.

The major studios have found the temporary final solution for movies: in technique and in destiny, their films *are* television. And there's no possibility of a big breakthrough in movies — a new release of energy, like the French New Wave, which moved from country to country and resulted in an international cross-fertilization — when movies are financed only if they fall into stale categories of past successes. But once the groups that are now subsidizing studio-made films begin to weary of getting TV shows when they thought they were buying movies, there should be a chance for some real moviemaking. And when the writers and directors have confidence in what they want to express, if they can't find backing from the studios they ought to be able to find backers outside the industry who will gamble on the money to be made from a good picture, once it is complete. It's easier to make money on movies now: there are more markets, and we know now that the films themselves have a much longer commercial life than early moviemakers could have guessed. The studios may find that they need great moviemakers more than the moviemakers need them. Billy Wilder may be right that you can't make pictures with 'em, but of course he's wrong that you can't make pictures without 'em. There are problems both ways, but there may be fewer problems without them, and less rage.

It would be very convincing to say that there's no hope for movies — that audiences have been so corrupted by television and have become so jaded that all they want are noisy thrills and dumb jokes and images that move along in an undemanding way, so they can sit and react at the simplest motor level. And there's plenty of evidence, such as the success of *Alien*. This was a haunted-house-with-gorilla picture set in outer space. It reached out, grabbed you, and squeezed your stomach; it was more gripping than entertaining, but a lot of people didn't mind. They thought it was terrific, because at least they'd felt something: they'd been brutalized. It was like an entertainment contrived in Aldous Huxley's *Brave New World* by the Professor of Feelies in the College of Emotional Engineering. Yet there was also a backlash against *Alien* — many people were angry at how mechanically they'd been worked over. And when I saw *The Black Stallion* on a Saturday afternoon, there was proof that even children who have grown up with television and may never have been exposed to a good movie can respond to the real thing when they see it. It was a hushed, attentive audience, with no running up and down the aisles and no traffic to the popcorn counter, and even when the closing credits came on, the children sat quietly looking at the images behind the names. There may be a separate God for the movies, at that.

The New Yorker, 1980

Index

Also by Pauline Kael

I Lost It At The Movies
Kiss Kiss Bang Bang
Going Steady
Deeper Into Movies
Reeling
When the Lights Go Down
Taking It All In
State of the Art
Hooked
Movie Love

5001 Nights at the Movies